Larry Buzan

OLD GLORY STORIES

An Association of the U.S. Army Book

OLD GLORY STORIES

American Combat Leadership in World War II

Colonel Cole C. Kingseed, U.S. Army (Ret.)

Naval Institute Press
Annapolis, Maryland

Naval Institute Press
291 Wood Road
Annapolis, MD 21402

Library of Congress Cataloging-in-Publication Data

Kingseed, Cole C. (Cole Christian), 1949–

Old glory stories : American combat leadership in World War II / Cole C. Kingseed.

p. cm.

Includes bibliographical references and index.

ISBN 1-59114-440-X (alk. paper)

1. World War, 1939–1945—United States—Biography. 2. United States—Armed Forces—Biography. I. Title.

D769.K48 2006

940.54'12730922—dc22

2005037912

Printed in the United States of America on acid-free paper ♾

12 11 10 09 08 07 06 9 8 7 6 5 4 3 2

First printing

To Three Great Company Commanders:

Major John Howard
D Company, Oxfordshire & Buckinghamshire Light Infantry Regiment,
British 6th Airborne Division

Captain Joe Dawson
G Company, 16th Infantry Regiment,
1st Infantry Division

Captain Dick Winters
E Company, 506th Parachute Infantry Regiment,
101st Airborne Division

CONTENTS

ACKNOWLEDGMENTS

AS IN ANY PROJECT OF THIS NATURE, innumerable persons contributed; without them I could never have completed my examination of combat leadership in World War II. First and foremost, I thank Colonel Robert A. Doughty, professor and head, Department of History, U.S. Military Academy, who graciously gave me a year-long sabbatical to conduct research and write this book. As an active duty officer, I could not have brought this project to a successful conclusion without time to research and interview the veterans whose stories I tell here. Nor would any acknowledgment be complete without paying fitting tribute to two great historians of the war: Martin Blumenson, the editor of *The Patton Papers* and the author of numerous leadership studies, and Stephen E. Ambrose, whose books on Dwight D. Eisenhower and D-Day have inspired an entire generation of historians. My participation on scholarly panels with such renowned authors and discussions with them on the intricacies of combat leadership were inspirational in the truest sense of the word. General Neil Creighton, former president of the Robert R. McCormick Tribune Foundation, and Lieutenant Colonel John Votaw, U.S. Army (Ret.), former director of the First Infantry Division Museum at Cantigny, also generously supported my research through a series of symposia that the McCormick Foundation cosponsored with the U.S. Naval Institute.

In addition to the McCormick Foundation, I drew heavily upon the resources of the Eisenhower Center for American Studies at the Metropolitan College, University of New Orleans. Stephen Ambrose admirably served as the center's first president; Douglas Brinkley not only succeeded him but maintained the high standards of professionalism that have always characterized the center. I wish to thank two friends, Kevin M. Hymel and Robert McDonald, who assisted me in the final stages of production of this work. And I would be negligent if I failed to acknowledge Mary Blake French, editor of *Army* magazine, for graciously granting copyright permission from a series of articles under the "Profiles in Leadership" series that I wrote for *Army* during the period 1996–97. These articles constitute all but the initial chapters of the first part of this book, which address the general officers who commanded during the war. I have greatly expanded the text to provide broader coverage of each commander.

Among the many veterans who shared their wartime experiences are several who merit special consideration. Largely through the efforts of the Eisenhower Center and my instructional duties at West Point, I met former First Sergeant Leonard "Bud" Lomell, D Company, 2nd Ranger Battalion. Bud and his wife, Charlotte, graciously opened their home in Toms River, New Jersey, to me for a short visit in the summer of 1998. Together we discussed ranger operations in the campaign in northwest Europe as well as Lomell's personal exploits at Pointe du Hoc and his "longest day" in the attack on Hill 400. Like Lomell, Lyle J. Bouck Jr. is a frequent visitor to West Point, where he has shared his proven principles of leadership with the U.S. Corps of Cadets. Sixty-odd years ago Bouck commanded the Intelligence and Reconnaissance Platoon, 394th Infantry Regiment, 99th Infantry Division, on the first day of the Battle of the Bulge. Paul Tibbetts, the officer who piloted the Enola Gay on the bombing mission over Hiroshima, Japan, also took time from his busy schedule to discuss combat leadership in the Army Air Forces. Vernon J. Baker, the sole surviving African American Medal of Honor recipient from the war, invited me to spend a few days in his cabin in Benewah Valley, Idaho. Over a bowl of venison stew we discussed the 92nd Infantry "Buffalo" Division, which fought gallantly in Italy's northern Apennine Mountains. In my research, I also met three superlative company commanders: John Howard, who commanded the British airborne company that seized Pegasus Bridge in the first action of D-Day; Joe Dawson, the first American officer to penetrate the German defenses on the bluffs overlooking Omaha Beach; and Dick Winters, who commanded both an airborne company on D-Day and a battalion of the 101st Airborne Division's Screaming Eagles at Bastogne. That these veterans consider me their friend is the greatest reward any author or any soldier can possibly possess.

And last, but certainly not least, my heartfelt thanks to my family, who have been a constant source of inspiration. My father served aboard the USS

MacDonough at Pearl Harbor on December 7, 1941. His own courage, and that of his entire generation, instilled in me a sense of patriotism and admiration for the American fighting man. My children, John and Maura, together urged me to record the achievements of the men and women who defended democracy a half century ago. And last, I owe an incalculable debt to my wife, Mary, who has returned so much happiness in my life and has taken a quiet pride in my association with the veterans of World War II.

To those named above, and to all others whom I may have inadvertently omitted, I express my gratitude and thanks. I alone am responsible for any errors that appear in this narrative. Such deficiencies are sins of omission rather than commission.

OLD GLORY STORIES

PROLOGUE

With the possible exception of the American Civil War, no generation has produced a finer array of combat commanders than the generation that defeated the Axis coalition in the twentieth century's greatest conflict. Approximately 16.3 million American men and women—about 12 percent of the U.S. population—served in uniform over the course of the war. Contributing 8.25 million men and women to the war effort was the United States Army, trained and organized by Army Chief of Staff George C. Marshall. Though Marshall's work was indispensable to the ultimate victory, training and organization alone were not enough. Sooner or later the war had to be brought to the enemy's doorstep, whether the windswept dunes of North Africa, the sweltering jungles of the Southwest Pacific, the mosquito-infested Philippine archipelago, the bloodstained beaches of Normandy, or the snow-covered forests of the Ardennes. Victory in World War II was the result of the spirited leadership and undaunted courage of all those who participated in it, from the individual rifleman to the upper echelons of army command. This book is about the combat leaders in the U.S. Army. Rather than a comprehensive history of battles and campaigns, of which there are already many, this work is an analysis of leadership in combat: how soldiers react in war, and how sergeants, lieutenants, captains, and generals direct soldiers in the most intense of all human dramas.

Recent years have witnessed a veritable avalanche of monographs and manuscripts examining the phenomenon of leadership in combat. Historian Stephen E. Ambrose and journalist Tom Brokaw have paved the way with a number of superb narratives that have introduced the members of the

"GI generation" to the modern generation. Both authors have drawn extensively on the memoirs of the American men and women who responded to Franklin D. Roosevelt's clarion call to arms in 1941. In addition to founding the National D-Day Museum in New Orleans, Ambrose was the most prolific author of the American participation in World War II with his *Pegasus Bridge*, *Band of Brothers*, *D-Day*, and *Citizen Soldiers*, to name but a few. Brokaw has reached a more general audience with *The Greatest Generation*, *The Greatest Generation Speaks*, and *An Album of Memories: Personal Histories from the Greatest Generation*. Perhaps the best recent publication that examines the intricacies of combat leadership during the war is Gerald F. Linderman's *The World within War*. As the nation commemorated the fiftieth anniversary of World War II, an increasing number of veterans also published their wartime memoirs, partly through their desire to preserve the legacy of their generation, but also, and more important, to pay a final tribute to their fallen comrades. The best of these include Paul Fussell, *Doing Battle: The Making of a Skeptic*; John Colby, *War from the Ground Up*; Leon Standifer, *A Rifleman Remembers*; Harold Leinbaugh and John Campbell, *The Men of Company K: The Autobiography of a World War II Rifle Company*, Charlton Ogburn Jr., *The Marauders*, and Dick Winters's *Beyond Band of Brothers*. The net result is a rich repository of literature matched only by that of and about the American Civil War. Why, then, another book on World War II? Quite simply, World War II was so vast in its magnitude and so cataclysmic in its effect that there is still a story to tell.

The men and women who played a role in the war are my most important sources. My association with Stephen Ambrose taught me to let the characters speak for themselves, and where possible I have done so. Before writing, I attempted to interview as many veterans as possible, particularly those whose stories appear in these pages. Absolutely indispensable in my research was the Army War College at Carlisle Barracks, Pennsylvania, which contains the most comprehensive collection of diaries, letters, operational reports, and unit histories of the U.S. Army in Europe and the Pacific. Regrettably, far fewer published accounts exist for the Pacific theater than the European theater, where the U.S. Army played the principal role in defeating the Axis enemy. Oral histories and private papers are also bountiful at various army installations and museums, and they provide an invaluable supplement and corrective to the official record. The Eisenhower Center in New Orleans alone has accumulated nearly fourteen hundred reports from the veterans of D-Day and the campaign in northwestern Europe. The Women in Military Service for

America Memorial Foundation has assembled a vast array of reports on the roles and contributions of American servicewomen.

A brief word about the organization of this book: When writing about senior officers I have tried to follow a more thematic approach, focusing on such topics as restoring the fighting spirit and analyzing the unique characteristics required to command special units in combat. I also examine some of the differences between the Pacific and European theaters, though some officers achieved dual-theater command as a result of the special requirements and demands of amphibious operations. Direction of large combat units—from division- to theater-level size—required a unique set of skills that few senior U.S. Army commanders had practical knowledge of prior to 1941. How Generals Douglas A. MacArthur, Dwight D. Eisenhower, Omar Nelson Bradley, George S. Patton Jr., Robert Eichelberger, and their fellow warriors responded to the demands of modern warfare on a fluid battlefield is the subject of the first few chapters. Airborne commanders Matthew Ridgway, James Gavin, and Maxwell Taylor likewise commanded special units that demanded a different set of leadership skills than those required of army-level commanders. A special breed of warriors fought the German and Japanese armies on the front lines. They are the subjects of the second part of the book.

Perhaps most striking to me as I compiled this narrative was the fact that the qualities of combat leadership that senior commanders so highly prized—initiative, physical and mental toughness, the ability to make coherent decisions on the spur of the moment under the most stressful circumstances—were the identical qualities that captains, lieutenants, and sergeants considered indispensable to victory on the tactical battlefield. Successful commanders in World War II, regardless of their rank and responsibilities, all had the ability to think clearly in combat. Though their levels of responsibility and the impact of their decisions varied greatly, Eisenhower's decision to launch the invasion of western Europe in June 1944 required the same degree of moral courage that Lieutenants Audie L. Murphy and Vernon Baker displayed at Holtzwihr Woods and Castle Aghinolfi, actions for which they were awarded the Medal of Honor. Likewise, George Patton, Matthew Ridgway, and Paul Tibbets all understood that imprinting their personalities on their respective commands would help them create organizations that considered themselves superior to any enemy they might encounter on the battlefield. I argue that the recognition by Patton and Lieutenant General William Simpson, the commanding general of the Ninth U.S. Army, that the initial German advance in the Battle of the Bulge created an unparalleled opportunity to exploit the enemy's weakness in artillery and supply differed little from Lieutenant Dick Winters's intuition that the enemy's shifting of machine-gun fire just prior to Easy Company's assault offered a few precious seconds to exploit a tactical weakness and to charge the enemy battery at Brecourt Manor on D-Day. In that sense, tactical and operational leadership are far more similar than disparate. Perhaps correspondent Ernie Pyle had it right. When his colleagues chastised him for talking to any officer above the rank of major, Pyle responded, "Well, democracy [and battle] include the big as well as the little, so I have to work in a general now and then just to keep the balance."

One final note: several commanders traversed multiple categories of analysis, but I have limited my study to a single category for each individual to avoid redundancy. General Robert L. Eichelberger, for example, restored the fighting spirit of the American army in New Guinea in 1942 but also commanded the Eighth Army under Douglas MacArthur throughout the Pacific war. In the chapter depicting army-level commanders in the Pacific, I thus exclude Eichelberger and focus on Walter Krueger, Jonathan Wainwright, and Simon Bolivar Buckner.

The formidable warriors I discuss in these pages were for the most part ordinary men and women caught in extraordinary circumstances. In today's society, the public relishes the debunking of its heroes. Not even our most revered presidents have escaped scrutiny. Military officers have fared little better—only George Marshall seems above the fray. And of the principal commanders of the war, only George Patton has seen his warrior reputation enhanced as that magnificent generation slowly passes from the American scene. World War II's warriors suffered the same human frailties and experienced the same exaltations as their civilian counterparts. Commanders in the Pacific, for example, chafed that the "glamour boys" in Europe received public adulation while the warriors of the Pacific remained virtually unknown. Within the respective theaters, commanders jealously guarded their reputations and sought to diminish the status of their rivals. Patton's diary and Robert Eichelberger's letters to his wife provide ample testimony of the intense rivalry among senior commanders. In the end, however, there existed a mutual respect and a hardening commitment to the task at hand: the defeat of the Axis powers.

The conclusions I reach in these chapters are my own, based on my interpretation of leadership in combat. Many veterans of the war still consider their experiences something to conceal in the hidden recesses of their mind, and I certainly respect their privacy. For others, to speak of the war is to honor courage and bravery under fire, comradeship in combat, and unspeakable hardship and unparalleled sacrifice in defense of liberty. This book is my tribute to their generation and the cause for which they willingly relinquished their youth so that future generations might enjoy the blessings of liberty. It is my sincere hope that a better understanding of their achievements will bridge the gap between their generation and the generation now embarking on a voyage through the twenty-first century.

PART 1
THE GENERALS

CHAPTER 1

THE THEATER COMMANDERS: MACARTHUR, EISENHOWER, AND STILWELL

The pace of modern war has increased greatly the burdens on leaders of all ranks. Highly efficient and energetic leadership is essential to success. No compromise is possible.

—*General of the Army George C. Marshall*

Generals of the Army Douglas A. MacArthur and Dwight D. Eisenhower emerged from World War II resplendent. The principal army architects of America's victory over the forces of fascism imprinted the force of their personalities on their respective theaters to such an extent that their names and faces remain familiar sixty years after the conclusion of the conflict. The officers who exercised theater command during the war held the most important command posts within the U.S. Army during peacetime as well. Both served as army chief of staff, their tenures separated by the war itself. In the century's greatest conflict, their theaters were separated by the world's largest oceans and the Eurasian landmass, and their paths crossed only intermittently. Each carried the title of supreme commander in addition to the exalted rank of five-star general, yet few senior officers have ever possessed such strikingly conflicting personalities. Likewise, their paths to the pinnacle of military success differed greatly, but the end results were the same: on May 7, 1945, "Ike" Eisenhower received the unconditional surrender of Nazi Germany in a schoolhouse in Reims, France, and on September 2 of that year MacArthur accepted the capitulation of Imperial Japan aboard the battleship USS *Missouri* in Tokyo Harbor.

No modern American commander has generated more controversy than Douglas MacArthur. President Franklin D. Roosevelt once described him as the second most dangerous man in America, the first being Governor Huey P. Long of Louisiana, an outspoken opponent of the president's New Deal. Army Chief of Staff George C. Marshall once chastised MacArthur for having a court rather than a military staff. His subordinate commanders viewed MacArthur's penchant for self-promotion and publicity as bordering on megalomania. The soldiers in the ranks had widely divergent views of him. Some saw "Dugout Doug," a man who avoided combat, while others saw a fearless commander who shared their misery. Future wartime air commander George C. Kenney may have penned the most accurate description of the controversial MacArthur when he stated, "Very few people really know Douglas MacArthur. Those who do, or think they do, either admire him or dislike him. They are never neutral on the subject."[1]

MacArthur was a man of remarkable contradictions with a fragile ego where matters of personal honor were concerned. His military career paralleled the emergence of the United States as a global military power. A veteran of forty-eight years of commissioned service, thirty-three of which were spent as a general officer, he fought in the three major wars of the first half of the twentieth century and was awarded every major award for valor—sometimes several at a time. His valedictory address to the U.S. Military Academy in May 1962, in which he extolled the virtues of Duty, Honor, and Country, is still considered one of the most dynamic speeches in American history.

If destiny ever smiled on an American soldier, that man was Douglas MacArthur. In a sense, MacArthur seemed destined to command. The son of a Civil War Medal of Honor recipient, MacArthur was born at Arsenal Barracks in Little Rock, Arkansas, on January 26, 1880. His first memories were of a forced march from Fort Wingate to tiny Fort Selden, some sixty miles north of El Paso. In later years he was fond of saying that the first notes he heard were not from his mother's lips but from a bugle. Douglas matriculated to the U.S. Military Academy in June 1899 and took the oath of allegiance as a member of the U.S. Corps of Cadets. At West Point the MacArthurian legend was born. As the son of one of the army's senior officers, young MacArthur was a marked man subject to more than the usual abuse heaped on plebes (first-year cadets) by upper-class cadets. His refusal to identify the cadets who ruthlessly hazed him and his classmates earned the young plebe the admiration of the senior members of the corps of cadets.

At the time of his graduation four years later, MacArthur ranked first in his class academically with an average of 98.14 percent—a figure that has been surpassed only twice in the academy's history. He also ranked first of ninety-four cadets in military demeanor and bearing, earning his chevrons as first captain, the senior cadet position within the corps. Upon graduation, MacArthur selected the Corps of Engineers, at that time the arm of the service that offered the best opportunity for accelerated promotion.

From 1903 through 1917 MacArthur served with distinction, first as an aide to his father in the Philippines, then as a military aide to President Theodore Roosevelt. Politically well connected due to his service in Washington and his parents' influence, MacArthur received choice assignments. He participated in the Vera Cruz expedition in 1914, where he was first nominated for the Medal of Honor for a daring reconnaissance behind enemy lines during which he killed several Mexican irregulars and saved the life of one of his men. Though the medal was not awarded on that occasion, Captain MacArthur was already establishing his reputation in Washington's social and military scene.

MacArthur obtained a much-sought-after assignment to the War Department's General Staff and befriended Secretary of War Newton Baker just as America's relations with Germany were deteriorating. As special assistant to the secretary in charge of public relations, Major MacArthur earned Baker's admiration, and when Congress declared war on April 6, 1917, Baker elevated MacArthur to the rank of colonel and assigned him as chief of staff to the 42nd "Rainbow" Division destined to deploy to France. MacArthur's record as chief of staff, and subsequently as brigade commander and, briefly, division commander, was miraculous. He soon emerged as the most dynamic commander of the American Expeditionary Forces (AEF) and was awarded seven Silver Stars and the Distinguished Service Medal in the course of the war. At thirty-eight he was the youngest division commander in the army, and unlike most of his counterparts, he retained his rank when the AEF returned home in 1919.

After the war MacArthur's star remained ascendant. From 1919 to 1922 he served as superintendent of the Military Academy and is generally credited with revitalizing the school's stagnant curriculum. His emphasis on intercollegiate and intramural athletics, coupled with his renovation of the Honor Code, gave rise to another aspect of the MacArthur myth: he became "the second father" of West Point, following the illustrious footsteps of Colonel Sylvanus

Thayer from a century before. In truth, MacArthur was a liberal reformer who consistently met resistance from the academy's academic board, and the majority of his policies were overturned by his successor. Subsequent superintendents resurrected MacArthur's reforms, so the general does deserve credit for dragging West Point kicking and screaming into the twentieth century.

Promoted to major general in 1925, MacArthur returned to his cherished Philippines for another tour and then was recalled to Washington when President Herbert Hoover nominated the fifty-year-old general to serve as army chief of staff. He was less successful in that post than at West Point and was frequently at odds with a parsimonious Congress over budgetary priorities.

MacArthur's performance at the pinnacle of army command was mixed at best. He lobbied Congress and two administrations to correct what he perceived to be budgetary allocations that would leave the army powerless to wage total war against the nation's enemies; he disbanded the experimental armored force that had been organized by Major Adna Chaffee; he disapproved funds for an air corps that he thought offered little prospect for success; and he dabbled in Republican Party politics at the expense of appropriate civil-military relations. His most noteworthy episode—and the one that alienated future president Franklin D. Roosevelt—was dispersing the Bonus Marchers from the capital in 1932. At MacArthur's side during these events was his junior aide, Major Dwight D. Eisenhower, who served as MacArthur's right-hand man and speechwriter for the next six years. Though Eisenhower admired his chief's intellectual gifts, he abhorred MacArthur's penchant for ignoring a clean-cut line between the military and their civilian political bosses. "If General MacArthur ever recognized the existence of that line," he later noted, "he usually chose to ignore it."[2]

When MacArthur's four-year term expired in 1934, Roosevelt extended it for an additional year, as much to keep an eye on MacArthur as to deny a MacArthur protégé the eligibility to serve as his successor. Unlike his predecessors, MacArthur chose to remain on active duty when his tour as army chief of staff ended. With no acceptable post awaiting an officer of his seniority, MacArthur accepted an invitation from Philippines president Manuel Quezon to serve as his military adviser. Roosevelt acquiesced, only too happy to place an ocean between MacArthur and the Republican Party base. With Major Eisenhower in tow, MacArthur arrived in Manila in late 1935. Aside from a brief visit to Washington in 1937, he would not see the mainland United States again until his abrupt recall by President Harry S. Truman during the Korean War in April 1951.

Douglas MacArthur was clearly an anomaly in U.S. political and military circles. In his mind, Asia, not continental Europe, held the key to America's economic and political future. He viewed Japan, and a decade later Communist China, as the real threats to U.S. security. In this regard MacArthur was a true "Asianist" who directed his efforts at strengthening the Philippines bastion against an inevitable Japanese onslaught. In 1937, with no sign of promotion on the horizon and fully aware of the increasing coolness between Roosevelt and Quezon, MacArthur requested relief from active duty, which the U.S. president approved "with great reluctance and deep regret."

His affection for the Philippines was genuine, and for the next four years MacArthur worked feverishly to prepare the Philippine archipelago for the war that he clearly foresaw. Again his efforts were mixed. His mobilization plans, most of which were written by Eisenhower before a falling-out sent Ike scurrying back to the mainland in 1939, were generally unrealistic and far beyond the meager resources available for their implementation. Washington ignored MacArthur's frequent requests for men and matériel, and with George C. Marshall now serving as chief of staff, there was little chance of reversing the trend. MacArthur later summed up the U.S. government's intransigence, noting that "Washington had not . . . offered any meaningful assistance to Filipino defense plans" since 1935.[3]

The situation changed when FDR implemented an oil embargo against Japan and froze Japan's financial assets in the United States in June 1941. At Marshall's suggestion, Roosevelt recalled MacArthur to active duty on July 27 and appointed him commanding general of the U.S. Army forces in the Far East. Accordingly, MacArthur began an "eleventh-hour struggle to build up enough force to repel an enemy" that he knew far outnumbered his own meager forces. He was still in the process of mobilizing the Filipino troops when, on December 8 at 1240 hours, Japanese planes appeared on the horizon and Douglas MacArthur's world began to unravel.

Why MacArthur's air force was caught on the ground and subsequently destroyed nine hours after his headquarters had received news of the Japanese attack on Pearl Harbor remains a subject of speculation. MacArthur's own apologia that he was under specific orders not to initiate hostilities against the Japanese lacks credibility. Unlike his counterparts at Pearl Harbor, however, MacArthur never found himself the subject of a War Department investigation to affix responsibility for the debacle. He emerged with his reputation intact, if slightly blemished. His premier biographer, D. Clayton James, notes that when all the evidence is sifted, however "contradictory and incomplete it may be, MacArthur still emerges as the officer who was in overall command in the Philippines . . . and must therefore bear a large measure of the blame."[4]

The Japanese air offensive was followed by major amphibious landings beginning on December 22 in the vicinity of Lingayen Gulf, one hundred miles northwest of Manila. Lacking sufficient air and naval support to contest the enemy's advance, MacArthur urged Washington to send immediate reinforcements "lest the Philippines be lost," and then, on December 23, ordered the implementation of War Plan Orange–3 (WPO-3), a withdrawal of his land forces to the Bataan Peninsula. Three days later Manila was declared an "open city," and Japanese forces entered the Filipino capital on January 2.

When stockpiling supplies on the peninsula, MacArthur's logistical planners had prepared rations and supplies for ten thousand men for six months. By the first week of January, however, Bataan held in excess of eighty thousand American and Filipino troops and twenty-five thousand refugees. MacArthur immediately placed the defenders on half rations, and in the following weeks the ration was reduced several times. Though MacArthur's critics—and there were many—cited the withdrawal to Bataan as an indication of his deteriorating martial abilities, the orderly withdrawal saved the garrison from immediate destruction in the open plains north of Manila where the Japanese had expected the decisive battle to take place. MacArthur regarded his decision to implement WPO-3 as the "most vital decision of the war." The withdrawal certainly surprised the Japanese, and the subsequent battle gave the American and Filipino publics a symbol of national pride. Successful resistance was impossible, of course, without substantial reinforcements from the United States, but the image of the "battling bastards of Bataan" generated widespread sympathy and resurrected the MacArthurian legend of America's "fightingest general." In truth, MacArthur had forfeited valuable days by delaying the withdrawal, and numerous supplies had to be abandoned when the primitive railroad network between the peninsula and Manila proved inadequate to handle the massive redistribution.

Safely ensconced on Corregidor at the mouth of Manila Bay, MacArthur relegated the daily military operations on Bataan to General Jonathan Wainwright and visited the peninsula's beleaguered defenders only once during the entire campaign—a far cry from the days in the Meuse-Argonne when young Brigadier General MacArthur was in the thick of the fighting. Still, his command responsibilities were different now. In World War I MacArthur was a tactical commander responsible for directing the employment of several thousand men on a narrow battlefield front; in 1941 he was an operational commander entrusted with conducting military operations within a specified theater of operations. Aside from peppering the War Department with daily calls for reinforcements and regular prognostications of doom, there was little MacArthur could do to stem the onslaught once the Japanese established a lodgment on Luzon.

MacArthur found relief in another way when, on February 22, President Roosevelt ordered him to proceed to Australia to establish and assume command of a new Southwest Pacific Theater. Gathering his principal subordinates at Corregidor on March 10, MacArthur announced that he would retain overall command of the Philippines but divided the command into four districts, with Wainwright receiving command of the Bataan force. Then he called Wainwright to his side, presented him with two boxes of cigars and two jars of shaving cream, and quietly informed him that he would be departing the following evening. MacArthur and his entourage slipped out of the bay aboard a PT boat skippered by Lieutenant John Bulkeley. On March 17, MacArthur was safe in Australia. At the Adelaide railroad station he met a group of reporters and announced: "The President of the United States ordered me to break through the Japanese lines and proceed from Corregidor to Australia for the purpose, as I understand it, of organizing the American offensive against Japan, a primary object of which is the relief of the Philippines. I came through and I shall return." And return he did, just as he had promised the defenders, but "too late for those battling men in the foxholes of Bataan [and] the valiant gunners at the batteries of Corregidor."[5]

MacArthur's failure to conduct a more coordinated and sustained defense of the Philippine archipelago is mystifying. He lost the majority of his air force at Clark Field during the initial hours of the war, and with some notable exceptions the Filipino forces were unable to coordinate any meaningful defense north of Manila. The mobilization and training plans MacArthur had fashioned since his arrival in 1935 were a complete failure. Even Eisenhower, his former aide, confided to his diary that he felt his former chief "might have made a better showing." Moreover, MacArthur's refusal to relinquish overall command of the islands after leaving Corregidor suggests that his ego overrode sound military considerations; he appeared insensitive and self-absorbed in the legend that had come to surround him. Nowhere was this more apparent than in his negative endorsement of Marshall's nomination of Wainwright for the Medal of Honor for his spirited defense of Bataan. Such an award, stated MacArthur, would cheapen the medal and serve as "an injustice to other USFIP soldiers who were more deserving." Marshall backed down, and

Wainwright had to wait three more years to receive the nation's highest decoration for bravery. Such, then, are the allegations against MacArthur.

As always, there is another side to the story. Though his mind seemed paralyzed during the opening hours of World War II, MacArthur conducted the withdrawal from central Luzon to Bataan with great vigor. Though inadequately supplied, he directed the Philippine defense with considerable skill and delayed the Japanese conquest for five months, completely disrupting the Japanese timetable for southward expansion. As the senior army commander actively engaged against the enemy, MacArthur inspired a nation during its darkest hour. Small wonder that the National Father's Day Committee named him "Number One Father for 1942" and literally hundreds of American mothers named their male offspring Douglas. Nor was it necessarily his desire to leave the Philippines when he did. Understanding the propaganda value that the Japanese would achieve with his capture, FDR ordered MacArthur to Australia and awarded him the Medal of Honor for "conspicuous leadership in preparing the Philippine Islands to resist conquest, for gallantry and intrepidity above and beyond the call of duty in action against invading Japanese forces and for the heroic conduct of defensive and offensive operations on the Bataan Peninsula." George Marshall wrote the citation that the president approved on March 25.

MacArthur can be excused for taking justifiable pride in the reconquest of the island group that had witnessed his greatest military defeat. The long and tortuous route back to the Philippines ran through New Guinea, a two-thousand-mile-long island that borders northern Australia. First to be cleared was the eastern portion of the island, where the Japanese had established an advance base at Buna Mission. While the Allies dallied, the Japanese deployed thousands of fresh troops in the hope of securing the southern flank of their Greater East Asia Co-prosperity Sphere. MacArthur had the mandate, but not sufficient troops, to seriously impede the Japanese advance. In March 1942, just one month after his arrival in Australia, the Joint Chiefs of Staff (JCF) designated Douglas MacArthur the supreme commander, Southwest Pacific Theater. His theater included Australia, the Bismarck Archipelago, the Solomon Islands, New Guinea, and the Netherlands East Indies except Sumatra. Allied concurrence followed on April 18, and the Southwest Pacific Area (SWPA) was born.

MacArthur's specific instructions were to hold Australia; to check the Japanese conquest of the SWPA; to protect the land, sea, and air communications within the SWPA and its closest approaches; and to prepare to take the offensive. Additionally, the Joint Chiefs directed MacArthur to establish a combined headquarters with his respective Allied governments and to form a staff that would include officers assigned by the respective governments concerned. Then came the caveat: the Combined Chiefs of Staff would exercise general jurisdiction over grand strategic policy, and the Joint U.S. Chiefs of Staff would exercise jurisdiction over all matters pertaining to operational strategy.[6]

MacArthur simply selected the portions of the mandate that best suited his purpose. His inability to find "any capable Dutch officers" or qualified Australian commanders to serve in his theater infuriated the Allies, and the ill will generated by MacArthur's insistence on establishing a headquarters that was "Allied" in name only hindered the smooth attainment of coalition goals throughout the war. To prevent American ground forces from serving under Australian commanders, MacArthur created the separate Alamo Task Force under the direct command of General Walter S. Krueger, who would eventually command the Sixth U.S. Army. Fortunately, inter-Allied cooperation quickly yielded to military expediency, and by fall 1942 a combined Australian-American force was gradually inching toward Buna. Unfortunately, the campaign produced disastrous results. Ill-led and ill-trained troops suffered more from the environment than from the Japanese defenders, and Marshall dispatched Robert Eichelberger to the theater as a corps commander. On reporting to MacArthur's headquarters, Eichelberger received a cordial welcome and was then told to "take Buna or not come out alive," a directive reminiscent of MacArthur's own boast in 1918 that he would take Châtillon "or my name will head the casualties." Eichelberger succeeded in taking Buna on January 2, 1943, but the Papua New Guinea campaign proved expensive. Moreover, Buna was only the initial step; a far more dangerous road lay ahead.

In his memoirs, MacArthur characterizes the movement across the littoral of New Guinea and the isolation of the Japanese garrison at Rabaul as a masterpiece of "triphibious warfare," a three-dimensional concept calling for the coordination of ground, sea, and air operations. From Papua to Manila, the SWPA chief concentrated on his primary target and avoided the frontal attack with its terrible cost in life, thus negating the Japanese strongholds and neutralizing them by severing their principal supply lines. Nowhere was this concept more successful than in the isolation of the Japanese base at Rabaul on New Britain, where one hundred thousand Japanese withered on the vine and were starved into irrelevance. By mid-1944 MacArthur had advanced eighteen hundred miles westward and seven hundred miles to the north by "leapfrogging" Japanese garrisons and delivering maximum combat power at weakly held enemy positions.[7] It was masterfully conducted, but to MacArthur the New Guinea campaign was merely a means to an end, and that end was the liberation of the Philippines.

To secure presidential approval and JCS acquiescence, MacArthur accepted Marshall's invitation to meet the president at Pearl Harbor in July 1944 to determine the future direction of the Pacific war. Summoning his finest display of theatrical oratory, MacArthur argued vigorously for a direct assault on Leyte followed by the invasion of Luzon. The Philippines were, after all, "American territory" where "unsupported" American forces had suffered a catastrophic defeat. Abandonment a second time, argued MacArthur, would be unforgivable. His words carried the day, and FDR approved the campaign. The Philippine campaign, notes historian Eric Larrabee, was MacArthur's "vindication, the culminating event of the SWPA war."[8]

American forces waded ashore at Leyte on October 20 and attacked the principal Filipino island of Luzon in December. At Christmas, MacArthur announced that the enemy forces on Leyte had capitulated, but in fact, fighting continued for months. The same intensity occurred on Luzon, where fanatical Japanese resistance extracted a fearful price following MacArthur's attack on January 9, 1945. Despite MacArthur's predictions of minimal casualties, the cost of retaking the Philippines was exorbitant. Total U.S. Army combat casualties in the Philippines were about 47,000, including 10,380 killed and 36,531 wounded, slightly less than the numbers incurred at Okinawa. Non-battle casualties were the highest of the war: 93,400 lost to sickness or injury.[9] Manila, or what was left of it, fell on February 27, the date MacArthur presided over ceremonies restoring constitutional government to the Filipinos at Malacanan Palace. He then dispersed Eichelberger's Eighth Army to liberate the remainder of the archipelago while Krueger's forces routed out pockets of enemy resistance on Luzon. The fighting continued until Japan surrendered, though MacArthur had officially announced the end of the Philippine campaign on July 4.

MacArthur's crowning achievement occurred on September 2, when aboard the USS *Missouri* he formally accepted the Japanese surrender. As Supreme Commander, Allied Powers (SCAP), he was the logical choice to preside over the surrender ceremony. Standing on the quarterdeck with "only God and his own conscience to guide him," Douglas MacArthur rose to the occasion with a spirited address: "Today the guns are silent. A great tragedy has ended. A great victory has been won. The skies no longer rain death—the seas bear only commerce—men everywhere walk upright in the sunlight. The entire world is quietly at peace. The holy mission has been completed. . . . We have known the bitterness of defeat and the exultation of triumph, and from both we have learned there can be no turning back. We must go forward to preserve in peace what we won in war."[10]

World War II ended at that instant, but the MacArthur legend would endure. As virtual viceroy of Japan in the years after the war, he engineered the transformation of the feudal island nation to a modern society. Five years later, "Mars granted an old soldier one last gift" when Communist forces invaded South Korea. MacArthur once again took active command and reversed the military fortunes with a dramatic turning movement at Inchon. His subsequent relief by President Truman severely tarnished MacArthur's image but in no way detracted from his sterling, albeit uneven, performance in World War II.

In retrospect, what did MacArthur contribute to the Pacific war? Not much, according to one senior military historian.[11] Certainly there is much to criticize. MacArthur clearly mishandled the initial defense of the Philippines. He repeatedly misrepresented his own accomplishments and forbade any communiqué to leave his headquarters unless it personally extolled his generalship. He exaggerated enemy losses to create the impression that his strategy and tactics were producing rapid victories at minimal cost. His own casualties were remarkably proportional to those suffered by other Allied commanders during the major campaigns of the war, but he inflicted a far greater killed ratio on the enemy than other senior commanders did. Nor was MacArthur reluctant to use political intrigue to galvanize political support for his own concept of operations. His frequent references to political backlash if FDR should abandon the Philippines in favor of a major offensive directed toward Formosa helped secure presidential approval of a drive that showcased MacArthur's theater and enhanced his reputation. Additionally, his frequent battles with the U.S. Navy and the Allies over military priorities and resource allocation clearly hindered military operations.

MacArthur enthusiasts disagree with this assessment. True, "leapfrogging" was not a novel concept and was forced on him by the Joint Chiefs, but MacArthur brilliantly exploited its inherent advantages. And if MacArthur pursued a personal agenda independent from that of his political and military chiefs in his advance from Papua New Guinea to the Philippines, he also maintained a fixed purpose from which he never deviated. His sole objective remained the liberation of the Philippines, and he adeptly manipulated available resources to achieve that purpose. That he diverted forces meant for the final conquest of Luzon and subsequent operations that had been approved by the Joint Chiefs in order to liberate other islands in the Filipino archipelago was inexcusable, but to a commander who fervently believed that his pledge dictated nothing else, it was the most honorable course to pursue. MacArthur's greatest failures were more the result of personality flaws than lack of military acumen. He remained to the last extremely sensitive to all affronts, both real and imagined, to his personal honor. In promising to "return to the Philippines" he assumed a near-divine mission. In the final analysis, his strengths far outweighed his weaknesses.

Dwight D. Eisenhower's rise to military prominence lacked both the brilliance and the notoriety that marked the career of Douglas MacArthur. When at long last he secured his brigadier general's star after a stellar performance in the Texas-Louisiana maneuvers of 1941, one prominent national newspaper mistakenly identified him as "Lieutenant Colonel D. D. Ersenbeing."[12] Even Ike later admitted that anyone who might have recognized his future potential while he was a cadet at West Point had chosen to ignore it. Although he lacked the highly publicized cadet career of MacArthur, Ike managed to achieve the rank of color sergeant and graduated sixty-first in a class of 164 that included future generals Omar N. Bradley and James Van Fleet. Fifteen years later, while Ike was serving in the nation's capital, Milton Eisenhower pointed out his brother amid the Washington elite and remarked that he was "going places." The response was hardly encouraging: "If he's going places, he better get started." Such assessments of Eisenhower's interwar career were understandable because Ike was virtually unknown outside the close community of the U.S. Army's elite officer corps. Nevertheless, periodic flashes of brilliance characterized Eisenhower's rise over the twenty-five years between his graduation from the Military Academy and his summons to serve in the War Department in the immediate aftermath of the Japanese attack on Pearl Harbor.

While MacArthur was establishing himself as one of the AEF's most brilliant frontline commanders, Ike Eisenhower was stuck at Camp Colt outside Gettysburg, Pennsylvania, where he commanded a tank training center. Within a year he was in command of more than ten thousand men, roughly the equivalent of a modern light infantry division. The task was monumental for a young officer just three years from West Point, and though he was denied the opportunity to participate in combat in France, Eisenhower earned the Distinguished Service Medal for his "unusual zeal, foresight, and marked administrative ability in the organization, training, and preparation for overseas service of the Tank Corps." Following the war, he remained with the Tank

Corps and befriended George S. Patton Jr. while both served at Fort Meade in Maryland. Ike's association with Patton evolved into a lifelong friendship and introduced Eisenhower to Major General Fox Conner, a distinguished officer who had served as John J. Pershing's operations officer during the Great War. Eisenhower later called Conner the "ablest officer" he ever knew. Ike's chance meeting with Conner was the first of three watershed events in the interwar period that led to his eventual rise to general officer.

Impressed with Ike's revolutionary ideas on armor tactics and the utilization of tanks as weapons of pursuit and exploitation, Conner requested Eisenhower's services as his executive officer in the Panama Canal Zone, where Conner commanded the 20th Infantry Brigade. Over the course of the next three years Conner meticulously groomed his protégé for senior command. Discovering that Eisenhower had virtually no interest in military history, Conner directed him to read Clausewitz and other theorists of war. He carefully supervised Ike's preparations of daily orders and honed his staff skills. And most significant, Conner secured an allocation for Eisenhower to attend the army's prestigious Command and General Staff School at Fort Leavenworth, Kansas, in 1925.

The Leavenworth course proved to be another of the major events that shaped Eisenhower's career. By graduating first in his class of 245 officers in June 1926 he earned a special efficiency report in which the commandant stated that Eisenhower "was especially qualified for chief of staff of a division and a corps."[13] For the second time in a decade his career had taken a dramatic turn. Subsequent tours of duty as a member of Pershing's Battle Monuments Commission and as military assistant to Assistant Secretary of War Frederick H. Payne broadened Eisenhower's staff experience. During the last year of his service on Payne's staff, Ike worked closely with Army Chief of Staff Douglas MacArthur. In the interim he attended the National War College and the Industrial War College, thus completing every senior service college that the military establishment offered. In the process he attracted the attention of some of the country's leading industrialists, including Bernard Baruch, who would oversee the nation's industrialization effort during World War II; Walter Giff of AT&T; and Daniel Willard of the Baltimore & Ohio Railroad.[14] By now Major Eisenhower was widely recognized as one of the army's premier staff officers, in large part because of his impressive analytical skills and ability to draw and communicate sound conclusions.[15] MacArthur was so impressed with Eisenhower's ability as an executive assistant and speechwriter that he invited the young major to accompany him to the Philippines. Realizing that it was probably not the best career move because it took him away from the center of army politics, the junior aide reluctantly accepted.

The four years that Eisenhower worked on MacArthur's personal staff were frustrating at best. Cut off from what he perceived was the mainstream of an army increasingly looking toward military events in Europe, Ike languished in splendid isolation half a world away. True, his service there gained him a much greater appreciation for civil-military relations, but the untimely death of his classmate and closest friend, Jimmy Ord, in January 1938 and a subsequent rift with MacArthur over Filipino mobilization plans and the staging of a public review to publicize his chief's efforts darkened Eisenhower's spirits. Finally, in 1939, Eisenhower secured an assignment to return to the United States. MacArthur was glad to see him go but nevertheless acknowledged that when the next war came, Eisenhower should be immediately promoted to brigadier general and given command of a division.

Eisenhower soon learned that his break with MacArthur carried a significant benefit. The officer corps had roughly split into two camps: proponents of Douglas MacArthur and those associated with Deputy Chief of Staff George C. Marshall, who was already earmarked for the senior slot once Major General Malin Craig reached mandatory retirement age in 1939. Clearly disassociating himself from the "MacArthurites," Ike performed brilliantly in a series of senior staff positions as chief of staff of the 3rd Infantry Division, IX Corps, and Third U.S. Army. Having finally attracted the attention of Marshall as a result of the army maneuvers in the late summer of 1941, Eisenhower received his first star. He could not have been surprised when on the morning of December 12 he received a call from Walter Bedell Smith, the secretary of the War Department's General Staff, telling him that Marshall wanted him in Washington right away.

By the time Eisenhower reached the War Department he had already established a reputation as a staff officer of extraordinary ability. Having proven his mettle working for Conner, Pershing, and MacArthur, three of the army's most distinguished officers, Ike now reported to Marshall, a stern taskmaster and keen judge of character. Officers who met Marshall's high standards were quickly groomed for high command. Marshall's modus operandi was simple: put the officer to the test, observe his qualities of leadership under pressure, and then assign a more demanding task if he met the first challenge. Above all else the army chief demanded selfless service. Writing to an elementary school class in March 1944, Marshall summarized the method he employed to select wartime commanders. Though he confessed it was relatively easy to select generals after seeing a display of their military qualities on the battlefield, a far more difficult task was to find the right men for the job prior to seeing them in active operations. Eisenhower fell into the latter category. The most important leadership factor, stated Marshall, was "character, which involves integrity, unselfish and devoted purpose, a sturdiness of bearing when everything goes wrong and all are critical, and a willingness to sacrifice self in the interest of the common good."[16] For the first six months of 1942, Eisenhower repeatedly passed Marshall's tests and was subsequently advanced to senior command far ahead of his contemporaries.

Eisenhower joined the War Plans Division of the War Department as deputy chief for the Pacific and Far East on December 14, 1941. Having served in the Philippines under MacArthur for four years, he was the logical choice. Immediately on reporting to the War Department Eisenhower faced his first challenge. After a brief welcome, Marshall outlined the general situation in the Pacific and then asked Ike what the U.S. Army's general line of action should be. "Give me a few hours," Ike requested. By early afternoon he had outlined the immediate steps to be taken: first, build up a base of operations in Australia from which supplies and personnel could be moved into the Philippines; second, influence Russia to enter the Pacific war.[17] A few hours later he briefed the chief, who enthusiastically accepted his recommendation and directed Eisenhower to "do your best to save them [the Philippine garrison]."

Over the course of the next several months, Marshall quietly groomed Eisenhower for senior command. In February, Marshall reorganized the War Department and placed it on a more efficient war footing. To lead the Operations Division, which constituted the department's command post, Marshall selected Eisenhower. Shortly thereafter Eisenhower passed another test when Marshall, knowing how desperately Ike wanted a field command, informed him that promotions were going to the commanders in the field, not to staff officers serving in the War Department. Never known for a mild temper, Eisenhower exploded, "General, I'm interested in what you say, but I want you to know that I don't give a damn about your promotion plans. . . . I came into this office from the field and I am trying to do my duty. I expect to do so as long as you want me here. If that locks me to a desk for the rest of the war, so be it!"[18] To Ike's amazement, three days later he discovered on his desk a recommendation for his promotion to major general.

It seems clear that Eisenhower rose to senior European command as the result of his superlative performance as Marshall's right-hand man and because his strategic vision coincided with those of Marshall and Roosevelt.

On March 25 Eisenhower proposed that the principal target for the first major U.S. offensive should be Germany, to be attacked through western Europe. Marshall made several revisions and then passed the recommendation to the president, who endorsed it immediately. The army chief then flew to London to discuss the plan with the European Allies. On his return in early June, Marshall called on Eisenhower to draft a directive for a commanding general of American forces in Europe and to make a recommendation for the organization that would be required. Eisenhower responded as ordered and also prepared a secret memorandum for Marshall in which he described the type of officer who should serve as commanding general of the U.S. forces. As a first condition, the designated commander ought to enjoy the fullest confidence of the chief of staff in order that he might efficiently, and in accordance with the basic strategic ideas of the chief, conduct all the preparatory work essential to its successful initiation. Next, he should be an officer who would fit perfectly into the final organization. If Roosevelt should direct Marshall to proceed to London and take active command of a subsequent invasion force, the officer previously serving as commander should be one who could fit in as a deputy or chief of staff.[19] Consciously or unconsciously, Eisenhower was describing himself, for he, more than anyone else, had Marshall's complete confidence and understood the intricacies of the latter's strategic thinking. Marshall read the memorandum and then informed Ike that he intended to brief Roosevelt. The president concurred and on Marshall's recommendation designated Eisenhower commanding general of the European Theater of Operations (ETO), with headquarters in London, effective June 24, 1942. He was promoted to lieutenant general on July 7.

Unlike most commanders, who perform their apprenticeship under fire, Eisenhower was thrown into the middle of a war with virtually no command experience and absolutely no combat experience.[20] Complicating his new position were the political complexities inherent in commanding military forces in the combined arena. To the British chiefs and field commanders, Eisenhower was an unproven commodity, and their analysis changed little over the course of the war. General, later Field Marshal, Sir Bernard Montgomery, who was to serve under Eisenhower from March 1943 to the end of the war, characterized Ike as a "great military statesman" but hardly a great soldier in the true sense of the word.[21] According to Montgomery, Ike's lack of command experience, coupled with the poor training of American ground forces, proved disastrous during the early stages of the war. Given the experience of exercising direct command of a division, corps, and army, Eisenhower might have refined his martial skills. In the view of General Alan Brooke, chief of the Imperial General Staff, one of the great victories of the war occurred in the Mediterranean in January 1943 when he and his chiefs were successful in "pushing Eisenhower up into the stratosphere and rarefied atmosphere of a Supreme Commander, where he would be free to devote his time to the political and inter-allied problems, whilst we [the British] inserted under him one of our own commanders [General Harold Alexander] to deal with the military situations and to restore the necessary drive and co-ordination which had been so seriously lacking."[22]

Though Montgomery later admitted that he grew to appreciate Eisenhower as supreme commander in northwest Europe, the truth was that he and Ike differed greatly in their views on command organization and operational strategy. Sixty years of postwar scholarship have not altered the fact that both Monty and Brooke felt that they were far more qualified to head the wartime alliance in combat. In recent years, American historians, citing the wartime papers of the principal American military leaders, have also cast aspersions on Ike as a wartime commander. Omar Bradley, who commanded 12th Army Group, assessed Ike as a political general of rare and valuable gifts, but not a battlefield commander.[23] George Patton, who commanded one corps and two armies under Eisenhower, frequently claimed that Ike "was more British than the British" and longed for John J. Pershing, the commander of the American Expeditionary Forces in World War I, who successfully resisted the wholesale amalgamation of U.S. forces into the French and British armies.[24] U.S. Army chief Marshall disagreed and credited his principal protégé with creating "great history for the good of mankind." Wherein lies the truth?

Any analysis of Eisenhower as a military commander must begin with the North African and Mediterranean campaigns and conclude with the campaign in northwestern Europe. Commanding the Allied task force that invaded North Africa as part of Operation Torch was Ike's first combat command, and he had only three months to get ready. As he prepared for the invasion, he initiated a series of messages to Marshall to keep his chief informed and to solicit advice on organization, selection of commanders, and allocation of resources. It was Marshall, not Eisenhower, who selected the assault corps commanders. Aside from requesting Major General Walter Bedell "Beetle" Smith as his chief of staff, Eisenhower assured Marshall that "anyone you name to important commands in that force will be completely acceptable to me." Marshall chose Lloyd Fredendall and Patton to play prominent roles in the upcoming invasion. Eisenhower's letters during this period were filled with uncertainty and frustration regarding the creation of a fully integrated Allied staff. Hesitancy could be expected, of course, but it did nothing to endear the American commander to the British, who already considered the American army latecomers to a conflict that for them had entered its fourth full year.

From November 1942 until he relinquished command in the Mediterranean theater, Eisenhower directed three major amphibious operations: North Africa (Torch) on November 8, 1942; Sicily (Husky) on July 10, 1943; and Salerno (Avalanche) on September 8, 1943.[25] In North Africa, Eisenhower quickly matured as a military commander. His political agreement with French admiral Jean François Darlan to head the Vichy French government in North Africa secured an armistice that enhanced the success of the forthcoming invasion but incurred the great ire of the American and British governments. Both had pinned their hopes on Henri Giraud, who was later named by the Free French as commander in chief of their North and West African forces. Eisenhower considered the deal politically expedient and militarily necessary, and regretted any political embarrassment he had caused.

The amphibious assaults were uniformly successful, in part because Darlan ordered the Vichy forces not to resist the invasion, but command problems, poor communications among various headquarters, and inclement weather slowed the Allies' advance into Tunisia. When Erwin Rommel struck Eisenhower's forces at Kasserine Pass in mid-February 1943 and inflicted severe damage, he caught Eisenhower flat-footed. Numerous factors—including faulty troop dispositions, poor communication, and inept American field commanders—contributed to the debacle, but Eisenhower as overall commander must share in the responsibility. He moved quickly to rectify the situation, first by relieving Fredendall as II U.S. Corps commander and replacing him with Patton, then by marshalling as many resources as possible to turn the tide. To assist Eisenhower, Marshall dispatched former classmate Omar Bradley to Tunisia to act as Ike's "eyes and ears." It was a fortuitous selection; the steady Bradley proved "a godsend." After Patton's victory over the Germans at El Guettar, Bradley assumed command of II Corps while Patton resumed planning for the invasion of Sicily, now scheduled for summer 1943. By mid-March all Allied forces, now including Montgomery's Eighth Army, had come under Eisenhower's command. By agreement within the Combined Chiefs of Staff at Casablanca, Eisenhower became commander in chief, Allied Force Headquarters. Commanding the respective ground, naval, and air forces under Eisenhower were General Harold Alexander, Admiral Andrew Cunningham, and Air Marshal Arthur W. Tedder. The campaign ended in May when the Afrika Korps capitulated, sending roughly 250,000 Axis troops into captivity.

By any assessment the Allied campaign in North Africa was successful, but Eisenhower's performance was inconsistent. North Africa had proven a testing ground not only for his command organization but also for American training, doctrine, and tactics. He would take the same command organization into Sicily in July. This time Ike's "hands-off" approach to the battle and Alexander's refusal to coordinate the efforts of Patton's Seventh U.S. Army and Montgomery's Eighth British Army produced victory, but victory tempered by the escape of thousands of German defenders. For all his efforts, Ike remained an unproven commander in British eyes. In fact, Ike, Bradley, Patton, and Mark Clark had matured into seasoned commanders by the summer of 1943. So had some excellent division commanders, most notably Lucian K. Truscott Jr. of the 3rd Infantry Division and Matthew Ridgway of the 82nd Airborne Division. More important, the American army had also come of age in the fighting in the Sicilian mountains. Better equipment, better officers, and improved tactics had made the American GI every bit as effective as the British Tommy. As for Eisenhower, his letters to Marshall reflected a growing confidence in his own ability and an increasing reluctance to discuss the intricacies of military operations with his chief.

In the attack against the Italian mainland, Eisenhower dismissed Marshall's suggestion that Clark's Fifth Army land farther north and directed Clark to land at Salerno. Ike's reasoning was sound: though Montgomery had encountered limited opposition when he landed on the toe of the Italian boot on September 3, intelligence indicated that the Germans were defending in greater strength in the north; consequently, any invasion beach ought to be within range of Allied air support. His concerns proved prophetic, for Clark made initial advances, then became bogged down when the enemy reinforced the Italian front with significant armor and infantry reserves. For the next nine months Italy proved a bloody stalemate, with Clark and his British counterparts paying a stiff price for limited territorial gains. By this time, however, Ike had been tagged to command the cross-Channel invasion now set for spring 1944.

Eisenhower's selection to command Operation Overlord was hardly a foregone conclusion. Roosevelt initially favored Marshall, and indeed both the army chief and Eisenhower assumed that Marshall was the natural choice. Roosevelt named Ike, however, and Prime Minister Winston Churchill immediately approved, quite content that Eisenhower had demonstrated a unique capacity to command coalition forces. Moreover, Ike had successfully managed three major campaigns within the span of a year. Though personally disappointed that he would have to remain in Washington, Marshall forwarded to Stalin Roosevelt's communiqué announcing the appointment of Eisenhower to command the invasion. Now assured of Marshall's continued support and armed with the knowledge that his greatest task lay before him, Ike relinquished command in the Mediterranean. Following a brief rest in the United States, he arrived in London in mid-January to assume command of the Allied Expeditionary Force.

The northwest Europe campaign was Eisenhower's crowning achievement as a military commander. He carefully selected his principal American commanders, sending Bradley to London in the fall to train the First U.S. Army and to command the American ground forces scheduled for the invasion. He picked Patton, still in the doghouse for slapping American soldiers in Sicily, to command the follow-on American army. He followed the suggestion of Montgomery, now serving as his ground forces commander and in overall tactical command of the invasion until Ike himself assumed direct command, and greatly expanded the size and area of the invasion. Eisenhower also increased the size of Supreme Headquarters, Allied Expeditionary Force (SHAEF), to manage the additional complexity of commanding a force that would eventually number five million men. He also demanded, and received, temporary command of the strategic air forces to implement his Transportation Plan, the destruction of the French transportation network in the lodgment area. Next he made the critical decision to support Bradley's recommendation that the American airborne divisions be included in the task list to facilitate the success of the amphibious forces. Finally, Eisenhower made the decision he was born to make—he gave orders to launch the invasion itself. Regardless of his other accomplishments, that decision ensures Eisenhower's place in history. At that moment Eisenhower went from being the most powerful commander in the world to being the most powerless, for henceforth the success of D-Day lay in the hands of the Allied soldiers, sailors, and airmen he had committed to the invasion.

In retrospect, D-Day was a spectacular success. By the end of June 6, fully 135,000 Allies were ashore. The subsequent campaign proved bloody and fearsome, but the Allies remained firmly ensconced on the Continent. The campaign was far from perfect, the most notable failure being the escape of nearly 50,000 German troops from the Falaise pocket. With the opportunity to completely annihilate the bulk of the German army in France, the Allied commanders, including Eisenhower, hesitated. Only Patton sensed the historic opportunity that had presented itself. By not intervening and ordering Montgomery and Bradley to close the pocket and destroy the enemy force, Eisenhower missed a great opportunity to shorten the war. Yet the Allies had destroyed the bulk of two German armies, and the enemy's inability to reestablish defensive lines short of the Netherlands and the Moselle indicated the enormity of the Allied success. When the Normandy campaign concluded on September 1, Eisenhower and his lieutenants had won a monumental victory. That same day he formally assumed direction and command of the land campaign, relegating Montgomery to command of his army group.

In the approach to the Rhine, Eisenhower repeatedly opted for a broad front approach, vice Montgomery's desire for a single thrust across the north German plain to capture Berlin. As supreme commander of the Allied Expeditionary Force, he insisted that it would be the Allied forces, not American or British forces, that would win the war. His detractors insist that he missed other opportunities by allocating his resources across such a broad front. Nor were Montgomery and Brooke disposed to favor Eisenhower's decision to personally command the land forces. Monty's periodic flirtations with the British press over Ike's direction of the land battle destroyed any semblance of military protocol and on more than one occasion were outright insubordination. Yet Eisenhower prevailed, never deviating from his emphasis on Allied solidarity. At the same time, Ike, more than any other American commander, fully understood what the war meant to the British. What other reason could there have been for him to call Montgomery's bluff and assign to him the vast majority of the Allied strategic reserve forces for the ill-fated airborne operation to seize the bridges over the Rhine in September 1944?

When Hitler launched the Ardennes offensive in mid-December, only Eisenhower immediately understood that the surprise assault was more than a local penetration. Rather than panicking, Eisenhower remained in firm command and reallocated forces for the Allied counterattack. To facilitate operational control of the battlefield, he released the SHAEF reserve for operational commitment and detached Courtney Hodges's First U.S. Army from Bradley's command and assigned it to Montgomery's 21st Army Group. As Bradley fulminated, Eisenhower remained firmly convinced that Allied victory was far more important than national prejudices and damaged egos. Repeatedly assuring Bradley of his continued support, Ike broadened his most trusted subordinate's control in the subsequent advance across the Rhine, and his insistence that both American and British forces receive priority ensured sufficient rewards and accolades for all.

Often neglected by modern historians is Ike's insistence that the destruction of German forces in southern Bavaria was more important than the capture of Berlin as a "strategic prize." Though Churchill urged Ike to race toward the German capital, Eisenhower never deviated from the orders enunciated in his directive from the Combined Chiefs of Staff: he was "to enter the Continent of Europe and in conjunction with the Allied nations, undertake operations aimed at the heartland of Germany and the destruction of her armed forces." Moreover, there was still a war to be won in the Pacific, and much of the American army in Europe might be needed for the invasion of Japan. Why risk an estimated one hundred thousand additional casualties to capture a city that, according to the Yalta agreement, would fall within the Soviet zone of occupation? History has proven Ike correct. By war's end, Eisenhower could claim with justifiable pride that victory in western Europe was the result of the complete integration of Allied ground, naval, and air forces. The unconditional surrender of Nazi Germany on May 7 prompted Eisenhower to compose a short but succinct communiqué to the Combined Chiefs of Staff: "The mission of this Allied force was fulfilled at 0241 local time, May 7, 1945."[26]

Tributes followed—and rightly so. Marshall wrote first, commending Eisenhower for "commanding with outstanding success the most powerful military force that has ever been assembled. . . . You have stood for all we hope for and admire in an officer of the United States Army." In his response, Eisenhower was effusive, noting that "since the day I arrived in England, indeed since I first reported to you in the War Department, the strongest weapon that I have always had in my hand was a confident feeling that you trusted my judgment, believed in the objectivity of my approach to any problem and were ready to sustain to the full limit of your resources and your tremendous moral support, anything that we found necessary to undertake to accomplish the defeat of the enemy. . . . Our army and our people have never been so deeply indebted to any other soldier."[27]

To King George VI Ike expressed his "heartfelt gratitude for the generosity" of the king's own message of congratulations. Churchill sent a personal letter of congratulations, then wrote President Truman to tell him "what General Eisenhower has meant to us. In him we have had a man who set the unity of the Allied Armies above all nationalistic thoughts. . . . At no time has the principle of alliance between noble races been carried and maintained at so high a pitch. In the name of the British Empire and Commonwealth, I express to you our admiration of the firm, farsighted, and illuminating character and qualities of General of the Army Eisenhower."[28]

Even Montgomery, who more than once had been a thorn in his commander's side, belatedly acknowledged that "honest differences of opinion are almost inevitable among experienced commanders, especially if they are also men with very definite views of their own. But such differences must never be allowed to overshadow the supreme need of Allied co-operation: this co-operation was brought to great heights under Eisenhower."[29] All in all, it had been a sterling performance from a commander who just one year before the war had been a lieutenant colonel with no combat experience. In the span of two and a half years, Eisenhower had emerged from war's darkest crucible as the most successful coalition commander since England's own duke of Marlborough in the early eighteenth century.

Any discussion of theater commanders in World War II would be incomplete without a brief word on General Joseph W. "Vinegar Joe" Stilwell in the China-Burma-India (CBI) Theater. A personal friend of the army chief of staff, Stilwell was the only officer alive who called Marshall "George." He, like Marshall, was an old "China hand," having served with the 15th Infantry Regiment in Tientsin in the 1920s. Several years later, Stilwell headed Marshall's tactics section at the Infantry School at Fort Benning, Georgia. As one of the army's senior commanders, Stilwell was dispatched to Burma at the outset of the war as the overall American military representative in a theater dominated by a British colonial army and inept Chinese forces under the command of Chiang Kai-shek. His instructions were ambiguous, as were the command arrangements. Stilwell's orders were to "co-coordinate, smooth out, and run the Burma Road, and get the various factions together and grab command and in general give 'em the works."[30] His general duties encompassed heading the U.S. military mission to China, supervising Lend-Lease to the country, and serving as Chiang Kai-shek's Allied chief of staff. An irascible officer who disdained alike both British and Chinese, Stilwell arrived in Burma just as the Japanese were commencing a major offensive. Allied preparations proved wholly inadequate to stem the determined Japanese advance. Chiang offered two Chinese armies to Stilwell, but he never clarified the command arrangements with his army commanders, who repeatedly refused to take orders from an American. Stilwell also had problems with the British, who were reluctant to accept the notion of dual command. The paucity of Allied resources and the overwhelming Japanese numerical advantage doomed the defense of Burma from the beginning; the campaign was an unmitigated disaster. Stilwell later described the subsequent withdrawal from

Burma in which he led a small group of refugees 140 miles across the mountains to India: "All retreats are ignominious as hell. I claim we took a hell of a licking and it's humiliating as hell."

The reconquest of Burma would require the full cooperation of British, American, and Chinese forces, and Stilwell immediately directed his efforts to achieve this union. It was an impossible chore. Burma was last on everyone's priority list, and Chinese field forces again refused to acknowledge his command authority. Now serving as Chiang's nominal chief of staff, Stilwell took the matter directly to the generalissimo, accusing the field commanders of gross ineptitude and misconduct. By "throwing the raw meat on the table" Stilwell sowed the seeds of his own relief. In the interim, however, he laid the foundation of a campaign to recapture Burma. American divisions, now destined for Europe and MacArthur's SWPA, were not forthcoming, and Stilwell had to be content with the return of the 10th Air Force to his command. The Chinese were not impressed. Chiang noted on May 25, 1942, that "Chinese confidence in their Allies will be completely shaken," and that this could presage the "total collapse of Chinese resistance."[31]

Still convinced that Anglo-American cooperation was feasible, Stilwell willingly placed himself under the command of Lord Louis Mountbatten, Supreme Allied Commander, South-East Asia Command. Like Patton, Stilwell had a difficult time controlling his mouth and frequently gave voice to his view that Chiang's government was so inherently corrupt that future operations would be imperiled by incompetent Chinese commanders. Nor did he make his feelings secret to visiting U.S. senators and to Secretary of War Henry Stimson. Not surprisingly, the generalissimo himself soon demanded Stilwell's recall for "losing the confidence of the troops." Considering Roosevelt's evolving policy toward Nationalist China, the relegation of CBI to a theater of tertiary importance, and the fact that even the British found him acerbic and irrational, Stilwell's relief was inevitable. Though Mountbatten never recommended that Stilwell be recalled, the relation between the two Anglo-American commanders was tenuous at best. Stilwell was not called Vinegar Joe for nothing.

Even as Stilwell's forces secured Myitkyina, the strategic key to northern Burma, in August 1944, the generalissimo renewed his demand for Stilwell's recall and insisted that as generalissimo, he, not Stilwell, ought to supervise the distribution of all Lend-Lease supplies. Caught in a political quagmire of his own making, Roosevelt acquiesced to Chiang's demands lest he lose Chiang's support—and possibly all of China. Knowing that Chiang could no longer tolerate Stilwell, the president directed Marshall to issue orders to bring him home. On October 21, 1944, Stilwell boarded an aircraft and returned to the United States. He arrived home on November 2, his wartime mission "of little glory and no thanks matched by his reception in Washington."

A political embarrassment to the Roosevelt administration and the most visible sign of American failure in the Far East, Stilwell was immediately placed under a gag order and told to disappear. As a full general he was hardly expendable, however, and he was far too senior to be assigned to either the SWPA or ETO. Appointed commander, Army Ground Forces, he spent the remainder of the war inspecting military camps before Marshall assigned him to replace Lieutenant General Simon Bolivar Buckner as Tenth Army commander following Buckner's death on Okinawa. Although he was slated to command the Tenth Army in the invasion of Japan, the Japanese surrender on August 14 negated his chance. "So it is over," he noted. "I don't care what they do with the god-damn emperor. . . . Hooray, Hooray. We have survived. No blanks in our list. Lucky people." For Vinegar Joe Stilwell, once given command of World War II's forgotten theater, the war was over. He died of cancer in 1946, five months before he was due to retire.

The U.S. Army's World War II theater commanders proved themselves officers of exceptional ability. MacArthur and Eisenhower were surely the principal stars and deserve full credit for their contributions to the ultimate Allied victory; Stilwell is all but forgotten. The command styles of MacArthur and Eisenhower differed significantly. MacArthur was a loner, consumed with his own place in history and waging battle with his own countrymen nearly as ferociously as he did with the enemy; Eisenhower was the ultimate "team player" and the personification of Allied harmony. Sixty years after the war, a substantial number of Americans are still familiar with Eisenhower's subordinate commanders while only a few recognize the distinguished officers who served under MacArthur in the SWPA. Personal idiosyncrasies aside, Douglas MacArthur and Dwight D. Eisenhower deserve to be remembered as outstanding commanders who fought on a global stage. Each made his share of mistakes and perhaps missed fleeting opportunities that might have shortened the war in his respective theater, but in the long run both achieved the ultimate goal of every combat commander—total victory over their nation's enemies.

CHAPTER 2

ARMY GROUP COMMANDERS IN EUROPE AND THE MEDITERRANEAN: TRAVAILS AND TRIUMPHS

> Supreme Headquarters, Allied Expeditionary Force, was responsible for the broad strategy, the direction of effort, and the allocation of resources, including supplies, troops, and air. These were its proper and necessary responsibilities and tactical arrangements and decisions were necessarily left to the three great tactical headquarters [army groups] we established.
>
> —*General of the Army Dwight D. Eisenhower*

PRIOR TO WORLD WAR II, the U.S. Army's only experience with army group command dated back to General John J. Pershing's direction of two field armies on the Western Front during the last two weeks of World War I. Various Command and General Staff College and War College classes studied army group functions in the intervening period, but, as Omar Bradley later claimed, only in vague and theoretical terms.[1] Contemporary regulations suggested that an army group should direct but not conduct operations, confining itself to broadly worded "mission orders" such as those that characterize the American army in the twenty-first century. Following the British model in the Mediterranean Theater, however, America's World War II army group commanders exercised more active control over the armies under their immediate command. As they gained battlefield experience, the U.S. Army's senior commanders became less and less reluctant to issue specific orders and to relieve corps and division commanders in whom they lost confidence.

As the war progressed, the essential task of the army group commander was to coordinate the operations of two or more armies. The Allied armies had increased in manpower and logistical resources to such an extent that they were beyond the capabilities of command and control of a single headquarters. General Dwight D. Eisenhower, the Allied supreme commander, was initially uncomfortable with such an organization, but later viewed the army groups as necessary to coordinate the actions of all the forces under his command. Though army group headquarters flourished in Europe, there was no comparable organization in the Pacific, where General Douglas MacArthur maintained personal control of the actions of his respective armies.

In the final two years of the war, three American officers served as army group commanders. Along with British Field Marshal Sir Bernard L. Montgomery, who commanded the 21st Army Group, Lieutenant Generals Omar N. Bradley and Jacob L. Devers were Eisenhower's principal subordinates in the campaigns in France and Germany. The third member of this illustrious trio, Lieutenant General Mark W. Clark, served in Italy under British Field Marshal Sir Harold Alexander. Clark, who earned his reputation primarily as commanding general of the Fifth Army, was elevated to army group command only in the final six months of the war on the Italian peninsula.

Foremost among the army group commanders was Bradley, commander of the 12th Army Group. At war's end, Bradley commanded the largest single American ground force in history—1.5 million men in four armies. Yet, sixty years after VE Day, the merits of Bradley's generalship are still being debated. Was Bradley the "GI's general" whom Ernie Pyle discovered in Sicily and Eisenhower proclaimed "preeminent among the commanders of major battle in this war"? Or are two recent Patton biographers, Carlo D'Este and Martin Blumenson, closer to the mark in speculating that had Bradley's and Patton's roles been reversed in northwest Europe, Germany would have never survived the catastrophic defeat in Normandy and the war might have ended in autumn 1944?[2] The verdict is still unclear.

Born in 1893 in Moberly, Missouri, Bradley came from a middle-class family. In the summer of 1911 he entered the U.S. Military Academy at West Point, where he was a classmate of Dwight Eisenhower. Bradley chose the infantry as his branch and missed combat in World War I. He attracted the attention of George Marshall while the latter was serving as the assistant commandant of the Infantry School in 1930. At Fort Benning, Major Bradley headed Marshall's Third Section, which was responsible for weapons and developing weapons doctrine. His supervision of a weapons demonstration involving a complicated tactical problem earned rare accolades from Marshall, who classified the quiet Missourian as an officer "conspicuous for his ability to handle people and his ability to do things simply and clearly." So delighted with Bradley's work was Marshall that he directed that the weapons section repeat "the best demonstration [he] ever saw" for every class that came to Benning as an illustration of how to simplify instruction.[3]

Simply and clearly—that was Marshall's style too. Consistently performing to Marshall's high standard, Bradley made a highly favorable impression on the future army chief of staff during the Benning years and entered Marshall's famed "black book," from which Marshall chose many World War II commanders. From his newly found mentor Bradley learned "the rudiments of effective command." Noting that Marshall seldom intervened after he had assigned an officer to his job, Bradley also carefully imitated Marshall's command style with respect to cultivating subordinate officers. If the officer performed, you left him alone. If not, you either counseled him or relieved him.[4] Marshall continued following Bradley's career, and a decade after their tour at Fort Benning, Marshall, now the deputy army chief of staff, selected Lieutenant Colonel Bradley to serve as a member of his personal secretariat.

Bradley's star continued to ascend when, in February 1941, he became the first active-duty member of the West Point class of 1915 to be promoted to brigadier general. His stellar performance again impressed Marshall, who sent him back to Fort Benning to serve as the commandant of the Infantry School and the post. Bradley's most innovative contribution to the mobilization effort of America's citizen-soldiers was the accelerated expansion of the Officer Candidate Schools (OCSs) designed to train junior commissioned officers recruited from the enlisted ranks or from the ranks of draftees with six months of basic training. Bradley's OCS program soon became the prototype for all OCSs at the army's various branch schools.

Repeated visits by Marshall cemented his professional relationship with Bradley, and in the immediate aftermath of the Japanese attack on Pearl Harbor, Marshall again nominated Bradley for accelerated promotion and assigned him command of the 82nd Division. As such, Bradley was instrumental in the selection of officers destined to command the army's first airborne division. Though Bradley transferred command of the "All-American" Division to Matthew B. Ridgway on the eve of the division's transition to an airborne unit, the cadre for the airborne division was drawn in large part from officers selected and trained by Bradley.

With the incorporation of National Guard divisions into the army's growing inventory, Marshall transferred Bradley in June 1942 to command the 28th National Guard Division at Camp Livingston, Louisiana. The 28th was typical of many National Guard divisions at that time: hastily assembled and poorly trained. Indeed, Marshall rejected Bradley's appointment to a corps four times so that he could straighten out the division. Bradley's fiftieth birthday on February 15, 1943, brought a congratulatory telegram from Marshall citing his splendid record with the 28th Division and promising him a corps-level command. The following day Marshall expressed his personal satisfaction with Bradley by delivering even better news. After superbly commanding two stateside infantry divisions in rapid succession, Bradley received orders to join his West Point classmate Eisenhower for "extended active duty" overseas.[5] Bradley understood that such an assignment meant combat duty in North Africa.

Rushed to Eisenhower's headquarters in the wake of the Kasserine Pass disaster, Bradley served as Ike's "eyes and ears" for the Tunisian campaign. Eisenhower gave Bradley broad latitude to go where he pleased in the American zone to observe and to report on anything that he felt worthy of Ike's attention. Eisenhower's confidence was based on his long friendship with Bradley, whom he knew to be a sound, painstaking, and broadly educated soldier.[6] The presence of his classmate reinvigorated Eisenhower, who expressed his deep appreciation to Marshall for dispatching Bradley so quickly to the theater. Bradley's arrival, Ike said, was "a godsend in every way and his utter frankness and complete loyalty are things that I count on tremendously."[7]

When Lieutenant General George S. Patton Jr. assumed command of II U.S. Corps in March, he asked Eisenhower for Bradley as his deputy commander. Bradley refined his knowledge of the art of war under Patton's tutelage, and then took command of II Corps in April when Patton left to concentrate on planning for the invasion of Sicily. Under Bradley, II Corps captured Bizerte.

Bradley's star continued to shine in Sicily, where elements of II Corps fought the Germans toe-to-toe up the rugged spine of the island. While Patton captured the glory in his thrust to Messina, Bradley encountered stiffer opposition inland. It was in Sicily that Bradley captured domestic headlines as a result of war correspondent Ernie Pyle's column entitled "Brass Hats." Told by Eisenhower to "go out and discover Bradley," Pyle left his usual station among the common soldiers to spend three days with Bradley. At times, Pyle noted, he "was so engulfed in stars he thought he must be a comet." Pyle developed great admiration for Bradley during his time with the II Corps commander, claiming that he had never known "a person . . . so unanimously loved and respected by the men around and under him." In Pyle's estimation, what endeared Bradley to the soldiers was his refusal to waste their lives in costly frontal assaults. When Pyle asked Bradley how he stood up under the responsibility of making decisions that would take human lives, Bradley's response was direct: "Well, you don't sleep any too well from it. But we're in it now, and we can't get out without some loss. I hate like the devil to order the bombing of a city, and yet it sometimes has to be done. It's really harder on some of the newer officers than it is on me. For although I don't like it, after all I've spent thirty years preparing a frame of mind for accepting such a thing."[8]

Nor was Pyle the only observer impressed with Bradley's ability to command American GIs in combat. In the tough fighting in Sicily, Bradley confirmed Eisenhower's opinion that he was "the best-rounded combat leader in our service."[9] Bradley had demonstrated a fine capacity for leadership and a thorough understanding of the requirements of battle. Equally important, Bradley never gave his commander one moment of worry, a quality, Eisenhower informed Marshall, that was of such great value "here in this sprawling theater with complicated problems of coordination among Allies" that it warranted favorable consideration for more senior command.[10] To Patton's mortification, it was Bradley who received the coveted appointment to go to England and prepare the American forces for the Normandy invasion. Since the job involved activating, forming, and organizing not only an army headquarters but also an army group, Bradley would play the dominant role in the impending invasion. Patton's reservations aside, there was much to commend Bradley for the job. He had demonstrated a talent for manipulating units in tightly contested fighting in the mountainous terrain of central Sicily, and though he had little experience planning amphibious operations, his ability was such that Eisenhower thought he could solve this part of the problem very satisfactorily. In short, the campaign in Sicily confirmed that Bradley had matured as a highly competent commander. It is thus not surprising that Bradley was the commander to whom Ike entrusted the American army that stormed ashore at Omaha and Utah beaches on D-Day. Simply put, Eisenhower selected his most trusted subordinate to perform the most difficult task. By day's end, elements of three infantry and two airborne divisions were rapidly expanding the beachhead. In the opening stages of the ensuing campaign, Bradley again demonstrated the cool leadership that had led to his selection as commander of the First U.S. Army.

Viewed in retrospect, however, D-Day revealed both the strengths and the weaknesses in Bradley's command style. His decision to commit the American airborne divisions to seal off the western flank of the invasion was certainly correct and greatly enhanced the success of the landing on Utah Beach. Omaha Beach proved a more difficult nut to crack, in large part because of Bradley's reluctance to employ the tactical lessons that had been learned in the Pacific in amphibious assaults against well-prepared beach defenses. Firing tables, the joint fire plan, and the amphibious doctrine for the D-Day invasion left much to be desired. Only the timely reports in late morning that individual groups of soldiers had finally penetrated the initial German defenses on the bluffs overlooking Omaha kept Bradley from abandoning the assault and diverting the follow-on forces to adjacent beaches. Consequently, Bradley attracted a fair amount of criticism for his orchestration of the battle. Historians Williamson Murray and Allan Millett severely chastise Bradley for the excessive casualties the First Army suffered in the expansion of the lodgment area, noting that Bradley was not the soldier's general of media legend but rather a man "jealous of Patton, suspicious of the British, unimaginative and dour."[11]

In late July, with his army bogged down in *bocage* that prevented employment of the maximum range of the weapons and mobility at its disposal, Bradley finally shifted from his broad-front approach and boldly conceived Operation Cobra. The operation entailed the massing of Major General Joseph L. "Lightning Joe" Collins's VII Corps on a narrow front against a weakened German line. Spearheaded by Collins, the Americans finally overwhelmed the entire German defensive line south of Saint-Lô. Cobra produced an unparalleled opportunity to destroy the German army in France. Yet, with the front burst wide open by Collins's advance and with Patton's newly activated Third Army at his command, Bradley, now commander of the 12th Army Group, failed to close the Falaise-Argentan gap. Though he later accepted full responsibility, stating that he preferred "a solid shoulder at Argentan to the possibility of a broken neck at Falaise,"[12] Bradley had the resources at hand to close the gap and did not do it. His error allowed the escape of an estimated fifty thousand German troops and, more important, a substantial number of officers and headquarters that would re-form to fight another day.

The reasoning behind the error reflects Bradley's personal approach to war. As an infantryman, Bradley tended to concentrate on the close-in battle. Keenly influenced by the Infantry School at Fort Benning, Bradley surrounded himself with officers who were careful and thorough tacticians. Regrettably, most of these officers, including his principal staff, lacked imagination and audacity. While Bradley was superb in planning the lodgment of the Normandy beachhead and in mustering his force for a breakthrough at Saint-Lô, he lacked operational insight beyond the confines of the immediate tactical battle. Given the fluidity of combat once the restrictions of mobility were removed, Bradley was forced to rely on subordinate commanders like Patton and VII Corps commander Lightning Joe Collins. While Patton, with his background as an armor commander, viewed battle as a series of movements over a number of map sheets, Bradley visualized grid squares. To paraphrase the Carthaginian Hamilcar Barca when he described Hannibal after the Battle of Cannae, Bradley knew how to gain a victory, but not how to use it.

In the subsequent drive to the West Wall, Bradley again proved his mettle. Not until the Germans attacked unexpectedly in the Ardennes in mid-December did criticism of Bradley's management of the front reappear. Eisenhower immediately grasped the severity and extent of the German penetration and cautioned Bradley to send two armor divisions to reinforce Troy H. Middleton's struggling VIII Corps. For his part, Bradley grossly misjudged the enemy's intention. Stung by the talk of his unpreparedness, a shocked Bradley reluctantly concurred with Eisenhower's transfer of Lieutenant General Courtney H. Hodges's First Army and Lieutenant General William H. Simpson's Ninth Army to Montgomery's 21st Army Group to facilitate command and control of both sides of the "Bulge." This left only Patton's Third Army at his immediate disposal. Bradley later concluded that his acquiescence was one of his biggest mistakes of the war. Instead of "standing up forthrightly to Smith [Ike's chief of staff] telling him that SHAEF was losing its head and that I had things under control," Bradley wrote in his memoirs, he knuckled under, largely due to what he confessed was the shock of the proposal and his deep reluctance to blow his own horn.[13] The subsequent elimination of the Ardennes pocket by Montgomery and Patton added to Bradley's growing frustration at having to work alongside egotistical allies and difficult subordinates.

Understanding Bradley's humiliation at losing his armies to Montgomery at the height of the German counterattack, the supreme commander cabled Marshall in late December to dispel any rumors that Bradley's faulty troop dispositions had contributed to the debacle in the Ardennes. Ike instead shored up his most valued subordinate, lauding Bradley for keeping a calm head and proceeding methodically and energetically to meet the situation. As if he realized that Marshall doubted Bradley's capabilities, Eisenhower added that he retained "his former confidence" in Bradley and recommended that he be immediately promoted to the rank of general.[14] Later in January, Eisenhower reiterated that Bradley's record of solid accomplishment since he had arrived in theater in February 1943 warranted favorable consideration for promotion to full general. The near disaster in the Ardennes, Eisenhower noted, was simply one of those incidents that must be anticipated along a great line where contending forces are locked in battle. In times of crisis, the real answer lies in the leadership exhibited by the commander in meeting unexpected problems. In this regard, Ike noted, Bradley had handled himself admirably after the initial offensive.[15] Some historians have been less kind.

Bradley's subsequent management of the 12th Army Group's crossing of the Rhine also reflected well on his military record. He was quick to reinforce the Remagen bridgehead, and he relieved a corps commander whom he believed acted too cautiously in expanding the bridgehead. Bradley also acted forcefully and, along with Eisenhower, developed a strategy that led initially to the encirclement and destruction of German forces in the Ruhr, and then to the final advance to the Elbe. It was Bradley's defining moment in the war. During the third week of April, the 12th Army Group was taking prisoners at the rate of 100,000 a day as the German resistance in the west crumbled. On April 16, the day Patton's army reached the frontier of Czechoslovakia, the army group captured 180,000 prisoners. In contrast, prisoner hauls for the entire Western Front were 344,000 in September, 109,000 during the November offensive, 81,000 in February, and 349,611 in March. In the six weeks after the first of March, 1,200,000 prisoners had been captured on the Western Front.[16] When Soviet forces met Bradley's troops at Torgau on April 25, the European war was essentially over. By May 9, the principal activity on Bradley's front consisted of rounding up Germans fleeing from the advancing Russians. Thus, eleven months and three days after D-Day, and three months to the day after the preliminary assault through the Siegfried Line toward the Rhine, the Wehrmacht laid down its arms in unconditional surrender.

At the close of the war in Europe, Bradley was undeniably Eisenhower's top lieutenant and most indispensable subordinate. Eisenhower described Bradley as a "quiet, but magnetic leader; [and an] able, rounded field commander; determined and resourceful; modest." Though latter-day historians may question Bradley's tactical competence, Eisenhower had no doubts about it. As he told Marshall, Bradley remained "the one whose tactical and strategic judgment I consider almost unimpeachable." In a final letter before Bradley left Europe to take up his new position as administrator of veterans affairs, Eisenhower conveyed his personal gratitude to Bradley for his leadership and forcefulness and for the professional capacity that made him one of America's great leaders and soldiers. "I cannot resist the urge," he wrote to Bradley,

> upon your departure to the United States, to attempt once more to give some expression of the personal sense of gratitude and admiration I feel toward you. Since you first joined me in North Africa in early 1943, I have constantly depended, with perfect confidence, upon your counsel and advice. In the Allied Command you have successively and successfully commanded a Corps, an Army and an Army Group. In my opinion you are pre-eminent among the commanders of major battle units in this war. Your leadership, forcefulness, professional capacity, selflessness, high sense of duty and sympathetic understanding of human beings combine to stamp you as one of America's great leaders and soldiers. I know that you are now going to a most important post and one that is fraught with possibilities for public criticism. These will be inevitable and the only word of advice I would like to submit is that you carry on that task with the same methods, the same objective attitude and the same devotion to duty that have made you so successful in the past. . . . My personal thanks are due you for the way you have always made my own tasks the easier to accomplish. With good luck and best wishes. From your old friend, Ike.[17]

Like Bradley, Mark Clark was a friend and confidant of Eisenhower. With the possible exception of Patton, Clark was Eisenhower's closest friend before the war. In fact, Eisenhower owed much of his prewar success to his association with the officer whom Winston Churchill later dubbed the "American Eagle." Born in Madison Barracks, New York, on May 1, 1896, Clark followed Devers and Bradley to the U.S. Military Academy. After graduating in April 1917, Clark served with distinction with the 11th Infantry Regiment, 5th Division in France during the Great War. While in temporary command of a battalion near the Vosges Mountains, Clark was seriously wounded, but he recovered sufficiently to join the General Staff Headquarters, First American Army. In that capacity he participated in the Saint-Mihiel and Meuse-Argonne offensives, but fame and glory eluded the ambitious young officer.

The interwar army found Clark attending the service schools that prepared talented officers for the responsibilities of wartime command. Clark graduated from the Infantry School in 1925 and from the Command and General Staff School in 1935. Upon graduation from the Army War College in 1937, Clark finally received his break. Assigned to the General Staff Corps with duty with the 3rd Infantry Division at Fort Lewis, Washington, Clark immediately earned a reputation as one of the army's premier trainers. At Fort Lewis, Clark also attracted the attention of George Marshall, who commanded the division's 5th Brigade at nearby Vancouver Barracks. As the division G-3, Clark's responsibility was to supervise the training of the division. Since the division commander and the chief of staff were not particularly interested in training, Clark frequently sought the advice of Marshall. Clark's evaluation of Marshall's performance in a mock exercise cemented the future chief of staff's favorable impression of Clark.[18] Subsequent exercises, organized by Clark, also gained Marshall's approval. It was only a matter of time before Marshall, as deputy chief of staff of the U.S. Army, would summon Clark to Washington. The army chief was gathering a cadre of highly qualified officers for services associated with the rapid expansion and mobilization of the army, and Clark was clearly an officer destined for increased responsibility.

The call came soon enough, and Clark joined General Headquarters, U.S. Army, as an operational planner and as Brigadier General Lesley J. McNair's principal assistant at General Headquarters, U.S. Army (GHQ). In that capacity Clark worked closely with Marshall, who later credited him with devising the method of raising and training new divisions as the American army expanded on the eve of the war. As he had with Bradley, Marshall recommended Clark for immediate promotion to brigadier general in July 1941, thereby skipping the grade of colonel. The 1941 Texas-Louisiana maneuvers justified Marshall's confidence in Clark's potential for senior command. As McNair's chief planner, Clark supervised the largest army field exercises to that date. By the time the maneuvers concluded in late September, Marshall had selected a new corps of officers for future command and dismissed others whom he considered too old or too lethargic for wartime command.

It was also on Clark's recommendation that Marshall ordered Brigadier General Eisenhower to the War Plans Division in the aftermath of the Pearl Harbor disaster. Henceforth, the names Eisenhower and Clark would be irrevocably linked. When Marshall later assigned Eisenhower command of the European Theater of Operations, U.S. Army, he simultaneously appointed Clark commander of II Corps, the principal invading force for Operation

Torch. As the date for the assault on North Africa approached, Clark, now Eisenhower's deputy commander in chief and principal trainer, made a highly publicized and dangerous trip to Africa to arrange details for the proposed landings. His mission was a success, as were the subsequent amphibious assaults on November 8, 1942.

In Eisenhower's opinion, Clark had clearly demonstrated his potential for army-level command. But Clark's penchant for self-promotion antagonized many of his colleagues, who doubted the wisdom of appointing Clark as Eisenhower's deputy. George Patton, for one, resented Clark's growing influence with Ike, noting that Clark was "too intrusive" for such an important post.[19] In early December, Marshall designated Clark the commanding general of the Fifth Army, the first American army to be activated in the European Theater. Although Patton was reportedly angry that Clark received the coveted assignment, Clark was the logical choice. He was, in Eisenhower's words, the "best trainer, organizer and planner" Ike had ever met, and the Fifth Army was essentially a training headquarters in early 1943. Ike needed an officer suited for army-level command—someone with organizational, training, and planning qualifications, and with broad knowledge of the entire situation.[20] Clark was once again in the right place at the right time. Although he was torn by his loyalty for his two old friends, Eisenhower heartily endorsed Marshall's decision. He was certainly aware of Clark's ambition; in fact, Ike once noted that "the title of Army commander was too attractive," and Clark had "begged and pleaded" for it for some time.[21]

In accepting command of the Fifth Army, Clark may, in fact, have missed a golden opportunity. Churchill was looking for an American adviser, and Clark's foremost biographer argues that had Clark accepted that job, he might have received the most coveted ground assignment of the war—command of the American invasion force in Normandy.[22] Clark, of course, had no desire to sit in London holding Churchill's hand. Nor could he have possibly foreseen Patton's fall from grace during the Sicilian campaign. And how could he reject a coveted army command? The bird in his hand was too attractive to release, and Clark was unwilling to look beyond the immediate promotion.

In September 1943, Clark and the Fifth Army launched Operation Avalanche, the invasion of the Italian mainland, with a determined assault at Salerno. The enemy outnumbered Clark's initial assault force, which consisted of the X British Corps and the VI U.S. Corps. Determined German resistance left the American corps badly bruised, and at the height of the battle Clark contemplated withdrawing his force. Only American firepower, coupled with timely reinforcement by a regiment from Major General Matthew B. Ridgway's 82nd Airborne Division, prevented disaster. Clark conspicuously toured the front, repeatedly exposing himself to enemy fire, and was later awarded the Distinguished Service Cross for his actions. His courageous leadership stiffened Anglo-American resolve, and he was instrumental in the final defeat of the German force.

Clark found the succeeding winter campaign particularly frustrating. Not only did the British commander of the 15th Army Group, to which the Fifth Army was assigned, downplay Clark's force, but Hitler's decision to defend Italy south of Rome created a situation in which terrain played the dominant role in delaying the Allied advance. Naples fell on October 1, 1943, but progress was excruciatingly slow. Determined to reach Rome as expeditiously as possible, Clark's army slogged northward against a series of heavily defended lines.

January 1944 was a bad month for Mark Clark. His forward elements had inched northward until they encountered entrenched German divisions behind the Rapido River. In one of the more controversial decisions of the campaign, Clark ordered Major General Fred L. Walker's 36th Infantry Division to cross the Rapido, hoping to ease the pressure on Major General John P. Lucas's forthcoming landing at Anzio, scheduled for January 22. The Rapido crossings were a disaster, with Walker's division losing almost seventeen hundred men. Clark accepted only minimal blame and directed his frustration at Walker.

Lucas landed at Anzio as planned but did not push forward to the adjacent Alban Hills, possession of which would have severed the Germans' communications lines and forced them to withdraw from southern Italy. Unfortunately, Clark failed to convey the urgency of the situation to Lucas, and Lucas in turn failed to display aggressive leadership. Clark believed that the establishment of the beachhead would suffice to weaken the German line, but he was sorely mistaken. Instead of withdrawing, the Germans counterattacked with greater ferocity than they had at Salerno. Again Clark contemplated withdrawal and relieved the VI Corps commander, this time replacing Lucas with Major General Lucian K. Truscott Jr., who had distinguished himself in Sicily. Truscott's appointment was one of Clark's most prescient decisions of the war.

During the several months in which the Fifth Army attempted to join with Truscott's besieged corps, Clark experienced further disappointment. Halted for weeks before the Benedictine abbey atop Monte Cassino, Clark's troops suffered increasing casualties as they tried to penetrate the Gustav Line. Clark needed a victory, but the Germans were in no mood to accommodate him.

Finally, the Fifth Army, reinforced by the Eighth British Army, surged forward in a combined 15th Army Group attack on May 11, 1944. German defenses along the Gustav Line collapsed, but Clark again failed to destroy the German force. Advancing sixty miles in fourteen days, the Fifth Army joined Truscott on May 25.

It had been a bitterly fought campaign. With his entire army once again intact, Clark disregarded British general Alexander's instructions to sever Highway 6 and to destroy the retreating German army. More concerned with capturing a prestigious objective than destroying the enemy, he directed the majority of his force toward Rome in an effort to seize the first Axis capital to fall into Allied hands. In a highly publicized ceremony, Clark led the Fifth Army into the Italian capital on June 5. The Germans had long since escaped, but Clark had his moment of glory. "Our capture of Rome . . . has been a great victory," he announced, "and we deserve it after the hell we have been through for so many months."[23]

The capture of Rome was Clark's greatest triumph, but it was hardly his last. As the Allied armies surged northward, Clark assumed command of the 15th Army Group in late November. At the same time, Alexander, promoted to field marshal, replaced Field Marshal Sir Henry M. "Jumbo" Wilson as supreme Allied commander, Mediterranean Theater of Operations. Clark's promotion was as much the result of Winston Churchill's esteem and admiration as it was due to the political ramifications of commanding an Allied army group. In accepting command of an army group that had previously been commanded by a British officer, Clark expressed his appreciation to the British prime minister: "I will be deeply honored to command the 15th Army Group. I fully realize the responsibility this assignment entails and the compliment His Majesty's Government has paid on me in consenting to place your glorious Eighth Army under my command. Please be assured that its welfare will be carefully guarded. . . . Please accept my great appreciation for the confidence you have always placed in me."[24] Promotion to full general followed on March 10.

In the ensuing campaign in northern Italy, Clark did not disappoint Churchill or the British Chiefs of Staff. Under its new commanding general, the 15th Army Group renewed its offensive as soon as the spring rains halted and sufficient infantry replacements arrived to fill the Fifth Army's depleted ranks. By midspring, Bologna and the Po River valley were in Clark's hands. On May 2, one day after Clark's forty-ninth birthday, German plenipotentiaries in Italy signed the instruments of unconditional surrender. Three days later, elements of the Fifth and Seventh U.S. armies joined hands at the Brenner Pass near Innsbruck, Austria. The war in the Mediterranean Theater was over. For Clark it was the moment of ultimate triumph. A lieutenant colonel in 1941, he was now a full general and, after Eisenhower, Bradley, and Patton, the most visible and highly acclaimed American general in the European Theater.

Though Mark Clark had played a leading role in the Allied victory in Italy, his leadership remains controversial. The commanding general of the 15th Army Group has not fared well in current historiography. Of all the senior American commanders in the European and Mediterranean theaters, Clark seems to have fallen far short of expectations. A far more competent staff officer than battlefield commander, Clark lacked the drive and compassion that characterized his more brilliant contemporaries. Historians Murray and Millett describe Clark as too ambitious, ruthless with subordinates, profligate with the lives of his soldiers, unsympathetic to the difficulties of other Allied armies, and more impressed with style than substance.[25] Theirs is a scathing indictment, but a fairly accurate one.

General Lucian K. Truscott Jr., who served as one of Clark's army commanders, would have concurred. Truscott found Clark an able staff officer and an unusually able executive and administrator, but thought that he "lacked training and experience in high command, his first major command having been Salerno—a rough lesson." Like MacArthur, Clark usually traveled with an entourage that included journalists and photographers. His public relations officer remained under strict orders to ensure that all dispatches included Clark's name and the name of his operational headquarters. Truscott concluded that Clark's concern for personal publicity was his greatest weakness and that it prevented him from acquiring that "feel of battle" that marks all top-flight battle commanders.[26]

In retrospect, Mark Clark is a classic case of an officer rising beyond his level of competence. Any assessment of Clark's capabilities as an army and army group commander must include his ill-advised order to attack across the Rapido River, his relief of two corps commanders in whom he had initially placed confidence, the unnecessary bombing of Monte Cassino, and his opting to seize Rome and stage a victory parade rather than overtake the retreating Germans. Though additional factors mitigated the costly campaign up the Italian boot, as army and subsequently army group commander, Clark must bear a certain degree of responsibility. His shortcomings have left serious questions concerning his tactical and operational acumen and a nagging doubt that Clark really understood the intricacies of waging modern war at a senior level of command.

Nor was Clark as successful as Eisenhower in mastering the nuances of coalition command, due in no small part to his mistrust of British and French forces. Clark's paranoia about a British conspiracy to deny him and his Fifth Army their due made him a begrudging Allied commander at best. Though George Patton voiced similar views toward the British, Patton remained a strictly national, not a coalition, commander. Even Marshall and Joseph T. McNarney, the deputy supreme commander for the Mediterranean Theater, were mystified by Clark's penchant for alienating his allies. In late October 1944, McNarney informed Marshall that "Clark's mental attitude is a curious mixture. He has the highest admiration for himself, his staff, his commanders and troops. He is consumed with bitterness against the British." The army chief of staff concurred, noting that Clark had not helped matters by his somewhat Montgomery-esque habit of permitting his people to give his name prominence over those of his subordinates.[27]

Yet it was Clark who stamped the indelible imprint of his personality on the Italian campaign. Perhaps remembering their prewar friendship and Clark's service as his deputy for Torch, Eisenhower repaid a long-standing debt to the "clever, shrewd and capable" Clark by ranking him fifth on his order of merit of senior American commanders. Churchill remained Clark's lasting champion. The day following the German surrender, Churchill cabled Clark: "Pray let me send you and your gallant men my most heartfelt thanks for all you have done to make this great victory possible." The prime minister also mentioned Clark in dispatches to President Truman, noting, "I also express British gratitude for the services of the highest quality, both in counsel and on the battle-line, of General Mark Clark of the United States Army, who commanded the fighting front . . . and whose comradeship with Field Marshal Alexander . . . will long be cherished in both our countries and commended by history."[28]

Unlike Bradley and Clark, Jacob Loucks Devers never enjoyed a close personal relationship with the supreme commander even though his contributions to victory were on a par with those of his more famous contemporaries. Born in York, Pennsylvania, in 1887, Devers graduated from the U.S. Military Academy in 1909, a member of the same class that produced army commanders George S. Patton Jr., Robert L. Eichelberger, and William H. Simpson. For the next thirty years Devers served in a variety of field artillery assignments and on the staff and faculty of West Point. From June 1939 to July 1940, he was chief of staff of the Panama Canal Department, a posting that Marshall considered extremely important given the priority of protecting the nation's lifeline between the Pacific and Atlantic oceans. In the autumn of 1940 Devers took command of Fort Bragg, North Carolina, and the 9th Infantry Division. He oversaw an intensive training program for draftees and National Guard troops, as well as an extensive building program as the army expanded on the eve of America's entry into the war.

Devers's most notable assignment before combat in World War II was as chief of the Armored Force at Fort Knox, Kentucky, where he was instrumental in the mobilization and training of the force that proved so decisive in ground combat in Africa and Europe. Under Devers's dynamic leadership, the armored contingent expanded from four to twelve armored divisions in twenty months. Marshall commended him for his achievement but simultaneously made it clear that he was not entirely satisfied with Devers's work. Following an inspection of the recently activated 4th Motorized Division in June 1942, the army chief chastised Devers because the division did not have a single tank, even though Marshall had personally authorized the advance activation of two armored divisions. In what could only be viewed as a serious rebuke, Marshall informed Devers that he feared that he had followed the same path "that separate corps chiefs have usually taken, that is, too little regard for units outside of their corps."[29] Marshall was disturbed because the army's only motorized division had "lost all this time in the development of tactics and technique so far as its tank echelon was concerned." Following the American defeat at Kasserine Pass eight months later, Marshall again cabled Devers (as he did his other branch chiefs) that he "had a real problem on his hands" as American divisions in combat had initially displayed a "certain softness or complacent attitude."[30]

Marshall set those reservations aside when he recommended that Devers be promoted to lieutenant general in May 1943 and then assigned him command of the European Theater of Operations. In that capacity Devers represented the United States in planning the cross-Channel attack and supervised the buildup of the American army in the British Isles. He also ran afoul of Eisenhower over the allocation of aircraft in support of Eisenhower's Mediterranean operations. When Bradley arrived in England the following September, Devers became largely superfluous. Bradley's arrival foreshadowed the appointment of another senior American officer, presumably Marshall or Eisenhower, to lead the American army in the upcoming invasion of France. The staid Bradley, already assigned a prominent role in the forthcoming invasion, was not unhappy to see Devers go; he found him "overly garrulous, egotistical, shallow and much too inclined to rush off half-cocked." Patton echoed Bradley's sentiments in early February 1944, stating that Devers was ".22 caliber."[31] Eisenhower agreed; he wanted battle-tested officers "accustomed to his views of combat," and Devers had yet to face the rigors of combat. With the greatest challenge of his career before him, Eisenhower favored members of the Mediterranean clique that had performed so well in North Africa and Sicily for the invasion of northwest Europe. The solution was simple. Ike recommended Devers to replace him in the Mediterranean, knowing that Devers "would be acceptable to the British."[32] In truth, Ike didn't like Jacob Devers; and he also knew that Devers, three years his elder, would be difficult to pass over for senior command of Overlord if he remained in England. The supreme commander was looking for a way to allow Devers a graceful exit from the United Kingdom. In his memoir, Ike was circumspect about the reasons for Devers's departure, noting that with both Bradley and Patton already in England, he foresaw little immediate need of Devers in the same organization. Devers enjoyed a fine reputation as an administrator, and his talents would be more valuable in the Mediterranean where Mark Clark would control tactical operations.[33] Devers received his new assignment from the War Department as soon as Eisenhower arrived in the United Kingdom to command the Allied Expeditionary Force.

In his new position as the deputy supreme Allied commander of the Mediterranean Theater under Jumbo Wilson, Devers's principal responsibility was to plan for Operation Anvil (also known as Dragoon), the invasion of southern France. In July 1944, with Anvil only a month away, Eisenhower wrote Marshall to express his support for Devers and to extinguish any rumors that Marshall might have heard concerning Eisenhower's reservations about Devers as commander of the operation. Aware of Marshall's interest in Devers, Eisenhower informed the chief that he had nothing against Devers personally and that positive reports he had heard from the theater had eliminated the "uneasy feeling" he once had held about him. Moreover, Ike confessed that he did not know Devers well, and that any doubts he had previously entertained concerning Devers's ability were based completely on impressions and, to some extent, on vague references that had no basis in positive information. Devers had been on the battle front a lot, Ike added, and had demonstrated a "happy faculty" for inspiring troops; that in itself was sufficient to warrant Eisenhower's favor.[34]

Marshall hardly needed an endorsement from Eisenhower. Earlier he had cautioned both commanders to pay closer attention to the troop replacement system and then suggested that each appoint a separate commander with that responsibility alone. Devers actually beat Eisenhower to the punch and briefed Secretary of War Henry Stimson in May 1944 of his own initiative to keep units fresh and vigorous. His rapid attention to an irritating problem overcame Marshall's reservations regarding the manner in which Devers was executing his duties.

Anvil commenced on August 15, 1944, with Alexander Patch's Seventh Army wading ashore against light opposition. On September 15, by agreement between Eisenhower and Wilson, the French and American forces that had participated in the invasion were passed over to Supreme Headquarters, Allied Expeditionary Force (SHAEF), and were placed under the 6th Army Group, which became operational on that date under the command of Devers. Devers's command thus consisted of Patch's Seventh Army and the French First Army commanded by General Jean-Marie de Lattre de Tassigny. In the ensuing campaign, Devers's forces merged into the main effort of Overlord and protected Bradley's right flank in the approach to the German border. Commanding the 6th Army Group with characteristic vigor, Devers made rapid headway until stiff German resistance in the Vosges Mountains, coupled with a long logistical tail, impeded his advance. A shortage of infantry replacements also prevented the 6th Army Group from fulfilling Devers's promise to sweep the enemy west of the Rhine. Though he had reached the Rhine ahead of schedule, Devers found himself the object of obvious displeasure at SHAEF. Bradley in particular lacked confidence in Devers, and his animosity infected Eisenhower's command structure.

Nor was the supreme commander pleased that the Germans still held a deep pocket west of the Rhine in the vicinity of Colmar. Historian David Eisenhower has confirmed that Devers, Marshall's one direct appointment in the European Theater, never enjoyed Eisenhower's complete confidence.[35] In late November 1944, Eisenhower had cautioned Devers about the staying capacity of the German Nineteenth Army in Alsace and the tendency of the French forces to operate independently of Devers's control. As German resistance stiffened, Eisenhower's temper flared. In Ike's view, Devers had ignored his advice and needlessly dispersed his forces for the drive west of the Rhine. Eisenhower informed Marshall in late January 1945 that Devers had been "badly mistaken" regarding the ability of the French army to eradicate the Colmar pocket. Furthermore, Devers had failed to concentrate his army group to eliminate the pocket, and the Germans now had a salient from which they could mount a major offensive. Ike noted that while Devers could scarcely be blamed for making a miscalculation with respect to the French, the pocket was nevertheless a "very bad thorn in our side." In fact, Devers lacked sufficient strength to break through the enemy defenses, and Bradley's group held a higher priority for replacements and matériel.

When the Germans launched their offensive in the Ardennes on December 16, 1944, Devers reluctantly halted his own offensive and relieved Bradley west of the Moselle River to facilitate Bradley's attack against the southern shoulder of the Bulge. With his own front exceeding 180 miles, Devers awaited the counterattack that Ultra intercepts foretold would strike between January 1 and 3, 1945. The German assault, code-named Nordwind, began near midnight on New Year's Eve. When Eisenhower suggested that he abandon Strasbourg and the surrounding territory to shorten and to strengthen his line, Devers instead prepared a forward defense. It was almost the final straw for the supreme commander. Exasperated with his 6th Army Group commander, Eisenhower ordered the SHAEF chief of staff, Lieutenant General Walter Bedell Smith, to "call up Devers and tell him he is not doing what he was told."[36] Smith's biographer claims that Eisenhower's exasperation over the Vosges campaign led him to consider relieving Devers and replacing him with Patch, but Eisenhower never petitioned Marshall for such a transfer.[37]

Though he eventually halted and then crushed the German attack, Devers earned what historian Russell Weigley terms the "unwonted coolness" of the supreme commander for the remainder of the war. Part of the problem lay in the fact that Eisenhower and his friends in the 12th Army Group never truly accepted Devers as an equal. Another factor was Devers's refusal to release Lucian Truscott from his post in the Mediterranean for duty as one of Overlord's assault corps commanders. In this matter Marshall repeatedly sided with Devers against Eisenhower. Eisenhower's cables to Marshall in the summer of 1944 indicate only a grudging endorsement of Devers for senior command. At best, Jacob Devers was "a good bet" if the Allies decided to activate another army group.[38] One gains the impression that a great deal of Eisenhower's support for Devers's promotion lay in his recognition that Devers was the man Marshall favored to command the attack up the Rhône River valley. Eisenhower's principal subordinates echoed his sentiments. Bradley and his army commanders felt that Devers had not earned his combat spurs before being elevated to army group command, although nothing was further from the truth. The existence of the Colmar pocket remained a burr under Eisenhower's saddle, for which he blamed Devers. The relationship between Eisenhower and Devers deteriorated considerably as a result, but

Eisenhower, ever conscious that Devers was Marshall's man, never seriously considered relieving him once the war entered its final stage.

January 1945 found the 6th Army Group once again attacking to clean up the Colmar salient. Led primarily by de Tassigny's army, Devers's forces finally eliminated the pocket, at a cost of eighteen thousand casualties. In the process the southern army group destroyed seven of the eight German divisional formations. Yet not even that victory gave Devers access to Eisenhower's inner circle. The supreme commander informed Marshall in mid-January that he was not yet ready to recommend Devers for promotion to four-star rank, even though Devers already held an army group command. Eisenhower noted that the 6th Army Group commander had not inspired the trust and confidence among the senior officers of the American organization (read SHAEF and Bradley's army group) that was so necessary to continued success. Damning him with faint praise, Eisenhower characterized Devers as "enthusiastic, but often inaccurate in statements and evaluations; loyal and energetic."[39] Ike had not yet determined the proper position of Devers with respect to the other commanders on his merit roster, he told Marshall, even though the overall results Devers and the 6th Army Group had produced were generally good, and sometimes outstanding. Marshall obviously disagreed. He recommended Devers for promotion to general on March 8, 1945, ahead of Bradley, Patton, and Clark.

The remainder of the war added luster to Devers's star. He crossed the Rhine on March 27 and drove rapidly to the south and southeast. His specific orders were to protect Bradley's right flank and to advance to meet the Russians in the Danube valley. By May 6, 1945, his forward units had captured Munich, reached the Brenner Pass, and crossed the Austrian frontier. That same day Devers received the unconditional surrender of German Army Group G, which comprised all German forces in Austria—nearly one million men. Representing Army Group G was General der Infantrie Hermann Foertsch, who freely admitted that he was powerless to prevent the capitulation. Among the prisoners were Hermann Goering, Albert Kesselring, and Gerd von Rundstedt. It was a climactic finish for the "outsider" who had served the supreme commander and his nation so well.

Regrettably, Devers ended his career somewhat embittered by the lack of recognition for his martial achievements. Following the war, Marshall brought him back to Washington to take charge of the army ground forces. He performed admirably, but Marshall, now retired, eventually soured on him. In an interview with biographer Forrest Pogue, Marshall admitted that Devers had done good work in Europe at first, but his personal ambition eventually got the best of him. While sitting on a War Department board to consider general officers for promotion, Devers moved his own name up on the list. When two other board members asked Marshall to reverse Devers's standing, he refused, but Devers's action offended Marshall's sense of selfless service to the nation.[40]

Bradley, Clark, and Devers played significant roles in the ultimate defeat of Germany. Elevated to a command position for which they had no prior training or experience, each overcame initial obstacles and performed well. The American military experience provided no clearly prescribed guidelines for the conduct of an army group command, and that lack added to the difficulties each man faced. Except for the final stages of World War I, when Pershing had established that command for himself, American commanders had never operated at a level higher than army level. The army group headquarters in essence acted as a glorified corps command, but without directly assigned troops and with an additional logistical function. How the army groups organized their respective headquarters was largely determined by the individual commanders. In meeting that challenge, Bradley, Clark, and Devers proved indispensable to victory.

CHAPTER 3

ARMY COMMANDERS IN THE PACIFIC: FORGOTTEN WARRIORS

I was interested [to hear] . . . about most officers not wanting to come out here [Pacific theater]. The officers who were here today say all the officers at home want to go to other theaters because there is more publicity there. . . . If I can get an army and do well with it . . . I will have no complaint about my part in the war. I only trust I can do whatever is given to me in a way that will be helpful to Uncle Sam. I sometimes think that the latter gentleman is not considered as often as he might be.

—*Robert L. Eichelberger, commanding general, Eighth Army*

MOST AMERICANS PERCEIVE WORLD WAR II in the Pacific as primarily a naval war. Images of battleships ablaze in Pearl Harbor, the great carrier battles at Midway, and marines raising the flag on Mount Suribachi have all but eclipsed the enormous contributions of the U.S. Army. Nearly sixty years after General Douglas MacArthur received the Japanese surrender aboard the USS *Missouri*, few but veterans and historians recall the heroic efforts of the army's frontline commanders in the Pacific. Over the course of the war, the United States employed three armies and twenty-one divisions in the Pacific Theater (excluding the units serving in the China-Burma-India Theater of Operations); most of those troops deployed in 1942.

After the army committed troops to the Mediterranean Theater and the cross-Channel attack, not one new division was sent to the Pacific.

Who led the American forces that served so gallantly in the jungles of New Guinea, the Philippines, and Okinawa? Aside from MacArthur, Robert L. Eichelberger, and Joseph W. Stilwell, three commanders in particular stand out. Jonathan M. Wainwright, Walter Krueger, and Simon B. Buckner Jr. served with great distinction in operations in the Pacific. Largely forgotten after the fall of Bataan and Corrigedor, Wainwright spent the remainder of the war in a prisoner-of-war camp. Krueger, the most successful of the three, commanded the Sixth Army in the campaigns "from down under to Nippon" (the title he gave his memoir of the Pacific war). Buckner, who commanded the Tenth Army, was killed in action. Each man met a different fate, but all three contributed mightily to the Allied victory.

In a sense, Jonathan Mayhew "Skinny" Wainwright IV was a magnificent anachronism, a soldier more suited for the cavalry of John Ford's cinema than a commander of modern warfare. Described by his principal biographer as at once "charming and profane, courtly and tough, a gentleman and a fighter, and a soldier to the core," Wainwright matured as an army commander between the world wars.[1] Born in Walla Walla, Washington, on August 23, 1883, Wainwright witnessed the closing of the American West. His father, a distinguished soldier in his own right, served in the First Cavalry, a unit in which Jonathan would later serve as well. Following Major Robert Wainwright's death in the Philippine Islands from a tropical disease, Jonathan threw himself into his studies at West Point. He entered the Military Academy in July 1902 and easily adjusted to West Point's academic and physical regimens.

Also attending the Military Academy in Jonathan's first year was a handsome cadet named Douglas MacArthur, whose father had also served in the Philippines. Little did Wainwright realize that his career and MacArthur's would be inextricably intertwined over the next thirty-five years. At West Point, Wainwright followed in MacArthur's illustrious footsteps, earning first captain honors himself for the class of 1906. Although not the top cadet academically that MacArthur had been—Wainwright stood twenty-fifth of seventy-eight cadets—he was first militarily. The accolades Skinny received in the *Howitzer*, West Point's annual yearbook, indicate the respect of his fellow cadets: "Corporal, Sergeant Major, First Sergeant, First Captain, Hop Manager, Marksman, Toastmaster New Year's 1906. This is IT—the summit toward which the Pampered Pets of the Powers that Be continually do strive, the goal of every good cadet's ambition. Many honors have been heaped upon his head—so many that it's a wonder his slender frame has withstood their bending moment without any more damage than giving to his knees a permanent set."[2]

Considering his personal history, it is hardly surprising that Wainwright selected the cavalry for his branch of choice. He received his commission on June 12, 1906, and departed shortly thereafter for his initial duty assignment with the First Cavalry at Fort Clark, Texas. A born hell-raiser, Wainwright balanced his reputation as a hard drinker with a compassionate command style that earned the respect of his contemporaries and his men. In 1909 he got his wish for combat duty when the First Cavalry was transferred to the Philippines to fight the insurgent Moros. As a platoon leader, Wainwright was frequently in the midst of the action, commanding small groups of soldiers on an endless series of jungle patrols.

On returning stateside in 1910, Jonathan was stationed at posts in Idaho, Wyoming, Kansas, and California. When World War I erupted, Wainwright yearned for combat but instead found himself attending the General Staff College established by General Pershing at Langres, France. Wainwright graduated high in his class and was detailed for duty as assistant chief of staff of the 82nd "All-American" Division, where he served with distinction during the Meuse-Argonne offensive that culminated in the final Allied victory. For his service in the war and as a member of the occupation forces, Wainwright received the Distinguished Service Medal, three campaign Bronze Stars, France's National Legion of Honor, and Belgium's Croix de Guerre. He entered the war a captain and came out a lieutenant colonel, though he reverted to his prewar rank in the postwar army. The day after he reverted to captain he was promoted to major.

As did many of his colleagues, Wainwright attended every military school of importance in the interwar army. Service on the War Department General Staff reacquainted Skinny with the military defense plans for the Philippines in the event of a Japanese attack. Working long hours on War Plan Orange, he helped develop the plans for a military withdrawal to the Bataan Peninsula and the defense of Corregidor Island. Subsequent duty with troops culminated in his selection to attend the Army War College in 1933.

Two years later, Wainwright was promoted to colonel and assigned to Fort Myer, Virginia, the home of the Third Cavalry. Fort Myer, adjacent to Arlington National Cemetery, was the most desirable of all the cavalry command posts, but it required someone with diplomatic as well as military skills. Wainwright enjoyed his tour among the nation's military and civilian elite immensely, but he soon found himself the object of innuendo—probably correct—that he was drinking too much. Never the most astute diplomat, Wainwright still regretted leaving the social scene at Myer.

Brigadier General Wainwright's new posting as commandant of the First Cavalry Brigade at old Fort Clark, Texas, appeared to signal an inglorious end to a respectable military career. Though rich in the heritage of the U.S. Cavalry, the obscure post had earned the reputation as "the country's most somnambulant Cavalry post, where superannuated officers . . . were usually allowed a pleasant last fling before retirement."[3] Too old for a wartime command in George Marshall's reinvigorated army, Skinny Wainwright resigned himself to spending his final years on the Texas frontier. To his surprise, the army chief of staff had other ideas.

When the USAT *Grant* sailed from New York Harbor on September 14, 1940, Wainwright and several hundred officers and men were on board. Their destination was Luzon, Philippine Islands, where Skinny Wainwright had first tasted combat against the Moros. Only in the expanding army of 1940 would an officer of Wainwright's age have received a second chance, regardless of his excellent military record.

Like most senior officers in the American army, Wainwright was convinced that war with Japan was rapidly approaching. The war in Europe was now a year old, with Germany triumphant across the continent. Though he would have preferred an assignment leading to combat in Europe, Skinny willingly accepted command of the Philippine Division, which included both a large contingent of Filipino troops and the largest American army unit in the islands. Theoretically, the Philippine Division was a square division with four attached brigades, but it was not equipped as such and lacked a brigade organization and some of its organic units. All the enlisted men in the division, except those in the 31st Infantry and a few military police and headquarters troops, were Philippine Scouts. The 31st was the only infantry unit in the islands composed entirely of Americans. In addition to this regiment, the Philippine Division contained the 45th and 57th Infantry Philippine Scouts (PS). (Of the 22,532 American soldiers assigned to MacArthur's Philippine Department on the eve of the war, 11,293 were Philippine Scouts.) The total strength of Wainwright's command in July 1941, including organic and attached elements, was 10,473 officers and men.[4]

In November, just weeks before the Japanese attacked Pearl Harbor, MacArthur, as commanding general of the U.S. Army Forces, Far East (USAFFE), divided his forces into four tactical commands: the North

Luzon Force, the South Luzon Force, the Visayan-Mindanao Force, and the Reserve Force. MacArthur offered Wainwright his choice of the commands. Wainwright's response was immediate. "Which do you consider the most important point in the Philippines to defend? Where do you think the main danger is—the place where some distinction can be gained?"

"The North Luzon Force, by all means," MacArthur replied.

"I'd like that," Wainwright said.

"It's yours, Jonathan."[5]

Now MacArthur's senior field commander, Wainwright assumed command of the North Luzon Force, which consisted of three Philippine army divisions—the 11th, 21st, and 31st—the 26th Cavalry Regiment (PS), one battalion of the 45th Infantry (PS) on Bataan, two batteries of 155-mm guns, and one battery of 2.95-inch mountain guns. One additional division (the 71st) could be committed only on the authority of MacArthur. Wainwright's orders were to protect airfields and prevent hostile landings in his area of responsibility. In the event of a successful landing, the enemy was to be destroyed. In contrast to War Plan Orange–3, which provided for a withdrawal to Bataan, MacArthur's plan stated that there was to be "no withdrawal from beach positions." The beaches were to be "held at all costs."[6]

Following the near annihilation of MacArthur's air force on Clark Field on December 8, the North Luzon Force prepared for the inevitable invasion. By Wainwright's own admission, the untrained and ill-equipped Philippine army units attached to his command were doomed even before they encountered the invading Japanese force. Following initial landings on December 10 in northern Luzon, the Japanese struck in force at Lingayen Gulf in the gray dawn of December 22. The transports carried the Japanese Fourteenth Army, whose main force included 43,110 men commanded by Lieutenant General Masaharu Homma. Philippine resistance was light, as many of the unprepared frontline units deserted their beach defenses. Homma's troops quickly forced Wainwright to withdraw to stronger defensive lines across the central Luzon plain. The scene, as described by MacArthur's principal biographer, was chaotic as the "defenders fell back, some fleeing to the hills never to return to their units and others regrouping later to resume the futile, uneven struggle."[7]

Lacking sufficient naval and air defenses to counter the Japanese amphibious assault, MacArthur issued a revised WPO-3 contingency plan that called for a withdrawal to the Bataan Peninsula and the evacuation of Manila on December 23. Wainwright's mission was crucial—he was to conduct a delaying action on successive lines to the final defensive position on Bataan. Of the five defensive lines, only the last was to be organized for a protracted defense. Skinny supervised the operation with characteristic efficiency, and soon MacArthur's forces were united on the peninsula. Unfortunately, MacArthur had not accumulated adequate supplies on Bataan to withstand a protracted siege.

The defense of Bataan officially began on January 7, 1942. On that day Wainwright took command of the west sector of the Bataan Defense Force, which became I Philippine Corps, consisting of three Philippine army divisions and miscellaneous troops—about twenty-five thousand soldiers in all. The Japanese effort was directed against the eastern defenses of the peninsula. Skinny conducted a series of limited counterattacks, but was forced to give ground when forces on his right flank withdrew to a more defensible position. His personal leadership galvanized his soldiers on more than one occasion. By late January, however, the limited depth of Bataan precluded further withdrawal. Throughout February, the Bataan force clung to a toehold, repulsing numerous enemy attempts to penetrate Wainwright's lines. On February 22, President Franklin D. Roosevelt ordered MacArthur to Australia to prepare for the Allied counteroffensive, and Jonathan Wainwright assumed command of the Luzon defenses. Though MacArthur had intended to retain command in the Philippines from his base in Australia, Marshall dismissed such an arrangement as ludicrous. Wainwright, not MacArthur, would command all U.S. forces in the Philippines effective on MacArthur's departure from the Islands. On March 19 Marshall wrote to the president recommending that the following message be dispatched immediately to Wainwright: "The nation is aware of the extreme difficulty of your task and of its vast importance. With confidence in your leadership and the superb gallantry and efficiency of that devoted band of American and Filipino soldiers under your command, I am today submitting your nomination as a Lieutenant General."[8]

Wainwright transferred his headquarters to Corregidor to direct the defense of Bataan. Command of the Luzon force was assigned to Major General Edward P. King Jr., an artillerist who had served as MacArthur's principal fire support officer since the outbreak of the war. For the next four weeks the line successfully resisted Japanese efforts at penetration and envelopment. In savage fighting, the Bataan force eliminated numerous pockets of enemy resistance and annihilated several amphibious task forces. In the process, the "battling bastards of Bataan" inspired a nation. On the verge of starvation and running dangerously low on supplies and ammunition, the American forces refused to capitulate; the outcome, however, was inevitable. On March 28, Homma launched a major offensive but was repelled. Three days later he renewed the offensive and was again beaten back by what Wainwright termed "the bayonets of malarial men with not enough food in their bellies to sustain a dog." The day of decision was April 6, when Homma mounted the largest attack to date. The exhausted American line crumbled. On April 9, unable to sustain organized resistance and without the approval of Wainwright, King finally surrendered. Regretfully, Wainwright wrote to MacArthur: "At 6 o'clock this morning General King . . . without my knowledge or approval sent a flag of truce to the Japanese commander. . . . Physical exhaustion and sickness due to a long period of insufficient food is the real cause of this terrible disaster."[9]

With the fall of Bataan, General Wainwright's days on Corregidor were numbered. Under direct artillery fire, the garrison on the island began a twenty-seven-day battle for survival. Refusing to fire on the tip of Bataan for fear of hitting his captured men, Wainwright prepared for the inevitable. It was not long in coming. On May 4, the tempo of the shelling increased significantly. On the following morning, Japanese forces landed on Corregidor. With no antitank guns, the garrison fought in vain to withstand the combined arms assault. On May 6, 1942, "with broken heart and head bowed in sadness but not in shame," Wainwright informed Roosevelt: "I must arrange terms for the surrender of the fortified islands of Manila Bay." And so, with "profound regret and with continued pride in his gallant troops," Skinny Wainwright went out to meet the Japanese commander.[10]

Wainwright spent the remainder of the war in a series of prison camps. Marshall sought to award him the Medal of Honor for his spirited defense of the Philippines, but MacArthur cravenly intervened, stating that it "would be a grave injustice to a number of other general officers of practically equally responsible positions who . . . exhibited powers of leadership and inspiration to a degree greatly superior to that of General Wainwright."[11] It was MacArthur at his vindictive worst—and high irony as well, considering that he himself had received the Medal of Honor under similar circumstances. Deferring to his commander in the field, Marshall quietly shelved the nomination, but he planned to resubmit it at a more opportune time.

In his memoirs Wainwright describes his first day of captivity as "the beginning of hell." Haunted for the remainder of the war for surrendering his command, and fearing that his name had been sullied by his action, Skinny endured unspeakable mental and physical hardships over the next three years. During that time he was moved from Formosa to Kyushu, then to Korea, and finally to Manchuria. Not until August 16, 1945, did Wainwright discover that the war was over. He had spent nearly twelve hundred days in captivity.

When Marshall was informed of Wainwright's release, he let MacArthur know that the people back home would be pleased if this commander, who had been forced to surrender the last regular army units in the Philippines, could witness the formal surrender of Japan aboard the USS *Missouri*. Aides quickly made the necessary arrangements. On August 31, 1945, Wainwright's plane landed at Yokohama and he was immediately ushered in to see his former commander. Grasping Wainwright's hand, MacArthur, for once in his life, was speechless. He reflected later that "the emotion registered on that gaunt face still haunts me."[12] To his great satisfaction, Wainwright occupied the position of honor behind the supreme commander during the surrender ceremony and received one of the pens used by MacArthur to sign the instrument of capitulation. On September 10, he received the ultimate tribute for a soldier. In a public ceremony at the White House, President Truman awarded Wainwright the Medal of Honor. Neither General Marshall nor a grateful nation had forgotten him after all.

Skinny Wainwright lived eight more years following his liberation. It would have been far better had he retired immediately after the war with his reputation intact. He decided instead to stay on in the peacetime army, but he had long since passed his prime. Popular on the speaking circuit, he longed for a major command, and Eisenhower, now army chief of staff, found one for him in 1946, assigning Wainwright to Fort Sam Houston, Texas, to command the Fourth Army. There he slowly deteriorated. "Alone in his hero's cage," a West Point classmate described him, "he worked for other men and made their speeches!"[13] Memories of the war haunted him. Frequently he broke down at reunion activities, and once again he hosted endless parties at his quarters. Rumors of his excessive drinking, reminiscent of Fort Myer in 1938, persisted. Finally, on August 31, 1947, Skinny Wainwright retired from the army he loved. He was the final member of his West Point Class of 1906 on active duty. He died on September 2, 1953, eight years to the day after he witnessed the Japanese surrender in Tokyo Bay.

General Walter Krueger, like Wainwright, served under MacArthur with gallantry and determined leadership. A sixty-one-year-old career soldier at the outbreak of the war, Krueger had first joined the army as a private during the Spanish-American War and had been commissioned in 1901. Krueger was a product of the army's institutional emphasis on professional education. A graduate of the Infantry-Cavalry School, the General Staff College, the Army War College, and the Naval War College, he fancied himself a military intellectual. He wrote a number of penetrating theses on amphibious operations and translated several European tactical manuals. Additionally, he had twice served in the War Plans Division (1922–25 and 1934–38) of the Army General Staff. During the latter assignment he had been chief of the division and a member of the Joint Army and Navy Board.

Krueger commanded various infantry units in the interwar army, including the 6th Infantry Regiment for two years, the 16th Infantry Brigade for eight months, and the 2nd Infantry Division for the better part of eighteen months. He commanded VIII Corps until May 16, 1941, before assuming command of the Third Army and Southern Defense Command. During the Texas-Louisiana maneuvers of 1941, Krueger's Third Army performed superbly, allegedly due to the organizational brilliance of its chief of staff, Colonel Dwight D. Eisenhower. Eisenhower certainly contributed to the Third Army's spectacular success, but Krueger was the unit's commander, and according to many, he actually devised the strategy that Eisenhower and his staff implemented. Krueger resented the public acclaim that went to his chief of staff and later claimed that Eisenhower had taken credit for his "brain-child."[14] In truth, it was the Krueger-Eisenhower team that captured national attention and the particular attention of the army chief of staff. Nor did Eisenhower fail to recognize his debt to Krueger. On the latter's assignment to the Pacific Theater, Ike cabled his congratulations, noting, "I cannot tell you the depth of my satisfaction and gratification that a tried and true war-horse, such as yourself, is to go where his talents will be of the greatest possible usefulness."[15] Of the forty-two division, corps, and army commanders who participated in the Texas-Louisiana maneuvers, only eleven went on to significant combat commands in World War II. Of these, only Krueger and George S. Patton Jr. commanded field armies in combat.[16]

Marshall's decision to keep Krueger spoke well of Krueger's potential for wartime leadership. Determined to avoid sending American soldiers into combat under general officers too old to command them in battle under the terrific pressures of modern warfare, Marshall decided to place the army's fate in the hands of leaders who could stand up to "the severest tests which he could devise in time of peace." Of all the senior line generals at corps and army levels at the time Marshall became chief of staff, he gave only Walter Krueger command of U.S. troops in battle.

On January 12, 1943, while inspecting the 89th Infantry Division at Camp Carson, Colorado, Krueger received the following radiogram from Douglas MacArthur: "I have just recommended to the Chief of Staff that you and the

Third Army Headquarters be transferred to this area. I am particularly anxious to have you with me at this critical time."[17] Krueger was no stranger to MacArthur, of course, after their long and intimate association on the War Department General Staff. MacArthur's estimation of Krueger's efficient operational and organizational abilities made him especially anxious to have Krueger assigned to the Pacific command. Krueger's gruff personality, disdain for publicity, and no-nonsense approach to the conduct of war made him ideally suited for a Pacific command under the vainglorious MacArthur. They had gotten along well in Washington, due in no small part Krueger's refusal to confront his chief and his preference for working behind the scenes to obtain what he wanted. Moreover, as chief of the War Plans Division, Krueger had established a reputation as the army's foremost expert in joint operations.

Though Marshall rejected MacArthur's request for the transfer of the Third Army, he did give him Krueger. Krueger received orders to organize and activate the headquarters of a new army, which he did in late January. Immediately thereafter, Krueger and the forward elements of his newly designated Sixth Army left for Brisbane, Australia, arriving in the Southwest Pacific Area (SWPA) Headquarters on February 7. To circumvent orders that would have had American forces serving under the Allied land forces commander, an Australian, MacArthur created an independent tactical organization known as Escalator Force (later called Alamo Force) to conduct operations. No one, least of all the Australians, was fooled by MacArthur's sleight of hand, but they were hardly in a position to argue. Direction of the Pacific war outside Southeast Asia remained in the hands of the United States, not the British Commonwealth. In any event, Krueger was far more senior than any Australian officer who might have been designated to command an Allied force. As he had done in the Philippines, MacArthur formulated all strategic plans, issued directives designating the operations and commanders, and provided the resources to conduct them, but he did not prescribe the tactical measures or methods to be employed. That was Krueger's responsibility. On February 16, 1943, MacArthur assigned all American combat units, including Robert Eichelberger's I Corps, to the Sixth Army.

In the ensuing campaign, MacArthur and the Third Fleet commander, Admiral William F. "Bull" Halsey Jr., launched a series of strikes to follow up Allied successes in New Guinea and the Solomon Islands. The ultimate prize was the Japanese stronghold at Rabaul on the island of New Britain. The immediate objective was the seizure of airfields along the New Guinea and Solomon coasts, from which Krueger and MacArthur intended to whittle down the enemy's strength and provide air cover for future Allied assaults. Krueger seized the Woodlark and Kiriwina Islands, then mounted a series of amphibious assaults on New Britain. Subsequent directives from the Combined Chiefs of Staff directed MacArthur to neutralize rather than capture Rabaul. During the ensuing campaign, dubbed Operation Cartwheel, Krueger superbly orchestrated a series of amphibious landings that demonstrated his expertise in conducting joint operations.

To complete the encirclement of Rabaul in February 1944, MacArthur and Krueger next turned to the Admiralty Islands in the Bismarck Archipelago. Again Krueger's efforts proved successful. By mid-1944 Krueger had ten American divisions under his command as he continued his advance up the coast of Dutch New Guinea. The substantial increase and the complexity of operations soon led the SWPA commander to activate the Eighth Army under the command of Robert Eichelberger, who had already earned a reputation as the army's premier fighting general in the Southwest Pacific. At the same time MacArthur formally dissolved Alamo Force, thus casting aside the thin disguise that Krueger's Sixth Army had worn for two years.

With two armies under his command, MacArthur began his greatest campaign, the reconquest of the Philippines. Not surprisingly, Krueger was his linchpin, commanding the ground forces in what MacArthur labeled the crucial battle of the war in the Pacific. On Krueger's shoulders rested the fate of the Philippines and the future of the ground phase of the Southwest Pacific Theater of Operations. On October 20, 1944, A-Day (in the Pacific, commanders used designations other than D-Day to indicate the date for launching a major operation), the Sixth Army stormed ashore. While the greatest naval battle in history raged in Leyte Gulf, Krueger's force secured the beachhead and moved inland. By December 26, MacArthur reported the Leyte-Samar campaign closed except for minor mopping up. As usual, the SWPA chief's reports were too optimistic; it took Eichelberger's veterans months to eliminate several "minor" pockets of staunch Japanese resistance. In the interim Krueger secured Mindoro, an island across the narrow Verde Island Passage from Luzon.

Relinquishing control of all troops, duties, and missions in the Mindoro area to the Eighth Army on January 1, 1945, Krueger prepared for the final assault on Luzon. His orders from MacArthur were clear: "Seize the Central Plains–Manila area by overland operations to the southward; prepare to conduct such operations as GHQ might later direct to complete the destruction of the enemy's forces and the occupation of Luzon; assume control of and direct the operations of Philippine forces on Luzon; establish facilities for minor naval operations at the earliest practicable date in the Lingayen Gulf area . . . and be prepared to initiate establishment of naval, air and logistical bases, as later directed by GHQ, in order to support subsequent operations to complete the destruction of Japanese forces in the Philippines and future operations to the north and west of the Philippine Archipelago."[18]

The major combat units initially available to the Sixth Army for the Luzon campaign were I Corps, commanded by Major General Innis P. Swift; XIV Corps, commanded by Major General Oscar W. Griswold; the 158th Infantry Regimental Combat Team; the 13th Armored Group; and two infantry divisions in reserve: the 25th Infantry Division and the 11th Airborne Division. The initial combat strength of the Sixth Army, excluding the airborne division, was 152,447. Other units joined the troop list when the full extent of the Japanese forces was finally realized.

To execute MacArthur's orders, Krueger devised a complicated three-phase operation. The first phase included the amphibious assault to seize and consolidate beachheads at Lingayen Gulf and the subsequent establishment of air and base facilities in that region. Next, Krueger would attack and destroy all enemy forces north of the Agno River, ten miles inland, and seize and secure crossings over that river. Finally, Sixth Army would destroy all enemy forces in the Central Plains area and continue the attack to capture Manila. The plan designated January 9 as the target date—or S-Day—for the operation and assigned 0930 as H-Hour for the assault landing.

Landings on Luzon commenced on schedule with an amphibious assault at Lingayen Gulf. Within a few days Krueger had 175,000 men ashore. Opposition was initially light but steadily stiffened as Krueger's forces advanced down the central Luzon plain that had witnessed Homma's attack three years earlier. Ever cautious, Krueger remained concerned about his exposed left flank, but MacArthur correctly gauged that the Japanese would neither counterattack nor sacrifice their army in the open plains of central Luzon. Accelerate the advance, he directed his principal ground commander. Krueger was not as confident, and the pace of his forward elements reflected his trepidation. Observing from afar, Eichelberger concurred with MacArthur, noting that old "Molasses in January" was hardly a great general, nor did he possess any of the elements of greatness.[19] In effect, Krueger based his operations on his estimates of Japanese capabilities, not on the enemy's actions.[20]

All the while, MacArthur continued to exert enormous pressure to recapture the Philippine capital as quickly as possible. To prod Krueger, MacArthur committed elements of Eichelberger's Eighth Army for an advance from the south. Inspecting the 1st Cavalry Division, which had just arrived to reinforce XIV Corps, MacArthur directed its commander, Major General Verne D. Mudge: "Get to Manila! Go around the Nips! Bounce off the Nips, but get to Manila! Free the internees at Santo Tomás! Take Malacanan and the legislative buildings!"[21] Haunted by the nightmare of a formidable Japanese counterattack into his exposed pickets, Krueger finally bowed to MacArthur's demands. It was a bitter pill to swallow, however, and Krueger bristled at his commander's lack of confidence in his abilities. According to MacArthur biographer D. Clayton James, Krueger ranked next to Lieutenant General Richard K. Sutherland, MacArthur's chief of staff, as the officer who most frequently incurred the wrath of the Old Man.[22] Krueger finally secured Manila on February 27, but desperate fighting continued on Luzon long after that date.

By June 30 the Sixth Army controlled most of the island, but an estimated 25,000 Japanese troops remained in the mountains. On July 1 Eichelberger's Eighth Army assumed responsibility for operations on Luzon and for clearing the remaining islands. MacArthur declared the Philippine Islands secure on July 4, but fighting continued until the war's end. As late as August 15, almost 115,000 Japanese, including noncombatant civilians, were still at large on Luzon and the central and southern islands. Though most of these forces were scattered and incapable of coordinated offensive operations, they still posed a danger to the liberators.

Overall, the cost of the campaign had been excessive. Battle casualties alone numbered 8,140 killed, 29,557 wounded, and 157 missing. Non-combat casualties were proportionately higher. As usual, the infantry had sustained the greatest losses. The infantry incurred roughly 90 percent of all Sixth Army casualties on Luzon.[23] In turn, Krueger and his men killed 173,563 and captured 7,297 of their adversaries while engaging and defeating the largest Japanese army encountered by the Allies in the Pacific war.[24]

Though MacArthur at times found Krueger less than enterprising, even timid, he certainly had reason to be pleased with his senior army commander. In February 1945, at the height of his dissatisfaction with the Sixth Army's progress, MacArthur recognized Krueger's distinguished record by nominating him for promotion to four stars. Eisenhower, now supreme commander in Europe, also endorsed his former boss. In response to Marshall's communiqué requesting Ike's recommendation on four-star promotions, Eisenhower noted that Krueger was a special case because there were no army group commanders in the Pacific. It seemed to Ike that Krueger's age would make it impossible for him to be an embarrassment to Marshall when the army chief reorganized the army after the war was over. Nor did he believe that any of his European commanders would be resentful if Krueger were promoted.[25] Marshall obviously concurred. Krueger received his promotion on March 5, days ahead of Omar Bradley and the European "glamour boys." It was a fitting tribute to a great soldier.

The Luzon campaign terminated Walter Krueger's combat service. Entrusted by MacArthur to command American ground forces for Operation Olympic—the initial invasion of Kyushu in November—Krueger was ecstatic when Japan accepted the Potsdam ultimatum on August 14. His remaining days in the Pacific were confined to occupation duty in Kyushu and western Honshu. On December 31, 1945, the Sixth Army relinquished its occupation duties to the Eighth Army and redeployed to the United States. Four weeks later, on January 26—MacArthur's birthday—Krueger arrived at Mac's Tokyo headquarters to bid farewell to his wartime chief. In a brief ceremony, MacArthur decorated Krueger with the Distinguished Service Cross and with an additional oak leaf cluster to his Distinguished Service Medal. Three days later he boarded the USS *New Jersey* and was homeward bound. For Walter Krueger the war was over. The accolades soon followed. MacArthur's civil affairs adviser confirmed an assessment that MacArthur was especially lavish in his praise of Krueger. "I have known all of our great army commanders of this century and in over-all accomplishment rate him [Krueger] at the top of the list."[26]

Unlike Wainwright and Krueger, Simon Bolivar Buckner Jr. never served in the Southwest Pacific Theater. His opportunity to command a field army occurred in support of Admiral Chester W. Nimitz's Central Pacific drive. His tragic death at the very moment of victory denied him his rightful place in the pantheon of American military heroes.

Born on July 18, 1886, to Simon B. Buckner Sr., a hero of the Confederacy, Buckner Junior spent two years at the Virginia Military Institute before receiving his appointment to the U.S. Military Academy in 1904. He graduated fifty-seventh in his class four years later and selected the infantry as his branch of service. During World War I, "Buck" Buckner earned his wings and trained the nation's first combat pilots for the fledgling U.S. Air Service, but did not see action. Like Eisenhower and Bradley, he was later criticized because he had risen to high rank without being tested in battle.[27] Exemplary service in

Panama and the Philippines, coupled with a distinguished record as a trainer and educator—including a tour at the Military Academy as an instructor of tactics—led to his appointment as commandant of cadets at West Point in 1933. Coincidentally, his future adversary on Okinawa, Lieutenant General Mitsuru Ushijima, held a comparable post at the Japanese Imperial Military Academy. The years before the war witnessed Buckner in a variety of training and inspection tours. He became a colonel in 1937 and attained the rank of brigadier general on September 1, 1940.

From 1940 to 1944, Buckner was the senior army officer in the Alaskan Defense Command (later redesignated the Alaskan Department) at Fort Richardson, Alaska. Buckner's command grew in importance in the spring of 1941 as tensions increased between Japan and the United States. By September, Marshall had dispatched more than twenty thousand additional men to the Alaskan Defense Command. Conflicting demands from other theaters, and particularly from Chief of Naval Operations Ernest King, however, led the army chief to shift his attention to more likely avenues of approach in the event of an Allied counteroffensive against Japan. In short, Marshall seemed content to adopt a "wait and see" policy for Alaska and directed Buckner to remain on the strategic defensive, with any troop augmentations to be used for defensive purposes only.[28] The Japanese attack that finally occurred in June 1942 was more a nuisance than a full-fledged threat of conquest.

As a major general, Buckner played an instrumental role in the recovery of Attu in the Aleutian Island chain in May 1943 and was cited for exceptionally distinguished and meritorious service. Regrettably, interservice rivalries over command arrangements coupled with Buckner's inappropriate remarks concerning the contribution of the U.S. Navy had deeply embarrassed Marshall the previous autumn. Buckner had always been impetuous, but his indiscretion in reciting a rhyme about the navy's reactions to the perils of navigation in the Aleutians to a group of senior naval officers had exceeded acceptable limits and created hard feelings with the navy. Buckner's poem included a verse that had Rear Admiral Robert A. Theobald, the senior military officer in Alaska and the commander of Task Force 8, saying:

> The Bering Sea is not for me, nor for my Fleet Headquarters
> In mortal dread I look ahead in wild Aleutian waters
> Where hidden reefs and williwaws and terrifying critters
> Unnerve me quite with woeful fright and give me fits and jitters.[29]

Though the chief generally admired Buckner, he abhorred his lack of judgment. Moreover, Buckner had violated one of Marshall's cardinal maxims, that of interservice cooperation in distant theaters of the war. Buckner was in great jeopardy of being relieved of his command, but Marshall decided to first send Buckner's immediate superior, Lieutenant General John L. DeWitt, to investigate the incident. Relations between the two services had deteriorated to a point, Marshall informed DeWitt, that there appeared to be no other cure but a complete change. He hesitated, though, not wanting the incident to reflect ill on Buckner, whom he considered an excellent organizer. DeWitt was able to smooth the navy's ruffled feathers, but the affair left a bad taste in Marshall's mouth and it took Buckner the better part of two years to regain the chief's confidence.[30] Indeed, when Marshall was considering officers for corps-level command and looking for a lieutenant general to replace DeWitt as commanding general of the Western Defense Command and Fourth Army at the Presidio of San Francisco, he passed over Buckner, apprehensive that such a promotion would irritate the navy. Consequently, Buckner remained in Alaska until mid-1944.

Buckner did eventually get his army command. Transferred to the Central Pacific Area in June 1944 after being promoted to lieutenant general, Buckner formally assumed command of the Tenth Army in September. The remainder of the year found him training the force that would participate in Operation Iceberg, the invasion of Okinawa. His training program was later recognized with the Navy Department's Distinguished Service Medal, though the award reflected interservice cooperation more than the navy's confidence in Buckner's ability as a commander.

Buckner's Tenth Army comprised seven combat-experienced divisions in two combat corps: the all-marine III Amphibious Corps of three divisions under Major General Roy S. Geiger and the XXIV Army Corps of four divisions under Major General John R. Hodge. The Tenth Army included a total of 183,000 assault troops and 115,000 technical and logistical troops. Although the Tenth Army had not previously directed combat operations as a field headquarters, its corps and divisions had seen combat before the invasion of Okinawa. III Amphibious Corps had captured Guam and Peleliu, and XXIV Corps had carried out the conquest of Leyte.[31]

American forces landed in Okinawa on Easter Sunday, April 1, 1945. Overall command of the invasion rested with Admiral Raymond A. Spruance; Buckner commanded the ground forces. The Tenth Army met virtually no opposition as it moved inland. Correspondent Ernie Pyle, covering a marine regiment, noted that the invasion beach was incredibly calm. "There wasn't a dead or wounded man in our sector. Medical corpsmen were sitting among their sacks of bandages and plasma and stretchers, with nothing to do."[32] The marines quickly eliminated resistance on the northern part of Okinawa, and the area was declared secure on April 20. The situation in the south was far different. There, General Mitsuru Ushijima had constructed a series of strong concentric defensive lines centered on the ancient castle town of Shuri in the south-central portion of the island. As casualties mounted, both on the ground and in the fleet, Buckner pushed steadily onward until he encountered the heavily fortified Shuri Line. Buckner's progress typified his personal approach to war—slow and methodical. Admirals Nimitz and Spruance, who were suffering heavy casualties from kamikaze raids, urged Buckner to accelerate his advance, but he reminded his naval superiors that the land campaign was his responsibility. Preferring to attack deliberately with massive firepower rather than risk yet another amphibious assault, Buckner eschewed any suggestion of conducting an "end run" to outflank the Shuri Line. There would be no Anzio on Okinawa.[33]

It was mid-May when the Tenth Army finally captured Maeda Ridge and Sugar Loaf Hill and renewed its advance. On May 27 Buckner ordered III Amphibious and XXIV corps to maintain unrelenting pressure on the enemy. Shuri Castle fell on the last day of May as Ushijima withdrew to a final defensive line. Buckner assured correspondents, "It's all over now but cleaning up pockets of resistance." That proved to be a colossal understatement. As the Americans advanced south from the Shuri Line, combat on Okinawa took its cruelest form. According to historian Allan R. Millett, every hill became a battleground of flying grenades and raking machine-gun fire. To clear caves, the attackers used what Buckner described as his "blowtorch and corkscrew" method. Tank-infantry teams drilled holes in cave roofs and then used phosphorus grenades to ignite gasoline or napalm poured through the openings.[34] Refusing to risk another amphibious assault to outflank the Japanese line, Buckner proceeded with World War I–style tactics, attacking straight up the gut against formidable defenses. Progress was excruciatingly slow and expensive in human lives.

By mid-June it was only a matter of time before the American advance completed the destruction of Ushijima's Thirty-second Army. In the process the Tenth Army lost its commander. On June 18 Buckner visited the forward observation post of the 8th Marine Regiment, 2nd Marine Division. Shortly after 1300 hours, a Japanese artillery observer spotted Buckner's party and launched a five-gun barrage. A round exploded overhead, sending shrapnel and a piece of coral into Buckner's chest. He was dead within ten minutes. No other member of his party suffered a scratch. General Geiger assumed temporary command of the Tenth Army until General Marshall dispatched General Joseph Stilwell to Okinawa on June 23. Okinawa was the only Pacific campaign that took the lives of both opposing commanding officers. With Americans closing in on his headquarters, Ushijima committed ritual seppuku on June 22.

In retrospect, the assignment of Buckner to command the Tenth Army was one of Marshall's few poor choices among the senior army leadership of World War II. Buckner repeatedly failed to demonstrate the tactical and operational acumen an army-level commander must have. Dismissive of his subordinates, all of whom had considerably more combat experience against the Japanese than he did, Buckner eschewed innovative tactics for a more cautious approach that not only endangered the lives of the ground troops but also kept the supporting Fifth Fleet in Ryukyian waters in order to sustain the land force. U.S. naval casualties during the Okinawa campaign were the highest of the Pacific war, mostly as a result of kamikaze attacks, which sank or severely damaged in excess of 120 ships.

Okinawa was declared secure on June 22 after eighty-three days of combat. American battle casualties were enormous, including 12,520 dead or missing and 36,631 wounded. Of the total, the Tenth Army endured 4,582 killed, 18,099 wounded, and 93 missing.[35] Japanese casualties exceeded 110,000 killed and 7,400 captured. Ushijima's tenacious and spirited defense, with a force far larger than American planners had anticipated, resulted in the costliest battle of the Pacific war.

As could be expected, Buckner attracted a great deal of criticism for his cautious tactics. Even MacArthur, quick to compare Operation Iceberg's high casualty figures with his own "moderate" totals for the entire Southwest Pacific Area from Melbourne to Tokyo, joined a chorus of marine generals and navy admirals claiming that the commanders on Okinawa had unnecessarily "sacrificed thousands of American soldiers." Ever jealous of the achievements of the navy's Central Pacific campaign, MacArthur also believed that Buckner was too strongly influenced by Nimitz.[36] Eichelberger noted that the Big Chief (MacArthur) stated that "if 'Buck' ever came under him he would bust him because he had sold out to one of our sister services."[37] Had Buckner survived Okinawa, it is extremely unlikely that he would have taken part in the final invasion of Japan, which MacArthur had been designated to command.

What MacArthur and the other detractors failed to appreciate was that Okinawa was the first battle in the Pacific in which a single American army opposed a Japanese army commanded by a defensive genius willing to sacrifice his entire force to forestall the impending invasion of the Japanese homeland. The proximity of Okinawa to Japan's home islands also contributed to the intensity and ferocity of the Japanese resistance.

Stung by MacArthur's personal attack against one of his primary subordinates, Admiral Nimitz supported his ground commander and refused to join the "Buckner-bashing" fray. Admiral Spruance, on the other hand, doubted if the army's slow, methodical method of fighting really saved any lives in the long run. Spruance believed such tactics merely spread the casualties over a longer period.[38] Moreover, the longer period greatly increased the naval casualties when Japanese air attacks on ships became a continuing factor.

Generals Wainwright, Krueger, and Buckner made contributions that have been largely forgotten amid the remembered carnage of the Pacific war. Skinny Wainwright functioned best at the division and corps levels, where he was free to execute the quick, bold strokes that were the hallmark of the cavalry to which he had dedicated his career. As for Krueger's performance, the SWPA commander, who had been more than a thorn in his side, said it best: "History had not given him due credit for his greatness. I do not believe that the annals of American history have shown his superior as an Army commander. Swift and sure in attack, tenacious and determined in defense, modest and restrained in victory—I do not know what he would have been in defeat, because he was never defeated."[39] Buckner's achievement is best reflected in the citation of his Distinguished Service Cross (posthumous), which states: "The outstanding leadership, tactical genius and personal courage of General Buckner thoroughly inspired his command, and culminated in final victory in Okinawa." It seems a fitting, yet somewhat unwarranted, epitaph. Collectively, Generals Wainwright, Krueger, and Buckner inspired the nation and led the U.S. Army to victory across the broad expanse of the Pacific, through the impenetrable jungles of the Philippines, and over the fissured surface of Okinawa. History has not accorded them the credit they deserve for their achievements. Future generations will do well to include this trio of warriors in the Valhalla of military heroes.

General of the Army Dwight D. Eisenhower and the commanders of the European Theater of Operations. Left to right, front row: Lieutenant General William H. Simpson; Lieutenant General George S. Patton Jr.; General Carl A. Spaatz, U.S. Army Air Forces Europe; Eisenhower; General Omar Bradley; Lieutenant General Courtney L. Hodges; and Lieutenant General Leonard T. Gerow, Fifteenth Army. Second row: Brigadier General Ralph F. Stearley, IX Tactical Air Command; Lieutenant General Hoyt S. Vandenberg, 9th Air Force; Lieutenant General Walter Bedell Smith, SHAEF chief of staff; Major General Otto P. Weyland, XIX Tactical Air Command; and Brigadier General Richard E. Nugent, XXIX Tactical Air Command. *Photo courtesy of National Archives*

Lieutenant General George S. Patton Jr. and Lieutenant General Omar N. Bradley sit in a C-47 during an inspection of the front in France, September 9, 1944. *Photo courtesy of National Archives*

General Douglas MacArthur, commander, Southwest Pacific Theater of Operations. *Photo courtesy of National Archives*

Brigadier General Frank Dorn, commander of Y-Force (left), greets Lieutenant General Joseph Stilwell in China during the Salween River offensive. *Photo courtesy of National Archives*

Major General J. Lawton Collins (left) and Lieutenant General Omar N. Bradley inspect the beach assault landings on Slapton Beach, England, March 1944. *Photo courtesy of National Archives*

General Jacob L. Devers, 6th Army Group; General Joseph C. McNarney, Mediterranean Theater; and Lieutenant General William Simpson, Ninth U.S. Army, at the Waldorf Astoria in New York on their return home, June 24, 1945. *Photo courtesy of National Archives*

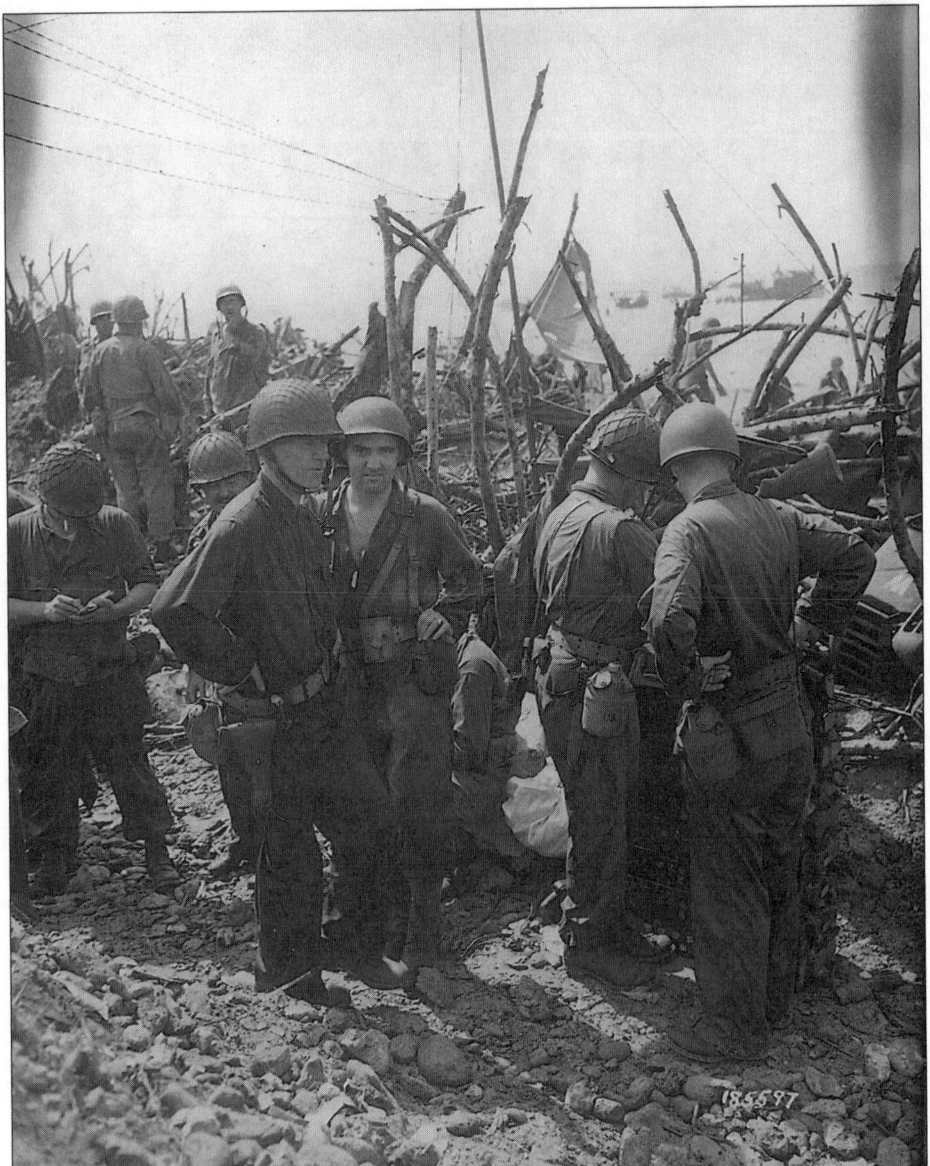

Major General Charles H. Corlett (left of center) and other officers of the 7th Infantry Division examining the remains of shattered Japanese defenses in the Kwajalein Atoll, January 31, 1944.
Photo courtesy of National Archives

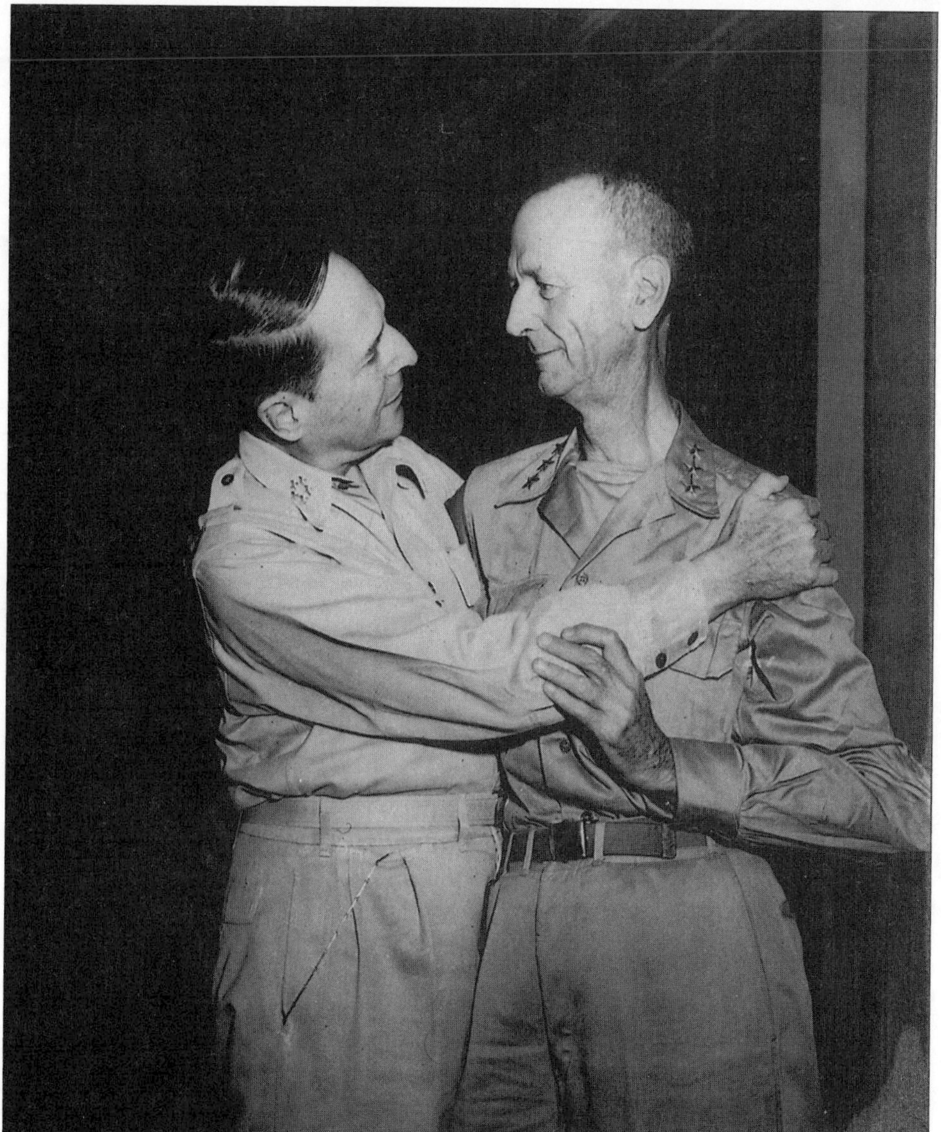

General Douglas MacArthur (left) greets General Jonathan M. Wainwright at the New Grand Hotel, Yokahama, Japan, August 31, 1945, after Wainwright's release from captivity. *Photo courtesy of National Archives*

Major General William M. Miley (left), commanding general, 17th Airborne Division, chats with Brigadier General Floyd L. Parks, chief of staff, 1st Allied Airborne Army, prior to an airborne mission over the Rhine River on March 24, 1945. *Photo courtesy of National Archives*

Lieutenant General Mark Clark; Major General Lucian K. Truscott, commanding general of VI Corps; Major General Ernest N. Harmon, commanding general of the 1st Armored Division; and Major General Alfred M. Gruenther, chief of staff to Lieutenant General Clark, receive British decorations, April 30, 1944. *Photo courtesy of National Archives*

Major General Maxwell Taylor prepares to lead the 101st Airborne Division into Holland on September 17, 1944. *Photo courtesy of National Archives*

Field Marshal Sir Bernard L. Montgomery, commanding general of the 21st Army Group, checks the situation map with Major General Matthew Ridgway, commanding general of the 18th Airborne Corps, during the Battle of the Bulge. *Photo courtesy of National Archives*

General George S. Patton Jr., commanding general, Third U.S. Army—the Allied commander the Germans feared most. *Photo courtesy of National Archives*

Major General James M. Gavin, commanding general of the 82nd Airborne Division, February 1945. *Photo courtesy of the National Archives*

CHAPTER 4

ARMY COMMANDERS IN EUROPE: A FORMIDABLE ARRAY OF WARRIORS

Another thing that would strike you [Marshall] is the high average of ability in our higher command team. . . . These Army Commanders, with Bradley, make up a team that could scarcely be improved upon.

—*General of the Army Dwight D. Eisenhower*

According to the U.S. War Department's 1942 field manual, the field army was not only the "fundamental unit of strategic maneuver, . . . the unit which the theater commander or commander of the field forces uses as a basis for planning and executing strategic and tactical operations," but also "the largest self-contained unit" and "a flexible combat force capable of independent operations."[1] In a statement before the 79th Congress, Prime Minister Winston Churchill, Britain's wartime leader, remarked that he had witnessed the creation of America's mighty army, which had emerged victorious in every theater against the most resolute enemies. To create great armies was one thing, noted the prime minister; to lead them into battle and to handle them effectively was quite another.

Four of the officers with whom Churchill was most familiar were the commanding generals of the armies that constituted General Omar N. Bradley's 12th Army Group in late 1944 and early 1945. By VE Day the field armies comprised twelve army corps, forty-eight divisions, and more than 1,300,000 soldiers—the largest purely American force in history. Leading Bradley's armies was a distinguished quartet of warriors: Lieutenant Generals Courtney H. Hodges, George S. Patton Jr., William H. Simpson, and—in the war's final months—Leonard T. "Gee" Gerow. They shouldered the principal burden at the operational level of war against the German Wehrmacht in the bitter fighting in northwest Europe.

Lieutenant General Courtney H. Hodges has long puzzled academic scholars.[2] Hodges was born on January 5, 1887, in the small hamlet of Perry, Georgia. At seventeen he entered West Point with George Patton, and like his future counterpart, failed mathematics. Resigning after his plebe year, he enlisted in the army in 1906 and received a direct commission through a competitive examination in 1909, the same year Patton graduated from the Military Academy. Hodges's and Patton's paths would cross several times before they joined Bradley's command in northwest Europe in 1944. Both served with distinction on the Mexican Punitive Expedition led by General John J. Pershing in 1916, and both earned their combat spurs in Pershing's American Expeditionary Forces in World War I. During the war, Hodges commanded both a battalion and a regiment; he was awarded the Distinguished Service Cross for his "fearlessness and courage," and the Silver Star and the Bronze Victory Medal with three battle stars as well.

Bradley first met Hodges during a tour at West Point in 1920–24, when Hodges was a major serving in the tactical department. According to his future commander, Courtney Hodges was a legitimate war hero and "a profound inspiration for the very corps of cadets that had earlier rejected him." Bradley viewed Hodges as the quintessential "Georgia gentleman" and the most modest man Bradley had ever met.[3] Later, Bradley and Hodges would be classmates at the Army War College. From there, their respective paths diverged. Hodges returned to the Philippines and served with Dwight Eisenhower on Douglas MacArthur's staff, and Bradley returned to West Point as a company tactical officer.

Like all the army commanders in World War II, Hodges owed his rise to prominence to his association with Army Chief of Staff General George C. Marshall, with whom Hodges had served on the Infantry Board in the early 1930s. Hodges later became commandant of the Infantry School, preceding General Bradley in that position. In May 1941, Marshall appointed Hodges chief of infantry, one of the most coveted assignments in the army. As a reward for his distinguished service, Hodges assumed command of the Third Army in the United States before its deployment to England in early 1944, and then served as Bradley's deputy commander for the upcoming invasion of Europe. In England, Bradley used Hodges to train the fresh divisions arriving from the United States so that he could concentrate on inspections and operational planning. Similarly, Hodges delegated many of the day-to-day operations to his chief of staff, Major General William B. Kean Jr., whom contemporary observers believed was the real brains of the First Army and whom Hodges had known intimately in the Office of the Chief of Infantry preceding the war.

Bradley and Hodges were similar in many ways. Both were career infantrymen who eschewed publicity. Even Marshall recognized their common qualities, informing Eisenhower that Hodges "is exactly the same class of man as Bradley in practically every respect. Wonderful shot, great hunter, quiet, self-effacing . . . [with a] thorough understanding of ground fighting."[4] Bradley himself called the soft-spoken and unassuming Hodges "unostentatious and retiring."

Keenly aware of the immense responsibility of army command, Hodges fancied himself a superb planner who maintained a firm grasp on the tactical and operational situation. One recent biographer notes that he preferred simple, direct solutions to complex maneuvers, arguing that "too many of these battalions and regiments of ours have tried to flank and skirt and never meet the enemy straight on."[5] By the time he wrote his memoirs, Bradley seems to have cooled on Hodges, noting that his understudy had grown cautious and conservative (two qualities similar to Bradley's own style of leadership); but there is no evidence that Bradley disapproved of Courtney Hodges in 1944. Perhaps Bradley's steadfast support was based on the fact that in neither temperament nor imagination did Hodges pose any threat to Bradley's conduct of the campaign in France and Germany. Nor is there sufficient evidence to indicate that Eisenhower was anything less than supportive of Hodges's assignment to a senior command for the impending invasion. The supreme commander, who was quite familiar with Hodges's credentials and also knew that he had Marshall's unwavering support, cabled Marshall in early January 1944 that he intended Hodges to accompany Bradley throughout the early stages of the campaign so that he could be fully ready to assume command of either the First Army or the army group in the event of Bradley's demise.[6]

According to the Overlord plan, Bradley would command the First Army until sufficient forces were available to activate a second American army, at which time he would move up to command the 12th Army Group and his deputy would take the reins of the First Army. Hodges served as Bradley's understudy until July 27, when in the midst of the Cobra breakthrough Bradley ordered him to keep close track of the three corps on the First Army's left, or eastern, flank. General Hodges's subsequent performance in Normandy was steady but uninspired. His First Army bore the brunt of Adolf Hitler's gamble to sever the American lines at Mortain. The destruction of the bulk of the German armor in the Falaise pocket was facilitated in no small part by Hodges's ability to hold the western side of the pocket while Field Marshal Montgomery and Bradley strove to close it. In the process, however, Hodges seemed to take a back seat in the major decisions surrounding the battle. With Patton grabbing most of the headlines, Hodges failed to impress his own persona on either his staff or his army.

The First Army, which under Bradley's leadership had achieved significant victories in North Africa and Sicily, never adjusted to Hodges's preference for working with a small group of inner advisers (i.e., his corps commanders). Moreover, Hodges's uneven support of his corps commanders in the campaign in northwest Europe caused undue friction and jealously among his principal subordinates. As historian Alfred Chandler notes, First Army headquarters evolved one type of relationship with VII and XVIII Corps, under J. Lawton Collins and Matthew Ridgway, respectively, and quite another relationship with III, V, and XIX Corps, under John Millikin, Gee Gerow, and Charles H. "Cowboy Pete" Corlett. Before war's end, Hodges relieved both Millikin and Corlett, and he contemplated relieving Gerow on several occasions.[7] It is thus not surprising that these commanders looked toward Bradley or Kean, and not Hodges, for inspiration and support.

In the advance toward Germany, Hodges once again proved steady but not spectacular in a fluid situation. Again he stayed in Patton's shadow and never achieved the public acclaim showered on his more flamboyant contemporary. At best, the First Army's operations reflected Hodges's background. An infantryman by trade, he thought it "safer, sounder, and in the end, quicker to keep smashing ahead" than to risk all in a campaign of maneuver. This perspective was more reminiscent of infantry operations during Lieutenant General Ulysses S. Grant's Wilderness Campaign and General Pershing's offensives in World War I than it was of an army in which mechanization and motorization had mobilized the battlefield. Not surprisingly, the First Army suffered heavy casualties on Germany's western frontier, particularly in the fighting in the Huertgen Forest. In sum, Hodges's direction of the First Army was sporadic at best. He received generally high marks in the early campaign in Normandy and the final assault against the German homeland, but much lower ones in the close-in fighting that characterized his approach to the Rhine.

The Battle of the Bulge was certainly not Courtney Hodges's finest hour. His faulty troop dispositions and poor intelligence reports contributed to the disaster in the Ardennes. When the Germans did attack, Hodges reacted slowly. At times he appeared dazed, never grasping the full impact of the size and speed of the enemy's advance. His aide later testified that Hodges was suffering from influenza and "feeling very badly because of what had happened" but was still providing "general overall guidance" and retained his presence of mind "except for very, very brief interludes."[8] Ignoring his own role in the debacle, Bradley, always the First Army's strongest supporter, said in his defense that Hodges had received a terrific blow. The problem lay much deeper, and Bradley knew it but did nothing about it. Hodges was physically and mentally exhausted and by all rights should have been relieved. Such a drastic measure was politically unthinkable with Eisenhower and Bradley because it would have reflected discredit on the American high command within the Allied Expeditionary Force. Simply put, Hodges lost control of the battle. Had it not been for his transfer to Field Marshal Montgomery's 21st Army Group and the injection of Matthew B. Ridgway's XVIII Corps and Collins's VII Corps into the breach, the disaster might have reached catastrophic proportions. What saved the First Army was inspired leadership at the corps, division, and regiment levels, coupled with the indomitable spirit of its soldiers.

Why did Hodges perform so poorly? Historian Russell Weigley and Major General James Gavin, commander of the 82nd Airborne Division, theorized that Hodges and his principal subordinate commanders displayed "unimaginative caution." Most of the First Army commanders likewise showed themselves "competent, but addicted to playing it safe." Moreover, Hodges had demonstrated a disturbing tendency "to resort too quickly to un-fair, ill-considered firings of division and corps commanders" in lieu of accepting personal responsibility. "Summarily relieving senior officers," Gavin concluded, "makes others pusillanimous and indeed discourages other potential combat leaders from seeking command. Summarily relieving those who do not appear to measure up in the first shock of battle is not only a luxury we cannot afford—it is very damaging to the Army as a whole."[9] Over the course of the war, Hodges sacked ten division and two corps commanders; in contrast, Patton fired three and Simpson none. Some of the reliefs were certainly justified, but Hodges seemed far too willing to sack commanders when the going got rough. The First Army achieved some spectacular successes, but it also left the most American dead in the wake of its long advance.

After a brief rest, the First Army and its commander were first to breach the Rhine at Remagen, and Hodges performed magnificently in the subsequent operations aimed at eliminating the Ruhr pocket. Recognizing the importance of establishing a bridgehead across the Rhine, Hodges pushed Millikin's corps across the river before telephoning Bradley, then later relieved Millikin for failing to develop the situation to Hodges's satisfaction. The seizure of the Ludendorff Bridge at Remagen was undoubtedly Hodges's finest moment of the war, and his superiors were ecstatic at the First Army's success.

Both Eisenhower and Bradley rated Hodges as the most capable all-around army commander in the European Theater. Eisenhower saw Hodges as the "spearhead and the scintillating star" of the final advance into Germany. As to Hodges's overall value, the supreme commander reminded Marshall that it was the First Army, not Patton's Third Army, that had always been given "the most difficult" jobs, and these "had been brilliantly and speedily executed, often against much resistance." In recommending that Marshall promote Hodges to four-star rank, Ike characterized Hodges's conduct of the pursuit and its exploitation to the northeast from the Normandy beachhead as a model of boldness and daring. During this pursuit, elements of Hodges's forces were constantly compelled to fight important battles—each of which, under his direction, was conducted with the greatest degree of tactical skill and resulted in the elimination of great numbers of the enemy. Choosing to ignore Hodges's mismanagement of the Huertgen and Ardennes battles in the interest of recognizing the many contributions of the First Army in northwest Europe, Eisenhower lauded Hodges for his "tactical masterpieces" that resulted in maximum gains and minimal losses.[10] Ike's communiqué reflected his desire to distribute credit for the impending Allied victory among all his principal commanders rather than allowing those (read Patton) who generated the majority of publicity to reap all the glory. Looking at the record as a whole, however, Eisenhower's previous ranking of army commanders, in which he placed Hodges behind Patton, Lucian Truscott, and Alexander Patch in overall effectiveness, was more accurate. Hodges remained on active service until 1949, when he relinquished command of the First Army.

Reflecting his increasing jealousy of George Patton, Bradley concurred with Ike's glowing appraisal of Hodges, stating that of all his principal subordinates, Hodges required the least supervision. When he ranked his commanders at war's end, Bradley rated Hodges highly. He was, Bradley said, a "general's general, blending dexterity and common sense in such equal portions to produce a magnificently balanced command." Only William Simpson matched Hodges's stature among senior army commanders. Bradley maintained implicit faith in Hodges's judgment, skill, and restraint, in no small part because Hodges was a mirror image of Bradley himself in these qualities. Because of the remarkable similarity between the two men, there was little in Hodges for Bradley to dislike.[11]

In sharp contrast to the methodical Hodges stood the mercurial George S. Patton Jr., who commanded the Seventh Army in Sicily and the Third Army in France and Germany. Like Hodges, Patton had attracted Marshall's attention in World War I and during the years preceding World War II. A 1909 graduate of the U.S. Military Academy, he also served on Pershing's Punitive Expedition, where he gained national acclaim for his heroism in a highly publicized engagement with Pancho Villa's band of raiders. While in France with the American Expeditionary Forces, Colonel Patton commanded a tank brigade and received the Distinguished Service Cross for valor during the Meuse-Argonne offensive.

During the interwar period Patton alternated between command and staff positions before commanding Fort Myer, Virginia, on the eve of the war. By the time of the Texas-Louisiana maneuvers of September 1941, in which he commanded the 2nd Armored Division, Patton had fashioned an image of a hard-driving, hell-for-leather cavalryman. Already a legend within the army, he burst into the public eye when he appeared on the cover of *Life* magazine, which praised the leadership of the most visible proponent of the army's armored force. Underneath the stern countenance that graced America's favorite periodical was the ultimate warrior. More than any of his contemporaries, Patton dedicated his entire life to the study of his profession, and when the war began, he responded with a single-mindedness of purpose reminiscent of Ulysses S. Grant a century earlier.

Generals Marshall and Eisenhower remained ambivalent toward the eccentric Patton. Both admired the manner in which he had rehabilitated II Corps in Tunisia in the wake of the Kasserine Pass debacle. Patton's restoration of that unit's combat spirit is well known and needs little elaboration here. Suffice it to say that he gave the U.S. Army its first major victory against German troops and emerged from the campaign as the American army's premier combat commander. At the same time, Patton's outspoken abrasiveness threatened to damage his reputation and reduce his role in the war effort. On

February 3, 1943, Ike cabled Patton "to assume a sphinx-like quality" lest he give the impression that he acted merely on impulse and not after study and reflection. Reminding Patton that superiors frequently "shy off from a man on account of impressions," he warned his subordinate to curb his "ready and facile tongue." Directing Patton to take this letter exactly as it was meant and to take a little time to think over what he was trying to say, Eisenhower added that his advice reflected both his own impressions and his interpretation of things said by some distinguished visitors.[12] Patton drafted a response in which he welcomed Ike's advice but asserted that his flippancy was the result of years of thought and study. If he seemed glib in the company of high personages, he wrote, it was because he was not "sufficiently over-awed in their presence" and tended to speak with candor.[13] Thinking better of it, Patton never mailed the letter and dedicated his efforts toward preparing for the upcoming invasion of Sicily.

In Sicily, Patton commanded the Seventh Army brilliantly, first traversing the island to Palermo and then beating Montgomery to Messina. In the process he earned the grudging respect of America's British allies and demonstrated that American forces were every bit their equal. Eisenhower was duly impressed and characterized the Sicilian campaign as a "model of swift conquest which would be studied by future classes in the staff college in Leavenworth." Patton's superb corps and division commanders, Ike stated, could have done nothing without his leadership. But Patton's personality remained a problem. Eisenhower informed Marshall that Patton continued "to exhibit some of those unfortunate personal traits of which you and I have always known." His habit of impulsively bawling out subordinates, extending even to personal abuse of individuals, had led Ike to take drastic steps. The slapping incidents further alienated Eisenhower, who initially attempted to cover up Patton's misconduct but later directed him to deliver a formal apology to the soldiers in question and to the 1st Infantry Division as a whole. Eisenhower recognized Patton's enormous value to the war effort and earnestly hoped that he was cured, for "aside from this one thing, Patton possessed qualities that the Allied High Command could not afford to lose unless he ruined himself."[14] Perhaps, Ike suggested, Patton's craving for recognition as a brilliant commander would help him suppress his self-destructive tendencies. Yet the damage was already done, for in the same communiqué Eisenhower described his growing admiration for Bradley as a combat commander who never caused him a moment of worry. From Sicily onward, Bradley's star was clearly ascendant and Patton's was in decline.

Marshall reluctantly concurred with Eisenhower's assessment, noting that General Patton's "love of violence, his needless profanity and obscenity and his gaudy showmanship" were "all serious defects in a commander." Although he questioned Patton's utility in subsequent operations, Marshall deferred to Eisenhower, who recognized Patton's value. Patton, Ike said, was a truly aggressive commander "whose troops [would] not be stopped by ordinary obstacles." When recommending his Seventh Army commander for promotion to permanent major general, however, Eisenhower remarked that Patton was more suited to operations in an exclusively American theater than in an Allied theater and emphasized to Marshall that under no conditions would he promote Patton beyond army-level command. In assessing Patton's performance during the latter half of 1943, Ike rated him "superior" and recommended that he be utilized in command of an army. Of twenty-four lieutenant generals Eisenhower knew, he graded Patton fifth in effectiveness and "outstanding as a leader of an assault force." He was also "impulsive and almost flamboyant in manner [and] [s]hould always serve under a strong but understanding commander."[15] Ike's reference to "a strong but understanding commander" was his way of saying that Bradley, already designated the American ground force commander for the impending invasion, would henceforth be Patton's immediate superior.

A review of the Marshall-Eisenhower correspondence reveals that both men clearly understood Patton's potential in army-level command. In assessing Patton's performance since the early days of Torch, Ike cabled his chief: "Many generals constantly think of battle in terms of, first, concentration, supply, maintenance, replacement, and, second, after all the above is arranged, a conservative advance." Patton's forte, Ike continued, "is that he thinks only in terms of attack as long as there is a single battalion that can keep advancing."[16]

Eisenhower's genius lay in his ability to extract the greatest performance from a diverse set of subordinates, and that was certainly the case with his friend Patton. Ike understood that Patton's emotional range was enormous and that he lived at either one end of it or the other. Patton's rudeness in a public forum led to yet another Eisenhower rebuke in the spring of 1944, and again Marshall placed Patton's fate in Ike's hands. This time Eisenhower chastised Patton and laughingly informed him, "You owe us some victories; pay off and the world will deem me a wise man."[17] Ike also admonished him that this was the final straw. Patton could stay, Eisenhower stated, "based solely on my faith in you as a battle leader and from no other motives." But all this was well in the future. In the interim Marshall had other jobs for Patton, usually connected with well-publicized tours of the Mediterranean region to deceive the Germans as to the role Patton would play in the upcoming invasion.

The months preceding the cross-Channel attack were frustrating for George Patton, who felt himself to be in limbo while Eisenhower and Marshall debated his future. In mid-February 1944 Patton confided to his diary that Eisenhower had an unfortunate habit of underrating all the Americans who served under him and overrating all the British and Americans who served elsewhere. Dissatisfied that he was "merely a pawn" for the upcoming invasion, Patton chafed under the tight reins of SHAEF. On the eve of the invasion, Patton entertained William H. Simpson, who was slated to command the Ninth Army after the Normandy campaign was concluded. Reflecting on their time together at West Point, Patton reminisced, "You, Hodges and I are older than either Eisenhower or Bradley, but we're going to do an awful lot of fighting for them . . . we older foxes are carrying the ball here"—or so he later recalled saying. Simpson's version of Patton's colorful language was far earthier: "Isn't it peculiar that three old farts like us should be carrying the ball for those two sons of bitches?"[18]

Patton's relationship with Omar Bradley, who had served as his subordinate in both North Africa and Sicily, has attracted its share of attention in postwar literature, but in fact Patton was a dutiful subordinate once he assumed command of the Third Army in August 1944. Command of the follow-up army in Normandy was hardly the command Patton coveted, but as he confirmed in his diary, it was "better than nothing." Though he privately railed against what he considered Bradley's timidity and lack of strategic vision, Patton publicly remained extraordinarily cooperative. Accordingly, when Bradley ordered a halt to Patton's northward thrust to Argentan, Patton complied, knowing full well that a golden opportunity to shorten the war had just passed. Bradley's decision, fully supported by Eisenhower and Montgomery, was arguably one of the greatest strategic errors of the war and needlessly prolonged the campaign in northwest Europe.

Patton's private diary reveals his true view of Bradley, whom he considered "a man of great mediocrity. At Benning in command, he failed to get discipline. . . . In Sicily when the 45th Division approached Cefalu, he halted them for fear of a possible German landing. . . . I told him I would take the blame if it [a battalion-size amphibious landing on Sicily's northern coast intended to envelop the German defenses] failed and that he could have the credit if it was a success." What bothered Patton most was Bradley's refusal to take risks that might result in tactical success. On the other hand, he noted that his chief had many of the attributes that were considered desirable in a general officer. Bradley "wears glasses, has a strong jaw, talks profoundly and says little, and is a shooting companion of the Chief of Staff [Marshall]."[19] Bradley countered in his postwar memoirs that Patton's memory of the campaign in Sicily was wrought with "distortions and fabrications." In the final analysis, Patton remained Bradley's dutiful subordinate because he realized that without Eisenhower's and Bradley's support he would not be allowed to fight the war he had spent his life preparing to fight. Command of the Third Army was his last real chance to participate in the war. Hence he would keep his frustration under wraps until Providence provided him the opportunity to fulfill his destiny.

Their personal differences aside, what really separated Patton from Bradley was their divergent perspectives of the most effective manner to wage mobile war. Whereas Ike and Bradley essentially advocated attrition through firepower on a broad front, Patton thought annihilation of the enemy through pursuit and envelopment was the best strategy. Alone of the senior American commanders, Patton clearly understood that the destruction of Germany's armed forces, not the gaining of territory, should be the guiding principle of the war. Utterly ruthless in battle, Patton focused on what he intended to do to the enemy, not what the enemy might do to the Third Army.

Contemptuous of caution and weary of commanders who preferred the comfort of their headquarters to personal reconnaissance of the forward battle area, Patton made his presence felt on the battlefield. In Sicily, he exuded confidence on his visits to the front. James Gavin, destined to command the 82nd Airborne Division in late 1944, recalled a chance meeting with Patton three days after the operation began. "It was good to see him," noted the aggressive Gavin, "first, because I liked him as a soldier, and second, because it was good to see an army commander in the midst of things."[20] British historian Max Hastings describes Patton's battlefield mystique another way. Alone of the senior American commanders, Patton understood that the cult of personality could be immensely valuable in war. Whatever men thought of Patton—and many scorned him—they all knew who he was.[21]

Patton's supreme moment lay not in Normandy but on the German border. When Hitler launched his last great offensive in the Ardennes on December 16, 1944, Eisenhower called on Patton and his Third Army to halt the German drive. Within three days, Patton turned his army 90 degrees, from east to north, and advanced to relieve the surrounded garrison at Bastogne. His performance in disengaging three divisions and shifting them to a major offensive in another direction was quite simply masterful. No other commander could have moved as quickly and assuredly. Patton expressed his immense pride in the Third Army to his wife, Beatrice, in a letter on December 29, informing her that the previous week's fighting was the most brilliant operation he had thus far performed and was in his opinion the outstanding achievement of the war.

Five weeks later, Eisenhower recognized Patton's achievement in a memorandum of record in which he listed all his senior commanders by order of merit. Basing his assessment primarily on his conclusions as to the value of the services each officer had rendered during the war, and only secondarily on his opinion of the officer's qualifications for future utility, Ike rated Patton ahead of all other army-level commanders. "Dashing fighter, shrewd, and courageous" were the words the supreme commander used to describe Patton.[22]

Bradley did not concur with Eisenhower's opinion and routinely attempted to downplay Patton's achievements, instead promoting Hodges as his most trustworthy and reliable army commander. If the truth be known, Bradley was jealous of Patton—jealous of his flamboyance and penchant for garnering headlines, jealous of his ability to decipher correctly the enemy's intentions, and jealous of his absolute refusal to allow his opponent to disrupt and halt Allied operations. Though one Patton biographer claims that Bradley was intimidated by Patton's professional assurance, there seems little evidence that Bradley either admired or coveted Patton's command style.[23] If anything, Bradley considered himself a far more balanced and effective military commander.

Like all military commanders, Patton has attracted his share of detractors. Eisenhower later noted that Patton tended to become pessimistic and discouraged when he became bogged down in the close-in fighting in the Moselle. In such instances the Third Army commander needed a great deal of "moral patting on the back." Nevertheless, it was Patton on whom Ike repeatedly relied when disaster threatened. Nor is it surprising that Patton was the Allied general most feared by the Germans. Two decades after the war, Eisenhower remembered his friend as "a genius in pursuit [and] a natural in exploiting the weaknesses of the Nazi forces" on a fluid battlefield. This was true in Sicily, in the dash from Normandy to Metz, and again when the Third Army traversed the Rhine in March 1945. At war's end, Patton's forward columns had crossed the Austrian and Czechoslovakian frontiers.

By Patton's own reckoning, the Third Army inflicted 1,486,700 casualties on the enemy while suffering 136,865 of its own.[24] The Third Army also captured more prisoners of war than any other army—more than 1,000,000. He had indeed earned his pay. Patton's untimely death in an automobile accident in December 1945, at the very pinnacle of his success, subsequently elevated him to mythical status—a status that was later confirmed by a major motion picture that earned actor George C. Scott an Oscar for his portrayal of the Third Army commander.

Rounding out Bradley's 12th Army Group in the fall of 1944 was William H. Simpson's Ninth Army. A classmate of Patton and the youngest member of his West Point class, Simpson graduated second from the bottom of his class, earning the nickname "Simp" in the process. Bradley later characterized Simpson as "a quiet but strong-willed Texan—tall, rawboned and bald as a billiard ball . . . whose four years at West Point were a desperate struggle to hang in academically."[25] Simpson served with Black Jack Pershing in the Philippines after graduation and later commanded an infantry company in Pershing's Mexican Punitive Expedition. Ever cognizant of Simpson's contribution to the success of the Mexican excursion, Pershing later championed his rise as an aspiring young officer when the United States entered World War I.

In spring 1917 Simpson was still serving in El Paso, Texas, with the 6th Infantry Regiment, but he soon received a coveted assignment as aide-de-camp to Major General George Bell Jr., the El Paso Military District commander. Accompanying Bell to France in 1918, Simpson joined his commander on a tour of the Allied armies in France, then attended the Army General Staff School of the American Expeditionary Forces at Langres, France. His unit's seven months of combat hardened Simpson into a battle-tested officer who quickly grasped the intricacies of ground warfare. At age thirty he was already chief of staff of the 33rd Division and had been repeatedly cited for bravery. During World War I, Simpson was awarded the Distinguished Service Medal, a Silver Star, and other medals. Like Hodges and Patton, he was a recognized war hero.

Simpson's interwar service was similar to that of most of his contemporaries, including a variety of school, command, instructor, and staff assignments. He served with distinction in the Office of the Chief of Infantry and later attended the Advanced Infantry School and Command and General Staff College. In August 1927 he joined Dwight Eisenhower at the Army War College and then was assigned to the War Department General Staff upon graduation in 1928. Promoted to full colonel one year before Nazi Germany invaded Poland, he assumed command of the Infantry Replacement Training Center at Camp Wolters, Texas, in April 1941. He straightened out two

National Guard divisions immediately preceding America's entry to the war and was earmarked by Marshall for senior command. Benefiting from the rapid expansion of the U.S. Army, Simpson received a corps command and, in October 1943, earned his third star and assumed command of the Fourth Army in the southern United States.

The Fourth Army, redesignated first the Eighth and then the Ninth Army, landed in Europe on August 27, 1944, and entered combat on September 5. Troops under Simpson's direct command initially included five combat divisions, most of which were besieging the port of Brest. When Brest finally capitulated, Simpson eschewed personal glory and allowed Troy Middleton, the VIII Corps commander, to accept the surrender. Finally free of major responsibility in the Allied rear, Simpson was now ready for a new assignment.

Despite the Ninth Army's successes in capturing Brest and guarding Bradley's southern flank, Eisenhower remained skeptical of Simpson's abilities. He remarked to Marshall that he believed Collins and Gerow had already demonstrated the capacity for leadership and for handling large formations, and were thus better suited to taking over a new army command than was an officer who had not actually demonstrated that ability. Ike's preference to promote either of the D-Day corps commanders to army-level command was understandable. Simpson was an unknown quantity. Moreover, both corps commanders were just beginning to come into their own as battlefield orchestrators. Marshall, however, could not afford to be so narrowly focused on the European Theater; his concerns were global. Convinced that generals who trained large armies in the United States should have the opportunity to command in combat, he overrode Eisenhower's objections. In the campaign ahead, Simpson would more than once prove his mettle and justify Marshall's confidence.

Following the surrender of Brest in September, Bradley positioned Simpson on the far left of his advance, between Hodges's First Army and Montgomery's British front in Holland. Bradley's purpose was twofold: the Ninth Army was less experienced and could be more easily spared than the veteran First or Third, and, according to his memoirs, Bradley anticipated that Montgomery would eventually wangle an army from Eisenhower to strengthen his British Army Group. Simpson performed well on the subsequent advance to the Ruhr River, outdistancing the veteran First Army, inflicting 1,264 enemy dead, and capturing 8,321 prisoners. Moreover, Simpson was far more suited in temperament for duty with the British field marshal than either the prickly Hodges or the egotistical Patton. After-action reports indicated that all headquarters had operated with a quiet efficiency seldom observed in units untested in combat, and Simpson earned what historian Russell Weigley terms "Bradley's affections as the army he could count on simply to go about its business."[26] The cost had been high, though, and the Germans continued to offer determined resistance as the Allies surged toward the Rhineland.

The achievements of Simpson and the Ninth Army in the advance to the German frontier pale in comparison with their accomplishments during the Ardennes offensive, where once again the commander's cool leadership during battle was particularly admirable. When the Wehrmacht launched its final offensive in the west, Simpson immediately recognized the true scope of the attack. Realizing that a team effort would be critical in halting the German offensive, Simpson massed the Ninth Army's full combat power and rushed his 7th Armored Division to bolster Major General Troy Middleton's VIII Corps at Saint-Vith. He then reconfigured his tactical dispositions to strengthen the northern shoulder of the Bulge. Of all the army commanders, it was Simpson whose thinking seemed closest to Eisenhower's assessment of the scope and intensity of the German offensive. By the tenth day of the campaign, seven of Simpson's divisions were heavily engaged in the First Army's sector. Within a month, the Allied armies had crushed the German offensive. Much of the credit for that success should go to William Simpson. Major General Alvan C. Gillem Jr., who commanded XIII Corps, Ninth Army, said of him: "We see leadership best reflected . . . when firmness is substituted for harshness, understanding for intolerance, humanness for bigotry, and when pride replaces egotism. General Simpson's every action exemplified the best of these traits of character. His integrity inspired a high degree of loyalty. His conduct on all occasions was scrupulous, and his associates of all ranks found him to be patient, impartial, courageous, sympathetic, and confident. They also found him equally loyal to seniors and juniors alike. He was an able, respected commander for whom all were willing to give their best endeavors."[27]

On the campaign from the Ruhr to the Rhine, Simpson again found himself under the operational control of Field Marshal Montgomery, a situation he accepted with his customary grace. He had worked well with Montgomery when his Ninth Army had been transferred to the 21st Army Group in the midst of the Ardennes battles. Following a brilliant campaign culminating in the Ruhr River crossings in February–March 1945, however, Simpson demanded and received a more autonomous role in crossing the Rhine as part of Montgomery's Operation Plunder. In the initial directive for the river crossing Montgomery had assigned command of the operation to General Sir Miles Dempsey's British Second Army, relegating the Ninth Army's participation to a single corps. Simpson protested, and Montgomery eventually relented and assigned a larger portion of the crossing to the Ninth Army. Shortly thereafter, on April 4, Eisenhower returned Simpson to Bradley's control. By mid-April, elements of the Ninth and First armies had effectively closed the Ruhr pocket, bagging a grand total of 317,000 Germans. Simpson's rapid advance to the Elbe, reminiscent of Patton's dash across France the preceding summer, made him the first Allied commander to reach the river and meet the Russians. Simpson was preparing to advance toward Berlin when he was halted by orders from the supreme commander. Whether Simpson could have traversed the final fifty miles and captured Berlin still remains a subject of speculation.

Of General Simpson's contributions to the Allied victory there can be little doubt. Although Ike was more comfortable with the Mediterranean clique with whom he had served since 1942, he rated Simpson a "clear thinker, [and an] energetic, balanced" fighter, and ranked him fifth on his order of merit list for army commanders, behind Patton, Truscott, Patch, and Hodges. Ike later revised his opinion of Simpson, ranking him nearly equal with Hodges and Patton. He certainly remembered him fondly after the war, stating that "if Simpson ever made a mistake as an Army commander, it never came to my attention. Alert, intelligent, and professionally capable, he was the type of leader that American soldiers deserve."[28]

Bradley, too, remained impressed with Simpson, but he would never concede that Simpson and his Ninth Army measured up to Hodges's First Army. Bradley still held emotional ties to the First Army, which he had commanded on D-Day. Nevertheless, as Bradley expressed it in his memoirs: "Ike and I left Simpson's headquarters [February 1945] convinced that the Ninth Army was destined for outstanding performance."[29] What most endeared Simpson to Eisenhower and Bradley was his quiet and balanced style of command. Unlike the temperamental Hodges and the outspoken Patton, Simpson remained "uncommonly normal" and caused neither the supreme commander nor the army group commander any problems.

Simpson retired immediately after the war, citing reasons of health. Promoted to four-star rank on the retired list in 1954, he died in 1980 at the ripe age of ninety-two.

Major General Leonard T. Gerow commanded the fourth army in Bradley's 12th Army Group. Like the army chief of staff, Gee Gerow attended the Virginia Military Institute, achieving high academic honors when he graduated in 1911. In 1914 he, like Douglas MacArthur, participated in the occupation of Vera

Cruz. One year later, Gerow found himself at Fort Sam Houston, Texas, with the 19th Infantry Regiment, where he befriended a young lieutenant fresh from West Point named Dwight D. Eisenhower. Gerow's and Eisenhower's paths would cross numerous times in the decades before World War II, and Gerow was probably the only officer with whom Eisenhower maintained a warm personal relationship longer than he did with George Patton. Unlike Eisenhower, Gerow served in France during World War I. He was promoted to lieutenant colonel and served as assistant to the officer in charge of purchasing and disbursing in the Signal Corps.

Gerow also knew Omar Bradley well. In 1924 Gerow finished the Infantry Officers Advanced Course at Fort Benning, Georgia, graduating first to Bradley's second. Gerow and Eisenhower were classmates at the Command and General Staff School at Fort Leavenworth, Kansas, in 1925. The two young officers were study partners for most of that year, cementing the friendship that had begun at Fort Sam Houston a decade earlier. At Leavenworth, Gerow graduated second in his class, several hundredths of a point behind Eisenhower. The Eisenhowers and the Gerows were also neighbors in the Wyoming Apartment Building on Connecticut Avenue in Washington during the 1930s.

In the decade before the war, Gerow established a well-deserved reputation as a general staff officer, serving initially as assistant executive officer in the Office of the Assistant Secretary of War from 1926 to 1929, and from May 1936 to March 1939 as executive officer of the War Plans Division of the War Department. Later, as chief of the War Plans Division, Gerow asked his friend Eisenhower to join him on the War Department General Staff. Eisenhower begged off, citing his desire to remain with troops and at least serve a "normal tour with them." If he should be asked to join Marshall's staff, however, Ike asked if Gerow could arrange for the Eisenhowers to secure an apartment in the same building where the Gerows resided. Friendships ran deep in the interwar army, and Gerow, noting Ike's reluctance to come to Washington, withdrew his request.

During this period Gerow maintained daily access to Marshall, who valued his unselfish approach to the rapidly expanding demands of war. What Marshall did not relish were Gerow's inaccurate assessments of the Soviet Union's capability to withstand the Nazi invasion and of Japan's plans for prosecuting the Pacific war. In December 1941, Brigadier General Eisenhower joined Gerow's staff as coordinator of Far Eastern military affairs and soon replaced his boss in Marshall's esteem. In fact, Marshall was looking for a replacement for Gerow even before Pearl Harbor, and Eisenhower fit the bill. As the army chief later informed Ike's principal naval aide, "I brought him to head the Operations Division to replace a good officer [Gerow] who had been in that job two years. I felt he was growing stale from overwork, and I don't like to keep any man on a job so long that his ideas and forethoughts go no further than mine."[30] Moreover, Gerow was tainted by the Pearl Harbor fiasco because his office had been responsible for sending out the war alerts to the army's various commands, including the Hawaiian Department. The Roberts Commission, appointed to investigate the circumstances of the debacle, implicated Gerow, among others, for his failure "to follow through" in deciphering Japan's intentions.[31]

When Marshall assigned Gerow to command the 29th Division, a National Guard division that sailed for France in October 1942, Eisenhower took over as Marshall's principal operational planner. When Ike himself arrived in England in midsummer 1942, he initially requested Gerow to serve as his deputy commander of U.S. forces in the United Kingdom, citing Gerow's "loyalty, sense of duty and readiness to devote himself unreservedly to a task." Marshall reluctantly approved the request, but Eisenhower later withdrew it and instead settled on Mark Clark as his principal subordinate.

Though he did not share Eisenhower's high opinion of Gerow's abilities, Marshall promoted Gerow to command of V Corps, then the highest U.S. field command in England, in July 1943. Gerow held the principal responsibility for planning the American component of the invasion until Bradley arrived in mid-September to serve as the First Army's commanding general. Gerow's responsibilities naturally diminished with the arrival of Bradley, but as one of only a few senior American commanders in England with battlefield experience, he was the natural selection to command the American invasion force that would assault the Normandy coast. With D-Day still five months away, Eisenhower tagged Gerow to command V Corps, one of the two assault corps. Because he was so familiar with the Overlord plan and had already spent a significant amount of time training in England, Gerow received the most dangerous mission on D-Day: the assault on Omaha Beach. Bradley, aware of Eisenhower's and Marshall's unflinching support of Gerow, acquiesced, albeit reluctantly.

Generally uncomfortable with any senior commander who had not served in combat in the Mediterranean Theater, Bradley viewed Gerow's abilities with considerable skepticism. Bradley would have much preferred Lucian Truscott for the Omaha assignment, but Truscott remained in the Mediterranean.[32]

In his memoirs, Bradley characterizes Gerow as "an outstanding gentleman and soldier—cool, hardworking, intelligent, well organized, competitive . . . self-confident, and steady . . . thoroughly schooled in the Overlord plan."[33] "Thoroughly schooled" did not equate with combat experience, but Bradley nevertheless accepted Gerow's role in the forthcoming invasion. Years later, Bradley recounted how he agonized over assigning green troops and a green commander to spearhead the Omaha Beach assault. Hedging his bet, Bradley assigned Major General Clarence Huebner's experienced 1st Infantry Division to the assault as well, a decision that proved essential to the corps's success. As it turned out, Gerow's vision for conducting an amphibious assault against a well-entrenched enemy coast proved more accurate than Bradley's. Historian Adrian R. Lewis credits much of the Allies' success on D-Day to Gerow's foresight and understanding of amphibious warfare.[34]

Gerow's performance in the subsequent fighting in the Normandy *bocage*, though unimaginative, was sufficient to merit Eisenhower's consideration for promotion to army-level command in late August. Following the Normandy breakout, V Corps remained in the forefront of Hodges's First Army. Under Gerow's command, the 4th Infantry Division and Jacques LeClerc's 2nd French Armored Division liberated Paris on August 25. From the French capital, Gerow renewed V Corps's assault beyond the Seine. By the eve of Montgomery's abortive Market-Garden offensive to take the bridges over the Rhine, Gerow was already positioned along Germany's West Wall. There he halted, starved for ammunition and fearful that he had reached the culminating point of his advance because Patton's dash forward had severely stretched Bradley's logistical resources.

With little encouragement and no significant support from Hodges, Gerow had little recourse but to slug his way forward. He had finally demonstrated his fighting ability, and Eisenhower confirmed his satisfaction with his friend's performance by informing Marshall in mid-September that Gerow was "doing beautifully." Only the rapid advance of Lieutenant General Jacob L. Devers's 6th Army Group up the Rhône River valley and the diversion of several American divisions to that sector postponed Gerow's promotion to army-level command.

For the next three months V Corps conducted the close-in fighting that characterized Hodges's campaigning. Casualties mounted as Gerow bore the brunt of the second battle of Huertgen Forest in early November. Mirroring Hodges, Gerow's overall conduct of this specific campaign was uninspired and resulted in a disproportionate number of American casualties. With the termination of the Huertgen battles, Gerow, now a seasoned corps commander, renewed his offensive toward the Rhine. While he was so engaged, the Germans launched the Ardennes offensive. Gerow was among the first to realize that the German thrust was not merely a local counterattack. Retracting his lines on his own initiative—and against the orders of his army commander—Gerow prepared to meet the onslaught. Concentrating all available artillery pieces and reinforced with elements from Major General J. Lawton Collins's VII Corps, Gerow held the Elsenborn Ridge and stymied the Germans' repeated attempts to exploit their initial success. All in all, it was a commendable performance and Gerow deserved much of the praise for halting the enemy drive.

After the Ardennes battle, Bradley, anticipating a prolonged campaign east of the Rhine, formed a fourth American army. Gerow was promoted to lieutenant general on January 1, 1945, and assumed command of the Fifteenth Army on January 16. So swiftly did the enemy resistance crumble west of the Rhine, however, that Bradley abandoned his plan to commit Gerow's army on the line and ordered it to hold the west bank of the river as a "semi-occupational army." In addition, the Fifteenth Army assumed responsibility for containing the enemy forces continuing to resist in Lorient and Saint-Nazaire, France. Gerow's chief contribution then became staging and equipping units newly arrived from the United States, a rather inglorious end to his combat service.

In Eisenhower's estimation, Gerow was the best corps commander in the theater: a "good fighter, balanced, calm, optimistic, [and a] selfless leader."[35] That assessment was probably more a reflection of Eisenhower's personal attachment to his old friend than an accurate portrayal of Gerow's martial abilities. Gerow eventually earned high marks from Bradley as well, who rated him just below Patton and Collins in overall effectiveness. Other commanders, most notably Patton, were not convinced of Gerow's ability. Patton characterized Gerow as one of the "leading mediocre corps commanders in Europe" and claimed that he "only got the Fifteenth Army because he was General Eisenhower's personal friend."[36] In this, Patton seemed to forget that Eisenhower had retained Patton himself in theater in part because he, too, was the supreme commander's personal friend.

Following the war, Gerow, now an army commander, became commandant of the Command and General Staff College at Fort Leavenworth, Kansas, where he served admirably from October 1945 to January 1948. With Bradley now the chief of staff, Gerow assumed command of the Second Army at Fort Meade, Maryland, until he retired in July 1950. Temporarily recalled to active duty in 1951 to serve on the Army Logistical Support Panel of the Office of the Chief, Army Field Forces, Gerow was promoted to full general in 1954.

The American armies that fought in the European Theater were led by able and dedicated commanders. Bradley's 12th Army Group commanders were no exception. Despite historians' tendency to attack the quality of the American leadership and the effectiveness of the U.S. Army in Europe, the successes of Bradley's army commanders far outweighed their failures. In one of his final communiqués to Marshall, Eisenhower remarked that aside "from the one feature of Patton's unpredictability so far as his judgment (usually in small things) is concerned, [t]hese Army commanders, along with Bradley, make up a team that could scarcely be improved upon."[37] Each made operational and tactical errors, but, on the whole, Hodges, Patton, Simpson, and Gerow commanded their respective armies with distinction, the campaign in the Huertgen Forest and the opening engagements of the Ardennes notwithstanding. When called upon, Bradley's commanders met the challenge of combat and constituted an integral component of what one historian has called "the most formidable array of warriors this country has ever produced."

CHAPTER 5

AMERICA'S DUAL-THEATER COMMANDERS: INTERLOPERS FROM THE PACIFIC

> I told Bradley to go up to the United Kingdom . . . get a real conception of what his requirements are . . . give us his ideas of what he wants. I have promised him that from every Corps and Division Headquarters we will produce some good individuals to help him in his very great task [command of American forces for Operation Overlord]. We will hold nothing back whatsoever . . . we should make such provision as is humanely possible to give ourselves a reasonable chance for success.
>
> —*General Dwight D. Eisenhower*

GENERAL GEORGE C. MARSHALL VIEWED THE SELECTION of officers for high command as one of his most complicated and important duties as army chief of staff. Only a handful of those he selected served with distinction in both the Pacific and European theaters of operations. Alexander M. Patch, J. Lawton Collins, and Charles H. Corlett head the list of such dual-theater commanders. Each member of this triumvirate graduated from the U.S. Military Academy, although none gave an academic performance indicative of the fame he would later achieve as a combat commander. Collins achieved the highest academic honors of the three, graduating thirty-fifth in the class of 1917, the same class that produced Mark Clark and Matthew Ridgway. Patch and Corlett ranked in the bottom third of the class of 1913. Both Corlett and Patch served with the American Expeditionary Forces

(AEF) in France in 1918. Captain Patch commanded a battalion in the 1st Infantry Division during the Meuse-Argonne offensive, and Corlett was the executive officer for the AEF's chief signal officer. Because of the nature of his assignment, Corlett did not serve in direct combat. Collins remained in the United States, but on his promotion to captain in 1919 he deployed to Europe as a member of the army of occupation.

All three men were also products of the Leavenworth system and the Army War College during the interwar period, and Collins was a graduate of the Army Industrial College as well. By the eve of World War II, the three future commanders were rising stars in an officer corps that Marshall was rapidly grooming for war. Each had demonstrated the vital qualifications of leadership, force, and vigor that Marshall demanded in his general officers. Collectively, Generals Patch, Collins, and Corlett were exceptionally well prepared for the challenge of high-level command. It is no surprise that the army chief of staff summoned each for combat duty when the war tocsin sounded in the immediate aftermath of Pearl Harbor.

Alexander "Sandy" Patch was the first to receive the call. Four months before the Japanese attack, he was relieved of his duties as a regimental commander in the 9th Infantry Division and placed in command of the Infantry Replacement Training Center at Camp Croft, South Carolina. In January 1942, Major General Patch assumed command of Task Force 6814 and the responsibility for the defense of New Caledonia and neighboring islands in the South Pacific. In cooperation with the military forces of the United Nations, Patch's mission was to hold New Caledonia against attack.[1] Japanese forces were advancing southward at an alarming rate, and New Caledonia was a critical part of the logistical lifeline to Australia. Patch's force of approximately sixteen thousand troops sailed from New York on January 23 and arrived in New Caledonia on March 12 after uniting with its equipment in Australia.

In addition to his operational challenges, Patch immediately became embroiled in local politics. The island's French colonial administrators were convinced that Patch intended to take over the island; local civilian officials were challenging the authority of the Free French provisional government leader, Admiral Georges Thierry d'Argenlieu, Charles de Gaulle's military representative on the island; and d'Argenlieu, for his part, was resentful that Patch would not take him into his confidence. The crisis came to a head when d'Argenlieu exiled Henri Sautot, the governor of the island and the man favored by the populace. Patch, who opposed d'Argenlieu's high-handed decision, refused to help the French military officials impose order after an action that he described as "devious and surreptitious and unknown to me." It was Free French leader Charles de Gaulle who finally settled the dispute. Following the Battle of the Coral Sea in May, and after considerable pressure from the British, de Gaulle urged the Free French in New Caledonia to cooperate with the Americans.[2] Once the immediate threat of Japanese invasion had been removed, Patch and d'Argenlieu concluded a satisfactory working agreement. Patch received the Distinguished Service Medal for "exhibiting marked military and administration ability . . . [and for] exceptional meritorious services in a position of great responsibility."

In May 1942 Patch assumed command of the 23rd "Americal" Infantry Division, a designation combining the words "America" and "Caledonia." Following several months of intense training, Patch deployed elements of the Americal to Guadalcanal to reinforce troops led by Marine General Alexander A. Vandegrift, who was engaged in a desperate struggle to seize the island. On November 19, Patch himself was on the scene, often operating within one hundred yards of the front lines. His presence there inspired the troops and resulted in the capture of Point Cruz, a critical terrain feature on the western portion of the island. On December 9, in accordance with the original plans, he then relieved Vandegrift in a simple ceremony and took over as the senior ground commander. He received orders from Admiral William F. "Bull" Halsey Jr. to "eliminate all Japanese forces on Guadalcanal," and from December to February, intense fighting flared on the island.[3]

On January 2, 1943, following an initial tactical setback at Mount Austen, Patch, now commanding XIV Corps—consisting of the 2nd Marine Division, the Americal, and the recently arrived 25th "Tropic Lightning" Division—launched a series of offensives that culminated in the total destruction of Japanese forces on Guadalcanal. On February 9, Patch cabled Halsey: "Total and complete defeat of Japanese forces on Guadalcanal effected today. . . . Am happy to report . . . Tokyo Express no longer has terminus on Guadalcanal." Halsey's response displayed his typical wit: "When I sent a Patch to act as tailor for Guadalcanal, I did not expect him to remove the enemy's pants and sew it on so quickly. Thanks and congratulations."[4] Other accolades followed. In May, Patch received the Distinguished Service Medal from the navy. The citation read in part: "By his skillful planning, inspired leadership and brilliant tactical generalship, he administered, in spite of all handicaps, a series of crushing defeats on the enemy which resulted, on February 9, 1943, in the extermination of all organized enemy resistance on Guadalcanal Island." Marshall echoed the navy's praise, informing Patch: "You have done a superb job both in New Caledonia and Guadalcanal."[5]

But victory had taken its toll. By the time the campaign on Guadalcanal ended, Patch was suffering from recurring bouts of malaria and pneumonia. His condition was so serious that his immediate supervisor in the Pacific, Lieutenant General Millard F. Harmon, prompted Marshall to recall Patch to the United States, where he could rest and recuperate while "advantage could be taken of his experience in the organization and training of new units." Marshall promptly accepted Harmon's recommendation and informed Patch that "for some time we have been considering the desirability of bringing senior battle-experienced officers from each theater back to the United States to strengthen our training program." Patch responded that while he personally preferred to remain closer to active operations, this was "no time for anyone to give the slightest attention to his own preference. . . . Hence, the least I can do is to be prepared to serve wherever it may be considered that I can be of use."[6] This was precisely the type of selfless service that the army chief desired in his general officers.

After Patch assumed command of IV Corps at Fort Lewis, Washington, on May 25, 1943, he may have thought life was easier in the jungles of the South Pacific. Already in trouble for a remark to Marshall in which he downplayed the fighting ability of the American soldier, Patch found himself in real hot water when a reporter revealed that the general had leaked the fact that naval code breakers had broken the secret Japanese code. Admiral Isoroku Yamamoto, the Japanese Combined Fleet commander, had been killed in an aerial ambush as a result. An angry exchange of telegrams with Marshall culminated in an "eyes only" message in which Marshall chided the newly appointed corps commander for his "alleged indiscretion." Patch responded on July 21 "that there was little or no secrecy" in the South Pacific regarding the use of messages based on code-intercept information and that he "was unaware or unconscious that there was any further need for absolute secrecy regarding an enterprise which had occurred many weeks previously." Although he was not really content with Patch's explanation, there was little Marshall could do, as he described the situation to the irate Chief of Naval Operations Ernest King, because "disciplinary action in the case of a corps commander inevitably involves publicity, which would make matters worse."[7]

What actually saved Patch from disciplinary action was his combat experience. Marshall was looking for a commander for the impending invasion of southern France in the summer of 1944, and he could not afford to bypass someone with Patch's proven combat ability. Early in March 1944, Patch and five members of his staff arrived in Algiers, then headquarters for the Allied Expeditionary Force, North African Theater of Operations. Although he was still nominally in command of IV Corps, it was no secret that Patch was designated to command the Seventh Army, the army that Patton had commanded so magnificently in Sicily. Marshall had cabled Lieutenant General Jacob Devers, the American deputy commander in the Mediterranean, in February stating that he was making Patch available for assignment. Though Devers preferred Mark Clark for command of the invasion, he readily accepted Patch, due in no small part to the chief's strong endorsement. Patch's immediate superior was General Sir Henry Maitland Wilson, Allied commander of the Mediterranean Theater; his primary mission was twofold: to establish a beachhead east of Toulon as a base for the assault and capture of Toulon, and thereafter to capture Marseilles and exploit toward Lyon and Vichy. In short, he was to clear the Rhône Valley of enemy forces and subsequently link up with Eisenhower's forces, which were scheduled to conduct the cross-Channel attack in June. The operation—code-named Anvil (changed to Dragoon in early July)—was originally planned as a supporting attack for Operation Overlord. To the Seventh Army commander's immense relief, his knowledge of amphibious war in the Pacific gave him instant credibility among the Allied Mediterranean leadership.

Spearheaded by Major General Lucian K. Truscott Jr.'s VI Corps, Patch's Seventh Army attacked on August 15 and met with immediate success. Ever cognizant of the importance of Allied harmony after his interaction with the French administration of New Caledonia, Patch insisted that French General Jean-Marie de Lattre de Tassigny's Army B participate in the capture of Toulon and Marseilles. The French captured both cities by August 28 while Truscott's three infantry divisions—the 3rd, 45th, and 36th—surged north, clearing Germans from their path. Truscott's movement was nothing short of miraculous, confirming his reputation as one of the best fighting generals in the war.

Three days after the invasion, Marshall cabled Devers and asked him to give Patch his personal congratulations on the "great success of the initial phase of his landing. It evidences planning of a high order and aggressive leadership."[8] Marshall immediately nominated Patch for the grade of temporary lieutenant general and also praised Patch's principal subordinate, Lucian Truscott. Marshall informed Eisenhower that Truscott's performance in Anvil "has been so outstanding . . . that [it] seems to me he has clearly established his right" to command an army. Ike concurred, noting that Truscott was "always my first choice for such assignment."[9] As for Patch, he continued to monitor the Seventh Army's advance and linked up with Major General Wade H. Haislip's XV Corps of Patton's Third Army on September 10–11, months ahead of schedule. On September 15, Patch relinquished operational control over Anvil's forces to Devers, the newly activated commander of the U.S. 6th Army Group.

By any measure, Patch had performed superbly since mid-August. The Seventh Army captured fifty-seven thousand German prisoners in the first two weeks of the campaign alone, at a loss of only four thousand French and twenty-seven hundred American casualties. Almost equally low casualty rates followed Anvil all the way up the Rhône Valley. Most important, the Mediterranean ports provided the logistical support that was crucial in maintaining Eisenhower's drive to the West Wall. Patch's finest hour, however, lay ahead. As Devers directed his army group eastward, Patch's Seventh Army was the first Allied force to reach the Rhine on October 19. Led by Lieutenant General Philippe Leclerc's 2nd French Armored Division, the Seventh Army captured Strasbourg on November 23. A month later, the Germans counterattacked in the Ardennes, and Patch was forced to halt his advance and to defend the portion of the Allied line vacated by Patton, whom Omar Bradley had ordered to smash the southern shoulder of the Bulge.

Fortunately for the Allies, Ultra intercepts warned them that the Germans were also planning a limited offensive against Devers's 6th Army Group beginning sometime between January 1 and 3. The attack, code-named Nordwind, began on New Year's Eve. The subsequent fighting in the Vosges Mountains produced some of the most intense combat of the war. By late January, Patch had halted the German offensive, destroying a large portion of the German Nineteenth Army in the process. On February 11, Patch received the Croix de Guerre with Palm and the National Legion of Honor, degree of Commander, from Charles de Gaulle for his leadership in halting the German drive.

For the remainder of the war, Patch performed with characteristic vigor and "played his role superbly," according to Eisenhower's wartime aide.[10] On March 15, the Seventh Army resumed the offensive aimed at piercing the Siegfried Line and securing the Saar-Palatinate region. The German defenses collapsed three days later. On March 26, Patch was across the Rhine. Nürnberg fell three weeks later, followed by the liberation of Dachau on April 29. In late April, Eisenhower issued a special order that read: "The whole Allied Expeditionary Force congratulates the Seventh Army on the seizure of Munich, the cradle of the Nazi beast."[11] Hitler's Eagle's Nest was next. The Obersalzberg mountain retreat fell to the 3rd Infantry Division and the 101st Airborne Division on May 4. The same day, Patch, along with Devers and Wade Haislip, received the surrender of German Army Group G, thus ending combat operations on the Seventh Army's front. The surrender occurred at the Thorak Estate at Haar, just southeast of Munich, the terms to be effective at noon the following day. Among the German captives were Field Marshals Gerd von Rundstedt and Albert Kesselring. Later, elements of the Seventh Army rounded up Reichsmarschall Hermann Goering. VE Day found Patch in the vicinity of Augsburg in southern Bavaria. For Sandy Patch, the war was over.

A warrior to the end, Patch was on the short list to return to the Pacific for the upcoming invasion of Japan. He seemed to have come full circle, from the Pacific to Europe and back to the Pacific again, but it was not to be. Japan surrendered on August 14 and formally capitulated to the victorious Allied powers on September 2. Dispirited after his dream of another wartime command collapsed, Sandy Patch made one final contribution to the U.S. Army. In late August he traveled to Washington to head what became known as the Patch Board, a group of officers charged with examining the organization of the War Department and proposing an appropriate postwar organization. He submitted his report on October 18, nearly one month to the day before he died suddenly on November 21 of the pneumonia that had plagued him throughout the war. He was fifty-five years old, two days short of fifty-six.

Eisenhower, by then the army chief of staff, eulogized his old friend, calling him a "soldier's soldier."[12] His leadership in battle, both in the Pacific and in Europe, had contributed immeasurably to the defeat of his enemies. Ike noted that Patch's most outstanding achievement in Europe was his brilliant leadership of the Seventh Army. In his assessment of army-level commanders, Eisenhower rated Patch third, behind only Patton and Truscott, and characterized him as a "cool fighter, balanced, energetic."[13] Marshall concurred, noting that Patch had "rendered a magnificent service to the country and died commanding the respect not only of the Army, but of the people."[14] As an army commander of Allied forces, Sandy Patch was unsurpassed.

Like Sandy Patch, General J. Lawton Collins served with distinction in the Pacific and Europe and commanded a division at Guadalcanal. Collins was born in New Orleans, Louisiana, on May 1, 1896. He arrived at West Point in 1913, overlapping with future commanders Eisenhower and Bradley for two years. Commissioned a second lieutenant in the infantry in 1917, Collins served in a series of stateside assignments before commanding a battalion in France in 1919.

Marshall was intimately familiar with Collins long before the war. Collins had served as an instructor at the Infantry School under Marshall from 1927 to 1931 and as assistant secretary to the General Staff during the last half of 1940. Detailed as chief of staff of VII Corps at San Jose, California, in January 1941, then-Colonel Collins earned a reputation as a superb staff officer during the corps's large-scale maneuvers in the summer and autumn of that year. Marshall was so impressed with Collins that he personally selected him—"the ablest officer" he knew—to serve as chief of staff to the commander of the Hawaiian Department, Lieutenant General Delos C. Emmons.[15] Emmons had relieved General Walter C. Short in the immediate aftermath of the Pearl Harbor debacle, and Marshall wanted a ground officer as department chief of staff.

Collins received his first star on February 14, 1942, while he was coordinating the ground defenses of Oahu. Three months later, he took command of the 25th Division and was promoted to the grade of major general. Collins immediately began preparing the division for combat, spending much of his time on battalion field exercises in the Koolau and Waianae mountains, and on two combat firing ranges that he had established on the slopes of the mountains while serving as department chief of staff. Concentrating his efforts on offensive combat in mobile warfare and close air support, Collins built a solid fighting force eager to go to war.

He did not have long to wait. In October he received orders to report to Douglas MacArthur's Southwest Pacific Theater, though CINCPAC Admiral Chester Nimitz warned him that the assignment was temporary. Reluctant to lose the services of an able army commander who had established cordial relations with the navy, Nimitz congratulated Collins on his combat assignment but added, "Collins, you may think you are going to MacArthur's command but I want to warn you that I am not going to let you get away. You have too fine a Division to lose from this theater [Central Pacific Theater]. The 1st Marines will soon be needing relief on Guadalcanal, so don't be surprised if your orders are changed while you are en route to Australia, and you are turned in there."[16] Sure enough, Nimitz cut through the bureaucratic red tape, and Collins reported to Admiral Halsey in New Caledonia on December 10.

Assigned to Alexander Patch's command, Collins received the mission of relieving one of the Americal's regiments without delay. On completion of that, he was to seize and hold a line approximately three thousand yards to the west in preparation for a coordinated attack to eliminate Japanese resistance on the island. On January 10, Collins launched his first attack. Although the division took heavy casualties, the initial assault was successful. In the process Collins received the sobriquet "Lightning Joe," not from the speed of his movements but after the telephone code name of division headquarters. Twelve days later, the 25th Division again provided the main effort, rolling up the enemy's southern flank as Patch launched XIV Corps in a final assault to destroy the Japanese defenders. Forsaking the official policy under which officers in the South Pacific did not wear their insignia of rank for fear of attracting snipers, Collins wore his two stars on his collar. His presence on the front lines electrified his forward battalions.

At the conclusion of the fighting, Patch cited the 25th "Tropic Lightning" Division for its rapid advance and skillful maneuver in breaking the enemy's power to offer further effective defense. It was largely through the sustained drive of the 25th Infantry Division, Patch noted, that the last vestige of organized resistance on Guadalcanal was crushed and possession of an island vital to projected operations was wrested from the hands of the Japanese. Subsequent fighting in New Georgia added luster to Collins's rising star. By year's end he had established himself as a first-rate combat commander and was eagerly awaiting his next assignment, which he anticipated would be corps-level command.

Collins was politically as well as militarily astute. Having worked closely with Marshall in the secretariat, he knew that the army chief closely monitored the performance of his principal commanders. In the immediate aftermath of the victory on Guadalcanal, following the time-honored military tradition of keeping the boss informed, Collins dispatched a personal letter to Marshall in which he described his division's successes against the Japanese in mid-January and noted that "the tactical doctrines taught at Benning [always dear to Marshall's heart] and other service schools have proven eminently sound." Collins concluded that "the Japanese have shown very poor tactical judgment here and an inflexibility of temperament and plan which has operated to our profit." For his part, Marshall was delighted with the army's contribution to the Japanese defeat. And as for Collins, he was rapidly emerging as "one of our youngest division commanders and one of the brilliant officers in our Army."[17]

While on leave in Washington in December 1943, Collins paid a courtesy call on Marshall. Collins was hoping to hear that he was about to receive a corps-level command in the Pacific, but the army chief never discussed such matters with subordinates. Instead he queried Collins on current operations in the Southwest Pacific Theater. As it happened, Eisenhower was also in town, negotiating with the chief for assault corps commanders for Operation Overlord. Above all else Ike needed an experienced combat commander to lead the amphibious assault, and he wanted both Collins and Lucian Truscott. Though he preferred Lucian Truscott, who had more combat experience than any general in the Mediterranean Theater, Eisenhower gladly settled for Collins when Truscott's presence was required at Anzio.

Though he regretted leaving his superb division, Collins was elated with the European assignment, as he had long been certain that the decisive battles would be fought in Europe. The War Department cut orders transferring Collins to Europe on January 19, with additional orders directing him to assume command of VII Corps on February 12. At age forty-seven, he was the youngest corps commander in active service. Three days before Collins assumed command of the corps, Bradley recommended—and Eisenhower approved—placing Collins in charge of the assault corps that would attack the eastern coast of the Cotentin Peninsula. Eisenhower explained to Marshall that Collins's combat experience was the deciding factor in his selection because Ike was "just a bit uneasy about our failure to get a greater leaven of combat experience among our formations."[18]

Collins commanded VII Corps for the remainder of the war in Europe, and the corps's performance was legendary. In preparation for D-Day, Collins drilled his men in the lessons he had learned in conducting amphibious operations in the South Pacific. He also rapidly endeared himself to Eisenhower, Bradley, and Patton by his commitment to intense training and teamwork. Though Collins had not really known Ike and Bradley at West Point except by reputation, he had subsequently served with them in the Philippines and at the Military Academy respectively. Like them, he was an infantryman. Later, Collins and Bradley had become close friends when they served together at Fort Benning during Marshall's tour. Both Ike and Bradley interviewed Collins for the VII Corps job and found him "speaking the same language" with respect to tactics and operations. Besides, with his year of combat experience, Collins could balance untested, but highly respected, Major General Leonard Gerow, who was scheduled to command V Corps in the upcoming invasion.

According to the Overlord scenario, Gerow would land at Omaha Beach and Collins would come ashore at Utah Beach. His mission was to land on the east coast of the Cotentin Peninsula between Varreville and the mouth of the Douve River, seize the beach, link with Gerow west of the Douve, and capture Cherbourg as quickly as possible. Under his immediate command were Major General Raymond O. Barton's 4th Infantry Division, which would conduct the main assault, followed by the 90th Division and possibly the 9th Division. Under his operational control once they landed would be Matthew Ridgway's 82nd Airborne Division and Maxwell Taylor's 101st Airborne Division.

The amphibious components of VII Corps landed against extremely light opposition in the early hours of June 6, moved rapidly inward, and linked up with the two airborne divisions. Ashore himself on D+1, Collins directed the efforts to sever the Cotentin Peninsula and isolate Cherbourg. After extensive operations aimed at expanding the bridgehead, VII Corps captured the crucial port on June 27, but only after the German garrison had destroyed most of the port's facilities. The remainder of June and July found Collins fighting through Normandy's hedgerows, combat that brought little progress and significant casualties. As at Guadalcanal, frequent visits to the forward battle areas kept the corps commander abreast of the fighting.

Finally, Bradley designed Operation Cobra to break the stalemate. Assigning Collins to lead the principal assault, Bradley kicked off the operation on July 25. Again the VII Corps commander performed brilliantly, transforming Bradley's breakthrough to a breakout. It was Collins, instinctively surmising that the German defenses were on the verge of collapse, who committed the armor divisions that swept first to Coutances, about a dozen miles ahead of the front line, then opened the door to Avranches, the gateway to Brittany. According to historian Martin Blumenson, it was Collins who carried the ball in Normandy.[19] And it was Collins who blunted the German counterattack at Mortain, thus enabling the Allies to close the Falaise pocket.

In the advance across France and Belgium, Collins was again in the vanguard of Lieutenant General Courtney H. Hodges's First Army. By September 5, VII Corps was on the Meuse. Liège fell two days later. Following a temporary halt because of insufficient gasoline, Collins plunged ahead, attacking Aachen and entering the dense Huertgen Forest about ten miles to the south. In both cases he misread the strength of the German resistance. The enemy surrendered Aachen on October 19, but the Huertgen Forest proved a tougher nut to crack. In retrospect, Collins called the Aachen-Huertgen campaign the toughest and most costly of VII Corps's operations in Europe.[20] Collins failed to display the imagination in this campaign that had characterized his previous battles in Normandy and the subsequent drive to the German border. True, the forested terrain of the Huertgen did not provide many opportunities for maneuver, but VII Corps's operations resulted in attrition that needlessly bloodied frontline divisions and resulted in unnecessary casualties. Collins did not clear the forest until December 9.

Within three weeks VII Corps was thrown back into the line to stem the German offensive in the Ardennes. Defending a portion of the northern shoulder, VII Corps again performed admirably. On January 3, 1945, Collins resumed the offensive with the 2nd and 3rd Armored Divisions in the lead. Attacking until January 22, when it was pinched from the line by the convergence of Ridgway's XVIII Corps and Patton's III Army, VII Corps achieved all its objectives. Long viewed as Bradley's and Hodges's "fair-haired boy," Collins also attracted the growing admiration of the supreme commander. As early as January 1945, Eisenhower cabled Marshall that the Battle of the Bulge only added to the excellent reputation Collins enjoyed at SHAEF. Ike often wrote that Collins was one of the finest officers in his command. Of the corps commanders in the AEF, only Collins was acceptable to the supreme commander to fill the impending vacancy of SHAEF operations officer.

In the war's waning months, Collins led VII Corps across the Ruhr to the Ruhr. In Cologne, VII Corps captured its 140,000th prisoner since D-Day. Crossing the Rhine on March 14, Collins formed the northern flank of General Bradley's thrust east of the river. Again Collins played a critical role in the destruction of a German army. Encircling the Ruhr pocket from the south, VII Corps joined Lieutenant General William H. Simpson's Ninth Army on April 1, surrounding more than 325,000 Germans. Shortly thereafter, Eisenhower formally recommended Collins for promotion to lieutenant general; it came through on April 16.

Ike's recommendation was based on Collins's performance from Normandy to the German frontier. The VII Corps commander had repeatedly demonstrated himself a master of tactics and a dynamic leader. Faced with difficult tactical situations, Collins had never failed to conduct his battles to the entire satisfaction of his army and army group commanders. In overall ability, Eisenhower rated the VII Corps commander second only to Gee Gerow, whom he had just elevated to command the Fifteenth Army. When Eisenhower listed Collins's most outstanding characteristics, he described a "particularly fine commanding general in a battle; energetic, always optimistic, a leader." Bradley obviously concurred, stating that Collins had proved himself the ablest of the five corps commanders. Had he created another ETO army, Bradley later said, Collins, despite his youth and lack of seniority, would certainly have been named to command it.[21]

After the Ruhr encirclement Collins completed another encirclement of enemy forces—this time in the Harz Mountains. In the process VII Corps collected another eighty thousand prisoners. In May, Collins went to Torgau, where he personally met the lead elements of the Soviet army on the Elbe River. And that ended J. Lawton Collins's combat experience in World War II. Directed to join MacArthur for the final invasion of Japan, Collins was in California when news of events in Hiroshima and Nagasaki signaled the end of hostilities. Like Sandy Patch, he had almost come full circle, from Guadalcanal to Europe to the Pacific. In the interim between his initial posting and scheduled return to the Pacific, he earned the respect of seniors and subordinates alike. Few corps commanders in the war matched his unparalleled success in diverse operations. Only two or three are even worthy of comparison.

Like Patch and Collins, Charles H. "Cowboy Pete" Corlett was an aggressive and well-respected corps commander. Born on July 31, 1889, in Burchard, Nebraska, Corlett arrived at West Point in 1909 and, like Collins, became acquainted with Cadets Eisenhower and Bradley. Fresh from West Point in the summer of 1913, Corlett drew the 30th Infantry, an element that was stationed at Fort Saint Michael, near the mouth of the Yukon River, as his assignment. World War I ended his isolation. Corlett deployed to France with the 1st Infantry Division, serving as director of Signal Corps supplies for the American Expeditionary Forces. During the interwar period Corlett attended the Army War College and then taught infantry tactics at the Coast Artillery School at Fort Monroe, Virginia, and at Fort Leavenworth, Kansas. Earning a reputation as an excellent staff officer, Corlett supervised the Eugene, Oregon, district of the Civilian Conservation Corps and received a plush assignment to Douglas MacArthur's general staff in Washington.

Now a brigadier general, Corlett was in command of Fort Greeley, Alaska, when World War II broke out. Corlett acquired his expertise in amphibious warfare in the Gulf of Alaska and the Shelikof Strait. A superb trainer, Corlett examined every aspect of amphibious operations, concentrating on indirect fire support for assaulting units, combat loads for individual soldiers, and command and control between ship and shore. Kodiak Island and the Aleutians, with their perilous tides and rugged terrain, were natural training grounds for amphibious warfare.

Even as the Japanese were invading the western Aleutian Islands, Corlett was beginning to attract Marshall's attention as a seasoned commander. In August 1943, Corlett, one of the few army officers in the Alaskan Department who courted positive relations with the navy, captured Kiska just as the Japanese defenders were in the process of evacuation, earning rave reviews for the manner in which he planned the attack by a joint American-Canadian task force. With American soil once again free of foreign invaders, it was time to reduce the Alaskan garrison, which had grown disproportionately high. On Admiral King's suggestion, Marshall shifted the U.S. 7th Infantry Division to the Central Pacific for further direction by Nimitz.

Corlett, now commanding general of the division, received his next assignment shortly thereafter: to capture Kwajalein Island in the Marshall Archipelago as part of a corps commanded by Major General Holland Smith of the Marine Corps. Training in Hawaii consumed the remainder of 1943. Improving on the amphibious techniques he had utilized so successfully in the Aleutians, Corlett attacked on January 30, 1944. Kwajalein fell a week later, at a cost of 372 Americans killed and 1,600 wounded; the Japanese casualties were more than twenty times that. The operation's success exceeded Corlett's and Nimitz's wildest expectations. According to official army historians, "except for the occasional failure of tank-infantry co-ordination, no important deficiency had been revealed in the execution of the plan."[22] The keys to the American victory were the well-coordinated naval and artillery fire coupled with close air support for the advancing infantrymen. Additionally, the ship-to-shore movement had been conducted expeditiously and without serious mishap. Supplies flowed ashore and to the front lines smoothly and without interruption. In short, the interservice cooperation exceeded that achieved in any campaign thus far in the Pacific war. For his sterling leadership Corlett received the Naval Distinguished Service Medal and the Silver Star for gallantry. Unfortunately, the rigors of Pacific combat exacerbated Corlett's lifelong struggle with pneumonia.

Corlett expected that following a short rest he would join MacArthur in the conquest of the Philippines, but Marshall thought otherwise. With the invasion of France just four months away, the army chief felt that Corlett's knowledge of amphibious operations might be useful to the Overlord planners. Writing to Eisenhower in London, he offered Corlett's services, noting that the "detailed reports of the 7th Division operation against Kwajalein . . . indicate that Corlett's training of the division, cooperation with the Navy plan of battle, landing, artillery support, tank and infantry action, organization of beaches for supply, continuity of methodical effort and even details of burial of his dead, approached perfection."[23] Preferring his own team but not wishing to alienate Marshall, with whom he had already had some personnel differences, Eisenhower replied that he had consulted his army commanders (read Bradley) and was certain that he wanted Corlett for assignment as a corps commander. Because planning was already in an advanced state, however, it was probable that Corlett would not command one of the two assault corps, but would instead take over one scheduled for later entry into action. Ike added that Corlett's early arrival in theater would be of great advantage to his staff and commanders.[24] Five days later Corlett was en route to England. On March 15 he assumed command of XIX Corps.

Once he was in England, Corlett found that the SHAEF planners had little interest in his combat experience in the Pacific; in fact, they were downright cool. Bradley, his nominal superior officer and someone he had known from his cadet days, was particularly unfriendly. Notwithstanding the comments in his first memoir, in which he characterizes Cortlett as a "canny commander who skillfully maneuvered his troops ashore at Kwajalein Island," the First Army commander considered Corlett abrasive, short fused, and somewhat indignant that he had not received more of a hero's welcome for his Pacific achievements. Patton, no stranger to amphibious operations and upset that the supreme commander had not drawn on his own knowledge of amphibious warfare, was equally unimpressed by Corlett's achievements. In the confines of his personal diary Patton noted that Eisenhower had sent for a general "who had captured a Pacific Island in a 'nearly perfect' maneuver." Of course, he added sarcastically, Corlett did not have to fight until after he got ashore.[25]

Corlett was indeed stung that neither Eisenhower nor Bradley ever mentioned his record in the Pacific, but he nevertheless offered his candid assessment of the Overlord plan. Corlett was particularly concerned about the ammunition support for Overlord; the Allies were taking to the Normandy beachhead only about one-fifteenth as much as he had taken to Kwajalein. (Bradley later attributed the small allocation of ammunition to necessary rationing and inefficiency on the part of the navy and the army service commands in England.) Corlett also noted the crucial lack of amphibious tractors to support the initial assault. On both counts, note historians Allan Millett and Williamson Murray, Corlett was completely correct.[26] Although he recommended alterations in the fire support plan and voiced his concern about the low ammunition allocation, Corlett rapidly realized that no one was listening; he was the proverbial outsider. He soon discovered that American generals in England considered anything that had occurred in the Pacific strictly "bush league stuff" meriting no consideration. Indeed, the only friendly faces Corlett encountered in England were those of Sandy Patch and the English, who were fascinated by the extent of the logistical lines in the Pacific. In his own words, Corlett felt like an expert according to the naval definition: "A son-of-a-bitch from out of town."[27] Bradley, of course, maintained that Corlett had been well received, and attributed any problems to Corlett's personality rather than to any innate preferences in SHAEF for officers who had served in North Africa and Sicily. Corlett never stopped believing that the Americans who landed on Omaha Beach on D-Day suffered far more casualties than would have been the case if Bradley had given his recommendations sufficient consideration.

Regardless of his peers' opinions, Corlett did know how to command large units in combat, and throughout the spring he concentrated on preparing his corps for action. On June 12, American forces overran Carentan and XIX Corps moved into the gap between V Corps and VII Corps. Fighting through the Normandy *bocage*, Corlett's corps finally captured Saint-Lô on July 18–19 after an exhausting twelve-day advance. His progress had been slow, however, and Bradley contrasted Corlett's methodical progress with Collins's lightning severance of the Cotentin Peninsula and isolation of Cherbourg. Corlett's corps protected Collins's exposed flank as Cobra became a reality, and blocked German counterattacks to reestablish a defensive line across the Cotentin Peninsula.

On August 31, Eisenhower informed General Marshall that Corlett had done so well and had demonstrated such capacity for leadership and for handling large formations that he merited consideration for an army command in combat. Courtney Hodges, the newly activated First Army commander, to which XIX Corps was attached, disagreed. Although Corlett's corps had been among the first Allied forces to enter Belgium, Hodges criticized Corlett's "snail's pace" as the First Army was attempting to close the gap around Aachen. XIX Corps had been ordered to penetrate the West Wall north of Aachen and then turn south to the area of Wurselen, east of the city. Hodges was dissatisfied at Corlett's progress against the fortifications of the Siegfried Line and demanded more speed. On more than one occasion he and Corlett had heated exchanges, once in front of subordinates, over Corlett's high ammunition expenditure. Corlett, who preferred to expend ammunition rather than lives, bristled at Hodges's criticism. Under terrific pressure and sustaining inordinate casualties, Corlett finally closed the gap with Collins on October 17. The action came too late to save Corlett's command.

On October 18, on Courtney Hodges's recommendation, Bradley relieved Corlett "without prejudice and without reflection of his ability as a commander."[28] Corlett's final meeting with Hodges was courteous but short. There was no love lost between the two commanders; nor was there any lost between Bradley and Corlett. The official explanation for Corlett's dismissal was declining health. In the relief order, Bradley noted that Corlett was not in good health and had shown signs of exhaustion. Corlett was indeed fatigued by the constant pressure of combat. Even Collins noted that he sometimes had difficulty arranging corps boundaries and supporting fire with his counterpart in XIX Corps. Two days later, Eisenhower cabled Marshall that he was sending Corlett home for a physical checkup and rest. Placing Corlett on sixty days' detached service so as "not to lose my hold on him," Eisenhower requested that he return to the theater as soon as the War Department determined that he was fit for duty. For Cowboy Pete Corlett, however, the war in Europe was over.[29] He never saw combat again.

Too professional a soldier to complain about what he obviously considered a severe injustice, Corlett hid his disappointment well. In January 1945, having received a clean bill of health, Corlett received command of XXXVI Corps from Marshall and prepared to return to the Pacific. Before he could deploy, the Ardennes offensive intervened and the divisions designated for XXXVI Corps were dispatched to Europe. Consequently, XXXVI Corps reverted to a training headquarters with no active units assigned. When VJ Day arrived, Corlett was preparing divisions returning from Europe for deployment to the Pacific.

In assessing Corlett's performance as a corps commander, Bradley ranked him twentieth among the active commanders in the theater. Corlett fared equally poorly with Ike, who failed to include Corlett's name on his list of the top thirty-eight officers in theater. Did Corlett receive a raw deal from Generals Bradley and Hodges? It is hard to say. By his own admission Corlett was tired, run-down, and perhaps sick. Moreover, his temper was short and he found himself at odds with his commander over battle strategies. As the supreme commander remarked to his successor on Marshall's staff, some officers did not realize their own exhaustion. Corlett fell into this category.

Corlett's relief should in no way detract from an extraordinary career that spanned thirty-seven years of military service. Since 1941 he had commanded in positions of increasing responsibility. Corlett had organized the army base at Kodiak and been in temporary command of the Alaskan Department during the naval battle at Attu and the intensive bombing and reconnaissance of Kiska. He had commanded the expedition against Kiska and had organized, planned, and commanded the expedition that seized Kwajalein. He had commanded XIX Corps through France, Belgium, Holland, and into Germany. And at war's end, Corlett stood ready to command an expedition to seize the Kuril Islands and then participate in the assault on the Japanese home islands. All in all, it was a sterling performance.

Generals Patch, Collins, and Corlett formed a unique triumvirate of commanders. Viewed by some officers in Europe as interlopers, the Pacific commanders usually overcame such prejudices and met the challenges of dual-theater command. All three were experts in conducting amphibious operations, and it was the combat experience they gained on Guadalcanal, Kwajalein, Kiska, and New Georgia that contributed most to Allied success in the campaigns in France and Germany. Of the three, Collins ranked highest in the estimation of Generals Marshall, Eisenhower, and Bradley. Collins may well have been the best corps-level commander of the war. General Patch also demonstrated superb leadership skills. His direction of the Seventh Army rivaled that of the more flamboyant Patton and exceeded that of Generals Hodges and Simpson in the supreme commander's estimation. As for Corlett, he never overcame the impression that he was a "son-of-a-bitch from out of town." Nevertheless, he performed with distinction at the corps level and was the only member of the trio who commanded a combat corps in both the Pacific and European theaters. Along with Patch and Collins, Corlett made a significant, but largely unrecognized, contribution to the Allied victory.

CHAPTER 6

COMMANDERS IN DESPERATE SITUATIONS: RESTORING THE FIGHTING SPIRIT

Confidence in battle comes with experience, with leadership, with comrades and weapons. It is absolutely necessary to inculcate a disciplined fighting spirit with a realization that a price must be paid for success and the willingness on the part of the individual officer and soldier to sacrifice himself to gain the objective.

—*General E. N. Harmon*

In his memoir of the Korean War, General Matthew B. Ridgway notes that every soldier learns that war is a lonely business. All a commander's study, all his training, and all his drill anticipate that moment when he alone must decide whether to stand, pull back, or order an attack that will expose thousands of men to sudden death.[1] No officer encountered a greater challenge than Ridgway when he assumed command of the Eighth Army in Korea in December 1950. After the Chinese intervention, the Eighth Army suffered a catastrophic defeat, and pessimism permeated its ranks. What was needed before the army could return to the offensive, said Ridgway, was the restoration of its fighting spirit. The Eighth Army required pride in itself, confidence in its leadership, and faith in its mission.

Three commanders in World War II faced similar challenges. Lieutenant General Robert L. Eichelberger, Major General Ernest N. Harmon, and Lieutenant General Lucian K. Truscott Jr. each received an urgent summons from the theater commander to restore a defeated army's fighting spirit. Each succeeded in reversing his army's fortunes.

Prior to World War II, Robert L. Eichelberger did not fit the popular image of a combat commander. A classmate of George S. Patton Jr. at West Point, Eichelberger served on the Mexican border in 1916 and later received the Distinguished Service Medal and the Distinguished Service Cross for his duty as the operations and intelligence officer for the American Expeditionary Force in Siberia. He then served as secretary of the War Department General Staff for both Douglas MacArthur and Malin Craig before being appointed superintendent of the U.S. Military Academy in 1940. The latter two assignments were prestigious positions, and his service in them earned Eichelberger the respect of most of the army's senior leaders, including George Marshall.

Fifty-five years old when Japan attacked Pearl Harbor, Eichelberger requested combat duty and received command of the 77th "Statue of Liberty" Division, a reserve unit from New England and the metropolitan New York area. At the time of the division's redesignation as the 77th Infantry Division on May 20, 1942, only Eichelberger and sixteen staff officers were present. They were soon joined by twelve hundred noncommissioned officers from the 8th and 30th divisions at Camp Jackson, South Carolina, and another six hundred regular and reserve officers. Much of the 77th Division's later success in the Pacific can be attributed to the high standards established by Eichelberger, who directed from the start that the division would maintain superior standards of discipline, police, and dress. To raise the morale of the incoming draftees, many of whom had no real desire to serve, he ordered that the new soldiers arriving at Camp Jackson would find clean quarters, hot showers, hot meals, and clean beds already made up for them. Cadre officers and noncommissioned officers worked long hours side by side to ensure a warm reception.

Eichelberger's superlative performance caught the attention of Marshall, who elevated Eichelberger to command of I Corps in June 1942. There he continued to excel and earned Marshall's undying admiration. His initial job was to host Winston Churchill and his entourage of British officers on an inspection tour of American military facilities. Eichelberger performed superbly, producing a carefully staged combined arms demonstration involving ten thousand men and hundreds of tanks and vehicles of the 8th, 30th, and 77th divisions with only three days' notice. Churchill was particularly delighted with the airborne drop of six hundred paratroopers, an operation he found both "impressive and convincing." In the corps commander's words, "the entire demonstration, almost providentially, went off without a hitch."

Several years later Marshall confessed to Eichelberger why the successful demonstration had been so important to him. Until that time Churchill had refused to believe the Americans capable of raising an army of sufficient size or excellence to manage a cross-Channel invasion in the foreseeable future.[2] It would take more than a training demonstration to convince the British that the growing American army was ready for combat, but Eichelberger had at least persuaded the prime minister that given time to train and organize, Americans would be ready to fight the German Wehrmacht at a place of Churchill's choosing. Far more important to Eichelberger's own professional development, he had passed yet another of Marshall's tests, and the army chief rewarded him accordingly.

Around this time, Eichelberger received word that he was to command a corps scheduled for an amphibious assault in North Africa. Fate intervened, and the deteriorating situation in the Southwest Pacific, coupled with the growing number of American combat troops assigned to that theater, dictated the deployment of a corps-level headquarters to coordinate MacArthur's impending ground offensive in New Guinea. Eichelberger was hardly a stranger to MacArthur. He had served as secretary of the General Staff when MacArthur was army chief of staff, and the SWPA chief's well-known penchant for West Point and army football was not lost on Eichelberger, who had served so well as superintendent of the Military Academy. Indeed, MacArthur himself was a former "supe," having served with a great deal of distinction and notoriety from 1919 to 1922.

The officer originally designated for a corps command in the Southwest Pacific, Major General Robert C. Richardson, objected to serving under Australians. Eichelberger had no such qualms. Since he and his staff were available, he received the job. Eichelberger's I Corps would consist of the 32nd Division, commanded by Major General Edwin F. Harding, and the 41st Division, commanded by Major General Horace Fuller, and would be nominally under the command of General Sir John Lavarak, commander of the First Australian Army. Eichelberger's principal responsibility in Australia would be to prepare I Corps for combat. This entailed direct supervision of the training programs of the two divisions.

Japanese ground forces had once again been on the march in the Southwest Pacific since midsummer 1942. On July 21 the Japanese landed a large task force on the Papuan peninsula, which lies at the lower end of the great island of New Guinea, directly across the Coral Sea from Australia. Seeking to anchor their southern boundary, the Japanese resolved to take Port Moresby, the capital of Papua. MacArthur countered on October 1 by issuing the first comprehensive plan to destroy the Japanese Buna-Gona beachhead on the northern Papuan coast. Unfortunately, the combined American-Australian offensive was poorly planned and even more poorly executed. By November, the tenacious Japanese defense had halted the Allied offensive in its tracks. To make matters worse, MacArthur had received reports that the American 32nd Division's "poor morale and discipline" had prompted the Australian land force commander, Sir Thomas Blamey, to request an Australian brigade in lieu of another American division because Blamey knew the Australians "would fight."[3]

With American pride at stake, to say nothing of the SWPA chief's enormous ego, MacArthur summoned Eichelberger to his temporary headquarters at Moresby on November 2. Opening the meeting with a long monologue on the condition of the 32nd Division and his humiliation at reports that Americans refused to fight, MacArthur ordered Eichelberger to go to the front and seize Buna. There was no mistaking the seriousness MacArthur attached to the mission. "Bob," he informed Eichelberger, "I'm putting you in command at Buna. . . . Relieve Harding and remove all officers who won't fight . . . put sergeants in charge of battalions and corporals in charge of companies—anyone who will fight. Time is of the essence." He then added, "I want you to take Buna, or not come back alive. And that goes for your chief of staff [Brigadier General Clovis Byers] too."[4] It was an awesome challenge. MacArthur tried to sweeten the directive by promising Eichelberger a Distinguished Service Cross and a recommendation for a high British decoration if he took Buna. "Also," he continued, "I'll release your name for newspaper publication."[5] The irony of the latter promise was not lost on Eichelberger, who departed early the next morning for the front.

What he found at Buna would have disheartened a weaker commander. The 32nd Division was tired, riddled with malaria, and demoralized. There was little evidence of discipline. The troops were in deplorable condition: long, dirty beards; clothing in rags; and little evidence of military courtesy. The forward elements were half-starved, and what meals they did receive were cold. Their medical condition was no better. In one company, every soldier was running a fever. Inspired leadership based on a genuine concern for the welfare of the soldiers was obviously lacking. To evacuate all the frontline troops would have invited disaster. Eichelberger decided to fight with what he had. A thorough reconnaissance of the front lines by vehicle and on foot convinced him that many of the commanders had not even visited the forward positions. Though the two wings of his force were only three miles apart, it took seven hours to walk from one flank to the other. Nor were the division's commanders familiar with Japanese troop dispositions. It seemed obvious that there had been no night patrolling. At one point Harding advised him not to go forward because the Japanese had recently launched a concerted counterattack against the American front lines.

Eichelberger refused to remain in the rear, determined to see combat conditions at firsthand. He was particularly distraught to find that his reconnaissance did not draw any enemy fire; there had been no recent Japanese attack. The inspection tour sealed Harding's fate. As the first order of business, Eichelberger recommended to Harding that he relieve his two regimental commanders. Harding refused and blamed hunger, fatigue, and fever for the Americans' failure to advance. When Harding repeatedly lost his temper following justifiable criticisms by the recently arrived corps commander, Eichelberger relieved him on the spot and sent him to Port Moresby for reassignment.[6] After replacing Harding with Brigadier General Albert W. Waldron, the 32nd Division's artillery commander, Eichelberger relieved the commanders of both wings of the division, replacing them with two members of his own staff, Colonel John E. Grose, I Corps inspector general, and Colonel Clarence Martin, his operations officer. Similar reliefs followed. All told, Eichelberger relieved one task force (regimental) commander and five of six battalion commanders. The responsibility for taking Buna now rested squarely on his own shoulders.[7]

After assessing the tactical situation, Eichelberger began the transformation of the 32nd Division. His first priority was to improve morale. Stopping all fighting, the general took the next two days to unscramble the units and establish an orderly chain of command. Two imperatives came first: reorganization of the troops and immediate improvement of supply. For the first time in weeks, troops received hot meals. In Eichelberger's view, hot food and full stomachs were elemental as morale builders and well worth the hazard of a sniper's bullet. Next, he ensured that positions of leadership were filled by leaders. The commanders Eichelberger placed in key positions were officers in whom he had complete confidence. They were aggressive and eager to engage the enemy. Grose, in command of Urbana Force on the left, remained committed to the capture of Buna Mission; Martin took command of Warren Force on the right, which had one flank on the sea.

With morale on the upswing and failed tactical leaders replaced, Eichelberger focused the division on the enemy. On December 5, he ordered a general offensive. The first day's advance was negligible. The following day the Americans continued the attack using different tactics. Eichelberger directed that there would be no more costly frontal assaults against the entrenched Japanese defenders. Instead, the troops were ordered to soften up the enemy line by attrition and infiltration, and to await the arrival of tanks before attempting the final breakthrough. Moreover, artillery was to work over the enemy emplacements before patrols knocked them out one position at a time.[8] Eichelberger also decided to direct the engagement from the front. Accompanying Urbana Force in its attack on Buna Mission, Eichelberger established his tactical command post within 125 yards of the front. The effect of his presence was electric. In his report to MacArthur's chief of staff after the first day of fighting, the I Corps commander stated, "The number of our troops who tried to avoid combat today could be numbered on your fingers."[9] His message was clear: although jungle fighting is generally done at the small-unit level, soldiers do best when they understand where they are going and why.

Eichelberger's seemingly rash actions had an exhilarating effect on his command. Realizing how important it was for his soldiers to see their commanders in the field, he always wore his silver stars on his collar. His activities during a normal day, according to one account, "could well be classified as interference, but were, as a practical matter, assurances of maximum effort . . . his three stars were . . . evidence . . . that the high command was taking a very personal interest in the fight." When an enemy soldier fired at the general's command group from a range of fifteen yards, a hail of bullets killed the sniper.

Over the next month the American forces inched forward. Command inspections, better rations, constant reconnaissance, and improved medical care had transformed the 32nd Division. Still, Buna was nip and tuck, and the casualties among officers and men were staggering. Reinforced by an Australian battalion and another regiment from the 32nd, together with a platoon of light tanks, Eichelberger continued the advance on December 18. Progress was slow but steady. By January 2, 1943, organized resistance at Buna Mission had ceased. It was a "grand day," Eichelberger wrote in a letter to his wife. Sananada followed, and on January 22 the Papua campaign ended after six months of bitter struggle.

The human toll had been high. According to the official army history, the campaign cost the Japanese 1,400 known dead. On the Allied side, 620 were killed, 2,065 were wounded, and 132 were missing. The 32nd Division sustained 1,954 of these casualties—353 killed, 1,508 wounded, and 93 missing. The total casualties were thus 2,818—a figure considerably in excess of the 2,200 men the Japanese were estimated to have had at Buna when the 32nd Division launched its initial attacks.[10] Eichelberger had been luckier than most of his officers, having suffered no wounds or illness. He was the only American general in the combat zone not to become a casualty, although he did lose thirty pounds over the course of the campaign.

Eichelberger took an exhausted and disheartened command and led them to victory—the first significant land victory against the Japanese. How did he do it? In his own analysis, General Eichelberger noted that in battle, the margin between victory and defeat is often narrow.[11] Under the pressures of combat, officers and men alike tend to forget that the enemy is hard-pressed too. Sometimes just plain stubbornness wins a battle that awareness and wisdom might have lost. At Buna, Japanese morale cracked before that of the Americans and Australians did. Eichelberger failed to mention his own contributions to the victory. The 32nd Division, which had performed so poorly in November, was the same division that won in December. The difference was General Eichelberger and the restoration of the division's fighting pride.

Biographer James Shortal notes that Eichelberger learned three important lessons at Buna that gave him a distinct edge in the future. First, he learned the importance of a realistic training program that stressed physical conditioning, night patrolling, live-fire exercises, and constant maneuvering in the jungle. Second, Eichelberger perfected his jungle tactics at Buna. He would never again make a frontal attack if he could avoid it, nor would he allow soldiers to probe enemy lines slowly or develop a siege mentality; in the future, speed became the hallmark of his operations. Third, Buna consolidated Eichelberger's philosophy of leadership. In the hell of jungle combat, the real margin between victory and defeat had been his style of leadership. Henceforth, his eyes burned with intensity and determination. He resolved never again to be in a situation similar to Buna. The next time it would be the Japanese who would have to worry about facing the veteran American soldiers. The next time, the Japanese would know fear.[12] In short, the jungle campaign matured Eichelberger as a combat commander.

For his inspirational leadership the general received an oak leaf cluster to add to his Distinguished Service Cross for displaying extraordinary heroism in action, extraordinary courage, marked efficiency, and precise execution of operations during the Papuan campaign.[13] From his viewpoint, MacArthur more than fulfilled the promises he had made to Eichelberger. In addition to Eichelberger's oak leaf cluster, his corps headquarters received a Presidential Unit Citation and Eichelberger received a coveted honor from King George VI, Honorary Knight of the Military Division of the Most Excellent Order of the British Empire. Additionally, SWPA communiqués revealed that Eichelberger had commanded the forces at Buna and Sananada. Articles in *Life* magazine and the *Saturday Evening Post* generated a great deal of publicity for Eichelberger—so much, in fact, that MacArthur gently reminded him that he could reduce him to the grade of colonel and send him home if he so desired. Later, Eichelberger wrote to a friend in the War Department's public relations bureau, "I would rather have you slip a rattlesnake in my pocket than to have you give me any publicity" in MacArthur's theater.[14] And to his brother, shortly before the end of the war, he confessed: "I am naturally worried before any article appears about me because . . . of the publicity that came out about me after Buna. I paid through the nose for every line of it."[15] Only later did he discover that the War Department had been set to approve his recommendation for the Congressional Medal of Honor but MacArthur had recommended against it.

Privately, Eichelberger resented MacArthur's refusal to acknowledge his achievements and his rejection of Marshall's three requests to transfer Eichelberger to Europe to command an American army, but his public utterances were always supportive of the "Big Chief," his nickname for MacArthur. Their professional relationship continued to deteriorate as the war progressed. In truth, both men were responsible, for both possessed immense egos that by war's end left each with only a grudging respect for the other. The establishment of the Sixth U.S. Army and the transfer of Lieutenant General Walter Krueger to the Pacific Theater in February 1943 further embittered Eichelberger, who resented the assignment of another officer to the command he felt was his due. During the course of the final year of the war, Eichelberger, always a proud and sensitive man, competed with Krueger for the Big Chief's attention, often to the detriment of their postwar reputations. Regardless of personality conflicts, however, MacArthur never ceased to value Eichelberger's combat abilities.

In 1944 Eichelberger finally took command of the Eighth Army and performed brilliantly, though he was often overshadowed by both Krueger and—of course—MacArthur. Over the course of the war Eichelberger conducted fifty-five amphibious assaults, each of them successful. Twice more he was summoned by the SWPA chief to put out another fire, first at Hollandia and

Biak and then in the final conquest of Luzon. In both campaigns, MacArthur's "fireman" repeated his previous success at Buna. Though he commanded the Eighth Army for slightly more than a year, few commanders matched Eichelberger's combat experience at corps and army levels. By war's end, even the Big Chief had to admit, "No Army of the war has achieved greater glory than the Eighth."[16] And it all began at Buna with the transformation of a single division.

Half a world away, in the desert of North Africa in early 1943, another commander received a summons to a desperate situation—a telegram ordering him to report to General Dwight D. Eisenhower at Allied force headquarters in the wake of a crushing defeat at Kasserine Pass. Field Marshal Erwin Rommel's audacious attack had caught American forces flat-footed and unprepared in their first full-scale combat against the Afrika Korps, and Eisenhower was less than satisfied with the performance of Major General Lloyd R. Fredendall, commander of U.S. II Corps. To complicate matters, Fredendall was hardly on speaking terms with Orlando Ward, his principal subordinate and the commander of the 1st Armored Division. In fact, Fredendall had requested Ward's immediate replacement. Eisenhower, thinking in terms of rehabilitation, which the American force might require after the recent debacle, concluded that relieving Ward might be inexpedient.[17]

On the receiving end of Eisenhower's cable was Ernest N. Harmon, a West Point graduate from the class of April 1917. A hell-bent-for-leather cavalryman by trade, Harmon had established a reputation as a hard-driving, somewhat irascible officer who got the job done. During the interwar years Harmon studied and taught in various service schools, graduating from the War College in 1934. Prior to the Torch landings, Harmon served as acting chief of staff of the Armored Force at Fort Knox, and in July 1942 became commanding general of the 2nd Armored Division. A devoted protégé of George S. Patton, Harmon was cut from the same bolt of cloth as his mentor—just as profane and just as intolerant of fools. Patton himself had once commanded the division that later earned the sobriquet "Hell on Wheels," and though he did not say so publicly, it was common knowledge among the troops that Hell on Wheels was Patton's favorite division. Right after he had been designated commander of the Western Task Force for the impending amphibious landing in North Africa, Patton summoned Harmon to his headquarters. "Do you want to go to war?" he greeted Harmon. "Sure," Harmon responded. "When do we start?"[18]

What Eisenhower had in mind for Harmon was far different from division command. On February 20, 1943, Ike ordered Harmon to report "for limited field duty." Arriving in Algiers, the commander of the 2nd Armored Division discovered that his mission was first to "restore the situation [at Kasserine], then [to] report directly to Eisenhower whether he should relieve Ward or Fredendall."[19] Officially, he was to serve as Fredendall's deputy corps commander and Ike's personal representative. Ike concealed his actual intent from Fredendall, merely stating, "I am making available to you as quickly as flying weather will permit . . . Major General E. N. Harmon. He is reported by every responsible authority that I know of as a determined officer and the best armored division commander in our service."[20] Ike later cautioned that he was sending Harmon merely to give Fredendall a "useful senior assistant" and that he had no thought of replacing Ward. Under the unusual conditions of the present battle, the II Corps commander might find a man such as Harmon useful; how Fredendall used Harmon was up to him as corps commander.

Harmon moved like a whirlwind. Within a day he was en route to General Fredendall's headquarters with absolutely no knowledge of the alignment of the American troops, the disposition of British and French forces in the area, or the actual tactical situation. After several unsuccessful attempts to find Fredendall's rear command post, he and his aide finally reached the II Corps headquarters near Djebil Kouif around three o'clock on the morning of Tuesday, February 23, only a few hours after Rommel had ordered his own forces to begin withdrawing. Harmon later recalled finding Fredendall sitting in a chair, looking rather glum. The corps commander's first words were, "We have been waiting for you to arrive. Shall we move the command post?" Harmon immediately rejected the notion, at which point Fredendall placed him temporarily in command of the "battle in progress," stating, "Here it is. The party is yours."[21]

Harmon thus found himself in direct command of the U.S. 1st Armored Division and the British 6th Armored Division, with his mission first to hold the Germans and then to drive them out of Kasserine. Fredendall stressed the urgency of the situation by telling Harmon that the Germans were already at Thala in the II Corps rear area. At that moment the phone rang and Fredendall began arguing with Ward's chief of staff about the belated delivery of thirty-three Sherman tanks. After confirming with Fredendall that he was indeed in command, Harmon seized the phone and gave Ward's chief a direct order to get those tanks to Thala by daybreak. Ward's chief of staff protested, but Harmon never wavered. The tanks were doing no good where they were; combat power needed to be forward in the front lines. Wasting no further time on amenities, Harmon then commandeered a halftrack and went forward to confer with Ward and Brigadier Cameron G. Nicholson, the assistant division commander of the British 6th Armored Division.

Fredendall's surrender of his command responsibilities to Harmon reflected the complete deterioration of his ability to command II Corps. In a sense, Harmon had inherited a far more dangerous situation than Eichelberger had faced the previous November. At Buna, Eichelberger had encountered a stalemate, with neither side able to swing the balance of battle in its favor. Both adversaries were exhausted and awaiting reinforcements, yet the chain of command, albeit somewhat incompetent, was intact. Here in Tunisia, the uppermost echelons were completely demoralized and the men had lost all heart. The latter was not surprising considering the paralysis of II Corps headquarters. Battle by its nature is chaotic. A commander's job is to ensure that the battle remains organized chaos, not disorganized chaos. Having lost touch with Ward and Nicholson, Fredendall had absolutely no concept of the condition on his front. And to wait for Harmon's arrival before taking decisive action was nothing short of dereliction of duty.

According to Harmon's memoirs, he had already decided on his course of action by the time he reached Ward's headquarters. His decision was simple: he faced a situation in which American troops had fled in the face of the enemy. The first order of business was to halt the flight, turn the men around, and recapture the lost ground. Harmon's first order was succinct: "We are going to hold today and counterattack tomorrow. Nobody goes back from here."[22] Next he countermanded the orders of General Sir Kenneth Anderson, the British commander of the First Army, to which II Corps was attached. Anderson had wanted to move an artillery brigade from the 9th Division north from the area of operations, but Harmon needed the support for his counterattack. Taking full responsibility for his decision, Harmon reasoned that if the attack were successful, no one would object; if the attack failed, no one would care. Directing Nicholson to hold his position, Harmon personally positioned Ward's Shermans when they arrived on the scene. He then reconnoitered the terrain to his immediate front and prepared for the forthcoming attack. Next he mustered all available artillery to support his impending offensive. Only after reporting his plan to Fredendall did Harmon get some rest.

In mid-afternoon on February 23, the Allies launched a concentrated attack to secure Kasserine Pass. Harmon's orders to Ward reflected the change in temperament at corps headquarters and served notice that the initiative had passed from the Germans to the Americans: "You will drive enemy from the valley, destroying as much of him as possible, and re-capture Kasserine Pass."[23] Allied infantry and armor moved forward with artillery support. German resistance was minimal, Rommel having withdrawn on his own initiative under cover of darkness. Two days later the German troops were back where they had started at the beginning of their own offensive on February 14.

By any measure of achievement, Harmon had performed miracles. The transformation that occurred on the Kasserine front within a single day was almost unbelievable. True, Rommel had already ordered a withdrawal, which he accomplished with his customary vigor, but the American commanders had no way of knowing that. More important was the fact that the Allied army in Tunisia, and the American II Corps in particular, gained confidence that they sorely needed. Never again would an American corps perform as poorly in combat as II Corps did at Kasserine Pass. And Ernie Harmon deserved much of the credit for the transformation. Though it would take Patton's brilliant performance in Sicily to convince the British that the American troops were battle hardened and field-tested, Harmon had taken the initial step. In Tunisia Harmon may not have prevented Rommel, the master of desert warfare, from winning, but he certainly prevented the Allies from losing.

How does Harmon compare with Eichelberger? Like Eichelberger, he produced order from chaos. In relatively short order he replaced defeatism with optimism. His willingness to assume responsibility in the face of adversity and to face possible charges of insubordination restored the fighting spirit of II Corps. Within twenty-four hours of his arrival, American troops had resumed the offensive; within two days they had recaptured Kasserine.

Fredendall dispatched Harmon back to Algiers as soon as the outcome of the offensive was decided. Reporting to Eisenhower, Harmon gave his chief a candid appraisal of both Fredendall and Ward. Ward was fine for now, although he had already displayed the battle fatigue that would later cost him his job, but Fredendall must go. Ike then offered Harmon command of II Corps, but he respectfully declined, stating that ethically he could not recommend the relief of a superior officer and then take that man's command. Recommending that George Patton get the job, Harmon returned to Morocco and his 2nd Armored Division.[24]

Harmon's subsequent notes on his combat experience during the Tunisian and African campaigns identify the fundamental problem confronting leadership in II Corps prior to his arrival.[25] The American soldier, he said, would follow a good leader practically anywhere and under any conditions of battle.

Therefore, placing the right men in positions of leadership was the most important safeguard for success in battle. After the initial battle, he surmised, all division commanders would place a higher premium on leadership than they had prior to the engagement. From Harmon's perspective, the American high command seemed inclined to stress administration, paperwork, and tactical knowledge above leadership prior to Kasserine. In this, Marshall and Eisenhower were egregiously wrong. Wherever possible they should have selected the natural leaders; administration skills and tactical knowledge, if lacking, could always be developed later. Officers like Fredendall, regardless of their qualifications on paper, should have been placed in staff jobs or in positions where they were not in contact with the men. Once the fighters were in command, the next step was to develop the offensive spirit and eagerness to close with the enemy that an effective fighting force exhibits. Confidence in battle came with experience, with leadership, and with comrades and weapons. It was absolutely necessary to inculcate a disciplined fighting spirit with an understanding that a price must be paid for success. Harmon's report was quite prescient, but he failed to acknowledge that it frequently takes the crucible of combat to determine if senior commanders are fit to command in combat.

For his service in Tunisia Harmon received a Legion of Merit. In a letter to General Eisenhower he respectfully requested a personal note reflecting Ike's assessment of the way he had handled the special mission during that critical period in late February. Eisenhower replied a month later, stating how impressed he had been with Harmon's "calmness, courage and leadership . . . during the final stages of the German advance and the beginning of his retirement." Ike added that without detracting in any way from the great value of the services rendered by other officers on the field, he thought it only just to say that Harmon definitely enhanced his already high reputation as a soldier and "demonstrated that kind of leadership that we need in the prosecution of this war." He concluded, "I am truly grateful to you."[26]

Not content with leaving Harmon in the rear, Ike then transferred him to command of the 1st Armored Division following his and Patton's assessment that Orlando Ward had been unable to recover from the initial shock of the battle and had failed to exhibit the necessary sturdiness of purpose to rehabilitate the morale and fighting spirit of his organization. Hoping to bring renewed energy and enthusiasm to the 1st Armored Division, Patton wanted Harmon for the final push in North Africa.[27] Harmon spent the remainder of the year in the Mediterranean Theater, where he continued to flourish.

Lucian Truscott, who eventually commanded the Fifth U.S. Army, viewed Harmon as one of the superior battle leaders of the war. "Tough, rugged, down to earth physical type, with boundless energy, Harmon possessed a keen mind, vivid imagination, and plenty of initiative," Truscott wrote after the war.[28] Though disappointed that General Mark Clark did not elevate him to corps-level command in 1944, Harmon impressed Truscott by making a point of extreme loyalty when Truscott received the command that Harmon so earnestly sought.

Others were not so impressed with Harmon. Despite his praise of Harmon's actions as a troubleshooter at Kasserine, Ike appeared lukewarm with regard to Harmon's ability to command a corps. His reservations centered on Harmon's brusque manner and questionable ability to work closely with allies. One Patton in the theater was enough. On the eve of the invasion of the Italian mainland, Eisenhower expressed his reservations to Marshall. In a candid letter, Ike recognized Harmon's battlefield abilities but questioned his judgment and common sense.[29] It was altogether reminiscent of an episode early in Harmon's career in which, fresh from West Point, Lieutenant Harmon sought to relieve the monotony of drill and took his recruits on a cross-country ride. When several emerged from the jaunt with broken arms and related injuries, Harmon's commander reprimanded him, saying, "Young man, I admire your spirit, but your judgment was God-damned poor."[30]

Harmon spent the majority of 1944 in Italy, on ground not conducive to the mobile warfare at which he excelled. He also lost the patronage of Patton, who was busy writing his own brilliant page in history. Mark Clark, commander of Fifth Army, and later Courtney Hodges, First Army commander, were also unimpressed with Harmon's gruff command style. Not until the very end of the war did Ernie Harmon command a corps, which he led with his characteristic distinction. Following the war, he organized and commanded the U.S. Constabulary in Germany in 1946 before retiring to become president of Norwich University in 1950.

Yet another disaster in the Mediterranean Theater required the services of a miracle worker. On January 22, 1944, Anglo-American forces under the command of Major General John P. Lucas stormed ashore at Anzio in an attempt to break the stalemate confronting Mark Clark's Fifth Army south of Rome. Initial resistance was light, Lucas's VI Corps having surprised the Germans, but VI Corps was still seventy miles from the Allied soldiers who were facing the strongly fortified German Gustav Line anchored at Monte Cassino.

General Lucas's mission orders from Clark were deliberately vague: "to seize and secure a beachhead and to advance on the Alban Hills" some twenty miles inland.[31] Whether Lucas was to move *toward* the Alban Hills and sever the main line of communication to the south or move *to* the Alban Hills was left to his own discretion. The vagueness was meant to keep VI Corps flexible and not commit it to any single course of action—at least, so Clark reasoned. Unfortunately, the strategic concept erred in two principal respects: it overestimated the effect the landings would have on the German high command, and it underrated the Germans' capacity to counter.

Cautious by nature and disinclined to take risks that might endanger his force, Lucas secured the beachhead and then awaited reinforcements and supplies before moving inland. Inclement weather also hampered the inward advance. Field Marshal Albert Kesselring, the German commander in Italy, seized the initiative from Lucas and counterattacked with every unit at his disposal. Within a week of landing, the Anglo-American relief force was under siege and in need of rescue itself. In one of the more controversial decisions of the war, Clark relieved Lucas "without prejudice" on February 22.[32] It was apparent that Clark was dissatisfied with the state of affairs on the Anzio front, and although he denied losing confidence in his VI Corps commander, Clark clearly had done so. Moreover, Clark reasoned that Lucas had lost confidence in himself. In Lucas's defense, it can be said that the entire beachhead was under constant artillery fire, but his inactivity in the days following the landing certainly contributed to the impending disaster. Sir Harold Alexander, 15th Army Group commander and Clark's immediate superior, echoed Clark's concerns. Writing to the chief of the Imperial General Staff, Alexander confessed, "I am disappointed with VI Corps headquarters. They are negative and lack the necessary drive and enthusiasm to get things done. They appear to have become depressed by events."[33] What Alexander wanted was a thruster, like George Patton, to turn the situation around. Clark, disinclined to have the flamboyant Patton in his theater, looked elsewhere.

To replace a commander whom he deemed tentative and "worn out," Clark selected Major General Lucian K. Truscott Jr., former commanding general of the 3rd Infantry Division and Lucas's deputy commander at the time. Truscott also ranked first on Eisenhower's list of division commanders best suited for corps-level command. In his twenty-six years in the army, Truscott, like Harmon, had earned a reputation as an aggressive cavalryman in the mold of Confederate General J. E. B. Stuart. Prior to the war he had never heard a shot fired in anger, but Truscott had applied himself in military and other studies during peacetime and had formed decided opinions concerning the techniques of combat and leadership. In addition, he had caught the eyes of both Marshall and Eisenhower. Summoned to Washington as a member of a special team to study commando operations, he served on Lord Louis Mountbatten's Combined Operations Headquarters staff.

Truscott, a veteran of North Africa and Sicily, had crossed swords with Patton more than once, and was one of the few commanders who dared to stand toe-to-toe with him. Which of the two commanders was more feared or more vulgar in speech was a subject of speculation among the soldiers of Truscott's 3rd Division and Patton's Seventh Army. Like Patton, Truscott possessed a cavalryman's penchant for aggressive action. Also like Patton, his philosophy in battle reflected a competitive nature that demanded victory at all costs. He once told his son, "You fight wars to win! Every good commander has to have some sonofabitch in him. If he doesn't, he isn't a good commander. . . . It's as simple as that. No sonofabitch, no commander."[34]

Truscott's first order of business was to assess the situation and ensure that the defenses were as secure as they could be. After that would come the task of restoring confidence in the men of VI Corps. Truscott was appalled to discover how close the beachhead had come to disaster. Corps headquarters had been neither positive nor confident in planning and directing operations. Nor was there understanding between British and American commanders and staffs, particularly between the corps headquarters and the British divisions. Lucas had placed little trust in the British commanders or their troops, and in Truscott's words, the British commanders returned the compliment. Nor was there any delineation between VI Corps and Fifth Army regarding responsibility for the management of rear-echelon assets. In addition, frequent German artillery and air attacks were creating havoc in the corps support area and causing Allied morale to plummet. Truscott's initial impression was that lower echelons of command felt that their corps and army commanders were unduly concerned for their own safety.

In his journal, Truscott's aide described the flurry of activity that characterized the new commander's first day on the job.[35] Summoning his subordinate commanders, the general supervised his first full-scale operations meeting to lay the groundwork for further support development. He then discussed subsequent operations with his ground commanders and ordered a realignment of the beachhead defenses. Whereas Lucas commanded from the safety of his command post, Truscott ventured to the front lines. Commanding from the rear—not that there was any rear area at Anzio—was anathema to Truscott. After touring his old division and the 45th Infantry Division along the forward lines, Truscott conducted a late-afternoon staff meeting and coordinated logistics and antiparachute defenses. The appearance of the commanding general quickly galvanized the beleaguered defenders of the beachhead. For the first time in a month, a feeling of optimism permeated the command. It was a full day, but Truscott had succeeded in producing substantial improvements. Unlike Buna and Kasserine, however, there would be no short-term reversal of fortune at Anzio. German strength was too great, and geography favored the enemy. Nevertheless, a subtle transformation in the unit's fighting spirit was under way.

Other changes quickly followed. Truscott was out daily, visiting troops on outposts and supervising training. In his own words, he "saw much, but said little, and that little usually only to officers on the subject of standards." Officers received his direct attention. Truscott had galvanized the soldiers of the Marne Division by insisting that they be able to march at a four-miles-per-hour clip when the infantry manual recommended a far slower pace. When one colonel questioned the "Truscott trot," its author looked upon him sternly and replied, "Colonel, you can throw that Field Manual and that order, too, in that wastebasket there. Will you issue that order or shall I detail someone else to issue it?"[36] The colonel got the message, and so did the officers of VI Corps when Truscott threw the book out the window once again.

To Truscott, commanders were "rather like old garments; the well-worn ones were usually the more comfortable. . . . [A] few officers who were thoroughly familiar with a commander and his methods could alleviate the pains of transition to a new command to some extent." Not surprisingly, Truscott looked to his old division and summoned his former chief of staff, his G-3 operations officer, and several 3rd Division battalion commanders to become members of his corps staff. He then organized and developed antiaircraft defenses and counterbattery fires. When told that his unorthodox proposal was not the technique employed by the Artillery School, Truscott responded, "Well general, I don't give a damn what the Artillery School teaches. I want this problem solved and I want it solved right now. I have suggested a possible solution. You have until dark tonight to find a better one."[37] Truscott never bothered to ascertain what modifications the artillerymen made to his suggestion, but within the next several nights they discouraged the Germans' use of self-propelled 88s. In truth, the near perfection Truscott achieved in the corps's artillery and antiaircraft fire was due in part to his insistence on the close cooperation between every command and staff echelon throughout the beachhead, a practice he had perfected in the 3rd Division.

Within a week of assuming command Truscott had revitalized VI Corps. The Germans' last-ditch effort to eradicate the beachhead on February 29 was met by determined resistance. Truscott's counterfire, coupled with intense air and artillery support and well-conceived counterattacks, halted the German advance. The worst was over. The Anzio beachhead would survive. Though it would take months for the corps to mount a full-scale offensive and link up with the Fifth Army, Lucian K. Truscott had saved the day.

Four months after his successful rehabilitation of VI Corps, Truscott conducted the breakout offensive that drove the German army from Rome. He remained one of the few commanders Eisenhower could not "steal" from the Mediterranean to participate in the cross-Channel attack. Later transferred to France, Truscott commanded a corps in Operation Anvil and subsequently assumed command of the Fifth Army in Italy in December 1944 when Clark was elevated to command the 15th Army Group. After the war, he succeeded his old mentor Patton as commanding general of the Third Army in Bavaria. In short, Truscott emerged from the war as one of the American army's best commanders. Eisenhower rated Truscott as second only to Patton in his effectiveness as an army commander. He was also an "experienced, balanced fighter; energetic; [one who] inspires confidence."[38]

When Truscott reflected on his experience in command at Anzio, he assessed his greatest contribution as restoring confidence and morale to all elements of the beachhead. Every successful commander, he wrote, must display a spirit of confidence, regardless of the dark outlook in any grim situation, and he must be positive and stern in the application of measures that will impress this confidence upon his command.[39] Truscott's location of his command post was indicative of this principle of leadership. When he arrived at Anzio, many headquarters were located in deep caverns or deep shelters insulated even from the sounds of battle. These shelters had an unfortunate psychological effect on the men who worked in them; a kind of claustrophobia magnified unseen dangers and drove the men toward panic. Since commanders and staffs depended on situation maps plotted from reports in visualizing any situation, situations often looked much worse than was actually the case. Visits to the front, however, usually restored the spirit of optimism. A much more alert, energetic, and elastic defense materialized once commanders left their subterranean headquarters and witnessed the battle with their own eyes. Truscott's own headquarters were in a converted wine shop over the entrance to the caverns.

The supreme commander, a longtime admirer of Truscott, repeatedly petitioned Marshall to transfer Truscott to his command because "he is the finest combat commander in the corps and divisional levels we now have on the front."[40] Later, Eisenhower requested Truscott to command one of Bradley's armies. Marshall's response was always the same: he could not spare Truscott from the Mediterranean. Proven combat commanders were at a premium in theaters outside Eisenhower's as well, and the Mediterranean Theater also needed skilled practitioners of the military art. Truscott was denied the fanfare that accompanied the war in northwest Europe and emerged from the war as the most unacknowledged of America's top commanders.

Several common elements of leadership become apparent in an appraisal of the contributions of Eichelberger, Harmon, and Truscott. Each commander made an immediate assessment at the front. Placing key leaders in positions of leadership, they then focused their troops' attention on the enemy and the mission, and away from thoughts of self-preservation. They directed all their thoughts and actions at improving the morale and the fighting spirit of the troops. At Buna, Kasserine, and Anzio, each clearly understood that the ability of a unit to fight has much to do with its frame of mind. Psychological strength, more than numerical strength or physical capability, is the key to success. Restoring the fighting spirit to a defeated army is perhaps the most difficult task a commander can undertake. Eichelberger, Harmon, and Truscott not only accomplished this task, they did it in the face of tenacious opposition. In the process they bequeathed a legacy of combat leadership to future generations.

CHAPTER 7

AIRBORNE COMMANDERS: THE STUFF OF INSTANT LEGENDS

Ridgway would cut your throat and then burst into tears. Taylor would cut your throat and think nothing about it. Gavin would cut your throat and then laugh.

—*Bill Moorman, communications officer, 82nd Airborne Division*

IN HIS ESSAY ON GENERALSHIP, British theorist J. F. C. Fuller notes that the three pillars of generalship are courage, creative intelligence, and physical fitness—attributes of youth rather than of middle age. General George S. Patton Jr. expressed similar sentiments about the need for competent, aggressive commanders. Wars may be fought with weapons, he said, but they are won by soldiers. It is the spirit of the men who follow the men who lead that produces victory. Nowhere were the physical and mental demands of leadership more evident than in the American airborne units and the officers who commanded these elite organizations during World War II. Airborne commands placed a greater premium on youth, vigor, and imagination than on experience. Although George Marshall initially selected proven and experienced officers to establish the airborne commands, these commanders routinely assigned far younger officers to spearhead the airborne drops. Generals Matthew B. Ridgway, James M. Gavin, Maxwell D. Taylor, William N. "Bud" Miley, and Joseph M. Swing exemplify the tenacity, spirit, and singleness of purpose required to command elite divisions in combat. Collectively, they embodied the essence of military professionalism during this century's greatest conflict.

American paratroopers, past and present, owe a special debt to Matthew Ridgway, arguably the finest combat officer this nation has produced. Ridgway personified battlefield courage. Gavin, who succeeded him in command of the 82nd Airborne Division, noted that Ridgway's "great courage, integrity, and aggressiveness in combat" instilled an esprit de corps that carried the division through the remainder of the war.

A second-generation West Pointer, Ridgway was born in March 1895 and lived the majority of his formative years on western outposts. He later recalled that his earliest memories were of guns and marching men, of parades and bands, of rising to the sound of the reveille gun and lying down to sleep at night to the sobering notes of taps. June 1913 found him at the Military Academy, where he joined the long gray line that also included Cadets Dwight Eisenhower and Omar Bradley, future officers who were destined to play instrumental roles in Ridgway's professional career.

Graduating in April 1917, Ridgway was denied a chance to demonstrate his leadership skills on the battlefields of Europe in World War I. Instead the army sent him to the Mexican border, where he remained until he unexpectedly received orders to report back to West Point to teach in the Department of Foreign Languages. He stayed at his alma mater for six years, serving first as a language instructor, then as a tactical officer, and finally as faculty director of athletics. Fortune finally smiled on Ridgway when he was assigned to Tientsin, China, with the 15th Infantry Regiment. It was his first contact with George C. Marshall, who was the executive officer of the regiment, and Ridgway made a favorable impression. In later years Ridgway, who freely acknowledged his debt to Marshall, would say that Marshall's character and achievements in peace and in war have been surpassed by no wearer of the uniform of the United States save only the nation's first commander in chief, General George Washington.[1]

Three years later, in 1929, they met again when Ridgway was taking the one-year Infantry Advanced Course and Marshall was commandant of the Infantry School. In 1936 their paths crossed yet again during military maneuvers in Michigan while Marshall was serving as the senior instructor of the Illinois National Guard. Ridgway procured the trucks Marshall needed to move his units in an expeditious manner. Returning to his headquarters in Chicago, Marshall cabled Ridgway and thanked him for "digging me out of a hole two or three times" and commended him for "such a perfect job," adding, "there should be some way of rewarding you other than saying it was well done."[2]

During this time Major Ridgway earned a reputation as an expert on Latin American affairs. Following graduation from the Army War College in 1937 he joined the War Plans Division, and he accompanied Marshall on a tour of Brazil in 1939. Anxious to get into combat after Pearl Harbor, Ridgway repeatedly lobbied Bedell Smith, the secretary of the General Staff, to intercede with the chief on his behalf. On one occasion Ridgway entered Smith's office and inquired, "Any word?" "Yes," Smith replied. "Tell Ridgway I'm tired of seeing him hanging around out there every time my door opens. When I have something for him, I'll send for him." Crestfallen, Ridgway returned to his office. Marshall finally "had something" for him in late January, assigning him as Bradley's second in command of the 82nd Division. The promotion brought the star of a brigadier general. After months of desk duty, Matthew Ridgway was finally on his way to war. When Marshall reassigned Bradley to another division, he appointed Ridgway to succeed Bradley in command of the 82nd Division. It thus fell on Ridgway's shoulders to transform the infantry division into an airborne division.

For the remainder of the war Ridgway's name was inexorably linked to airborne warfare; and so it is today. As commanding general of the army's first airborne division, Ridgway was instrumental in the development of American parachute and glider units. A list of his protégés reads like a virtual "Who's Who of Airborne Operations"; nearly every airborne divisional and regimental commander served with Ridgway in some capacity. Miley, Gavin, and Swift all served as assistant division commanders (ADCs), and Taylor was Ridgway's chief of staff in the 82nd Airborne Division. Ridgway had no knowledge of airborne tactics—to say nothing of the configuration of an airborne division—when he began the transformation. What he did possess was unflinching courage, iron discipline, and the complete confidence of the army chief of staff. In the ensuing months he developed a rigorous training program that produced what he described as "twelve thousand hardy characters who weren't afraid to jump, or duck in over tree tops and hedges to crash in a rocky field in a glider."[3]

In May 1943 Ridgway deployed his division to Africa in preparation for the upcoming invasion of Sicily. The invasion proved to be a sobering test for the 82nd and its tactics. Gavin's 505th Parachute Infantry Regiment made a widely scattered drop on July 10, and elements of Colonel Reuben Tucker's 504th fell victim to friendly fire the following evening. Twenty-three troop transports were mistaken for bombers and shot down by American naval and coastal fire. The American parachute regiments suffered 82 dead (including

Brigadier General Charles L. Keerans, the assistant division commander), 131 wounded, and 16 missing.

Eisenhower halted all planned airborne operations and demanded an immediate inquiry. Within a month of the disaster, Eisenhower's headquarters issued a training memorandum that stated emphatically that "the use of airborne troops should be confined to missions suited to their role, and the force commander's decision to use them must be made only after he is positive that the mission cannot be accomplished by other means more economical or equally well suited to the mission."[4] In weighing the decision, the memorandum continued, "it must be recognized that airborne operations are both hazardous and difficult of coordination, and can be justified only by a situation which clearly shows the use of such troops to be imperative." Unless the deficiencies that led to the loss of so many men could be corrected, a strong possibility existed that the Allies might follow the example of the Germans, who ceased large-scale airborne operations after suffering disproportionate casualties in the airborne invasion of Crete. Undoubtedly influenced by John P. Lucas (West Point, 1911), who served as his "eyes and ears" and who considered the concept of an airborne unit of division size "unsound," Eisenhower seriously considered disbanding the airborne divisions until an investigation could determine the reasons for the catastrophe. Fortunately, Marshall sided with the paratroopers and kept the airborne units on the rolls of active duty divisions.

Going ashore by amphibious landing craft on July 10, Ridgway did his best to restore order. So far forward was his command post (CP) that Patton allegedly chided him. "That damn Ridgway has got his CP up where his outposts ought to be. Tell him to get it back."[5] Coming from Patton, who was notorious for visiting troops on the front line, Ridgway considered the rebuke a compliment. Extensive fighting raged on Sicily for the better part of a month, and Ridgway was usually in the thick of it. The effectiveness of the 82nd in Sicily was best summed up by General Kurt Student, Germany's foremost authority on airborne operations, who recalled in 1945 that "the Allied airborne operation in Sicily was decisive. . . . [H]ad not the airborne forces blocked the Hermann Goering division from reaching the beachhead, that division would have driven the initial amphibious forces back into the sea."[6] Eisenhower's airborne forces adviser concurred, noting that "there is little doubt that the action of the American airborne troops speeded up the landing and advance inland by at least forty-eight hours."[7]

Sicily was Ridgway's initial test in commanding a division in combat, but it was hardly his last. His rapid deployment of the division to Salerno in September 1943 helped relieve the pressure on Lieutenant General Mark Clark's invading force. Nor were all of Ridgway's battles against the enemy. On more than one occasion he placed his career on the line and argued vehemently against committing the 82nd Airborne Division to an ill-conceived and poorly planned operation. One such case was a planned drop in the vicinity of Rome, to be followed by a quick advance by Allied ground forces to seize the Italian capital within five days. Ridgway doubted the feasibility of the assault and took his reservations directly to General Sir Harold Alexander, the Allied supreme commander in the Mediterranean. Just as the planes were preparing to take off for what Ridgway was sure would result in the deaths of thousands of American soldiers, Alexander reluctantly canceled the mission. Ridgway's willingness to stand up for his men and for what he believed was right saved his division. In the end, it took approximately seven months for the ground forces to capture Rome.

If Sicily and Italy provided the testing grounds for the American airborne divisions, D-Day brought them their greatest glory. On June 6, 1944, Ridgway jumped with the 82nd into Normandy. Thirty-three days later, on July 8, Ridgway and the 82nd were relieved of combat duties. In the interim, according to historian Clay Blair, they had become the stuff of instant legend. Under Ridgway's dynamic leadership the division had established a remarkable record of combat performance. Colonel Ralph P. "Doc" Eaton, the division chief of staff, noted with justifiable pride that the men of the 82nd were "a pack of jackals; the toughest, most resourceful and bloodthirsty infantry in the European Theater of Operations." But the cost had been excessive. After a month of continuous combat, Ridgway's paratroopers had suffered 46 percent casualties: roughly 1,282 dead and 2,373 wounded severely enough to require evacuation. When the division embarked for England, Ridgway was able to assemble only 6,545 officers and men.[8] Reports of Ridgway's tenacity reached Washington, prompting Marshall to send a personal dispatch to Bradley in which he complimented the American corps and division commanders for their fine performances. He then asked Bradley to give Ridgway and Maxwell Taylor "a pat on the back for the superb performance of their divisions and the long endurance under heavy losses."[9]

Ridgway also earned the praise of his immediate superiors. Bradley expressed his personal appreciation for a magnificent job, and Major General J. Lawton Collins, the VII Corps commander, awarded Ridgway the Distinguished Service Cross, commending the 82nd Airborne for "having broken the back of the German resistance in the Cherbourg Peninsula." The highest accolades came from Eisenhower, who promoted Ridgway to command of XVIII Corps, which comprised the 82nd, 101st, and newly arrived 17th airborne divisions.

Two of Ridgway's divisions, the 82nd and the 101st, participated in the ill-fated Arnhem operation, code-named Market-Garden, but Ridgway remained in England while the command of the operation went to British General Frederick A. M. "Boy" Browning. Though his two divisions remained in the line until November, and he paid occasional visits to them, Ridgway held no command responsibility over them. Ridgway maintained his headquarters in England until mid-December, when he received word that the Germans had launched an unexpected attack in a quiet region of the Allied lines abreast the Ardennes. Releasing the XVIII Airborne Corps from theater reserve, Eisenhower ordered Ridgway to deploy elements of his corps to the front as expeditiously as possible. Rushed into combat, Gavin's 82nd and Taylor's 101st performed magnificently, but Ridgway and Courtney Hodges relieved several division commanders for their inability to measure up to the rigors of combat. Ridgway then steadied the American line along the northern shoulder of the Bulge. All in all, it was an inspired performance. After the battle, Eisenhower wrote that Ridgway had added significantly to his already high reputation. One month later Ike described Ridgway as "magnetic; courageous; balanced, a fighter," and "one of the finest soldiers this war has produced."[10]

Over the course of the remainder of the war, twenty-two divisions served under Ridgway's direct command at one time or another. In addition to the American airborne divisions they included some of the most valiant outfits in the Allied service: the U.S. 1st Infantry Division and the 3rd Armored Division, and the British 6th Airborne, the Commando Brigade, and the 6th Guards Armored Brigade.

In 1945 Ridgway's name appeared repeatedly in dispatches between Marshall and Eisenhower. Ridgway and his fellow corps commanders Gee Gerow and Joe Collins were universally regarded as the three finest officers in the Allied Expeditionary Force; any vacancies that occurred in army command were slated to be filled by them in order of seniority. Following the war, Eisenhower recommended Ridgway for promotion, informing Marshall that Ridgway had never undertaken a job that he had not performed in a soldierly and even brilliant way. He had commanded airborne operations and a corps in a normal battle line, and everyone with whom Ridgway had served spoke of him in the highest terms. It was the ultimate compliment from the supreme commander.

Ridgway continued to serve his nation with characteristic vigor in the decade after the war. In 1950 he was the army's deputy chief of the staff for operations and plans before assuming command of the Eighth Army in Korea on Walton Walker's death. Four months later, he succeeded General of the Army Douglas MacArthur as commander in Japan and Korea. Demonstrating his ability to work well within an Allied coalition, Ridgway later succeeded Eisenhower as supreme commander of NATO. He served as the army chief of staff from 1953 to 1955, before retiring from active service in 1955. His tour as chief of staff constituted the toughest and most frustrating job of his career. Ridgway remained at constant loggerheads with President Eisenhower on the size and missions of the nation's premier ground forces. Matthew Ridgway died in 1993 at the age of ninety-eight, lamented by thousands of airborne veterans and a new generation of young paratroopers serving around the world.

When Ridgway was promoted to corps command, Brigadier General James M. "Slim Jim" Gavin, Ridgway's hand-picked successor, assumed command of the 82nd Airborne. Gavin represented a new generation of airborne officers who epitomized the dash and élan of elite combat forces. Born in Brooklyn, New York, on March 22, 1907, Gavin attended West Point, graduating in the class of 1929. An indefatigable student of military history, he read everything he could find on strategy and tactics. Gavin was brash, confident, and cocky, and he was never one to suffer fools, but he was also a natural leader of men. Ridgway would later write that Jim Gavin was "one of the finest battle leaders, and one of the most brilliant thinkers the Army has ever produced."[11] Many of Gavin's colleagues concurred then, but in the days when the army was first forming the airborne regiments, most thought Gavin was crazy. When virtually everyone jumped from primitive aircraft using a static line, Gavin would free-fall hundreds of feet before pulling the ripcord. Above all, he was absolutely fearless in the face of adversity. An iron disciplinarian, he demanded that his officers lead by example.

In July 1942 Gavin received a promotion to full colonel and command of the 505th Parachute Infantry Regiment. One staffer recalled that the thirty-five-year-old Gavin's regiment was one of the best-trained and most highly motivated regiments in the army. "They were awesome," he said, "every man a clone of the Commanding Officer. . . . Tough? God, they were tough! Not just in the field, but twenty-four hours a day." Ridgway's own chief of staff, Doc Eaton, said that he had never before seen such killers.[12]

Like his mentor, Gavin earned his combat spurs in the Mediterranean. Spearheading the Allied invasion of Sicily, Gavin's 505th Regimental Combat Team conducted the first mass combat drop in American history. Although their drop was widely dispersed across forty-five miles, Gavin's men performed heroically, seizing the high ground and road junctions six miles east of the Gela beachhead and delaying the Hermann Goering Division's concentrated counterattack against Patton's Seventh Army. The day following the jump was the longest in Gavin's memory. Surrounded by the sound of guns, he assembled as many paratroopers as he could find and attacked the first Germans he encountered. On July 11 Gavin personally led a 250-man battalion in a spirited defense against a German armored column. Both Patton and Bradley cited Gavin's defense of Biazza Ridge, just beyond the Gela beachhead, as among the finest, most dogged displays of leadership during World War II. Gavin was more reflective, summarizing the airborne drop as a "self-adjusting foul-up" that taught airborne commanders "the intangible and indefinable difficulties of fighting at night in hostile territory when every object appears to be, and often is, the enemy."[13] No matter; the fact that Patton's Seventh Army was firmly established in Sicily by the morning of July 13 was due in large part to Gavin. Although British commanders downplayed the contributions of the 82nd and other American units in Sicily, the Americans' consensus was that Gavin had made a significant impact on the operation and had demonstrated coolness under fire that instilled confidence among his paratroopers. Ridgway awarded him the Distinguished Service Cross.

Following his distinguished service in Italy, Gavin was promoted to brigadier general in September and became the 82nd's assistant division commander on October 10, 1943. He arrived in London in November 1943 as the senior American airborne planner for the upcoming invasion and worked closely with Omar Bradley, the commander of the American invasion force. In Bradley, Gavin and the American airborne divisions found their greatest ally. Bradley demanded and received an expanded role for the 82nd and 101st airborne divisions, and Gavin was instrumental in developing the plans for their deployment.

As the assistant division commander of the 82nd, Gavin also served as Ridgway's principal adviser. It was in this capacity that Gavin, designated commander of Task Force A—consisting of the 505th, 507th, and 508th Parachute Infantry Regiments—jumped into Normandy. Gavin distinguished himself once again at the Merderet River crossing west of Sainte-Mere-Eglise. Landing with his lead regiment, he personally supervised the defense of the

Merderet crossing and then led the counterattack that drove back the German forces. Though some historians would later question some of Gavin's tactical decisions on D-Day, his personal leadership was nothing short of inspirational and confirmed his potential for division-level command.

In the month following D-Day Gavin remained in the thick of the action. As casualties drained the combat strength of the 82nd's forward battalions, Gavin kept up his routine. He visited his battalion command posts every day, and his company command posts as often as circumstances allowed.[14] Strongly opposed to the policy of keeping airborne troops in sustained combat, Gavin expressed his reservations directly to Ridgway. But he actively supported his commander when Ridgway ordered another costly attack in early July. The result added new laurels to the division's reputation, but losses were excessive. Many rifle companies left Normandy below 40 percent strength. As for Gavin, he emerged from Normandy a public figure who personified the dash and daring that characterized the American airborne divisions. His personal path to glory now lay before him.

Ever the student of airborne warfare, Gavin next supervised a debriefing conference for the division in Leicester, England, on August 13. Each commander present who had commanded a unit of battalion or larger size was instructed to speak freely regarding any aspect of the operation in an effort to eliminate the problems of conducting massed airborne assaults. The conference's final report noted that basic procedures were relatively sound, but severe deficiencies existed at the squad through company levels. Specific areas needed improvement: additional radios were needed to facilitate rapid assembly of personnel; quick-release devices for parachutes would help the men disentangle themselves and begin fighting right away; an additional Browning Automatic Rifle per squad was needed; parachute field artillery had to be developed and perfected; and, most important, twice-weekly night reorganization and assembly exercises were a must. Gavin's personal observations served as a blueprint for future airborne operations.

On July 17, prior to this exhaustive after-action review, Gavin was summoned to Ridgway's headquarters and informed that Ridgway was moving up to command an airborne corps and that Gavin would take command of the 82nd Airborne Division. Though only a brigadier general, Gavin assumed command of the division on August 16. Within a month of his elevation to division command Gavin made his fourth combat jump, leading his proud division in Operation Market-Garden, Field Marshal Montgomery's abortive attempt to seize crossing sites across the Rhine at Arnhem. The mission assigned to the 82nd Airborne was to seize a series of bridges from Nijmegen to Grave, in the center of the Allied axis of advance.

On September 17, 1944, Gavin led 7,250 parachutists into Holland with the bridges at Nijmegen as their primary objectives. Although initially successful, Gavin's paratroopers soon ran into intense German resistance. September 20 rivaled the most difficult hours of the 82nd Airborne Division in Normandy. Gavin himself called it a day unprecedented in the division's combat history. Under heavy counterattack by two German combat teams, Gavin positioned himself where the decisive fighting was taking place and became, in historian Clay Blair's term, "a one man fire brigade." Issuing orders under fire, Gavin conducted a personal reconnaissance and made appropriate alterations to his plan. He ordered several counterattacks and supervised a river crossing under fire. By evening, all of the designated bridges were in the 82nd's hands. General Miles Dempsey, British Second Army commander, called Gavin's men "the greatest division in the world."

Although Market-Garden failed, Gavin's performance had been commendable. Promotion to major general quickly followed, making Gavin at thirty-seven the youngest division commander since George Armstrong Custer in the Civil War. Both the commanding general of the British Airborne Corps and XVIII Airborne Corps commander Ridgway heartily endorsed Gavin's promotion despite his age and junior rank. Gavin had been a brigadier general for only nine months, but he had proved to be, in Ridgway's words, "a proved battle leader of the highest type." Army Chief Marshall personally forwarded the recommendation to the president, noting that the promotion was an acknowledgment of Gavin's gallant and brilliant leadership over the course of the preceding month.[15]

Nor were airborne operations Gavin's only contributions to the Allied victory. From November through early December, his principal chore was to train the vast number of replacements that filled the depleted ranks of the 82nd Airborne Division. Gavin established a ruthless training program and drove the troops relentlessly. His efforts bore fruit when the Germans burst through the Ardennes on December 16. Gavin's division was once again rushed into the breach. Summoned by Courtney Hodges to First Army Headquarters, Gavin jotted in his war diary: "things in an uproar, the Germans about 10 miles away and coming on."[16] Gavin, temporarily in command of XVIII Corps until Ridgway arrived from England, ordered the 101st Airborne Division to Bastogne and sent his own 82nd to Werbomont on the northern shoulder of the German offensive. Once Ridgway arrived, Gavin reverted to divisional command and again performed magnificently. The 82nd was in continuous contact with the enemy until it was relieved by the 75th Infantry Division on January 9. Gavin's frontline leadership had more than once been the critical factor holding together the thin line of American paratroopers.

Jim Gavin remained in command of the 82nd Airborne Division until the end of the war. Subsequent fighting on the Siegfried Line and in the Huertgen Forest, which he likened to the lower levels of Dante's Inferno, added to his bitterness against senior commanders who failed to conduct personal reconnaissance prior to sending troops into battle. Two divisions, the 9th and the 28th, had been virtually destroyed in the Huertgen Forest; but not the 82nd. Having learned from their mistakes, Gavin used a combination of luck and personal observation of the battleground to discover a route by which a costly battle could be avoided. Rather than attacking German defenses in a direct assault, Gavin kept to the high ground and simply outflanked the enemy.

The spring of 1945 heralded preparations for an airborne assault on Berlin, in which the 82nd planned to land south of Tempelhof Airfield. When the attack was canceled, Gavin led his division across the Elbe at Bleckede, and on May 2 he received the surrender of the German 21st Army Group, commanded by General Kurt von Tippelskirch, totaling 150,000 prisoners. For Gavin and the 82nd Airborne Division, the war in Europe was over.

Gavin was not the only Ridgway protégé who earned his spurs in combat. Like Ridgway and Gavin, Maxwell D. Taylor was a veteran of the 82nd Airborne Division, having served as the division's chief of staff from 1942 to 1943. Indeed, Taylor was Ridgway's personal choice for chief of staff when he assumed command of the 82nd in June 1942. At the time Taylor was still serving in Marshall's secretariat, but like his new chief, he had been actively campaigning for field duty.

A 1922 West Point graduate who had finished fourth in his class, Taylor had a reputation for being too intellectual for his own good. Army Chief of Staff Marshall saw command potential in him, however, and invited Taylor to serve as assistant secretary of the General Staff in the War Department. Ever loyal to assistants who demonstrated the potential for increased responsibility, Marshall presented Taylor with the opportunity to display his capacity for field duty by assigning him to Ridgway's division. Ridgway respected Taylor's intellectual gifts but deplored his lack of urgency on administrative matters, and he was never really comfortable having Taylor as his chief of staff. The matter was resolved when Taylor was promoted to commander of the 82nd Airborne Division's artillery.

Arriving in North Africa in March 1943, Brigadier General Taylor helped prepare for the 82nd's first combat jump. He also briefly served as assistant division commander following the untimely demise of Brigadier General Charles L. Keerans Jr. in Operation Husky. Though he had accompanied Ridgway to Sicily aboard an assault craft and had not jumped as Gavin did, Taylor performed well once the entire division arrived in combat. In Sicily, Taylor's performance so impressed Ridgway that he was given responsibility for planning the airborne portion of the subsequent invasion of Italy. A highly successful covert reconnaissance mission to Rome in early September 1943 to determine the feasibility of airborne operations in the vicinity of the Italian capital raised Taylor's stock in the estimation of the Allied high command, Eisenhower in particular. In his memoirs, Eisenhower remarks that "the risks he [Taylor] ran were greater than I asked any other agent or emissary to undertake during the war—he carried weighty responsibilities and discharged them with unerring judgment, and every minute was in imminent danger of discovery and death."[17]

When Major General William C. Lee, commander of the 101st Airborne Division, suffered a heart attack in February 1944, Eisenhower and Bradley selected Taylor to replace him. The staff of the 101st did not particularly welcome the appointment. Taylor was viewed as an outsider because he had never served with the division, and his combat experience was limited. While Gavin had already made two combat jumps, Taylor had made none; indeed, he, like Ridgway, had made only one jump in his career prior to assuming command of an airborne division. Still, war presents strange opportunities, and Taylor was in the right place at the right time. As he himself admitted, "I became the beneficiary of a stroke of good fortune with a most unfortunate cause."[18] In the months ahead, however, Taylor proved his mettle.

On D-Day, Taylor's mission was to seize and hold the four causeways spanning the marshes behind Utah Beach and then to occupy the line of the Douve River to shield the southern flank of VII Corps. Taylor's drop of roughly sixty-six hundred men was not quite as dispersed as Ridgway's force was, and they captured most of their objectives, although casualties mounted throughout the day. Taylor himself assembled and led a provisional company of ninety soldiers toward Exit 1, at Pouppeville. All the exits were in Allied hands by midday, but sporadic fire continued throughout the next three days as Taylor gathered his division for a sustained push toward the base of the Cotentin Peninsula. Stubborn German resistance hindered the capture of Carentan until June 14, a full week later than the overly optimistic D-Day prediction. Casualties had been severe—nearly thirty-eight hundred men, according to Taylor, including Brigadier General Donald F. Pratt, the assistant division commander and the senior airborne commander killed on D-Day.[19] Yet the division had endured its baptism by fire and Taylor had justified Bradley's confidence. For his service in Normandy Taylor received the Distinguished Service Cross.

Redeployed to England, Taylor prepared the 101st for its next operation. On September 17 Taylor conducted the division's second combat jump, which involved 6,695 paratroopers as part of Market-Garden. His specific objectives included the bridge at Zon over the Wilhelmina Canal, to be followed by an attack to clear Eindhoven. Although the initial landing was highly successful, the Germans succeeded in destroying the Zon Bridge, delaying the capture of Eindhoven until the following day. The British armored column, harassed in its own right, finally passed through Taylor's position on D+2, a full twenty-four hours behind the expected arrival time. Taylor likened the operations of the 101st in defending its sector of the Eindhoven-Arnhem highway to the operations of the U.S. Cavalry defending the railroads as they pushed westward through Indian country. In the end, the 101st performed well in a lost cause—the British 1st Airborne Division was virtually destroyed at Arnhem. Taylor's division, like Gavin's, remained in the line until late November, when it reverted to Ridgway's command.

In early December, Taylor was ordered to Washington to represent the XVIII Airborne Corps in discussions regarding the organization and equipment of the airborne divisions. Dismissed by some historians as an attempt by Taylor to obtain a more lucrative command, the mission was important enough to merit special mention in Ridgway's memoirs. In fact, the mission was made at Ridgway's personal request and was of supreme importance to the future of the airborne. As planners in Washington tried to limit the size of the airborne divisions to eighty-eight hundred men, Ridgway sought authorization to maintain the peak strength of the airborne divisions in Normandy of approximately fifteen thousand soldiers so that the divisions could sustain themselves during prolonged combat. Marshall listened to Taylor's arguments and immediately authorized a substantial increase in the size of the divisions by attaching the previously independent airborne battalions and regiments.

While in Washington, Taylor learned of the German attack in the Ardennes and the plight of the 101st Airborne Division, under the temporary command of Brigadier General Anthony C. McAuliffe, at Bastogne. The defense of Bastogne quickly passed into legend and needs little recounting here. Suffice it to say that the attitude of the individual soldiers in America's airborne units was summed up on the first day of the battle: "They've got us surrounded, the poor bastards!" Taylor later recalled that his two greatest disappointments of the war were the canceled airborne assault on Rome and his own absence during the first ten days of the Battle of Bastogne. His chagrin was tempered by his pride in the division's accomplishment. During the days between McAuliffe's defiant "Nuts!" and Taylor's return on December 27, the "Screaming Eagles" had written the brightest page in the division's proud history.

On March 15 Eisenhower presented a Presidential Unit Citation—the first ever awarded to an entire division—to the 101st Airborne Division for gallantry in action. Demonstrating his penchant to secure favor with officers serving in senior positions, Taylor arranged to have a special formation of about two hundred Kansas paratroopers and the state flag of Kansas on hand when fellow Kansan Eisenhower reviewed the division.

The remainder of the war was anticlimactic for Taylor and the 101st Airborne Division. Assigned to Alexander Patch's Seventh Army, on May 4 Taylor received his final combat mission of the war, an attack to seize Berchtesgaden, Adolf Hitler's Alpine retreat. The honor went to the 506th Parachute Infantry Regiment. Three days later, the end of the war concluded all combat operations. VE Day found Taylor's veterans occupying Berchtesgaden, where they captured Field Marshal Albert Kesselring.

Earmarked to join Douglas MacArthur in the Pacific for the final offensive against Japan, Taylor was in France when news of VJ Day reached his headquarters. On August 22 he took leave of the 101st Airborne to assume the superintendency of West Point, bidding an affectionate farewell to the division he had led from Normandy to Berchtesgaden.

Major Generals William N. Miley and Joseph M. Swing, commanding generals of the 17th and 11th airborne divisions, respectively, are not as well known as the commanders of the 82nd and 101st airborne divisions. Their lack of fame is not a reflection of their accomplishments.

"Bud" Miley was born at Fort Mason, California, on December 26, 1897, into an old army family that included three generations of West Pointers dating back to the classes of 1823 and 1827. Miley himself graduated from the

Military Academy in June 1918 after excelling as a champion gymnast. Like many of his contemporaries, Miley attended the full range of army schools during the interwar period, receiving his diploma as top officer in his Advanced Infantry Course from Colonel Omar Bradley. An early devotee of airborne warfare, Bud Miley commanded the 501st Parachute Battalion in October 1940. The 501st was the first airborne battalion in the U.S. Army, and Miley was the perfect man for the job. "He was one of a kind," recalled one of his colleagues. "He could do a standing backflip, things like that. He was the perfect choice. . . . We were a wild, hell-for-leather outfit, but we were a bit ragged militarily."[20] Ironically, Miley, a personal friend of Ridgway, broke his shoulder on his very first jump.

Under Miley's dynamic leadership the 501st developed the parachute infantry techniques that later characterized the army's most successful airborne operations. Much of the time Miley concentrated on tactical operations following the initial deployment of paratroopers, developing tactics that proved instrumental to the survival of the airborne divisions. Miley assumed command of the 503rd Parachute Infantry Regiment (PIR) when he was promoted to ADC of Ridgway's 82nd Division. As ADC, Miley assisted his commander in the transformation of the 82nd from an infantry to an airborne division. Shortly thereafter he received command of the 17th Airborne Division, activating his command on April 15, 1943.

Deploying to Europe in the autumn of 1944, Miley joined Generals Gavin and Taylor as divisional commanders when Ridgway activated the XVIII Airborne Corps. His initial test of combat came on January 4, 1945, when the 17th Airborne Division participated in Major General Troy H. Middleton's VIII Corps attack to destroy the Bulge. The results were hardly surprising. Hastily thrown into combat with inadequate artillery support and in a dense fog, Miley's green troops ran into a buzz saw. Determined German attacks soon pushed him back to his starting point, but he regrouped and attacked again three days later, this time with three regiments abreast. The outcome was similar, with Miley suffering what he himself called "terrific" casualties. Two of his battalions were almost annihilated. Although he contemplated relieving Miley, Patton reconsidered because he did not want to "act too fast." Still, the Third Army commander was not pleased with Miley's performance. "The 17th Airborne . . . got a very bloody nose and reported the loss of 40% in some of its battalions," he noted; " . . . General Miley did not impress me when I met him at Bastogne. . . . He told me he did not know where his right regiment was, yet he was not out looking for it."[21] Another attack on January 13 proved far more successful, and by the time the Germans were eradicated in the Bulge, Miley had matured as a combat commander. Patton also noticed the improvement, stating that Miley had "finally found himself and had done well."

Miley and the 17th Airborne had successfully endured their "trial by combat." Two months later the 17th passed yet another test. As part of the final airborne operation of the European war, Miley and the 17th Airborne joined the British 6th Airborne Division in Operation Varsity, Montgomery's much-ballyhooed crossing of the Rhine. Varsity kicked off on March 24, 1945. It was a massive undertaking, with the American airborne armada consisting of 9,777 men: 4,964 parachutists and 4,613 who deployed by glider.[22] Heavy smoke obscured the landing zones, and Miley's division was dropped more than one mile from the intended drop zones. An unusually high number of C-46 Commando aircraft, which were not equipped with self-sealing fuel tanks, were hit by flak en route and burst into flames. Once on the ground Miley moved rapidly to consolidate his dispersed units. Although historians will long debate the merits of Varsity—Bradley considered it one more example of Montgomery's penchant for "overkill"—Miley was pleased with his unit's performance. By the end of the day, at a cost of 159 killed and 522 wounded, the 17th had accomplished all of its objectives and had captured more than 2,800 Germans. Varsity proved to be the 17th Airborne Division's only combat jump.

For the remainder of the war in Europe, Miley and his division performed occupation duty in the Ruhr near Essen. Command of the 17th Airborne Division was the crowning achievement of Miley's forty-year military career. He retired in 1955 and passed away in Starkville, Mississippi, on September 24, 1997, three months shy of his one hundredth birthday. He was the last of the surviving division commanders of World War II.

On the other side of the world, Major General Joseph M. Swing's 11th Airborne Division deployed to the Southwest Pacific Theater in May 1944. Swing was a U.S. Military Academy classmate of Eisenhower and Bradley, and had been division artillery commander under Ridgway in the 82nd. He served as Eisenhower's airborne adviser during the early stages of the Mediterranean campaign. Perhaps Swing's most notable service before his deployment to the Philippines was as the leader of the Airborne Operations Board, better known as the "Swing Board," a special War Department board convened in the wake of the Sicily debacle to determine policy on the mission and scope of airborne programs and operations. Swing forwarded several recommendations to the

War Department that led to important modifications in troop carrier requirements; the proportionate number of troop carrier units required for training of replacement crews; proportionate readjustment required in the current program of production of airborne divisions and troop carrier groups; and revision of current training doctrine, operational procedure, and techniques for airborne and troop carrier units in the light of recent combat experience.[23]

In February 1943 Swing activated the 11th Airborne Division, consisting of the 511th Parachute Infantry Regiment and two glider infantry regiments, the 187th and 188th. Over the next year he prepared the division for combat, overseeing every aspect of its training before its deployment to the Southwest Pacific Theater. The 11th was never used in the airborne role for which it was established because troop carrier planes and gliders were in short supply in the theater. Instead the division was committed to combat as regular infantry on the island of Leyte in the Philippines in October 1944; it was the only airborne division that actually saw combat in the Pacific. In Luzon the following February, the division's two glider regiments landed by ship, and the 511th PIR and the 457th Parachute Field Artillery Battalion jumped over the course of two days. Elements of the division conducted airborne assaults on Tagaytay Ridge and Aparri on June 23 during the fighting on Luzon. The ensuing campaign toughened the division and earned Swing a reputation as one of America's premier division commanders.

February 1945 also witnessed elements of the 11th Airborne participating in some of the most dangerous exploits in the unit's history. On February 23, while Swing and the remainder of the division pierced the Japanese Genko Line outside Manila, B Company of the 511th, commanded by Lieutenant John M. Ringler, joined the division's Provisional Reconnaissance Platoon in the liberation of 2,147 Allied civilians and prisoners of war interned at Los Baños. Writing to former army chief of staff General Peyton March, Swing described the raid as something "that would have made Knute Rockne envious in his heyday." Not only did the raid go off without a hitch, he wrote, "Old 'Doug' [MacArthur] sent a wire, saying it was 'magnificent,' and old Walter K[rueger] made a sour face and said he was pleased."[24] Only the rapid collapse of Japanese resistance in the aftermath of Hiroshima and Nagasaki prevented Swing's division from spearheading the final invasion of Japan.

The strategic mobility of the airborne division was demonstrated when 11,300 troops from the 11th Airborne Division were transported by air from the Philippines via Okinawa to Japan within seventy-two hours of the Japanese surrender. To the surprise of no one in the 11th Airborne Division, Swing was in the first aircraft that landed at Atsugi Airfield near Yokohama on August 30 to begin the occupation. He immediately took charge of the air base and was there to meet MacArthur, whom President Truman had designated to receive the formal Japanese surrender. The division remained in Japan until 1949, when its new commander, Bud Miley, former commander of the 17th Airborne Division, returned it to Fort Campbell, Kentucky.

As a side note, an independent airborne unit, the 503rd PIR, deployed to the Southwest Pacific in the summer of 1943.[25] Though Swing attempted to incorporate the regiment into the 11th Airborne Division, MacArthur kept it apart to use for special tasks. In February 1945 Colonel George Jones, commanding the 503rd Regimental Combat Team (RCT), recaptured Corregidor in what was arguably the most difficult American combat jump in World War II. The 503rd RCT had made combat jumps at Nadzab (September 1943) and Noemfoor (July 1944) prior to the Corregidor operation. Long after the war, the regiment was finally incorporated into the 11th Airborne Division.

A fifth airborne division, the 13th, commanded by Major General George W. Griner and later by Major General Elbridge G. Chapman Jr., was activated on August 13, 1943, and deployed to Europe in the final stages of the war. It saw no combat as a divisional entity and was frequently called on to furnish replacements for the 17th, 82nd, and 101st divisions. At war's end, Chapman's 13th Airborne Division, comprising the 515th PIR, 517th PIR, 88th GIR, and 326th GIR, was on standby near Auxerre, France, for possible airborne operations. Like Taylor's 101st Airborne Division, the 13th was destined for Japan when the war abruptly ended, but unlike Taylor's unit, the 13th was scheduled to deploy as a regular, nonairborne infantry division because MacArthur planned to use only two airborne divisions in the invasion of the Japanese home islands.

Following the war, the three principal airborne commanders—Ridgway, Taylor, and Gavin—dominated the 1950s U.S. Army. Ridgway and Taylor were both elevated to army chief of staff, and each ran afoul of President Eisenhower over the army's diminished role in a defense establishment that emphasized massive retaliation at the expense of a large conventional ground force. Ridgway, a true professional out of kilter with his civilian leaders, retired in 1955. Taylor remained army chief for two terms, then retired himself and immediately wrote a scathing indictment of Ike's defense policy that he entitled *The Uncertain Trumpet*. Taylor's views soon attracted the attention of President-elect John F. Kennedy, for whom he served as special military representative in the aftermath of the abortive Bay of Pigs disaster. After a short stint as American ambassador to the Republic of Vietnam, Taylor was selected as chairman of the Joint Chiefs of Staff under Lyndon Johnson.

Gavin too emerged as a controversial figure, arguing vehemently against Eisenhower's strategy of massive retaliation. His antipathy toward Maxwell Taylor eventually led to his professional demise. Gavin and Taylor remained polar opposites: Gavin the total warrior immersed in his profession, Taylor far more comfortable in the political environment. Seven years Taylor's junior from West Point, Gavin found his Pentagon responsibilities curtailed under Taylor's watchful eye. Denied an opportunity for advancement as long as Taylor remained army chief, Gavin became increasingly frustrated with Taylor's direction of the army and retired in 1958. Later years only increased the bitterness that characterized the relationship between the former commanders of the most glamorous divisions of World War II.[26]

Their postwar differences aside, America's airborne commanders were a special breed of warrior. Dedicated professionals, they had matured in the interwar army, taking full advantage of the service's emphasis on institutionalized education. Ambitious and tough as steel, all relished their role in the pioneering effort of conducting airborne operations. Unaccustomed to leadership from the rear, each preferred to command from the forward echelons, none more so than Gavin, who jumped with his division in every major airborne operation from Sicily to the Rhine and earned the nickname "Jumping General." Eisenhower's wartime naval aide described the élan of Ridgway, Taylor, and Gavin in March 1945 on the occasion of a meeting with the supreme commander: "They all looked superbly fit and keen in every way . . . they were straining at the leash, never knowing from day to day just what their next show will be; [all] were in quick and complete agreement [that Bradley should expeditiously exploit the Remagen bridgehead]."[27]

Gavin summed up what was required of airborne commanders in his description of Ridgway in Sicily: "Lots of courage, he was right up front every minute. Hard as flint and full of intensity . . . sometimes it seemed as though it was a personal thing: Ridgway versus the Wehrmacht." Not surprisingly, the legacy of combat leadership bequeathed by the commanding generals of America's elite divisions endures to the present day.

PART 2
THE WARRIORS

CHAPTER 8

ENOLA GAY: PAUL TIBBETS OF THE ARMY AIR FORCES

I am content that we did what reason compelled and duty dictated.

—Brigadier General Paul W. Tibbets

Brigadier General Paul Warfield Tibbets is a member of the most exclusive fraternity of warriors in the world, a band of brothers that consists of but two officers: the pilots who initiated the nuclear age in warfare. Moreover, Tibbets is the chairman of the board. As commander of the 509th Composite Group in 1945, he delivered the first atomic bomb on Hiroshima. From the pilot's seat of the Enola Gay, Tibbets saw the city shimmer in the morning light and then suddenly disappear. Three days later, Major Charles Sweeney, one of Tibbets's squadron commanders, flew the second atomic mission. Had there been a third strike, General Curtis LeMay, commander of the Twentieth U.S. Army Air Force, had already directed that Tibbets would pilot the plane. To Tibbets's relief, a third mission was unnecessary; Imperial Japan quickly accepted the Potsdam ultimatum and surrendered to the Allies.

There was little in his youth to suggest that Paul Tibbets would someday play an important role in the twentieth century's greatest conflict. Tibbets was born February 23, 1915, in Quincy, Illinois, the son of Enola Gay Haggard and Paul Warfield Tibbets. The family moved to Davenport, Iowa, when he was five, and then to Iowa's capital, Des Moines, before finally settling in Florida to escape the harsh midwestern winters. In the interim, young Tibbets acquired an interest in flying. When he was five years old, a barnstormer buzzed the family farm as part of a promotion for a local carnival. Rides were one dollar, a considerable sum in those days, and Enola Gay forbade her son to get into the airplane. His father, who had served in France as an infantry captain in the trenches, concurred. Tibbets remembered that his father always said that the two most dangerous things he had ever done were riding in a motorcycle sidecar for a dispatch rider and flying in an airplane. Seven years later, Paul Tibbets made his initial airplane ride in January 1927 as a "bombardier" dropping candy bars to a crowd attending the races at the Hialeah track. Tibbets later claimed that the Hialeah mission was far more exciting than the one to Hiroshima eighteen years later because nothing could ever match the thrill of a twelve-year-old's first flight. That first flight changed his life; having tasted the exhilaration of flight, nothing else would ever satisfy Tibbets.

Declining business fortunes brought the Tibbets family back to Illinois in the late 1920s, and Paul enrolled at the Western Military Academy in Alton, Illinois. After enduring what he termed "five years of iron-fisted discipline," Tibbets graduated in 1933 and enrolled in the University of Florida at Gainesville. An average student, Tibbets transferred to the University of Cincinnati after his sophomore year to complete his premedical studies. He continued flying during this time, taking private lessons.

Becoming less infatuated with the medical profession and more interested in flying, Tibbets dropped out of school in 1937 and joined the U.S. Army Air Corps cadet program.[1] Shortly thereafter Tibbets reported to Randolph Field at San Antonio, Texas, to begin his flight training. He soon proved to be an above-average pilot. When he graduated in February 1938, Tibbets pinned the gold bars of a second lieutenant on his shoulders and a pair of silver wings over his left breast pocket. Equally important, Tibbets opted for observation training, *vice* pursuit aircraft, which opened the way for him to fly multiengine aircraft instead of the single-engine fighters. Transferred to Fort Benning, Georgia, he spent a year piloting George Patton's personal airplane and accumulated nearly fifteen hundred hours of twin-engine flying time. While on a routine mission the first Sunday in December 1941, Tibbets, a newly promoted captain, heard over the radio that Japan had bombed Pearl Harbor.

Because of his flight experience Tibbets was selected for training in the new Boeing B-17 Flying Fortress. Assigned to the 29th Bomb Group in Savannah, Georgia, Tibbets spent the first months at war on antisubmarine patrol along the East Coast from Cape May, New Jersey, to the Yucatán Channel between Cuba and Mexico. The army began purchasing B-17s in greater quantities, and Tibbets reported to MacDill Air Base near Tampa, Florida, as the first officer in the new 97th Bomb Group (Heavy). There he received his first command—squadron commander of the 40th Squadron.

He found the job of making "a fighting outfit" of the command rewarding but exhausting; often he was in the air sixteen hours a day. By June 1942 the 97th was en route to England. The first B-17 in the 29th Bomb Group arrived at Prestwick, Scotland, on July 1. Tibbets followed a couple of days later. By June 27 the entire group was in the United Kingdom, and it was soon deployed to Polebrook, an airfield a few miles northeast of London. Within weeks the group commander was relieved and Colonel Frank Armstrong assumed command; he appointed Tibbets his executive officer.[2] On August 17 Tibbets piloted the first plane from the Eighth Air Force to hit the railroad marshaling yards at Rouen; his copilot was none other than Colonel Armstrong. Together they led the first attack formation that struck Hitler's Festung Europa. Major Paul Tibbets was finally at war.

Daylight precision bombing was a controversial subject in 1942. Two American generals, aviation pioneers Carl "Tooey" Spaatz and Ira C. Eaker, staked their careers and thousands of lives on its efficacy. The two were convinced that daylight bombing, coupled with nighttime bombing by the British Bomber Command, would maintain maximum pressure on Hitler's Germany. It fell to Tibbets and other commanders to devise the tactics to make the daylight raids effective. Which routes to fly, at what altitude, at what speed, in what formations? All of those questions had to be answered, and there was little room for error. "Our trouble was that we were untrained and nobody there knew what to train for or how to begin," recalled Tibbets. "It was reasonable to believe that the more firepower we could mass for ourselves, the better off we would be [against German fighter planes]. So it seemed to me that the first move was to learn to fly tight formations. . . . The compactness and tightness of that kind of formation flying would give us the benefit of all those ten machine guns all the way around those three airplanes [Tibbets and his two wingmen]."[3]

Over the course of the late summer, the Eighth Air Force received its baptism of fire. Tibbets led nearly every mission while the 97th remained in England. In the process he matured into a tough, combat-tested commander. On October 9 he flew lead plane on the first one-hundred-plane raid against Lille, an industrial city in northern France. Thirty-three American bombers were shot down or had mechanical problems, a casualty rate of one-third. The raid was proclaimed a success despite the losses, and Tibbets, as lead pilot, was accosted by reporters eager to hear his story. Within days, Paul

Tibbets had become a household name. Reflecting on those early bombing raids, Tibbets recalled that they proved less important for what they contributed directly to the Allied war effort than for what they added to the doctrine of daylight strategic bombing.

As a prelude to the invasion of North Africa in November 1942, Allied headquarters decided to send Major General Mark Clark, Eisenhower's deputy, on a secret mission to determine if the French Vichy government would resist the invasion. General Spaatz, commander of the Eighth Air Force, was directed to pick his two best pilots to fly the two B-17s involved in the mission. One of those he selected was Tibbets. From Tibbets's perspective, the flight to Gibraltar was "a comedy of errors which, with more than a little bit of luck, ended happily." Less than a week later, Tibbets flew Eisenhower to Gibraltar for the beginning of Operation Torch. The weather at the departure airfield was so bad that Eisenhower turned to General James C. "Jimmy" Doolittle and asked if the mission was going to be scrubbed. Pointing to Tibbets, Doolittle responded, "He's doing the flying; he's making the decisions." Ike then turned to Tibbets and repeated the question. Tibbets said, "I wouldn't hesitate myself to take off and go, but with you on board and all these other people—there's a certain risk being incurred." Ike smiled and said, "Son, they're going to start a war down there. I'm supposed to fight it." "OK," Tibbets replied. "Let's go." It was touch-and-go for the first few hours; the fog was so dense that Tibbets could not see his instrument panel. After he finally broke out into the clear, the twelve-hundred-mile flight proved to be an enjoyable experience. The supreme commander conversed with the newly promoted twenty-seven-year-old lieutenant colonel throughout the entire journey.

After the invasion, Tibbets and many other experienced pilots were transferred to the Twelfth Air Force to carry out the war in the Mediterranean. In his autobiography, Tibbets calls the North African campaign his real introduction to warfare. He witnessed aerial warfare on an unprecedented scale and saw the true effects of bombs on a civilian populace. On more than one occasion his crews were bombed on their own airfields when the Germans achieved local air superiority. On November 16 he led a small formation of B-17s on the first raid on Bizerte, a Tunisian port where German reinforcements were arriving. The raid was a complete success and added immeasurably to Tibbets's reputation as a seasoned pilot. As the end of the year approached, Tibbets was transferred to the Twelfth Air Force headquarters in Algiers, where he served as General Doolittle's bombardment chief. It was the beginning of the lowest point in his career in the European theater.

A desk job, no matter how important, was not command of a combat squadron. For weeks prior to his transfer Tibbets had served as the de facto commander of the 97th Bomb Group. He had flown forty-three combat missions in England and North Africa, usually as lead pilot. Now he was relegated to working for Doolittle's chief of operations, Colonel Lauris Norstad, whom Tibbets later described as "one of most vain and egotistical officers" he had ever met.[4] A clash between the two might have been avoidable had Norstad "been less arrogant and Tibbets . . . more tactful."[5] In early January, Colonel Norstad blackballed Tibbets's promotion to full colonel, allegedly claiming that there was going to be only one colonel in the operations division. Shortly thereafter Norstad convened a meeting to discuss the resumption of bombing attacks on Bizerte. Norstad had decided to send in the bombers at six thousand feet, an altitude Tibbets, who had flown numerous missions over Bizerte, considered sheer suicide. When Norstad accused Tibbets of combat fatigue, the veteran pilot placed his career on the line and announced that he would lead the raid if Norstad would come along as his copilot. Norstad backed down, but the damage was done.

Embarrassed that a junior officer had challenged him in front of his men, Norstad petitioned Doolittle to court-martial Tibbets for rank insubordination. Doolittle thwarted the court-martial and instead transferred Tibbets back to the United States when General Henry H. "Hap" Arnold requested that Doolittle's "most experienced B-17 pilot and combat commander" return for assignment to the B-29 program. Meanwhile Norstad inserted a derogatory letter in Tibbets's military personnel file. The two antagonists would meet twice more after the war, and on neither occasion were they excessively cordial.

The project to which Tibbets returned in February 1943 was the B-29 bomber built by Boeing. By the time the B-29s began rolling off the line in July, Tibbets was a seasoned twenty-eight-year-old lieutenant colonel who had amassed more than three thousand air hours. On reporting to "Boeing Wichita," Kansas, Tibbets found the YB-29 "Super Fortress" ready for service testing. With a wing span of 141 feet and length of 93 feet, the B-29 was the largest bomber that had been built to date. The plane contained a fire-control system that permitted guns mounted outside the airplane to be fired by a gunner who had no manual contact with the weapons. Its airspeed was well above 300 miles an hour, and it could ascend to more than thirty-five thousand feet; B-17s, in contrast, had a maximum speed of 220 plus miles per hour and generally flew below twenty thousand feet. Additionally, the plane contained a pneumatic bomb-bay door and a fully pressurized cabin and front crew section that reduced the crew's fatigue on long missions. In short, the B-29 was designed to fly faster and longer and to deliver a heavier bomb load than any aircraft that had ever been built. As the primary test pilot for the B-29 program, Tibbets rapidly accrued more flying time than any other American pilot. The pace was hectic, with Tibbets advising the various training commands about the intricacies and idiosyncrasies of the bomber as he discovered them. In a series of test flights, he determined that at between thirty thousand and thirty-five thousand feet he could turn in a shorter radius than an attacking P-47.

Tibbets was on station at Alamogordo, New Mexico, when he received the phone call that changed his life. Tibbets's work in the States had been an "emotional letdown" after the excitement of combat over Europe and North Africa. On September 1, 1944, he reported to Major General Uzal G. Ent, commanding general of the Second Air Force, the training unit for the Army Air Forces deployed overseas.[6] At the time, Tibbets was testing B-29s at Clovis, New Mexico, to determine their vulnerability to fighter attack. Unbeknownst to Tibbets, Hap Arnold had called Ent and given him three names for consideration for a special mission. After reviewing the men's files Ent selected Tibbets, but he wanted to confirm his choice with a personal interview. Though Tibbets did not know the specific reason for his summons, he surmised the urgency of the interview when Ent indicated that he was to pack his bags because he would not be returning to Alamogordo. The interview was destined to change not only Tibbets's career, but the nature of future warfare as well.

Upon arriving at Ent's headquarters in Colorado Springs, Tibbets was taken aside and interrogated by Lieutenant Colonel Jack Lansdale, the chief of security for the Manhattan Project. In addition to questions about his military record, Lansdale wanted to know about an embarrassing moment from Tibbets's youth when he was arrested during a lovemaking episode in Florida. Tibbets acknowledged the incident and was then ushered into Ent's office. Also present were two other men, something Tibbets found somewhat unusual. Dispensing with formalities, Ent introduced the two as Captain William S. "Deak" Parsons, a naval officer and gun expert, and Dr. Norman Ramsey, a Columbia University professor. Lansdale assured Ent that he was fully satisfied with Tibbets. "I knew you would be," replied Ent, who then informed Tibbets that he had been selected to perform a top-secret task that was extremely important. He would be expected to organize a combat force to deliver a new type of explosive so powerful that its full potential was still unknown.

Ent's charge to Tibbets was threefold: (1) he was to organize and train a unit to drop atomic bombs simultaneously on Japan and Germany; (2) Tibbets's private air force would be semi-independent of the armed services, and the project must remain top secret; and (3) he would use the code word "silverplate" as a last resort to request what he needed. From there the discussion moved on to the best method to deliver the bomb. Parsons, an associate director of the Los Alamos laboratory in charge of atomic bomb ballistics, stated that the minimum safe distance to withstand the shock waves generated by the atomic explosion was eight miles. It would be up to Tibbets to devise a way to increase the distance between the blast and the bomber, which would release the bomb from an altitude of thirty thousand feet, roughly six miles.

Other questions arose as well. How should the bomb bays of the B-29 be modified to accommodate the pumpkin-shaped bomb? Where would the unit be based, and where would Tibbets get the men for his air force? The secrecy associated with the Manhattan Project dictated an isolated spot. Ent gave Tibbets a choice of three airfields: Wendover, Utah; Great Bend, Kansas; and Mountain Home at Boise, Idaho. Ent also provided Tibbets with three B-29 squadrons of the 504th Bomb Group in training at Harvard, Nebraska. The general had already identified the 393rd Bomb Squadron there for detachment from its parent wing, subject to Tibbets's approval. Tibbets's task would require 100 percent of his resources and personal attention until the end of the war. In his own words, his mission was to organize an air force for the purpose of dropping a bomb that hadn't been built on a target that hadn't been chosen.

Why was Tibbets selected for the mission? The two other officers being considered were Brigadier General Frank Armstrong, Tibbets's former commander and one of Army Chief George Marshall's favorite officers, and Colonel Roscoe "Bim" Wilson, Hap Arnold's personal representative to the Manhattan Project. Both men were highly qualified. Tibbets, however, held certain advantages over them. He had a proven combat record that included planning the strategic bombing campaign against Germany. He was the youngest of the three and had demonstrated an exceptional capacity for leadership in combat. Having served as Eisenhower's personal pilot during the early stages of the war in North Africa, Tibbets's ability in the air was unquestionable. Moreover, he was the most qualified pilot available with B-29 experience, having tested the aircraft for more than a year. Additionally, he was known to be an independent operator and had devised novel tactics that eventually became the pattern for the combined bombing offensive against Germany. This independence had proved a mixed blessing on Tibbets's tour in North Africa when it offended Norstad, who was now the chief of staff of the Twentieth Air Force (Rear). In short, the demands of the Manhattan Project required a commander who could anticipate problems and ruthlessly execute a highly dangerous mission, and Lieutenant Colonel Paul Tibbets, though junior in rank, was the right man for the job.

Only when he departed Ent's office did Tibbets, only twenty-nine years old, comprehend the enormity of the task before him. The first order of business was to reconnoiter the various air bases that Ent had recommended. For security purposes Tibbets selected Wendover Air Base, which was situated in a virtually uninhabited section of Utah. Next he flew to Harvard, Nebraska, where he inspected the 393rd Bomb Squadron, commanded by Lieutenant Colonel Tom Classen. Tibbets liked the squadron and its commander, and he appointed Classen his deputy commander.

Although the 509th Composite Bomb Group would not be officially activated until December 17, 1944—ironically, the forty-first anniversary of the Wright Brothers' flight at Kitty Hawk—Tibbets established his own headquarters at Wendover on September 8. With virtual autonomy over personnel selection, he then requested his old B-17 crew from Europe, including bombardier Tom Ferebee; Staff Sergeant George Caron, his old tail gunner; Dutch van Kirk, navigator; and Staff Sergeant Wyatt Duzenbury, flight engineer. The real gem of the team was Charles Begg, an ordnance expert who had been nominated by Tibbets's security officer. Next was Bob Lewis, another B-29 test pilot whom Tibbets quickly assigned as his copilot. The remainder of the crew consisted of personnel recommended by men whom Tibbets personally trusted: bombardier Kermit Beahan, navigator James van Pelt, radar specialist Jacob Beser, and pilots Charles Sweeney and Don Albury. Sweeney, destined to fly the Nagasaki mission, had met Tibbets at Eglin Air Base, Florida, in September 1943 when Tibbets and copilot Lewis had flown a prototype B-29 to Eglin in order to test a central fire-control gunnery system. At the time, Sweeney was Eglin's base security officer and had never heard of the B-29. He flew as Tibbets's navigator on a mission to Marietta, Georgia, the following week and so impressed Tibbets that he had Sweeney assigned to his command.[7]

For the remainder of 1944 Tibbets concentrated on security issues and on organizing his command. Each airman assigned to the 509th Composite Bomb Group underwent a security investigation and received security briefings on a routine basis. Only Tibbets knew the true mission of the group, but he understood the natural curiosity of men in combat and offered as much information as he could. To relieve the monotony of sixteen-hour training days, he authorized the married men to bring their families to Wendover. He also briefed the men that they would eventually deploy overseas and would take part in an effort that could end the war. Any breach of security, he warned, would result in immediate dismissal from the command. To ensure the men's compliance he requested FBI support to follow them when they took Christmas leave. Several airmen let slip that they were involved in a top-secret project. When they returned to Wendover, they were summoned to Tibbets's office and summarily dismissed. The word got out to the rest of the command, and that was the end of security violations.

Tibbets also embroiled himself in the mechanics of the mission. The projected weight of the atomic bomb was ten thousand pounds, a weight that would reduce the maneuverability of the B-29 at thirty thousand feet. To compensate, Tibbets ordered most of the armament removed from the planes. Using "silverplate" he also ordered the delivery of fifteen specially designed B-29s with modified bomb bays. When his request for transport airplanes was denied, Tibbets informed Bim Wilson, who was now serving as Hap Arnold's aide. Arnold immediately approved the request and sent the serial numbers of the planes to Tibbets the very next day. He also demoted one of his deputy chiefs of operations from brigadier general to major for disapproving a silverplate request.[8]

Next Tibbets addressed the problem of how to put eight miles—the minimum safety distance—between the plane and the blast. Even at that distance the shock waves would hit the plane exactly forty seconds after the explosion, and he had to devise a tactic to ensure the crew's safety. Tibbets studied the problem and decided that if he could put the B-29 into a sharp 155-degree turn as soon as the bomb was released, he could escape the worst of the shock wave from the blast. Since such a maneuver demanded precision flying beyond the normal capability of most pilots, he initiated a training program that included extensive maneuvering drills as well as high-precision navigational and bombing exercises. When the time came to release the bomb, he wanted to be able to place it within two hundred feet of the aiming point. As winter gave way to early spring, Tibbets had trained his crews into a highly effective force. His initial orders had been to prepare his command to deliver bombs against both Germany and Japan, but Germany surrendered unconditionally in early May and only Japan remained as a potential target.

Tibbets could refine his preparations and his crews' techniques, but he could not dictate the pace of the scientific experiments. Early spring brought numerous meetings with Robert Oppenheimer and his associates. Tibbets remembered that "Los Alamos was playing percentage games" throughout June and July, trying to come to the perfect solution concerning the firing mechanism before the projected test date in late July. Well aware that Washington had consulted the best team of meteorologists that could be assembled and had decided that the period from August 5 to 11 would have the requisite clear skies over Japan to permit the precision bombing that the atomic mission would require, Tibbets made the critical decision that only he could make as a combat commander. Having just been promoted to full colonel, he exercised his full authority and transmitted to Washington the code word that ordered the 509th to be processed for deployment to Tinian Island in the Marianas chain. Tinian had been picked as the 509th's Pacific base in early February 1945, and an engineering team had already begun constructing the field where Tibbets's team would settle. Because he had not cleared his request with senior headquarters first, Tibbets then sat back to await the expected backlash. Sure enough, within hours Major General Leslie R. Groves, the Manhattan Project director, summoned him to the Pentagon for what Tibbets later described as a "classic chewing-out, complete with profanity." After being kept waiting outside Groves's office for an hour to "cool his heels," Tibbets entered and stood at attention while Groves threatened to reduce the thirty-year-old colonel to second lieutenant for his insubordination. Then, with a twinkle in his eye, Groves said, "Paul, you did something I could never do, but in the future, no more surprises." In retrospect, Tibbets's reasoning was sound. As long as the flight crews were at Wendover, the scientists had no reason to hurry; if the command was actually in position to deliver the bomb, the scientists would realize the urgency and stop dragging their feet.

Tibbets later remembered the months of May, June, and July as the most frenzied of his military career. Within two weeks of giving the order to deploy, Tibbets and two-thirds of the 509th were en route to Tinian. The majority of the command reached their destination on May 29. The eighteen B-29s arrived the next week. By this time the 509th was a self-contained unit comprising the 393rd Bomber Squadron, the 320th Troop Carrier Squadron, the 309th Air Service Group, the 603rd Air Engineering Squadron, and the 1027th Air Matériel Squadron, plus the newly arrived 1st Ordnance Squadron to handle the atomic bombs when they arrived.[9]

Tibbets's command was headquartered in an isolated corner of the island's major airfield. Practice bombing runs began almost immediately. Most of the bombing runs were conducted by two or three planes on the fringes of Japanese cities that had previously been decimated by General LeMay's daylight incendiary raids. Each plane carried a single bomb designed to replicate the size and shape of "Little Boy," the code name for the atomic bomb. LeMay personally approved Tibbets's move to single-plane strikes and gave him a list of twenty targets on which to practice. The only restriction LeMay imposed was that no lone-plane strikes could be near Kyoto, Hiroshima, Niigata, Kokura, or Nagasaki, the cities that had been designated as potential targets.[10] During the last half of July, Tibbets's crews made twelve such strikes on Japanese cities. Tibbets did not participate in any of these raids; he was forbidden to fly over Japan lest he be captured and forced to reveal that the United States was nearing completion of an atomic bomb. The raids had an unforeseen benefit in addition to the practice they provided: they familiarized the Japanese defenders with single-plane missions that accomplished relatively little damage.

As Tibbets prepared his crews for their mission, logistical and administrative problems temporarily plagued his command. At that time the Twentieth Army Air Force required all B-29 crew members to attend a three-week orientation course to review their qualifications and to acclimate themselves to conditions in the Pacific. The first day one of the 509th's crews attended the school, Tibbets was summoned to the office of Brigadier General John Davies, commander of the 313th Bombardment Wing. Davies asked Tibbets if all his crews were as well trained as the first one. "Yes," Tibbets responded. "I didn't select any special one to begin things." Then Davies said, "Hell, they are demoralizing my whole school. They know more about airplanes and navigation and everything else than my instructors know. You can't send them to school any more. They are embarrassing my instructors."[11] Davies promptly exempted the 509th crews from all future instruction. Such preferential treatment alienated Tibbets's command from the other air wings on the island, many of whom had served on Tinian far longer than the 509th. The universal gripe among the Twentieth Army Air Force crews that the 509th Composite Bomb Group was too elite to train with the other B-29 crews is evident in a famous "razzing" rhyme put together in the 313th Wing's headquarters by several anonymous pilots.

Into the air the secret rose,
Where they're going nobody knows.
Tomorrow they'll return again,
But we'll never know where they have been.
Don't ask us about results or such

Unless you want to get in Dutch,
But take it from one who's sure of the score,
The 509th is winning the war.

When other groups are ready to go,
We've a program for the whole damned show,
When Halsey's Fifth shells Nippon's shores
Why shucks we'd known it the day before.
MacArthur and Doolittle give out in advance,
But with this new bunch we've not a chance,
We should have been home a month or more,
For the 509th is winning the war.

On July 16 Tibbets received a coded message from General Groves advising him that the Alamogordo test had been a success; the atomic bomb was a reality. Tibbets began readying the crews for the actual strike. He prepared seven planes for the first mission. Two would accompany Tibbets, one carrying scientific instruments to measure the intensity of the blast and the other with photographic equipment to record the actual event. Another B-29 would land on Iwo Jima and serve as a backup if the bomb-carrying plane ran into mechanical trouble. Three planes would precede Tibbets and arrive at each potential target to give early weather data. As commander of the 509th, Tibbets had already decided that he would pilot the first plane. On the morning of July 26, the cruiser *Indianapolis* delivered the firing mechanism for the atomic bomb, and the bucket, with a slug of uranium (U-235), was taken to the bomb assembly hut to be fitted into one of the three casings already on hand.[12] Two B-29s from Hamilton Air Force Base in California delivered a second slug of uranium as well as the plutonium for the second bomb. Tooey Spaatz arrived on Guam on July 29 to take command of the U.S. Strategic Air Forces in the Pacific. Spaatz carried a top-secret order drafted in Washington by General Groves authorizing the dropping of the "the first special bomb" on one of four cities: Hiroshima, Kokura, Niigata, or Nagasaki. Unless Japan accepted the Potsdam ultimatum and surrendered unconditionally, the atomic bomb would be dropped on the first feasible day after August 3.

On receiving Groves's order authorizing the bombing missions, Tibbets prepared a detailed order and sent it to LeMay. LeMay approved it, designating Hiroshima as the primary target for Special Bombing Mission No. 13. The secondary target was to be Kokura; the third, Nagasaki. Tibbets and Tom

Ferebee studied an aerial photograph of Hiroshima, and Ferebee selected a geographical feature east of the city as the initial point from which Tibbets would begin his bombing run. As the aiming point, Ferebee put his finger on a T-shaped bridge near the heart of the city. The code name for the mission was "Centerboard," and the target date was set for August 6. The second strike was tentatively scheduled for August 9.

Having decided that he would pilot the plane that carried the atom bomb, Tibbets gave serious consideration to a name for his plane. Remembering how his mother, albeit reluctantly, had encouraged him to pursue his dream of flying, Tibbets selected the name Enola Gay. Tom Ferebee and Dutch Van Kirk, who had served with Tibbets in Europe and North Africa, heartily concurred with Tibbets's choice. Later Tibbets claimed he chose that name "because I have a quiet sense of history. I thought the plane and our mission might be remembered a long time." For the Hiroshima mission, Tibbets also selected the aircraft—B-29 number 82—and the crew who would fly with him. "I already had the essentials," he recalled in an interview. "[Bombardier] Tom Ferebee and [navigator] 'Dutch' Van Kirk are still the best friends I've got."[13] He selected Bob Lewis as his copilot because he regarded him as completely competent and dependable.

On the day before the mission, Tibbets busied himself with last-minute preparations. Since the weight of the (simulated) bomb had caused problems for several pilots during takeoff, Tibbets and the scientists decided that Little Boy would be assembled in flight by Captain Deak Parsons. A premature explosion would vaporize not only the airfield but the entire island of Tinian as well. At approximately 2300 on August 5, the three crews that would be making the flight gathered at the Quonset hut that served as the unit's operations headquarters for the mission briefing. Winds and weather were predicted and reviewed. Communications were checked and rechecked. Addressing the rendezvous at Iwo Jima with the two instrument B-29s, Tibbets said: "I'll circle the island once—then it's up to you to slide in. I can't wait." Then he advised the crew of the mission: "Tonight is the night we have all been waiting for. Our long months of training are to be put to the test. . . . Upon our efforts tonight it is possible that history will be made. We are going on a mission is that is different from any you have ever seen or heard about. This bomb contains a destructive force equivalent probably to twenty thousand tons of TNT."[14] Tibbets then reviewed the flight procedures, and Chaplain William B. Downey concluded the briefing with a prayer for their safe return and a rapid end to the war.

In the hours before takeoff, Paul Tibbets contemplated the magnitude of the mission he was about to fly. He never seriously doubted his ability to get the bomb-laden Enola Gay off the runway. He knew more about the B-29's capabilities than any other pilot in the U.S. Army Air Forces. Nor did he once consider assigning someone else to pilot the plane. That was not his command style. On the most important bomb mission of the war, he, the commander, was the logical choice. Confident, even overconfident, that the mission would be successful, he ignored the twelve cyanide capsules, one for each member of the crew, that he had placed into the pocket of his coveralls. After enjoying a quick breakfast, he prepared for his personal rendezvous with destiny.

Shortly after 0100, Tibbets returned to his quarters and picked up his flying gear, including cigars, cigarettes, pipe tobacco, and pipes. Then he, Parsons, Van Kirk, and Ferebee jumped into a jeep and headed for the flight line. Awaiting them was the Enola Gay, bathed in floodlights. Surrounded by photographers, the twelve crew members were photographed just prior to entering the plane. The twelve were Tibbets, copilot Captain Robert A. Lewis, bombardier Major Thomas W. Ferebee, navigator Captain Theodore J. Van Kirk, radar countermeasures officer Lieutenant Jacob Beser, weaponeer and ordnance officer Navy Captain William S. Parsons, assistant weaponeer Second Lieutenant Maurice Jeppson, radar operator Sergeant Joe Stiborik, tail gunner Staff Sergeant George R. Caron, assistant flight engineer Sergeant Robert H. Shumard, radio operator Private First Class Richard H. Nelson, and flight engineer Technical Sergeant Wyatt E. Duzenbury. Tibbets settled into the left-hand seat beside Lewis and completed the preflight checklist. At 0230 Tibbets began to taxi down the runway. Fifteen minutes later, Dutch Van Kirk made the notation in the Enola Gay's log: "Time Takeoff 0245. Destination: Hiroshima." Eight minutes later, Parsons and Jeppson lowered themselves into the bomb bay and inserted a slug of uranium and the conventional explosive charge into the core of Little Boy. With Lewis monitoring the automatic pilot, Tibbets closed his eyes and fell into a brief sleep.

Twenty-five minutes later, Tibbets awoke and took control of the Enola Gay. Climbing to 5,000 feet, he reached Iwo Jima at 0555 and departed at 0607 after circling Mount Suribachi until the two planes carrying the instruments and cameras joined him. As the formation departed Iwo Jima, Tibbets was right on schedule and approximately three hours from his target. At the time, he had not received any report from the weather planes, so he was still unsure of his final target. At 0730 Deak Parsons confirmed that the bomb was armed and ready. Copilot Lewis made an annotation in the log: "The bomb is now alive. It is a funny feeling knowing it is right in back of you. Knock wood." Climbing to his bombing altitude of 30,700 feet, Tibbets finally received a message from Major Claude Eatherly in Straight Flush, high over Hiroshima. Cloud cover was less than three-tenths at all altitudes, perfect to allow for a visual drop. Over the intercom Tibbets announced, "It's Hiroshima." Proceeding on a course toward the Japanese island of Shikoku, Tibbets made minor adjustments in the flight path. Hiroshima lay just beyond the narrow Iyo Sea. Eight minutes from the designated drop time, Hiroshima came into view and Tibbets confirmed its identity with the crew. Making a leftward turn of 60 degrees, he passed over the initial point on a heading of 264 degrees. Groundspeed for the Enola Gay was calculated at 285 knots, roughly 330 miles per hour, as Ferebee made an 8-degree correction to account for drift and wind speed. Ten miles out Ferebee saw the T-shaped bridge that had been designated as the aiming point. Tibbets and Van Kirk confirmed his sighting. Ninety seconds out, Tibbets turned the plane over to Ferebee on autopilot. "It's all yours," the colonel said, slipping back into a relaxed position. At 0915 plus 17 seconds—0815 Hiroshima time—Little Boy tumbled out of the belly of the Enola Gay.

As soon as Ferebee released the bomb, Tibbets put the plane into a 155-degree diving turn to the right to avoid the shock wave generated by the bomb. Forty-three seconds later, Little Boy exploded at the preset altitude of 1,890 feet above Hiroshima. Though many would later ask Tibbets what his thoughts had been after he released the bomb, Tibbets was far too busy concentrating on putting as much distance between ground zero and the Enola Gay to think about anything else. Nearly a minute later, nine miles distant from the blast, the first of two shock waves struck the B-29. Tibbets likened the experience to flying through enemy flak over targets in Europe and Africa. Once he was certain that the Enola Gay was safe from the effects of the explosion, Tibbets circled to view the results. Over the intercom he announced, "Fellas, you have just dropped the first atomic bomb in history." As the mushroom cloud reached 45,000 feet, Tibbets viewed the ground below. At the base of the cloud, raging fires engulfed Hiroshima. In his memoirs Tibbets notes: "If Dante had been with us in the plane, he would have been terrified!" He later likened Hiroshima to a tar barrel, "a hot one. You can see that little white smoke powder that hangs up above that boiling tar, and this is exactly what the city looked like." A wave of horror swept over the crew, prompting Lewis to write a final entry in his log: "My God!"[15]

What thoughts were in Tibbets's mind then? No accurate record exists. He was certainly grateful that the mission was successful. He felt relief that the bomb had worked, satisfaction that the job was done, and a letdown now that it was over. Tibbets immediately jotted some notes on a pad and passed them to Dick Nelson for radio transmission back to Tinian. The final message was curt and concise: "Clear cut, successful in all respects. Visual effects greater than Trinity [the July test at Alamogordo]. Hiroshima. Conditions normal in airplane following delivery. Proceeding to regular base." Privately, Tibbets turned to his copilot and confided, "I think this is the end of the war." Four hundred miles from Hiroshima, the mushroom cloud disappeared from tail gunner Bob Caron's view.

Hoping that the new weapon had made future war unthinkable, Tibbets reflected on the damage of the atom bomb. He was still thinking about the futility of future war when the Enola Gay touched down at Tinian at 1458. The mission had lasted twelve hours and thirteen minutes, and the weapon had been delivered just seventeen seconds behind schedule.

Awaiting the return of the Enola Gay were Generals Carl Spaatz, Nathan Twining, Thomas F. Farrell, and John Davies, and Rear Admiral W. R. E. Purnell. Farrell and Purnell were members of the project staff from Los Alamos. To Tibbets's surprise Spaatz stepped forward and pinned the Distinguished Service Cross on his flight coveralls. Cameras recorded the event for posterity. The next day President Truman announced to the world that the United States had dropped an atomic bomb on Japan. Concurrently, aerial photographs confirmed the tragic consequences of the world's first nuclear explosion.

After a lengthy debriefing Tibbets caught some well-earned rest and set about preparing the second bomb for delivery. LeMay had assumed that Tibbets would fly the next mission, but Tibbets had already decided that Chuck Sweeney would have that honor; no need to hog all the glory for himself. In fact, that was the reason Tibbets had selected Sweeney to fly one of the instrument planes that accompanied the Enola Gay. As the 509th's commanding officer, Tibbets had flown the Hiroshima raid to demonstrate that it could be done. Such leadership by example was Tibbets's modus operandi. If any initial mistakes were going to be made, Tibbets wanted to be the man who made them. That the Hiroshima mission went off like clockwork was a tribute to his organizational, technical, and leadership skills.

Sweeney was not so fortunate. A malfunctioning fuel pump delayed takeoff for the second bombing mission for more than an hour. Sweeney lost precious time over Iwo Jima when the escort planes carrying the scientific instruments failed to rendezvous at the prescribed time. Intense cloud cover over Kokura then forced Sweeney to fly to his secondary target, Nagasaki, where cloud cover forced him to approach by radar. A small break in the clouds allowed Sweeney to drop the bomb, but it hit more than a mile and a half from the planned aiming point. Due to the topography of Nagasaki, the bomb's effect was slightly less than at Hiroshima, but it was nevertheless extraordinarily devastating.[16] One day later Japan offered to surrender, and on August 15 (Japanese time) Japan accepted the Potsdam ultimatum. The war in the Pacific was over.

Following the official Japanese surrender aboard the USS *Missouri*, Tibbets toured Nagasaki and viewed firsthand the effects of the atomic bomb. On his return, he was whisked off to the Pentagon with an interim stop at Roswell, New Mexico, to bid farewell to the crews who were returning to civilian life. In Washington, Tibbets ascertained that the 509th would remain in existence and keep its headquarters in Roswell. Tibbets's future in the Army Air Forces seemed assured, but bureaucratic intrigue and petty jealousy would mar his career in the years to come.

In early 1946 Tibbets was relieved of command of the 509th Composite Bomb Group. The change of command was hardly a surprise. For years Tibbets had been the "golden boy" of the Army Air Forces, first in Europe and Africa, then in the Pacific. Many contemporaries were jealous of the attention he had received. Nowhere was this more evident than in Operation Crossroads, the test-firing of two atomic bombs, billed as the "greatest laboratory experiment in all history." Tibbets and Ferebee ranked first in the competition to determine which pilots would participate in the Bikini Atoll testing, but senior colonels and lower-ranking generals whom Tibbets had alienated during the war altered the selection criteria. The result was a public relations fiasco when the nuclear testing failed to achieve the desired results.

Two years later, Tibbets served as director of operations in the Office of the Chief of the Air Force Requirements Division. After that he tested the B-47 jet and was instrumental in its adoption by the air force. In the decade of the 1950s, Tibbets continued to serve with highest distinction, both in the United States and in NATO. He later called the decade "his troubleshooting years" because he was repeatedly summoned to bring substandard units up to par. The results were always the same: within a year Tibbets's command ranked top in the organization's pecking order. Long denied promotion, Tibbets finally received his general's star in 1957.

In retrospect, Paul Tibbets had an extraordinary career. He had participated in the most successful air operations in history in Europe, Africa, and the Pacific. He had been selected to form the atomic bombing unit that accelerated the end of the Pacific war. As commander of the 509th Composite Bomb Group, Tibbets demonstrated a capacity for command seldom equaled in combat. He selected the personnel, developed the tactics and training plan, deployed the unit on his own authority, and flew the first atomic mission with such precision that a host of observers called it the "most phenomenal flight in history." If there was ever a better B-29 pilot than Tibbets, he has not come forward. All in all, Tibbets's was a stellar performance.

As an epilogue to a distinguished career, Tibbets returned to the national limelight on the fiftieth anniversary of the Hiroshima strike when the Smithsonian Institution decided to construct an exhibit featuring the Enola Gay. For years Tibbets's plane had languished in a warehouse in Suitland, Maryland, while Sweeney's Bock's Car was visited by thousands at the Air Force Museum at Wright-Patterson Air Force Base outside Dayton, Ohio. The Enola Gay exhibit immediately generated an inordinate amount of controversy when the museum dictated an accompanying script that hinted that World War II was an attempt by the Japanese to "defend their unique culture against Western imperialism." Tibbets, who made no apology for his role in ending the war, labeled the Air and Space Museum's text "historical distortion." Bowing to public reaction and congressional objection, the Smithsonian scrapped the exhibit and replaced it with the fuselage, flight deck, and bomb bay of the Enola Gay. Nearly four million visitors viewed the exhibit before it closed in 1998. Tibbets, his crew, and the Enola Gay will finally get their due when the Smithsonian opens its new annex at Dulles Airport and features the airplane in its entirety. For Paul Tibbets and the crew of the Enola Gay, it has been a long wait.

I had the good fortune to visit General Tibbets in the late spring of 1998. As I was preparing for the interview, I realized that he lived in east Columbus, a mere thirty minutes away from where I had attended Ohio State University as a graduate student twenty years earlier. It was frustrating to realize that I could have contacted him then and did not, but now I would have the chance to make up for the lost opportunity. The meeting was hastily arranged because Tibbets maintained a hectic schedule. I had asked him to visit me at the Military Academy the preceding December, but he declined, stating that advanced age had impaired his hearing and it was somewhat embarrassing for him when he was unable to hear questions. He suggested that if we could find a mutually agreeable time, I ought to consider visiting him in Columbus the next time I happened to be in Ohio. He then outlined his schedule and gave me a few hours in the only afternoon he would be available. Needless to say I adjusted my plans accordingly and appeared at the designated time. I was graciously received at his home and spent an enjoyable afternoon sitting across the table from a man who had shaped history some fifty-odd years ago. Here was the commander whose very action had initiated the atomic age in warfare.

On that brisk May afternoon, Tibbets and I discussed a variety of topics that ranged from his formative years as a pilot to his postwar career. I was pleased to hear that he was in the process of revising his autobiography in the light of the recent controversy surrounding the Smithsonian Institution exhibit. I was astounded when he claimed that the mission over Hiroshima was "the most boring flight" he ever made. "Everything went according to plan," he said. "We had rehearsed the mission countless times. The bomb would explode exactly forty-three seconds after Tom Ferebee released it from the plane." When I asked to what he attributed the mission's success, he responded emphatically, "The crews of the 509th Composite Group." I should not have been surprised, because every commander takes pride in a unit that he has trained and prepared for war. The 509th Composite Bomb Group was Tibbets's personal creation in every sense of the word. He had selected the crews personally, developed a meticulous training plan, deployed them to Tinian, and then conducted the final rehearsals. As commander, he had flown the initial mission.

When I queried Tibbets about the notoriety that has accompanied him since that August day more than a half century ago, he said that he had not thought much of it at first; the mission was simply a duty that had to be done. With a tinge of sadness, he then reflected on the dwindling ranks of the World War II generation. "There really is little interest [in the war] today except by the veterans, who are slowly passing from the stage."

Our final discussion revolved around leadership, and Paul Tibbets was quick to offer his view: "Leaders are not made; they are born. My focus has always been on the 'instincts' of a leader. You can make a manager, but not a leader. The keys are the ability to assess a situation and the willingness to make the difficult decisions. Leaders must make decisions." I asked him if there is a difference between leadership and command. He paused briefly, then elaborated on the subject of wartime command: "You must understand that command is a lonely business. When you command a unit, and my unit was more important than most, you must distance yourself from the men. Regular human relationships do not enter into the equation. You cannot afford to be too close to the men in your command because you have to make the life-and-death decisions on a daily basis. The job of being in command is lonely by definition."[17]

Asked how he would like to be remembered, Tibbets said that he desired no special recognition. The name of the plane means more to him than any personal attention given its pilot. Repeatedly asked over the years if he has any regrets, his response is always the same. "No, I am content that we did what reason compelled and duty dictated." With his grandson and namesake now the mission commander of a B-2 Stealth Spirit bomber, the Hiroshima pilot prays in earnest that the nation will never again need to call upon a Tibbets to demonstrate America's nuclear might.[18]

CHAPTER 9

MEASURING UP: THE EPIC TALE OF JOE DAWSON

I have got to answer those guys because I wear bars. I've got the responsibility and I don't know whether I'm big enough for the job. But I can't break now.

—*Captain Joe Dawson*

No U.S. Army division has a more heralded history than the fabled 1st Infantry Division. Among its members when the Big Red One deployed to England in the summer of 1942 was Lieutenant Joseph Turner Dawson of Waco, Texas, the gangly twenty-eight-year-old son of a Baptist preacher. Dawson's personal journey to war took a path familiar to thousands of his countrymen who enlisted when unbridled hatred threatened their lives. Convinced that his country's existence was jeopardized by Hitler's conquering legions and that his precious freedom was in peril from a force bent on the destruction of democracy, he joined the army in May 1941 and embarked on a military career that would carry him across the Atlantic to battle the forces of totalitarianism on two continents. By the time he returned to the United States three years later, he had fought the Germans in North Africa, Sicily, France, Belgium, and Germany, and had suffered three wounds. In the interim he exemplified the motto emblazoned on the 1st Division's colors: No Mission Too Difficult, No Sacrifice Too Great—Duty First.

Joe Dawson adapted easily to military life. A graduate of Baylor University, he achieved the highest score on the intelligence test that the army administered to his group of 250 inductees. Private Dawson was not impressed with the caliber of the troops with whom he trained. In a letter to his parents, he noted, "the United States Army will not last two minutes if we have to depend upon what I've seen thus far. Everyone works harder to keep out of work than lifting a feather's weight. All the NCOs whom I've met are a very low average mentally and are unwilling to cooperate with each other. The officers seem to be extremely anxious to get out of anything that might in any way interfere with their personal pleasures."[1] This was hardly a ringing endorsement of an army gearing up for war.

Along with most of the army units in the United States, Dawson's company participated in the Texas-Louisiana maneuvers of late summer–early autumn 1941. Assigned to a chemical unit, Dawson, who had been promoted to corporal in June, described the maneuvers as "interesting and . . . enjoyable." Although he did not intend to remain in that unit any longer than necessary, he was pleased to witness a broader view of army operations than would have been possible had he been in an actual combat unit. More important, Dawson developed a better understanding of the American army—an understanding that would prove pivotal in his development as a combat leader.

No longer content to remain a soldier in the ranks, Dawson applied and was accepted to Officer Candidate School. The end of 1941 found Dawson at Fort Benning, Georgia, the home of the infantry. Reflecting on how his life had changed over the course of the previous year, he noted that the company of men with whom he was associating were the "*cream* of the entire country." His fellow officer candidates were "men with intelligence, ability, initiative, and moral and physical stamina," a distinct contrast to those he had seen over the past seven months.

A more significant change transpired in Dawson's assessment of the officers at the Infantry School. Unlike the officers he had once described as "morons who couldn't make a good supervisor for fourth grade school children," the Benning officers were peerless leaders who inspired the candidates to exert every effort in their power to make the most of their experience. Each seemed to possess the ability to instill a sense of the tremendous responsibilities that now belonged to the men and a deep-seated urge to merit the officer's approval. Undoubtedly humbled by the realization that he was now training with men who were his equals or superiors in ability, Dawson expressed concern as to whether he would "measure up" to his comrades. Such fear of failure remained the single constant throughout Dawson's career as a combat commander.

Placed in a greater context, Joe Dawson personified the American citizen-soldier on the eve of World War II. Imbued with patriotism and what he himself described as the seriousness of America's position, Dawson decided then and there to devote his life to protecting his home and heritage. Impelled by a personal sense of duty, he dedicated himself to meet the challenge with every ounce of moral and physical strength at his command. Unsure of what destiny had in store, Dawson viewed the situation as so serious that the entire nation must consecrate itself to the cause. The task at hand required complete application on the part of every man, woman, and child in the country. In short, Dawson experienced a personal epiphany as he prepared for war. His drama was replayed thousands of times in a hundred camps across the nation.

When the United States officially entered the war, the War Department increased OCS enrollment eighteenfold. Chief of Staff George C. Marshall directed the commandant at Fort Benning to prepare to handle 3,600 men per quarter, or a total of 14,400 candidates per year. There was no shortage of volunteers. Dawson's graduation and commissioning took place on March 27, with Dawson graduating in the top ten of his class. He had earned his commission after three months of "combined torture and trials," and Dawson now wore bars on his shoulders instead of stripes on his sleeves. Normally the top graduates were assigned as instructors at the Infantry School, but Dawson eagerly sought combat. His age, efficiency rating, and scholastic standing earned him the assignment he requested with the 1st Infantry Division at Camp Blanding, Florida.

All in all, Officer Candidate School had been a harrowing experience. Dawson wondered just what his decision would be if he were told he had to go through it again, for he could not adequately express the rigors to which he had been subjected. He could only assure his father that he had earned his bars the hard way. If he had it to do again, though, he hoped the Reverend Dawson would send him to Texas A&M, where one could obtain a commission "without working for it!"[2]

Dawson and the 16th Infantry Regiment, to which he was assigned, were back in Georgia in June, then moved to Indiantown Gap outside Hershey, Pennsylvania, to prepare for overseas deployment. The two months that the division was stationed at Indiantown Gap passed quickly as the men updated their service records and prepared unit rosters, emergency addressee cards, and individual and unit reports. The 1st Division was going to deploy to England ahead of the majority of the army's other divisions, and that was fine with Joe Dawson. Thoroughly indoctrinated in the combat heritage of the Big Red One, Dawson confessed his utter satisfaction with its fighting ability. Since arriving in the regiment in April, the unit had undergone a drastic shakeup to effect a more strongly knit organization. As a result, Dawson found himself with Headquarters Company in the capacity of reconnaissance officer and assistant S-2 (intelligence officer). On the last day in July he wired a telegram to his parents in Waco: "The road may be long and the traveling hard but within my heart is the strength gained through faith to ever carry on. May God keep you one and all and know that your son has drawn his strength and courage from the most precious father and mother in all the world. I have a date with destiny and some day we will be rejoined in glorious peace. My heart full of tenderest love." Joe Dawson was going to war. He would not return for another two years; in the interim he would carve his name in the history of the 1st Infantry Division.

For the next three months the Big Red One prepared for the upcoming invasion of North Africa. Under the command of Major General Terry Allen, the division crashed ashore near Arzew, east of Oran. Dawson now served as the division's assistant G-3 operations officer, but he would later be assigned as the assistant regimental S-3 of the 16th Infantry Regiment. Amid the doughboys of the Big Red One, Dawson honed the skills that would later make him such an effective commander. At about the same time, the tone of his letters changed, doubtless reflecting the actual heartache and grief that result when men die for their country. While in Tunisia, he also developed a healthy respect for his German adversaries, whom he characterized as cunning and artful fighters.

As a staff officer, Dawson frequently visited the front, often in the company of assistant division commander Brigadier General Teddy Roosevelt and General Allen, for whom he occasionally served as a junior aide. In the process he observed the leadership techniques that best motivated the American GI. At one point he remarked on the simplicity of Allen's orders to hold in place: "IN PLACE; no retreat, no strategic withdrawal, no surrender—just plain IN PLACE." It would prove an invaluable lesson in a time yet to come on a critical ridge above Aachen.

Promoted to captain in February 1943, Dawson repeatedly requested company command, but he had to wait until a vacancy appeared. In the interim he remained on staff. The final days of the Tunisian campaign were grim and fierce, with intense combat the order of the day. By May the Afrika Korps had surrendered and the 1st Division was preparing for yet another amphibious assault, this time in Sicily. Dawson wrote that the detailed planning such an endeavor required made it the most strenuous of all military operations. A certain fatalism now permeated the soldiers of the division. Dawson's own morale was high, but he knew that every time he went into action his chances of survival were much less than before, because combat took something away that could never be replaced. Though he wrote that he considered himself fortunate "that the bullet with [my] name on it [has] yet to strike," he had been through a hell in North Africa that had burned away the naiveté that had veiled his outlook as a youth. Whatever its outcome, he was ready for the invasion and promised to do his best.

When the 1st Division landed near Gela on July 10, Captain Joe Dawson was in the thick of it. Landing just behind the assault waves amid a hail of machine-gun fire and artillery shells, he ordered the coxswain to beach the craft on the dunes, but heavy fire twice drove them back into the sea. On the third attempt, Dawson's craft managed to land. He characterized the assault as a "ticklish moment that could be likened to stepping into the Great Unknown." For the next five weeks Dawson experienced combat at its most brutal level, and that combat transformed him. In Sicily, the fear became so overpowering that Dawson felt his inner soul almost strangled. Years later, Dawson noted that he had not seen anything of value in Sicily that was worth the trouble to send home, but he had experienced "a lot of hard earned combat." The fighting itself had been "grueling. We marched and fought clear across the island in practically nothing flat." He also witnessed cowardice that hurt him "more deeply than a knife stab" because it demonstrated the weakness that is "the gravest of all mankind." The Germans were "sores that festered and erupted to create the terrible consequences" that his generation was now facing. At one point, the enemy displayed a white flag and then commenced fire with an antitank gun and machine guns when the Americans approached to accept their surrender. Nineteen of Dawson's men were killed. It was a mistake he would not repeat. Joe Dawson now understood that only a bloodbath would suffice to crush the evils of Nazism. When the campaign was finally over, Dawson recognized that command carried far more important responsibilities than he had understood before.

Assigned command of G Company, 2nd Battalion, 16th Infantry Regiment in mid-August, he was ready to do his part.[3] Taking command of a battle-hardened company proved a mixed blessing, however, as many of the officers and NCOs remained loyal to its previous commander. Fortunately, the relatively long period of inactivity between the end of the campaign in Sicily and the debarkation of the 16th Regiment for England in November gave Dawson the opportunity to familiarize himself with the strengths and weaknesses of the company before he led them into combat. Writing to his family, Dawson noted that G Company was beginning to "perk up as a result of the cessation of hostilities, so my trouble really starts now, for it means keeping all the men in line and also trying to find suitable means of relaxation." That proved to be a tough chore, because "after living a carnal life on the battlefield, subordinates' moral ethics deteriorate so the iron hand must be used occasionally."

General Omar Bradley, the commander of the First U.S. Army, selected the 1st Infantry Division to spearhead the assault on the Calvados coast of Normandy. The Big Red One was Bradley's most experienced infantry division. It had combat experience in North Africa and Sicily and had participated in more amphibious assaults than any division in the European Theater. The "Fighting First" thus drew the toughest challenge: Omaha Beach, a four-mile stretch of sand at the base of 150-foot bluffs. The division deployed to Dorset, England, in November 1943 to train and refit for the formidable task that lay ahead.

For the next six months Dawson trained his infantrymen for the cross-Channel attack. Along the way he gained the respect of his battle-hardened officers, sergeants, and privates, who were becoming confident that he would come through for them when the chips were down.[4] As he prepared his own company for the "big show," Dawson also prepared himself mentally. G Company was as good as any company in the division. Dawson likened it to a football team, a coach's dream. The men were ready, and he predicted success. "When the whistle blows for the kickoff," he informed his family, they could know that he would be "in the middle of the scrimmage and not cooling my heels back in some supply depot far removed from the gridiron." Though many had thus far gained greater glory in this war than he, none had experienced more frontline action than Dawson, and he was glad to have this privilege. All he asked from his family was that they not worry about him; the final achievement would be worth the price—whatever it might be. He concluded by saying that when the big day came he would "give everything within my power" and the enemy would know that there was "*one* outfit led by a long, lanky Texan who *means business*."

Having made peace with his Creator, Dawson and his company moved to the embarkation site at Weymouth Harbor. The 1st Division began its movement to the marshaling areas on May 7 and completed it four days later. Once in the marshaling areas, the troops were "sealed" in their camps pending deployment to the points of embarkation. On June 3, all troops of the 1st Division went aboard their craft. Dawson's company climbed aboard the USS *Henrico*. On board the ship he spoke to his men individually, telling them that he wished them all the best and that he expected each to do his duty. Dawson wasn't sure how successful he was at raising their morale. He later noted that he received "a mixed reaction from them. I think I still was an outlander and, frankly, to be perfectly honest, I didn't know when I landed whether I was going to get shot from the back or the front." In any event, there was no more time to contemplate his personal fate. The Allied Expeditionary Force was about to embark on a "great crusade." Ike's order of the day stated: "The eyes of the world are upon you," and the eyes of G Company rested squarely on Captain Joe Dawson, an officer who had never commanded a company in combat. How would he react under fire? Would he measure up? The answer to those questions rested on a four-mile stretch of sand in the Calvados region of Normandy known as Omaha Beach.

For the soldiers, sailors, and airmen who experienced it, D-Day was a day like no other in history. The Allied armada set sail on the evening of June 5. H-Hour in the 1st Division's sector of Omaha was 0630, with Company G scheduled to land at Easy Red in the second wave at approximately 0700. Nothing in the 1st Division's history or Dawson's personal experience could have prepared the men for what they encountered on Omaha Beach that day. Withering enemy fire decimated Companies E and F of the 16th Regiment as they stormed ashore on Easy Red in the first wave. Utter chaos reigned, Dawson recalled, "because the Germans controlled the field of fire completely."[5] Most of the first wave lay dead or dying, and their equipment and the flotsam of battle clogged the shoreline. Omaha Beach was an inferno, dwarfing even Tarawa in its initial intensity.

Landing under intense fire, Dawson was first off his LCVP, followed immediately by his communications sergeant and his company clerk. As they jumped, an artillery shell struck the boat and destroyed it, killing every man left aboard. Within seconds, soldiers from the company's six remaining boats landed. Remarkably, most of Dawson's 227 officers and men survived the initial landing intact, but German fire quickly whittled down G Company's numbers.[6] Although he was overwhelmed by the sheer horror of the spectacle, Dawson seized the initiative and took command of the survivors, who by now were huddling behind the scanty protection of the dune that marked the high-water mark of the beach. He realized then that "there was nothing I could do on the beach except die. I knew no one else was going to do it. I was going to have to do it. Some things one does automatically, some by circumstance, but I knew it had to be done. There is no other way to say it." Unless he could galvanize his men into action, they would be cut to shreds on the beach. It was the toughest decision he ever made as a company commander. At one point Dawson found a sergeant and two soldiers who ignored his order to advance. He exhorted them to follow him and moved on. When he looked over his shoulder and saw them still huddled behind one of the beach defenses he again shouted for them to come along. And then he realized that they were dead. The encounter reinforced Dawson conviction that it was crucial to advance.

The distance from the shingle to the crest of the bluff was approximately 750 yards. Ordered by his battalion commander to advance, Dawson moved rapidly forward and collected his men at the base of the bluffs. As he looked about him he saw a path—blocked with obstacles and obviously mined—leading toward the crest that dominated the beach. The veterans from North Africa and Sicily knew what to do. Sergeant Ed Tatara and Private Henry Peszek fastened two bangalore torpedoes together, shoved them under the strands of concertina wire, and blew a gap through which Dawson and a small contingent of men passed. Having survived the dangerous stretch from water's edge to the foot of the bluffs, Dawson now began the dangerous ascent. German bullets "sounded like a bunch of bees that seemed to swarm everywhere," he later recalled. Midway up the slope he met Lieutenant John Spaulding with the remnants of his platoon from E Company. Spaulding had been one of the first junior officers to make it across the seawall, across the beach, and up the bluff.

Directing Spaulding to cover his advance, Dawson proceeded toward the summit. The last ten feet were nearly vertical. The change in topography provided complete defilade from the entrenched enemy above. A machine-gun nest on the summit was firing at the beach, and Dawson could hear rifle and mortar fire coming from the crest as well. "There was a machine gun about thirty feet to the east of where I thought we would be able to get through," he later recalled. "I knew he had to be taken out if we were going to reach our objective. I was able to get within a few feet, below him where he couldn't see me." Gathering his men, Dawson caught his breath and tossed two grenades, eliminating the enemy crew that was creating havoc on the beach below. Without waiting for reinforcements, Dawson and his men pressed on until they had silenced the remaining German positions.

As soon as his men reached him, Dawson debouched, firing on the retreating enemy and moving toward a gate in the right corner of an open field. Through the gate was a roadway leading into a heavily wooded area and toward Colleville sur Mer, the 16th Regiment's objective on D-Day. To Dawson's knowledge, no one had penetrated the enemy defenses until this moment. It was approximately 0900.

The men of G Company encountered German small-arms fire as soon as they entered the woods, and it was noon before they reached the outskirts of Colleville. As in most Norman towns, the dominant building was a church. The Germans were using the steeple as an observation post. Dawson collected a sergeant and a private, entered the church, and killed the three German defenders; Dawson shot an artillery observer hidden in the tower while his men disposed of the other two Germans. As Dawson emerged from the church, a bullet went through his carbine, shattering the stock and sending fragments through his kneecap and leg. Pausing only long enough to bandage the wound, he led his company through yet another "very severe firefight" on the outskirts of the village as the enemy launched a massive counterattack. In the interim, his men suffered seven casualties as a result of friendly fire. U.S. Navy ships lying off the coast of Normandy suddenly "bloodied [the company] from one end of the town to the other." There was little Dawson could do about it. Having lost his naval fire coordinator in the initial assault, he was unable to send the coordinates of his forward elements as expeditiously as he would have liked.

By now Dawson's knee had swollen to twice its regular size, and the medics thought his chance of survival would be better if it were treated in a hospital rather than in the field. Evacuated on D+1, Dawson was taken to a hospital in England. After doctors removed the fragments, he obtained a pass to go to town and promptly caught a train to Bournemouth, where he pleaded with the navy to take him across the Channel to Omaha Beach. "I thought I belonged with my company," he later explained.

By nightfall on D-Day the Americans had landed 35,000 men on Omaha. "But it took 250 to open the way," recalled Dawson at the end of the most important day in his life. He took justifiable pride in what G Company had accomplished. When other units had been overwhelmed by the awesome defense the enemy had prepared, the men of G Company—no less overwhelmed and frightened—had accomplished their assigned job. Company casualties on D-Day numbered fourteen killed, thirty-two wounded, and three missing in action. Not once had the men under his personal leadership faltered. Other commands had performed equally well, but G Company had been the first to penetrate the German defenses.

In retrospect, Dawson attributed his success to poor German marksmanship and his ability to control his command, both in landing together and in maneuvering up the bluff together as a fighting unit. Once his men reached the summit, they engaged the enemy directly with small-arms fire, forcing the Germans to cease the concentrated rifle, machine-gun, and mortar fire with which they were sweeping Omaha. Three weeks later, General Eisenhower presented twenty-two 1st Division soldiers, including Dawson, with Distinguished Service Crosses for heroism under fire.[7] Two other soldiers received the Legion of Merit. Dawson was immensely proud when Ike announced that he had recommended the 16th Regiment for a Presidential Unit Citation for what it had accomplished on D-Day. The supreme commander then asked each recipient to convey his personal best wishes and congratulations to every member of their respective commands.

In mid-July, Dawson and his executive officer returned to Omaha and recreated the company's assault. His heart stopped as he placed himself in the enemy positions. They seemed unassailable. He asked himself how and why G Company had succeeded. The answer, Dawson concluded, was that God alone had so willed it. From a purely abstract point of view and as a military problem, a place such as this could not be successfully taken by assault troops. It was just too perfect a defensive position. Too many men had paid for that crest with their lives that day, and for every inch they gained in the succeeding weeks. Dawson's reward was the looks of confidence they gave him; it was the highest tribute life had yet bestowed on him. Yet, fully aware of the challenges that lay ahead, he wondered anew if he would measure up to the demands of combat.

Summer 1944 was a heady time for Dawson and G Company. Early July brought some respite as the Big Red One took stock of its losses and refitted. Dawson's regiment was in division reserve, but they were in the thick of it again as the Allies finally broke the back of the German defenses in Normandy. Never was there a day when the 1st Infantry Division was not under fire. The rapid disintegration of the Wehrmacht in France produced undue optimism in the ranks, and Dawson was hardly immune. "It might appear that the enemy is beginning to crack," he wrote home, but the realization that he was on borrowed time was ever present. "Fate has decreed I remain in the middle of things till the final blow, so I am no longer wondering where I'm going, but how long I'll last on the way! I've used up all the luck of a dozen blokes and the Lord and I just happen to be awfully good friends else I would never have left Africa."

The strain of daily combat was beginning to take its toll on Dawson. In early August he lost one of his officers and temporarily buckled under the pressure. At night he could no longer sleep, he wrote, for "the awful hurt that gripped me. I prayed earnestly for God to somehow relieve me of the oppressive burden that sometimes weighs so very heavily. 'Tis indeed something that cannot be placed in words on a letter—this responsibility of men's lives, yet it becomes so personal and heart-breaking now after so many months of this. . . . [T]he road to glory is a one way road, each milestone a monument to the fallen." The ferocity of the fighting still amazed him. "With all the rumors and reports, the German still fights savagely and bitterly. I know it will end soon, but even so I am growing *so tired.* God knows how I've stood it this long, yet still there is the old drive, drive, drive, putting one foot in front of the other. I'll continue somehow, but the old heart is beginning to slow a bit. Maybe *this is* the real test now. Let's hope I measure up."

The juggernaut of war moved through France and into Belgium. As the Americans approached Germany's western border, every GI expected the German resistance to stiffen. Despite his personal foreboding of disaster, Dawson gallantly led his company into Belgium, where he personally captured thirty-seven Germans and received the Silver Star for rescuing an isolated platoon. Now in Germany, the Big Red One penetrated the Siegfried Line and approached the medieval town of Aachen.

Company G's accomplishments on D-Day and on the advance into Belgium were "merely episodes in a long war," remembered Dawson, reflecting on his career fifty years later. The most brutal fighting G Company encountered during the war occurred outside Aachen. As the former capital of Charlemagne's empire, Aachen held a special significance for Adolf Hitler, who ordered that it be defended to the last man. The "eyes of Germany are upon you," the Führer admonished the city's defenders. Against increasing resistance, Courtney Hodges's First Army battered Germany's Western Wall in early September and encircled the ancient city. There they paused and prepared to meet the expected German counterattacks. G Company, 16th Infantry, reinforced and still under Joe Dawson's command, bore the brunt of several of those counterattacks.

Moving into position in mid-September, Dawson established his defense along an 838-foot-high ridge running approximately 400 yards in its highest point. The ridge would be his home for the next five weeks. The men of G Company dug in on the far side of a railroad embankment that divided the town of Eilendorf just outside Aachen. From his position, Dawson could look into Belgium and Holland as well as Germany. What he saw startled him. In the distance the enemy was assembling tanks and infantry and moving up; they were in the woods about 1,000 yards to the northeast, in the orchard to the southeast, and in patches of rough ground in between. It was, he realized, going to be one "helluva fight."

Unlike the offensive tactics that had characterized G Company's attack across the Low Countries, the order of the day was now to defend. Stateside training had always emphasized the attack, not the defense. It was an undesirable change of pace. The 16th Regiment had chased the retreating Germans across France and Belgium, fighting sharp engagements along the way and capturing much matériel and thousands of prisoners. Dawson's own casualties had been light in proportion to the devastation wrought by the 1st Division. Now, on the frontier of Germany, his men met resistance of a character they had never before encountered. Every inch of ground was bitterly contested. Nazi fanaticism and resolution were exceeded only by what Dawson termed the "marvelous courage and irresistible force" of his own men. There, on the summits overlooking Aachen, G Company met its severest test since D-Day.

Two days after Dawson initially moved into position, a German infantry division attacked G and I Companies. The Germans hit first with artillery and mortars and then attacked in battalion strength. The intensity of the assault carried them into the American defenses, but the GIs held. The battle raged with a ferocity that eclipsed even the inferno of D-Day. Dawson recalled, "I lost men. They weren't wounded. They weren't taken prisoners. They were killed. But we piled up the Krauts." Amid constant shelling the Germans attacked again. "Every day," wrote Dawson to his family, "has seen the enemy try to throw us back, but somehow we've managed to hold him. To be truthful, it has been the supreme test for us all, and the terrific losses he has suffered lay before us as mute evidence of his all-out efforts. They've penetrated a little only to find us with that little extra something and back he goes—or rather his shattered remnants. The carnage has been frightful and recalls to mind some of the stories earlier in the war of his efforts in Russia. . . . [S]o goes the war. It's terrible beyond imagination, and only our grim resolve to end it as quickly as we can sustains us through these awful days."

Nor were enemy attacks the only problem confronting Dawson. The troops on the front line were freezing, and the support network had broken down. Dawson's requests for overcoats—submitted through proper military channels and via telephone calls to friends in the command post—had proved fruitless. One evening after G Company had repelled a particularly heavy German attack, Dawson called to request the overcoats again, hoping that the men's success might have earned a reward. Such deeds of valor always pleased General Clarence Huebner, the 1st Division's commanding general, so when the chief of staff heard Dawson's voice on the field phone, he signaled across the room to Huebner to listen in on the conversation. Dawson was a bit "hot under the collar" about not receiving the overcoats, and Huebner picked up the conversation just in time to hear Dawson tell the chief that if that "damned Santa Claus of a commanding general who promised the overcoats doesn't get off his duff and do something about it, I'm going to march my entire company off the lines and leave a hole big enough for the whole German army to come through."[8] Dawson would have been horrified had he known that the general was listening, but the chief of staff noticed a twinkle in the general's eye. The next afternoon, overcoats replaced ammunition when the division trucks brought up supplies.

On October 4, following two weeks of intense artillery bombardment, a second German division attacked.[9] By that time G Company had already repulsed three German counterattacks and endured five hundred shells per day from the German 105s.[10] After yet another bombardment, Dawson later recalled, "that other infantry division hit us. We had had constant shelling for eight hours and we had had twelve direct hits on what was our command post then because we were taking it from 270 degrees on the compass. When they stopped coming we could count 350 that we ourselves had killed—not those killed by our artillery or planes, but just by one lousy little old GI company all by itself."[11] Enemy casualties littered the battlefield, comprising "a figure unprecedented in the division's history" according to the 1st Division's operations officer.

For thirty-nine days and nights, Dawson's company held the ridge. At times the front lines were no farther than fifty feet apart. More than once Dawson called in protective artillery fire within ten yards of his own command post. Often the combat was hand to hand, and at times it seemed that the American defenders could not hold another minute. On October 15, a final assault, this time spearheaded by an SS panzer division, collapsed in the face of Dawson's artillery and infantry fire. Again the intensity of the attack carried the enemy into Dawson's lines. In the midst of the assault, the American battalion commander, who had commanded the unit gallantly since D-Day, cracked under pressure. Until a replacement was named, it fell to the frontline company commanders to coordinate the defense. Once again commanders like Joe Dawson, Ed Wozenski, Karl Wolf, and Kimball Richmond were up to the task.

How did they hold in the face of overwhelming enemy numbers? The answer lies in Dawson's own words: courage and determination. War correspondent W. C. Heinz spent several days in Dawson's headquarters, which were situated in a cellar in the village. The furnishings were sparse. There was a table with maps and magazines scattered about on its surface. On another table against the far wall a small radio was playing dance music. In addition to the radio there were two field phones—black phones resting on tan leather cases—that connected the captain with his platoons, out in the mud less than a hundred yards away, and with units at his regimental command post in the rear. One candle and one small kerosene lamp provided all the illumination.[12]

Before long, Heinz got Dawson to talk. After five weeks in the line, the beleaguered commander reflected on the loneliness of leaders who must make the crucial decisions in war. "Nobody will ever know what this has been like. You aren't big enough to tell them, and I'm not big enough to tell them, and nobody can tell them," Dawson said. Heinz promised to do his best and asked Dawson to address the strain of sending American boys to die. The captain responded, "I had a kid come up and say, 'I can't take it anymore.' What could I do? If I lose that man, I lose a squad. So I grab him by the shirt, and I say: 'You will, you will. There ain't any going back from this hill except dead.' And he goes back and he is dead." He continued, "How do you think I feel when I tell them there is no coming off the hill? They come in and say . . . 'I can't stand it any longer. I can't. I can't' . . . and I . . . say . . . 'you will . . . you will . . . you've got to stand it in spite of yourself,' and what do they do? They go back up there and die."

When Sergeant William Cuff and Private First Class James Mullen reported to the command post, Dawson announced: "I'm sending you both to Paris for a six-day furlough." "Thanks," Cuff replied. "Well, you had better like it," Dawson added, "and you had better stay out of trouble, but have a good time and bless your hearts." Heinz asked Dawson why he had selected those two for a furlough. "Two of the best boys I've got," the captain replied. "I've said right along that when I got a chance to send somebody back they'd be the first. Wire boys, they've had to run new lines every day because the old ones were chopped up. One day they laid heavy wire for 200 yards, and by the time Cuff got to the end and worked back, the wire was cut in three places by shell fire." Pausing for a moment, Dawson continued, "Another time they put a phone up to one of my machine-guns, and by the time Cuff got back to tell me to try the phone, the machine-gun had been blown up. So I have been thinking for a long time that they would be the first to have some fun when I could send somebody back." The next morning, a lieutenant came in and spoke to Dawson. "Captain," he said, "Cuff and Mullen say they don't want to go." "All right," Dawson sighed, "Get two other guys—if you can."

Dawson informed Heinz that some of his men who had been wounded in mid-September had returned because they were concerned for their buddies who were still defending the ridge. Just as Dawson had done after he was hit on D-Day, they went AWOL from the field hospital and returned to their command. Dawson couldn't explain it. What made men want to return to this inferno? It was absolutely crazy. "Somehow they get out of those hospitals, and the first thing I know they show up again here, and they're grinning from ear to ear."

Dawson talked long about his men and his responsibilities as their leader, and in the process he gave Heinz perhaps the most vivid portrayal ever recorded of a company commander in combat in the European Theater. How did Dawson manage? "I have got to answer those guys because I wear bars. I've got the responsibility and I don't know whether I'm big enough for the job. But I can't break now." He continued, "I've taken this for thirty-nine days and I'm in the middle of the Siegfried Line and you want to know what I think? I think it stinks."

For thirty-nine days in the fall of 1944, the men of G Company, under the inspirational leadership of the son of a Waco preacher, fought and died in their foxholes along what entered 1st Infantry Division lore as "Dawson's Ridge." When the history of these campaigns is written, Heinz reported, "they will tell you that this ridge was the key to Aachen. This is where three German divisions tried to crack through the shell we had thrown out beyond Aachen while we cleaned up the city." When the battle ended, Aachen remained secure. For their role in the defense of the city, G and I Companies, 16th Infantry Regiment earned the Presidential Unit Citation. It was Dawson's proudest professional achievement, far more significant in his eyes than any personal honors he had received from the supreme commander. Eisenhower also nominated the Big Red One to receive the Distinguished Unit Citation, stating that the fighting surrounding Aachen was the 1st Infantry Division's most outstanding operation in the European Theater. All that had stood in the way of German success was what Dawson termed "just one lousy little old GI company"—one lousy company and the indomitable spirit of its commander.

Following the battle, Dawson was evacuated for treatment of his wounds; he returned to the United States in November. Rehabilitated and strong once again, he returned to Europe in February, this time in service with the Office of Strategic Services. Promoted to major, he spent the remainder of the war at his Paris field station, far from his beloved company. Like most combat commanders, he missed serving on the line. Writing to a former commander, he stated that command of Company G had been a privilege and an honor, and that command in combat would remain the outstanding event of his life.

Measured in terms of the scale of the war, G Company's contribution had been large. The men had never once faltered or failed to accomplish their assigned mission, though the cost was sometimes high. Unsurpassed courage and indomitable will were the foundation of their greatness. Added to that was the men's concern for one another—even to their willingness to return to the battlefield to protect their friends. G Company was a family. It was certainly a home for Dawson, and he never forgot the men who were his brothers.

Dawson is actually representative of most of the company commanders who served in the 16th Regiment. Too humble to credit himself for his unit's achievement, Dawson turned to the junior leaders. "The real leaders in Company G were the sergeants, the squad leaders. Real success rested almost exclusively on the squad leaders. The junior officers were not well equipped for the task at hand, perhaps due to the explosion for demand. The officers didn't have time to mature since they were thrown into battle" during the later stages of the war, Dawson reflected. "The spirit of the army was centered in the NCO corps, not the officer corps. The best platoon leaders earned their commissions in the field, having emerged from the unit. They seized the initiative and exerted the requirements of leadership. They performed nobly."[13]

Had it been worth the price? Dawson thought so. Before returning to the United States a final time, he toured a Nazi concentration camp now in the hands of the French. The camp—surrounded by an electrically charged barbed-wire fence and guarded at each corner by a tower fitted with powerful searchlights and containing guards armed with machine guns and automatic rifles—was unlike anything Dawson had ever envisioned. Just to the left of where he was standing were two gallows, one for men and one for women. Like "evil reminders of the bestiality of man these two structures stood silhouetted in the gloom of silent witnesses of criminal atrocity." He then viewed the torture rooms and the crematorium. On September 23, 1944, he was told, one German SS master sergeant stood at the head of the steps and shot ninety-six men and women before he finally went mad. The visit was one of the most unforgettable experiences in Dawson's life. Though he had known war in all its bitterest forms, even his jaded senses were shocked at this house of horror. Yes, it had been worth it.

After retiring from the regular army in 1946, Dawson returned to his native Texas. He was appointed commander of the 2nd Battalion of the 142nd Infantry Regiment of the 35th Division and reached the rank of lieutenant colonel before resigning his commission in 1948 to assume greater professional and civic responsibilities. In 1951 he embarked on a new career as an independent oil operator. For the remainder of his life he was extraordinarily active in civic affairs. He served on the city council of Corpus Christi from 1947 to 1949, and later was chairman of the Civil Service Commission, the Corpus Christi Red Cross, and the Corpus Christi Heart Association, as well as president of the Reserve Officers Association of Corpus Christi.

His community rewarded him by naming an elementary school in his honor on September 14, 1997. "I don't deserve it," Dawson remarked, "but it's very sweet. I love this city, and I've loved everybody in it. I'm just deeply proud that they see fit to do it." Especially honored that through the school he would leave a legacy for Corpus Christi youths, he said, "The thing that makes it so tremendously moving to me is the fact that I'll be a part of the heritage of this city. I appreciate it more than I can say." In 2002, the city of Corpus Christi erected a bronze statue of Joe Dawson in front of the school that bears his name.

For Joe Dawson there was one additional honor from a grateful army and a grateful country. As a prelude to the fiftieth anniversary of D-Day, the Department of the Army selected Joe Dawson to introduce the president of the United States at the final ceremony in Normandy. Humbled by the honor, Dawson informed his community, "I will not be there as Joe Dawson. I am a symbol of all those veterans." Almost too ill to attend, Joe was unsure if he could make the trip. He need not have worried. When the big day arrived, Joe Dawson once again "measured up." On June 6, 1994, he introduced President William Jefferson Clinton to an audience composed of eight thousand World War II veterans and visiting dignitaries at the American cemetery at St. Laurent-sur-Mer, overlooking Omaha Beach. With tears streaming from his eyes, G Company's former commander spoke softly:

> In the face of crisis, men rise above themselves to accomplish great things. Here, on this hallowed ground is where the battle was joined. What better examples of courage and bravery were ever displayed than by the men of the assault elements of the 16th Infantry Regiment of the 1st Division, and the men of the 116th Infantry Regiment of the 29th Division, who were our comrades here on Omaha Beach. . . . I cannot tell you what it means to me to stand on this spot. . . .
>
> Where we landed at 0700 on the beach below was total chaos. Men lay dead or dying, and the equipment and wreckage of battle

> was choking the shoreline. I recall how I was overwhelmed with a feeling of anger and hate, and I knew we had to get to the enemy before we were destroyed. . . .
>
> We are here to recognize and pay homage to those who shaped the course of history. Only one who holds the highest office in the land can express to the world the pride and gratitude of our nation to you, the men of D-Day. And so, on behalf of the soldiers of my company and all other Army warriors who stormed these beaches and bluffs, and on behalf of our Navy, Coast Guard, and Air Force comrades who fought with us and for us on D-Day . . . it is my special privilege and great honor to present the President of the United States.[14]

As he stood on the spot where Dawson first penetrated the German defenses, the president's first words were, "Mr. Dawson, you did your men proud today." It was Dawson's proudest moment and his highest personal honor in a life dedicated to God and country.

On November 28, 1998, four years after the commemorative ceremonies, Joseph Turner Dawson died of complications from cancer in the city he loved. Two weeks later the family held a memorial service in his honor in the sanctuary of the First Baptist Church in Corpus Christi. In attendance were old friends and comrades as well as soldiers from the 1st Infantry Division. The congregation joined in and sang the "Battle Hymn of the Republic," a song that would have thrilled the captain who first breached the German defenses above Omaha Beach. Mourners then heard a grandson play taps, the warrior's farewell to a fallen comrade.

I first met Joe Dawson in June 1998. We had corresponded for four years, but had never seemed to be able to get together. I wanted Joe to come to West Point to address the Corps of Cadets on leadership under fire. He was quite willing to come, but cancer had already begun extracting its deadly toll. "No problem," I said, "I'll come to Corpus Christi." Then, in mid-May 1998, I received a phone call late one evening. "I've lost my beloved Melba [his wife of fifty-two years], and I don't know if I can go on. Will you come to Texas and see me?" I tried to reassure him, but my words proved inadequate, as would any words on such an occasion. "Of course I'll come, but don't pick me up at the airport. I'll grab a cab." You can figure out the rest. I flew to Corpus Christi and went outside to hail a cab. Sure enough, there was Joe.

We spent two days together discussing leadership and the qualities that make a successful commander. He gave me his wartime letters to read. I commented that a constant theme appeared to be "measuring up." I asked what he meant by that term, and he responded, "I was not even aware of that. It was certainly an unconscious thought. What I was asking myself was 'Do I measure up to my own standard?' I have always set high goals. If I measured up to them, I'm over the hill." I asked what his future plans were, and he announced that he hoped the country would remember the veterans the next June, on the fifty-fifth anniversary of D-Day. "We must remember our veterans," he said, shaking a long finger directly at my chest. "I'm counting on you to help." I then asked a final question: "How would you like to be remembered?" "As a leader," he responded without a second's hesitation. And that's how I like to remember Joe Dawson—as a leader who measured up to the crucible of combat at Omaha Beach and Dawson's Ridge, and a man who always found time for his friends and his community.

CHAPTER 10

RANGERS LEAD THE WAY: LEN LOMELL AND THE 2ND RANGER BATTALION

Don't waste time with losers.
I have seen very few losers turn out to be winners.

—First Lieutenant Leonard G. Lomell

THE HISTORY OF THE AMERICAN RANGERS is a colorful saga of courage and determination under fire. Tracing their lineage to Major Robert Rogers in the French and Indian War, today's rangers can reflect upon nearly 225 years of dedicated service to the nation. During World War II, Major William O. Darby organized and activated the 1st Ranger Battalion on June 19, 1942, at Carrickfergus, Northern Ireland. Approximately fifty of its members participated with British and Canadian commandos in the Dieppe raid on the northern French coast in August 1942, refining battlefield techniques that proved instrumental to their success in later campaigns. Thus the rangers were the first American soldiers to fight and die on foreign soil in World War II. The 1st, 3rd, and 4th Ranger Battalions fought in the North African, Sicilian, and Italian campaigns, and the 2nd and 5th Ranger Battalions participated in the Normandy invasion. The 6th Ranger Battalion, operating half a world away, conducted reconnaissance and long-range raids throughout the Southwest Pacific Theater of Operations, including among their exploits the liberation of Allied prisoners of war from the Japanese prison camp at Cabanatuan. A ranger-type unit, the 5307th Composite Unit (Provisional), organized and trained as a long-range penetration unit for employment behind enemy lines in Burma. The official unit designation was later changed to the 475th Infantry Regiment, commanded by Brigadier General Frank D. Merrill. Its 2,997 officers and men became popularly known as "Merrill's Marauders."[1]

Members of the ranger units remain immensely proud of their heritage, but no ranger holds his head higher than Leonard G. "Bud" Lomell of Toms River, New Jersey. Tough, rugged, and uncommonly courageous, Lomell remains the quintessential World War II American warrior. Historian Stephen Ambrose considered him the soldier more responsible than any individual other than Eisenhower for the success of D-Day.

Born in Brooklyn, New York, on January 22, 1920, the adopted son of immigrant Scandinavian parents, Bud Lomell graduated from Point Pleasant High School in New Jersey in 1937. His family was so poor that the only path to a college education lay in Bud's athletic ability. He enrolled at Tennessee Wesleyan College on a combination athletic scholarship and work program. While participating in the Golden Gloves boxing competition at the welterweight division, he was also a substitute "scatback" on the school's football team.[2] After his graduation in 1941 Bud returned to New Jersey and worked as a freight brakeman on the Pennsylvania Railroad for several months. Lomell tried to gain admission to one of the service academies in order to advance his education, but the process was delayed while he tried to locate his birth certificate. The Japanese attack on Pearl Harbor changed his plans.

The draft board notified Lomell that he was eligible for induction even though he was supporting his elderly mother and father, and Bud was drafted. In June 1942 the army shipped him to Fort Meade, Maryland, where he became a member of the 76th Infantry "Liberty Bell" Division. Bud rose quickly in rank to platoon sergeant in the Intelligence and Reconnaissance Platoon of the 417th Infantry Regiment. Along with two hundred other soldiers from the division, Bud attended ranger training. Only sixty graduated from the rigorous program, and Lomell was among them. In May 1943 his divisional executive officer telephoned him and inquired if he would like to be a ranger. Looking both for excitement and for the extra pay that would accompany promotion to first sergeant, and after talking to his company commander and platoon leader, Lomell accepted and became first sergeant, D Company, of the soon to be activated 2nd Ranger Battalion.

Deploying the company to Tullahoma, Tennessee, Lomell and his future company commander trained their unit and several groups of volunteers until Lieutenant Colonel James E. Rudder arrived to assume command of the battalion. Intense training dominated Lomell's life for the next twelve months.

Everything the rangers did was at the double quick, and everything D Company did was under the watchful eye of Lomell. An officer may have commanded D Company, but commanding officers often had additional duties that prevented them from directly supervising the training of their men. The men knew who really ran the unit. Lomell particularly emphasized discipline, physical fitness, and marksmanship. The men often ran five miles before breakfast. On twenty-five-mile forced marches at seven miles per hour the cadre rationed a single canteen per soldier per day. At the end of the day the men were bone-tired, every muscle aching. The trainees learned how to scale sheer cliffs and how to tumble and roll if they slipped. Lomell recalled that they never used safety lines. The men also learned how to survive in the wild by eating plants and small animals. Mostly, the potential rangers endured the toughest physical and psychological training techniques known at the time. In a word, the training was brutal, with the men suffering numerous injuries, some deaths, and some permanent disabilities. Their motto was Be the Best of the Best. Lomell and his men believed that their record in combat would soon speak for itself.

Of the two thousand men who started the training, only five hundred finished and were chosen to form the 2nd Ranger Battalion. That was typical of the rangers: only the fittest survived. In November 1943 the rangers boarded the *Queen Elizabeth* and sailed for Scotland, where they continued their training. Prepared to fight in all types of weather and terrain, the men frequently practiced on the four-hundred-foot stone cliffs of the Isle of Wight. There they trained with the Royal Marine Commandos and refined the teamwork that would later prove essential for their first combat mission. They also experimented with mortar-propelled grapples designed by the British commandos to catapult scaling ropes over the cliffs. Other innovations included lightweight sectional steel ladders that could be rapidly assembled and run up the face of the cliff. To accelerate their climbing, they added long extension ladders borrowed from the Fire Department of London. By late May the 2nd Battalion had evolved into a finely tuned unit.

D Company was now a crack outfit, but it was still untested in combat. How well it would measure up would depend on the men's cohesion and the training they had undergone since arriving in England. Unlike their counterparts in the line divisions, each ranger company consisted of only three officers and sixty-five enlisted men. Lomell later attributed D Company's cohesiveness to its small size and to the fact that all rangers—officers, NCOs, and men—had to endure identical training. In May, the battalion finally received its long-anticipated mission.

For the invasion of Europe, the rangers drew what Omar Bradley called the most dangerous and difficult task of D-Day: they were ordered to land under fire at the face of the hundred-foot cliffs of Pointe du Hoc and to destroy a battery of 155-mm coastal guns set atop the heights.[3] The battery at Pointe du Hoc had long been a prime target for the invasion planners. With an estimated range of twenty-five thousand yards, it was capable of firing on Allied forces landing all along the coast from Port-en-Bessin in the British zone to Taret de Ravenoville north of Utah Beach.[4] To eliminate the battery, Rudder devised an elaborate plan that required D, E, and F companies to land at the base of Pointe du Hoc along a ten-yard-wide beach and then scale the cliffs. On reaching the summit, the rangers had to destroy the battery before it could bring effective fire on the armada and the invasion beaches. Rudder set H-Hour at 0630. If the mission proved successful, the remainder of the battalion would land, quickly followed by the 5th Ranger Battalion. If after thirty minutes Rudder had not passed along the signal that the battery was destroyed, all subsequent reinforcements would be diverted to Omaha Beach in support of the 29th Division's 116th Infantry Regiment. There they would consolidate, march overland, and take the battery from the land side.

As the date for the invasion approached, D Company was a tight family itching to go and rarin' for a fight. Lomell was still D Company's first sergeant, but he now assumed the additional duty of acting platoon leader for the 2nd Platoon because Rudder selected Captain H. K. "Duke" Slater, the regular company commander, to be his executive officer on the eve of the invasion. Lieutenant Marton McBride, the 2nd Platoon's leader, was promoted to acting company commander, leaving a vacancy that Lomell filled. Such transfers were routine in a ranger company because all leaders were expected to perform equally well at the next higher level of command.

General Eisenhower often stated that plans are everything before the battle is joined, but once the battle begins, the plans go out the window. Nowhere was that more true than at Pointe du Hoc. Each of the three assault companies had been assigned three LCAs (Landing Craft Assault) to land them on the beach. One of D Company's boats swamped immediately after departing the transport area, taking Captain Slater and Lieutenant McBride with it. Both officers survived, but four of the twenty-five men aboard drowned.[5] As the remaining LCAs approached what they thought was Pointe du Hoc, Rudder noticed that the strong tidal current was carrying them eastward and that the coxswain was actually steering toward Pointe de la Percée, three miles east of their objective and about halfway between Omaha Beach and Pointe du Hoc.

Rudder directed the coxswain to turn right ninety degrees, so for a time the LCAs were actually moving parallel to the coast. The navigation error proved costly, for the rangers were now thirty minutes behind schedule. Moreover, German fire from the cliffs sank another of the LCAs. The remaining rangers were saved by gunfire from the destroyers USS *Satterlee* and HMS *Talybont*, which commenced firing just then and drove many of the Germans back from the edge of the cliff.

Now back on course, the rangers headed for the small beach just to the east of the point. Lieutenant James Eikner, the battalion communications officer, later remembered "bailing water with our helmets, dodging bullets and vomiting all at the same time."[6] D Company had been scheduled to land on the western side of the point, but too much time had been lost already. Rudder signaled Lomell and Lieutenant George Kerchner, leader of the 1st Platoon, to land east of the promontory with the remainder of the detachment. By this time the enemy was pouring a withering fire on the beach below, despite the gunfire from the *Satterlee*. In addition, the German 352nd Division, anticipating commando assaults on the cliffs, had placed 240-mm artillery shells hooked to trip wires along the crest at 100-yard intervals. They were designed to roll down and explode over the water with an effective radius of about 650 yards. The attackers immediately fired their rocket-propelled climbing ladders, but the ropes were waterlogged and many fell short. Still, at least one grapnel and rope from each LCA made it, and the rangers began their ascent.

Lomell was first off his LCA and immediately took a round through the right side. As he later recalled it, "The ramp was dropped presumably where you could stand. But there was a bomb crater eight to ten feet deep I stepped into and I got soaked." He had no sooner turned to rally his men, he said, than "I felt a burning sensation in my side. I spun around and didn't know who it came from. I didn't see anyone shoot me, but behind me was a ranger, Harry Fate, with whom I had a nasty confrontation a few days earlier. I had recommended to the commander that he be busted from the rank of sergeant because I didn't think he was hacking it. At the time Fate said, 'You know, Top, what they do with first sergeants in combat.' I asked him if that was a threat, but thought nothing more of it until I saw him standing behind me. I immediately yelled at him, 'You son of a bitch!' Fate protested, 'Honestly Len, I didn't do it.'"[7]

With no time to waste, Lomell and his platoon continued on. The primary means of climbing was by rope, and the rangers moved fast, providing covering fire as each man ascended. Within five minutes of landing, the first ranger was up the cliffs. Within fifteen minutes the majority of the fighting men were locked in mortal combat with the German defenders. Rudder established his command post at the edge of the cliff and ordered his signal officer to send the message "Praise the Lord," which meant "all the men are up the cliff." That wasn't exactly true, but enough were up to satisfy Rudder that he had a sufficient force ashore to accomplish the mission. The attack now continued with unabated ferocity. Due to the earlier delay, the rangers were on their own. Their reinforcements had already been diverted to Omaha Beach.

The scene that greeted Lomell and his platoon at the crest of the cliffs defied imagination. The area around the point resembled the surface of the moon. For five months, Allied naval and air forces had pounded Pointe du Hoc, creating a gray, pock-marked landscape that seemed to belong to another world. The massive concrete observation post at the edge of the cliff remained intact and operational, but the tunnels and trenches were all but obliterated and the concrete gun emplacements were badly damaged. Kerchner recalled that "it didn't look anything at all like what I thought it was going to look like. It was just one large shell crater after the other." The craters themselves were several yards across and anywhere from two to three yards deep. The assaulting rangers used them for cover and concealment, one group providing fire support as another maneuvered to the next hole.

Each company had been assigned two or three artillery positions to destroy, and Lomell and his men moved to silence the guns on the western portion of the battery. Miraculously, he still had twenty-two rangers from the 2nd Platoon. They rushed as quickly as they could to the gun emplacements, relying on speed to keep the enemy off-balance. To reach their objective they played it like a football game, charging hard and low. Reflecting on the battle, Lomell later recalled, "When we got over the top, nothing stopped us. We went right into the shell craters for protection because there were snipers around and machine guns firing at us. We wait for a moment. If the fire lifted, we're out of that shell hole into the next one. We literally ran as fast as we could go."

When the rangers arrived at the casements, they were amazed to discover that the "guns" were merely telephone poles! Aerial photographs had not detected the shift. The defenders had obviously moved the battery to an alternate location. What to do? The rangers' mission was to destroy the battery and then establish an ambush or roadblock on the coastal road connecting Grandcamp and Vierville, which was roughly twelve hundred yards from the observation post, and sever communications between the defenders of Omaha and Utah beaches. Lomell and Kirchner moved inward, fighting all the way. D Company was first to reach the road. By this time enemy fire had shrunk their ranks to barely twenty men of the sixty-eight who began the assault. E and F companies shared a similar fate. Only one company commander was still on his feet.

While Rudder directed the action on the point itself, fighting continued on the coastal road, where twelve rangers from D Company's 2nd Platoon quickly established the roadblock. Lomell led the first patrol to reach the road, and Technical Sergeant Harvey W. Koenig destroyed the communication lines used by the Germans. Establishing the roadblock was the unit's second mission; they still had the first one to accomplish. Lomell quickly dispersed his remaining men. A distinct clanking noise was approaching. The rangers laid low in an adjoining ditch while a forty-man German combat patrol laden with heavy equipment passed by a mere twenty feet away. Rather than risk an engagement that might jeopardize their ability to destroy the battery, Lomell let the enemy proceed toward Utah Beach. As the Germans disappeared around a bend, Lomell emerged from his concealed position.

Their primary mission was to destroy the battery, but where were the missing guns? Lomell and his platoon sergeant, Staff Sergeant Jack Kuhn, decided to find out. Coming across a dirt road leading south, Lomell noticed tracks that might indicate where the enemy had moved the battery. He decided to investigate. With no men to spare, he took only Kuhn and proceeded down the sunken road between two high hedgerows. At that time he and Kuhn had made the deepest penetration of D-Day.

After proceeding about 250 yards, they came upon a camouflaged vale. When he inched his head over the top of the hedgerow, Lomell could not believe his eyes. Before him in an apple orchard was the entire battery, set up in textbook battery position and ready to fire on Utah Beach. Piles of ammunition surrounded the guns. The closest Germans, approximately seventy-five men, were about 100 yards away, apparently having withdrawn to avoid the initial bombardment. They appeared to be checking their equipment and preparing to return to the battery, and they obviously had no idea that the rangers had penetrated their second line of defense along the coastal road. The Germans did know that their forward observation post was under attack by the rangers of E Company, because no firing orders were coming through. Lomell thought the Germans were waiting for a roving observation post to replace the one the rangers had destroyed on the point before returning to the guns.

Realizing that thousands of American lives might be lost if the battery remained intact, Lomell sensed a fleeting opportunity. Directing Kuhn to cover him, he said, "Keep your eyes on them and if one starts toward here, get him between the eyes. . . . Give me your grenades. . . . I'm gonna fix 'em." Lomell first destroyed the traversing and recoil mechanisms of the two nearest guns, then wrapped his field jacket around his submachine gun to muffle the sound and bashed the sights of the remaining guns. "Jack," he whispered, "we gotta get some more thermite grenades." Sprinting back to the coastal road, he and Kuhn gathered all the grenades they could carry and returned to the battery. Lomell quickly rendered the remaining guns inoperable by placing the incendiary thermite grenades on the traversing mechanisms and elevation mechanism, thus welding all the moving parts together. Kuhn was getting impatient: "Hurry up and get out of there, Len." Lomell joined him, and together they ran back to the coastal road to report that they had accomplished the mission. Sometime later, and unknown to D Company, a second patrol led by Sergeant Frank Rupinski of E Company discovered an ammunition dump a short distance south of the battery. It too was unguarded, and Rupinski blew it up. Lomell immediately sent two runners, Sergeant Harry Fate and Sergeant Gordon Luning, by different routes to inform Rudder that D Company had destroyed the battery, severed all communications, and established the first roadblock, and would maintain it until properly relieved. It was roughly 0900.

Around midday, remnants of E and F Companies gathered in the general area of the big guns and the D Company roadblock. The site became known as the inland battle area. It was there that the rangers suffered the greatest number of casualties. In the afternoon, Rudder signaled the *Satterlee*, "Located Pointe du Hoc—mission accomplished—need ammunition and reinforcement—many casualties." Survivors of a platoon of rangers from A Company of the 5th Ranger Battalion, who had landed at Omaha Beach, joined the defensive position between about 1900 and 2000 hours, bringing the total number of defenders to about eighty-five rangers.

It would be two days before reinforcements arrived. In the interim the rangers battled for their lives. The heavily outnumbered rangers endured three horrendous counterattacks from the German 1st Battalion, 914th Regiment on D-Day alone. The three-hundred-man German force finally withdrew after the third attack. The surviving rangers, except for D Company, withdrew back to Pointe du Hoc on the morning of D+1 to support Rudder's group. Lomell's company remained behind. Only thirteen men remained, but they were determined to defend the roadblock to the last man or until relieved, as ordered.

When the ranger battalion was relieved on June 8, only 90 of the original 225 rangers remained combat effective, and many of these were walking wounded, including Lomell. To this day Lomell has seen no sadder sight than his dead ranger buddies laid out along the roadside. "When I saw them, their faces and uniforms caked with dirt and blood, I couldn't believe it. I wanted to yell at them, 'C'mon, get up!' We were trained so well I didn't believe anything could kill us." The memory still haunts him.

For their heroic action on D-Day, the 2nd Ranger Battalion received the Presidential Unit Citation. The citation read in part: "Three companies of the battalion landed on the beach at Pointe du Hoc under concentrated rifle, machine-gun, artillery, and rocket fire of the enemy. The companies faced not only terrific enemy fire, but also mines and hazardous underwater and beach obstacles. Despite numerous casualties suffered in the landing, these companies advanced and successfully assaulted cliffs 100 feet in height. By grim determination and extraordinary heroism, large enemy coastal guns, which had been interdicting the beach with constant shellfire, were reached and destroyed."[8]

The War Department also recognized Kuhn and Lomell. Kuhn received the Silver Star; Lomell received the Distinguished Service Cross for extraordinary heroism in action against the enemy. Citing Lomell's bold leadership in the face of superior numbers, the citation on his award noted that "First Sergeant Lomell had led a patrol of men through the heaviest kind of automatic weapons fire to destroy an enemy machine-gun nest. While leading another patrol later in the morning, he penetrated through the enemy lines to the rear and discovered five enemy 155mm guns, which were shelling the beachhead. Though these guns were well guarded, nevertheless he gallantly led his patrol against the enemy and personally destroyed the guns as well as the ammunition supply." Though some of the facts were wrong, the bottom line was clear—Len Lomell had destroyed the German battery at Pointe du Hoc single-handed.

Some historians, including Cornelius Ryan in *The Longest Day*, have concluded that the rangers' mission was a failure. Because the enemy had withdrawn the battery from the fortified area around the promontory and because the casualties were so high, they say, nothing was gained. Quite simply, notes Ryan, it was a heroic but futile effort—to silence guns that were not there.[9] Ryan is wrong. The guns were there—just not where army intelligence had reported them to be. The battery was in working order with a panoramic view of the largest armada in history in its sights. Could the battery at Pointe du Hoc have halted the entire invasion by itself? Probably not, but it could have inflicted immense casualties on the invasion force had not a single ranger and his ranger buddy found the guns and destroyed them by 0815 on the morning of D-Day. Lieutenant Eikner said it best when he stated, "Had we not been there we felt quite sure that those guns would have been put into operation and they would have brought much death and destruction down on our men on the beaches and our ships at sea. But early on D-Day morning, the big guns had been put out of commission and the paved highway had been cut and we had roadblocks denying its use to the enemy. By 0900, our mission was accomplished. The rangers at Pointe du Hoc were the first American forces on D-Day to accomplish their mission and we are proud of that."[10] They had every reason to be proud.

On D+2 Lomell was evacuated for wounds. He rejoined D Company at the end of June as sergeant major of the 2nd Battalion. His duties were different now that he was no longer an acting platoon leader, but he still participated in an extremely costly campaign in Normandy over the course of the summer. The battalion initially moved to Brest, then back to northern France. By the end of the summer the battalion had suffered more than 100 percent casualties, though many of the rangers, like Lomell, had rejoined the outfit. D Company still contained the nucleus of veterans from D-Day, but only two or three had escaped wounds since the day they had assaulted Pointe du Hoc.

As the battalion's sergeant major, Lomell was responsible for the delivery of munitions, arms, and supplies, and for coordinating all the units. Helping to train replacements became his primary duty. During this period the rangers were usually attached to an infantry division, where they operated in two task forces: A, B, and C companies in one group, D, E, and F in the other. Clearing up German holdouts or pockets of resistance that the fast-moving armies didn't have time to eliminate remained the primary focus of the elite rangers.

As for Bud Lomell, his legend grew. On October 7 he became the first ranger in the 2nd Battalion to receive a battlefield commission. Assigned to B Company, he went directly to Rudder and requested a transfer back to D Company. Rudder hesitated, fearing that there might be a problem with familiarity if he assigned Lomell to his original company. He finally relented, but not before giving Lomell and D Company's entire chain of command a stern warning that if a problem arose, Lomell was out of the company for good.

John Carona, Dog Company's first sergeant, laid down the law to the enlisted men in the company. Needless to say, there was no problem.

By December 1944 the 2nd Battalion had been attached to the 1st, 4th, 8th, 9th, and 28th divisions. In every instance the battalion had accomplished all of its missions. During the first week in December, it was the 8th Division's turn as the rangers moved into the Huertgen Forest. The battalion had already served with the 28th Division in the Huertgen, sustaining a number of casualties from mines and artillery. It was not the kind of combat for which Lomell and his men had trained. James Eikner, who was still the battalion communications officer, later explained, "We were a very specialized unit. All volunteers—highly trained in special missions—putting us out on a front line in a defensive position wasn't utilizing our skills and capabilities. The attrition not only from the shelling but also from the weather, the trench foot, just sitting there in those foxholes making a furor every now and then and a little scrap now and then—we were very disappointed about this."[11] All that changed when the battalion joined the 8th Infantry Division on 5 December.

As the Allied advance swept toward the German border in late 1944, the Germans held the high ground in the Ruhr Valley, including the formidable towns of Schmidt and Bergstein, which included Castle Hill, also known as Hill 400, on the eastern edge of the forest. The highest spot in the region, Hill 400 offered its defenders excellent views of the Ruhr River half a mile to the east as well as all the avenues of approach to the river. By the time Lomell's rangers moved into the area, Courtney Hodges's First Army had already thrown elements of four divisions at Hill 400. The result had always been the same: massed casualties and no gain to justify the loss of lives. Lomell later recalled, "The roads approaching Bergstein and Hill 400 were jammed up and heavily cluttered with bombed-out and burnt tanks and vehicles of all descriptions. There were mine fields on both sides of the muddy roads and constant and continuing artillery attacks on all roads leading to Hill 400."

After so many futile attempts to take the heights, it was obviously time to try something new. The 2nd Battalion drew the short straw. Why the rangers? The men themselves believed that the tactics they had used so successfully since June—stealth and speedy infiltration coupled with surprise—were needed to conquer the hill. Detrucking at Kleinhaus, a town about two miles from Bergstein, under cover of darkness, the rangers deployed into attack formation along a sunken road on the edge of the town. The plan was to assault Hill 400 with two companies abreast—F Company on the left, Lomell's D Company on the right. E Company was in reserve, with the remaining companies garrisoning the town. Upon reaching Bergstein, Major George Williams, who that morning had replaced Rudder as battalion commander, dispatched two patrols to reconnoiter Hill 400.[12] Lieutenant Tex McClure took a five-man patrol from F Company to reconnoiter his company's objective; Lomell led the patrol from D Company. Both returned with enough intelligence to finalize the plan of attack, now scheduled for 0730 on the morning of December 7. Williams had two options: attack the hill in a frontal assault across open fields some one hundred yards wide, or try a flanking attack through known minefields. Williams decided on the former. The men fixed bayonets and prepared to charge at first light. Sergeant Bill Petty, who had distinguished himself on D-Day, recalled that "tension was building up to the exploding point."[13]

At 0730, 130 rangers crossed the line of departure and began the assault. Lomell's 1st Platoon led the D Company attack. One ranger recalled, "The commanding officer gave the word 'Go!' With a whooping and hollering as loud as possible, firing a clip of ammo at random from their weapons in the direction of the hill, the rangers ran as fast as they could across the cleared field."[14] Immediately they encountered small arms and mortar fire. The Germans had been caught by surprise but recovered just as the rangers began their ascent. Unlike Pointe du Hoc, where the rangers utilized grappling hooks and ropes to reach the summit, they climbed hand over hand while maintaining a steady stream of fire. Four machine guns fired point-blank at the attacking rangers, killing a number of them before Private Sigurd Sundby single-handedly silenced the guns in D Company's zone.[15] Casualties were heavy. Lomell's company commander, Captain Morton McBride, and his platoon sergeant, Sergeant Joe Stevens, were hit in the opening minutes. There was no alternative but to continue the attack as German mortar fire began extracting an increasing toll on the rangers. Led by Lomell, D Company's attack was swift and effective. By 0830 the two ranger companies had reached the top, where they quickly consolidated and reorganized their position. Technical Sergeant Harvey Koenig, who led D Company's 2nd Platoon, took about half of his remaining men and chased the retreating Germans almost to the Ruhr River before he returned to his lines to prepare for the inevitable counterattack. It wasn't long in coming.

At 0930 the enemy launched the first of five counterattacks to retake the hill. As an added incentive, Field Marshal Walter Model, the commander of Army Group B, promised Iron Crosses and two weeks' leave to each man who took part in the recapture of Hill 400. The first attack hit D Company hard. The Germans were repelled, but the rangers paid a terrific price. Major Williams later told historian Forrest Pogue, "In some cases Germans were in and around the bunker on the hill before the rangers were aware of their presence. Once on the hill they attempted to rush the positions. They used machine guns, burp guns, rifles, and threw potato masher grenades. Hand-to-hand fights developed on top of the hill in which some use was made of bayonets."[16] By noon, D Company had forty-eight men so seriously wounded that they were unable to fight.

It seemed to Lomell that the situation could not get any worse. Now the senior officer on the hill, he could get no reinforcements, medical supplies, or much-needed ammunition. Though there were at least thirty thousand Americans within a few miles of his position, none could break contact and come to the aid of the rangers. Men were bleeding to death only a few yards away and there was absolutely nothing anyone could do to help them. Lomell later recalled, "The counterattacks were horrendous. At times we were outnumbered ten to one. We were helpless, no protection, continuous tons of shrapnel falling upon us, hundreds of rounds coming in. Survival was a matter of luck. Guys were lying all over the hill. . . . If the Germans had known how many men, or really how few we had up there, they would have kept on coming." At one point he witnessed one of his section sergeants, Staff Sergeant Ed Secor, "a very quiet man, out of ammo and unarmed, seize two machine pistols from wounded Germans and in desperation charge a large German patrol, firing and screaming at them. His few remaining men rallied to the cause and together they drove the Germans back down the hill."

Lomell seemed to be everywhere, posting outposts and directing the defense. He later recalled, "In times like this, a platoon leader must do all he can do to put the men at ease. I assured the wounded that help was on the way. I never had time to be afraid. I was too preoccupied with the success of the mission and saving as many lives as I could."[17] By now, he had been wounded himself, his hand mangled, one finger attached by a single sinew. In great pain, the beleaguered platoon leader shifted BARs around the ragged perimeter in anticipation of the next German attack. Fortunately for Lomell, the enemy attacked his perimeter from only a single direction at a time. The enemy attacked at 1300 hours from the east, then again at 1450 from the north. The rangers held on by the skin of their teeth. Guts and determination were key weapons. By the time dusk fell at 1600, only a handful of survivors remained to defend the hill.

Evacuating his wounded now became Lomell's primary obsession. The afternoon attacks had resulted in numerous casualties, many of whom lay for hours where they had fallen. With the ground too hard to dig foxholes, far too many wounded rangers succumbed to secondary wounds from flying shrapnel. The medical bunker filled so quickly that there was soon no additional room available for the wounded. Not sure they could hold on, Lomell gathered his noncoms and offered them a proposal: "If we retreat, they'll take care of our wounded. We can come back and take the hill later." To a man they urged Lomell to stay, and he agreed. They would not abandon the fallen men. That evening, litter teams from C and E Companies arrived to evacuate the most seriously wounded. It was no easy task carrying litters down the steep hill, around tree stumps and under and over fallen trees in the snow, ice, and darkness. Worse yet, German shelling continued throughout the night. At 2100, Lomell sustained a second wound while assisting with the evacuation.

How did Lomell and his rangers hold on against apparently insurmountable odds? Pride was certainly a factor, but pride can carry a man only so far. What truly saved the rangers was American artillery. In mid-afternoon Lieutenant Howard Kettlehut, a forward observer from the 56th Armored Field Artillery Battalion, made it to the top and began calling in every piece of indirect fire at his disposal. Battalion commander Williams later informed Pogue, "At one point Kettlehut brought down fire from all artillery available in Corps—18 battalions in all; 155s, 75s, self-propelled 8-inch and 240mm guns placed a ring of explosive shells around the hill."[18] No enemy could withstand such ferocious fire support, but somehow the Germans continued their attacks on December 8. By then, however, an infantry regiment and tank destroyer battalion had relieved the embattled rangers.

Although the 2nd Ranger Battalion had been told that they would be relieved in twenty-four hours, it was almost two days before D and F Companies descended Hill 400. Only twenty-two rangers walked down the hill on their own two feet. Total casualties among the assaulting companies numbered 90 percent, including 22 killed and 111 seriously wounded or captured.[19] In turn, they had killed 300 and wounded several hundred more of their enemy. The 2nd Battalion had barely survived its toughest fight of the war. A half century later, Lomell commented, "June 6, 1944, was not my longest day. December 7, 1944, was the longest, worst, and most dangerous day of my eighty-one years. Climbing the cliffs on D-Day was easier on me personally, compared to assaulting and climbing a steep and slippery hill about four hundred feet high in the Huertgen Forest."[20]

On December 9, the rangers limped back to their reserve position to lick their wounds and wait for replacements. Exactly a week later the Germans began the Ardennes offensive. In the process they recaptured Hill 400, which they held until February 1945 when the American 508th Parachute Infantry Regiment recaptured the hill in a three-day battle. As for Len Lomell, he was evacuated to a field hospital that contained eight operating tables. On each table was a wounded ranger. He remained in the hospital until he was discharged on December 30, no longer fit for combat duty.

When the war ended, Lomell returned to the United States and led the victory parade down the main street of Point Pleasant, New Jersey. At the same time he renewed his acquaintance with Charlotte Ewart, a striking young woman whom he had dated before deploying overseas. A year later they married—on June 6, of course, two years to the day after Lomell led the 2nd Platoon up the cliffs of Pointe du Hoc. As Charlotte says now, "Every wedding anniversary we share with the surviving rangers, because it is also the anniversary of D-Day."[21] Together Len and Charlotte raised three daughters of their own, and when Charlotte's sister died leaving a teenage son and daughter, they took them in, too. Through it all they stayed close to Len's ranger buddies, who were always considered a part of the Lomell family.

Immediately after World War II, Lomell studied law at LaSalle University and Rutgers under the GI Bill. He was admitted to the bar in 1951 and established his own law firm in 1957. In the half century since the war, Bud Lomell has been active in civic affairs, including the Veterans of Foreign Wars, the American Legion, and the local board of education, to name but a few. Over the years he has served as the director of the First National Bank of Toms River, the president of the Garden State Philharmonic Symphony Society of Ocean County, and president of the Ocean County Bar Association. A frequent lecturer at the U.S. Military Academy, he is still the epitome of the American soldier. West Point cadets are proud to meet the first enlisted ranger to be inducted into the Ranger Hall of Fame at Fort Benning, Georgia.

Developing these future leaders of the army remains one of Len's top priorities. He tells the young men and women of the U.S. Corps of Cadets to be physically tough and morally upright. He also shares his personal philosophy of leadership: "Don't waste time with losers. I have seen very few losers turn out to be winners. A leader's ability is based on demonstrated integrity, honesty, the way he lives his life, his desire to do the right thing. If he possesses that image early on, he will be a success. If he is fair-minded, if he is willing to listen, you have a leader whose men will take over when the chips are down or the need arises. You will also have a winning team. Good leaders inspire their men to win whatever the challenge. There is always pride in winning."

His financial security long since assured, Lomell spends most of his free time granting interviews, speaking at high schools, and urging the youth of America to become good citizens. When asked why he devotes so much time to such endeavors, he replied, "I do it for the rangers who died. The question, 'What does a ranger do?' has haunted me for fifty years. Each time I tell someone, I educate him. I have an ongoing memorial to my deceased ranger buddies. I have been doing this since my retirement in 1985. The rangers never had a public relations section, so I volunteered to be just that." Today the Lomell home in Toms River is frequently the site of ranger reunions. Every ranger who passes through that section of New Jersey pays his respects to Bud Lomell. There is always a meal on the table, a room for the night.

Lomell returned to Hill 400 in 1989 with some fellow ranger survivors. By chance they encountered a group of young German officers who were conducting their own staff ride. The Germans showed Lomell their army textbook, which claimed that the Germans had been greatly outnumbered that day. Lomell exclaimed, "That's ridiculous! We were the ones . . . outmanned by at least ten to one." The Germans were politely incredulous that two ranger companies could have inflicted so much damage.

I first met Lomell in the spring of 1994, a month before he led his rangers back to the scene of their greatest triumph. His toughness, his candor, and his devotion to his comrades in arms impressed me. I relished his story of how he escorted Charlotte to Pointe du Hoc in 1960. In his inimitable style, he asked her if she would give him bragging rights among his fellow rangers by being the only ranger wife to scale the cliffs. Although she was dressed in her finest attire and had not expected such a challenge, Charlotte worked her way to the beach using old ropes, sections of broken ladders, and such aids as were available. Then, accompanied by the former first sergeant from D Company, Charlotte retraced the path of the rangers' assault. When they finally reached the summit, their clothes were covered with mud and slime but Bud had his bragging rights. Charlotte may be a tougher ranger than her husband. Today, Charlotte's many ranger friends would rather talk about her culinary talents than about her cliff-climbing adventures, but Bud is quick to remind them that his is still the only wife to climb Pointe du Hoc.

In August 1998, and again three years later, I traveled to Toms River to interview Bud Lomell. His house is a shrine, not to himself but to his fellow rangers. Their photographs and citations cover the wall of his small den. He lives, breathes, and sleeps "ranger." I was fortunate enough to spend the better part of two days with him and Charlotte. We discussed combat leadership and heroism under adverse conditions. Never once did he mention his personal achievements, only those of his men. The lack of the use of the first-person pronoun is typical of Bud Lomell.

As the twenty-first century dawned, the citizens and governing body of Bud's old borough of Point Pleasant Beach, New Jersey, honored its favorite son by proclaiming December 4, 1999, "Bud Lomell Day." The city's fathers held a small ceremony in his honor at Veteran's Park only a few blocks from where the skinny kid from Trenton Avenue worked summers at neighboring Jenkinson's beaches. In attendance were roughly three hundred friends and family, many of Lomell's fellow rangers, and another Point Pleasant Beach native, former Marine Corps commandant General Alfred M. Gray (USMC, Ret.). As the clouds gave way to a clear late autumn sky, a Coast Guard helicopter flew over to open the ceremony. Then speaker after speaker paid tribute to Bud Lomell and his rangers. Gray, himself a highly decorated veteran of several wars, noted that combat by its nature is violent and often lonely. Speaking of Lomell, Gray noted, "True warriors fight for what they believe in and they fight like hell for each other. Bud Lomell is such a warrior."

Then the assemblage moved to a covered monument in the center of the memorial park. Amid the pomp and circumstance, Lomell cut the ribbon and slipped the covering from a brick monument on which a steel grappling hook was mounted. The grappling hook is one of two of the original climbing implements still in existence from D-Day. The other is located at the ranger monument at Grandcamp, a small town just a few thousand yards from the site of the ranger assault. A plaque on the side of Lomell's monument reads:

DEDICATED TO:

1st Sgt. Leonard G. Lomell, a former member of Company D, 2nd Ranger Battalion, United States Army, World War II, in recognition of his Distinguished Service to his unit and country. On June 6, 1944, D day, 1st Sgt. Lomell, as an acting platoon leader, was the first Ranger wounded as his L.C.A. landed on the narrow beach below the 100-foot cliffs of Pointe du Hoc, Omaha Beach, Normandy, France.

Notwithstanding his wounds, he and his 2nd platoon climbed the cliffs despite the overwhelming odds against the success of their mission and the heavy firepower of the many German soldiers defending the fortress known as Pointe du Hoc. Topside in the assault, he neutralized a machine gun position, infiltrated two enemy lines of defense and personally found and destroyed the five large 155-MM (6") coastal guns located in an alternate position a mile inland from Pointe du Hoc. The guns had a range of 12 miles and could easily reach the landing beaches and the invasion armada of ships. Many thousands of lives were saved by 1st Sgt. Lomell's heroic action. The mission, said by General Omar Bradley to be the most dangerous mission of D day, was accomplished by 8:30 AM that morning.

1st Sgt. Lomell was awarded the United States Distinguished Service Cross, the second highest medal for valor in America. He also received the French Legion of Honor Medal for valor, the highest such award in France. England decorated 1st Sgt. Lomell with its British Military Medal for outstanding valor. Upon discharge as a Lieutenant, he was one of the highest decorated Rangers of World War II. Leonard "Bud" Lomell was truly a "citizen soldier." After the war he studied law under the G.I. Bill and became a successful lawyer in our county of Ocean, New Jersey. He continued to contribute significantly to his community and country.

Presented by the grateful citizens of
Point Pleasant Beach, New Jersey
December 4, 1999

When his own turn to speak arrived, the old ranger spoke not of himself but of his men. Asking the veterans to stand, he spoke of the immense pride each had for his fellow soldiers. As for himself, Bud said, he was simply lucky, "lucky to come from Point Pleasant Beach, lucky to have so many good friends who had made a man of me, lucky to have been in the right place at the right time." With utmost humility, he set past glory aside and said that he "only did what I was trained to do—nothing less, nothing more."

I asked Len what he wanted history to say of him. He responded instantly, "A damn good ranger, honorable, capable, what a leader should be. I've worked over fifty years to be just that, to do the right thing and to be respectful. I'll be proud to be remembered as a good ranger, as a good man, and as a respectful one."

CHAPTER 11

HEROISM OUTLASTS PREJUDICE: VERNON J. BAKER AND THE BUFFALO SOLDIERS

. . . for conspicuous gallantry and intrepidity in action at the risk of his life above and beyond the call of duty.

—Citation from Vernon Baker's Medal of Honor

MORE THAN ONE MILLION BLACK MEN AND WOMEN faithfully served their country over the course of World War II. In the racially segregated army of World War II, however, while Jim Crow ruled America in general and the army in particular, no African American received the Medal of Honor, the nation's highest decoration for heroism in combat. On January 13, 1997, President William Jefferson Clinton belatedly addressed this fifty-two-year-old injustice by presenting the Medal of Honor to seven black Americans for conspicuous gallantry and intrepidity in action at the risk of their lives above and beyond the call of duty. In the name of Congress the president bestowed six medals posthumously.[1] The seventh recipient was First Lieutenant Vernon J. Baker, who distinguished himself by extraordinary heroism at Castle Aghinolfi in the northern Apennine Mountains of Italy on April 5, 1945.

Vernon J. Baker was the unlikeliest of heroes. Orphaned at four, Baker, the youngest of three children, was raised by his grandparents in Cheyenne, Wyoming. His grandfather, Joseph Samuel Baker, imparted a series of aphorisms to guide Baker's life. "Use your brains, not your fists, boy," he admonished many times.[2] "Just be yourself and you will be successful." Growing up in a town of twenty thousand that contained only twelve black families, Baker encountered Cheyenne's unspoken and unstructured prejudice both at home and at school, but his quest for his grandfather's approval overcame most obstacles. Still, by age eleven he had evolved into a "damned little hellion," according to his sister. Several years later, Baker spent two years in Father Flanagan's Boys Home outside Omaha, Nebraska, before returning to Cheyenne in the summer of 1933.

Casting about Cheyenne was monotonous at best as Baker alternated between various jobs with the railroad. By his own admission he was "an angry young black man" in June 1941 when he enlisted in the army to escape the menial servitude he perceived to be the lot of black males in the rural West. His initial experience was not encouraging. The white recruiter told him, "We ain't got no quota for you people," and then ignored Baker and went about shuffling papers on his desk. Though his pride was hurt, Baker returned to the recruiting office a few weeks later and was welcomed by a different sergeant. This time the reception was more positive and Baker signed his name on the dotted line. Hoping to remain in Wyoming where the army had a quartermaster depot, Baker requested duty with the Quartermaster Corps. Peering across the desk, however, he noted that the recruiter ignored his request and wrote "Infantry." Within a week Baker was en route to Camp Wolters, Texas, where he encountered racial prejudice from both white and black officers, commissioned and noncommissioned alike.

Baker's first experience with the segregated South was hardly pleasant. After getting off the train in Mineral Wells, Baker boarded a nearby bus, dropped his duffel bag in the seat behind the driver, and sat down for the dusty ride to Wolters. The bus driver hollered, "Hey, nigger! Get up and get to the back of the bus where you belong." Before Baker, long accustomed to using his fists to settle disputes, could lunge at him, a strong arm caught his wrist. "Come on," said a shriveled black man who had been sitting on the back of the bus. "You trying to get killed on your first day in Texas? You're a black man. You tried to sit up front like's alright for black folks to sit anywhere they pleases. Nobody who lives here would try that on a dare unless he wanna be kilt." Explaining the facts of life to Baker, the old man told him to keep his fists in his pockets and not to make waves. "Clenching your fists in the presence of white people's liable to get you assault or 'tempted murder charge. Black man's justice in these here parts is done with a tree and a rope. . . . You in shock, son, you in shock. But you gotta listen. Stuff like this'll get you kilt. You're lucky this here driver's too lazy to tangle with you. Be a point of pride to most any other Southern man to beat you silly. Don't give 'em no opportunity." In later years Baker credited his unknown traveling companion with saving his life.[3]

Prejudice and professional jealousy, however, were not the exclusive property of the white race. Resentment followed Baker to his first assignment at Fort Huachuca, Arizona. Because he could read and write, he was made company clerk and was soon promoted to staff sergeant, accruing sixty dollars a month. By the time the Japanese attacked Pearl Harbor, Baker was the company supply sergeant. His rapid rise in rank brought Baker into direct conflict with older NCOs, who took considerable umbrage at the brash twenty-two-year-old "smart nigger" who was now their senior in rank in an army where promotion was based primarily on longevity of service. Three corporals met Baker outside the orderly room one evening and administered a beating designed to demonstrate that experience, not a high school diploma, was the proper path to military promotion.

Baker was thus somewhat relieved when his regimental commander summoned him and informed Baker that he was "volunteering" for Officer Candidate School to fill the growing need for a cadre of black officers to command the rapidly expanding military force. Baker performed well at the school and earned a commission as a second lieutenant. To his delight, his first posting was back to Arizona as a platoon leader in Dog Company, 25th Infantry Regiment. Later, when the 92nd Infantry "Buffalo" Division was reactivated, the unit evolved into C Company, 370th Infantry Regiment. Commanding the division was Major General Edward M. "Ned" Almond, a Virginian and avowed racist whom the army, in its infinite wisdom, assigned to the all-black division. In addition to Almond, the division was commanded above platoon level by white officers who considered the assignment professionally demeaning.

According to historian Stephen Ambrose, it is one of the great ironies of history that in World War II the world's greatest democracy fought the world's greatest racist with a segregated army. To the black soldier it was worse than that: the army and society together conspired to degrade African Americans in every way possible.[4] By the spring of 1944 the army's racial policies were under heavy attack by organizations like the NAACP, which alleged that the army was unjustly excluding black soldiers from the combat arms of the service. Under intense political pressure, the Roosevelt administration finally approved the assignment of black units to combat divisions in a combat role rather than the service support roles they had previously been allotted. The announcement came just in time. By mid-1944 the need for infantry replacements had increased tremendously as casualties had taken an excessive toll on the units serving in the forward battle areas.

Following corps field exercises outside Camp Polk, Louisiana, Almond announced that the Buffalo Division would join the Fifth U.S. Army in the Mediterranean Theater of Operations. The 92nd Infantry Division deployed to Italy in July, with the 370th Infantry Regimental Combat Team (RCT) in the lead. The combat team, consisting of the 370th Infantry, the 598th Field Artillery Battalion, and detachments from each of the special units of the 92nd Division, including the Headquarters Company, sailed from Hampton Roads on July 15. After transshipping at Oran, the regiment arrived at Naples on July 30.[5]

The deployment of the forward elements of the all-black division received a lion's share of the publicity accorded the frontline troops. A number of distinguished visitors dropped by, including Winston Churchill and Brigadier General Benjamin O. Davis, the first black West Point graduate to earn general officer rank. On October 18, the 371st Infantry Regiment, the second of the division's regiments, arrived in theater and relieved the 370th Infantry. The remaining regiment, the 365th Infantry, completed its deployment on November 8, at which time the entire division took over a six-mile front on the Fifth Army's western flank. Prior to deployment, Almond's chief of staff called all the officers together and told them it was time "for you black boys to go get killed." Not surprisingly, morale among the black soldiers in the division plummeted. According to Baker, the perception among the junior officers was that no commander above battalion level gave a damn about the men.[6]

Now a platoon leader, Baker commanded a group of "poor black rural southern men with no other way to make a living and with nothing to lose by being drafted into a segregated, racist army."[7] Getting to know his platoon and gaining the men's trust proved a challenge because the men initially regarded him as a "white man's tool." Most of the men were considerably older than Baker, who by his own admission had never before spent so much time in close contact with so many black soldiers. During his previous three years in the segregated army Baker had kept to himself as much as possible, still uncomfortable with a situation for which growing up in the rural West had not prepared him. Only the test of combat would break down the barrier that existed between officers and men, and in that regard Baker and his platoon were no different from thousands of other platoons.

Combat remained the final arbiter of respect between officers and their men. In preparing for that eventuality, Baker studied past missions and every manual he could find. For weeks the platoon trained in an extinct volcano crater outside Naples, with Baker getting to know the platoon and the platoon gradually taking stock of its commander. If anything, Baker later recalled, "he got too close" to the men, acting as their mother and father, reading their letters to them, and generally doing everything for them in order to develop the type of teamwork that he knew was essential for survival. Initially the men were somewhat skeptical and suspicious, but after the second patrol, in which they suffered a few casualties, the platoon coalesced around Baker. After five months of constant patrolling, Lieutenant Vernon Baker had matured as a dynamic combat leader in the intense crucible of war. In October, Baker himself suffered a wound that confined him to a field hospital through December.

While Baker recuperated, the 92nd Division established a reputation as a "problem division." The crisis reached such epic proportions that Army Chief of Staff George C. Marshall became personally involved. Following a tour of the front, Marshall described the 92nd Division as untrustworthy under fire. Writing to Eisenhower, he requested that Ike shift the Japanese American 442nd Infantry Regiment from France back to Italy to participate in the upcoming spring offensive. Referring to the Buffalo Division's soldiers, Marshall noted that "the Infantry literally dissolved each night abandoning equipment and even clothing is some cases." The artillery, engineers, and other divisional troops appeared excellent, he said, and the command and staff were superior. "But as matters now stand, the division itself is not only of little value, but weakens the front by necessitating the putting of other divisions in the rear to provide the necessary security against a local German thrust through . . . to supply lines, divisions that should otherwise be disposed in the center of the army." This trend was particularly disturbing to the army chief, who had taken special pains to see that the 93rd Division and other black units in the Pacific had received special training and preparation before going into action. Similarly, he had insisted that the 92nd Division be thoroughly prepared for its assignment to Italy. Substandard performance in battle might strengthen the reluctance of army commanders to use the black soldiers in combat.[8]

Marshall's assessment was shared by most of the senior army leadership in the Mediterranean Theater. When the 92nd Division arrived in Italy, Fifth Army commander Mark Clark planned to break in the division gradually by giving it "appropriate" tasks at the outset. "I do not feel it is wise," he wrote, "to count on its offensive ability in a slugging match with the Germans to the same extent as a white division." He was willing, however, to "give it every opportunity to develop its full 100% offensive power if it has the inherent capability of doing so." Years later, Clark reflected that "the Negro soldier needed greater incentive and a feeling that he was fighting for his home and country and that he was fighting as an equal." Clark was also against the indiscriminate mixing of black and white troops. Such dilution of combat troops, he thought, would surely lead to "our biggest defeat."[9]

The 92nd Division's commander, Ned Almond, seconded Clark's reservations. The unit's unsatisfactory performance was, he felt, directly attributable to the "undependability of the average Negro soldier to operate to his maximum capability, compared to his lassitude toward his performing a task assigned. While there are exceptions to this rule, the general tendency of the Negro soldier is to avoid as much as possible."[10] Almond later expanded his assessment to a general statement that black troops should not be utilized as combat troops. Acknowledging that "the Negro is a useful individual" and a citizen who should play a role in the nation's defense, Almond warned that "to expect him to exhibit characteristics that are abnormal to his race is too much and not recommended by me."[11]

Why the reluctance to integrate combat units? According to the army's official history, there were signs from the beginning that the troops of the 370th Infantry Regiment, though willing, were neither thoroughly trained nor thoroughly motivated.[12] Most of the problems were of the sort endemic to newly arrived troops. Failure to communicate, badly organized attacks, and a shortage of officers were often at fault.

A few senior commanders were willing to reserve judgment until the Buffalo Soldiers had experienced prolonged combat. General Jacob Devers disagreed with Clark's view that the 92nd Division was wholly unreliable in combat. Devers, who had served as deputy supreme Allied commander, Mediterranean, and as commanding general, Mediterranean Theater of Operation (U.S.), before organizing the 6th Army Group in September 1944, was convinced that "colored" troops had not yet had a fair chance. He was confident the 92nd Division would fight if properly indoctrinated and given an opportunity to gain some self-assurance.

In his memoirs, General Lucian Truscott claims that he initially agreed with Devers but altered his assessment in early February 1945 after the Buffalo Soldiers incurred excessive casualties in a limited-objective attack that should have been well within their capabilities. In the war's final months, Truscott, now newly appointed Fifth Army commander, noted that the failure of the division to reach assigned objectives was "due entirely to the unreliability of [its] infantry units." Though he remarked that the 370th Infantry Regiment was superior to its counterparts, Truscott concluded that the disorganization of units, the lack of cohesiveness in small units, and the excessive amounts of equipment and matériel lost to the enemy were all evidence of lack of control by company-grade officers. It was Truscott's assessment that 370th personnel exhibited no pride of race and little pride in accomplishment—harsh criticism indeed from the army commander.[13]

The white regimental commanders concurred with Truscott. Colonel James Notesteio, commanding officer of the 371st Infantry Regiment, Baker's sister regiment, stated categorically that initiative was "not a racial characteristic [of blacks]. Only one in ten has or has developed initiative, which I think it reasonable to expect. Generally, results are obtained only through the imagination and pressure provided by white officers." In reviewing his own command at the end of the war, Notesteio could not find a single black officer whom he considered wholly dependable over a long period during stress. There were "far too many cases of fear and cowardice" in the regiment. If the United States had to mobilize again "within the next two generations [sixty years]," he concluded, he would recommend that "no colored infantry divisions be organized. Colored officers should not be commissioned in the infantry."[14]

An equally serious problem involved the level of illiteracy within the Buffalo Division.[15] By the end of 1944, the division's Army General Classification Test (AGCT) score percentages disclosed that none of the enlisted men scored in the Class I intelligence category; 10 percent were in Class II, 15 percent were in Class III, 41 percent were in Class IV, and 21 percent were in Class V. Approximately 13 percent had no score at all because they were illiterate and unable to take the test. The poor test scores simply reflected the lack of educational and cultural opportunities and the lower socioeconomic status of black soldiers relative to white soldiers in other combat divisions.[16] Moreover, the army officers administering the series of tests tended to rate the black soldiers as stupid and far less intelligent than their white counterparts.

The division's problems were compounded by the lack of trained replacements for the black battalions on the front line—an armywide problem not confined to black units. Combat units in France and Belgium experienced similar problems as the war extracted its toll on frontline GIs. Almond later stated that the low intelligence level of his division meant that significantly more time had to be spent on training activities. "Rifle marksmanship, for example, required three to four times as much ammunition for instructional practice before we went to record practice and consequently more time in combat firing was required than we should have [taken] for [these] men."[17]

At Truscott's insistence, Almond reorganized the 370th Infantry Regiment in the spring of 1945. Transferring experienced battlefield leaders from sister regiments, Almond assigned only white officers to company command, in spite of the fact that there were a number of black officers—including Baker—with superior ratings. Like most of the junior officers in the regiment, Baker bristled at being overlooked and also at the condescending attitude toward the lower enlisted ranks displayed by white officers at the regiment and division levels. Even worse, when the "new" 370th Infantry moved into the battle area, only a few of the white officers had any experience with the troops under their command. They were strangers, for the most part, to one another, and many noncommissioned officers were in similar positions with enlisted men.[18] That situation proved detrimental in the campaigns to follow.

On returning to his unit in December, Baker found himself the senior officer in the company until Captain John F. Runyon and two additional white officers arrived in late March to occupy the senior leadership positions. In early April, Baker received word that the company was preparing for a "big push" to seize the enemy defenses confronting the division. Reverting to weapons platoon leader just as he learned that Charlie Company would lead the next attack on Castle Aghinolfi, Baker again prepared his men for combat. The company now comprised one black and two white officers and 142 enlisted men. Baker's platoon consisted of two mortar squads and two machine-gun squads, all below their designated strength. The objective occupied the summit of a small hill that anchored one leg of what the Italian partisans called the "Triangle of Death." Used primarily as an artillery observation post, the castle dominated the coastal highway on the western end of the Gothic Line, a defensive position that followed a natural barrier of rugged terrain stretching across the Italian peninsula. The line was so strong that small units using a series of well-placed machine guns supported by indirect artillery fire could hold off vastly superior forces. In the vicinity of Castle Aghinolfi, Allied strategy had been to send the infantry up a trio of small peaks, named Hills X, Y, and Z, toward the castle from the south. Three previous attacks had met with unmitigated disaster. Now the 1st Battalion would get its turn, moving along routes similar to those used in the preceding attacks. The assault was scheduled to begin before dawn on April 5. Fully 70 percent of Baker's men were replacements with little or no combat experience.

Describing the British airborne assault on Pegasus Bridge on D-Day, Stephen Ambrose notes that sometimes a single day's combat tells more about the character of an army and a nation than a sustained period of combat. For Vernon Baker, April 5, 1945, was such a day. Awakened at three in the morning, Baker discarded his combat helmet and his utilities and donned his dress uniform and his customary wool helmet liner. The day foreshadowed death, and if Baker was going to die, he intended to do it in style. Wrapping two bandoleers of ammunition around his waist, he next attached four grenades to the pockets of his Eisenhower jacket. Baker remembered that he was lucky "to have ninety-six rifle rounds to take into battle." Next he grabbed his M-1 rifle and instinctively checked it thoroughly. He was ready for battle, but he was without the services of his senior noncommissioned officer. The preceding evening his platoon sergeant had shuffled in and said he was going to the dispensary and would be unavailable to join the platoon on the attack. Disgusted by the sergeant's cowardice and dereliction of duty, Baker dismissed him and told him to get the hell out of the platoon area. There would be no room for cowards on the upcoming mission.

At 0500, following a fifteen-minute artillery preparation, Baker's company crossed the line of departure. What followed is best told in Baker's own words.[19] "On the morning of April 5, Charlie Company was to attack and take the high ground to the right of Highway #1 in the vicinity of Porta, Italy. I, the leader of the weapons platoon, was ordered to follow the second rifle platoon. The second platoon was close on the heels of the third rifle platoon, three-fourths the way up the hill. . . . Single file, rock to rock, my men followed with .30-caliber light machine-guns, 60mm mortars, and ammunition. I carried nine pounds of M-1 rifle, stretched hand-to-hand in front of my waist." He refused to use a sling to carry his weapon. "That meant I had to pull my rifle off my back when the bullets started flying—a shortcut to death."

Baker, at the head of his weapons platoon, and Company C's three rifle platoons advanced toward their objective, Castle Aghinolfi, approximately two miles away. Initially they met little resistance. As dawn arrived and the rolling barrage of artillery commenced, Baker advanced to keep ahead of the terrific volleys that were falling at ten-minute intervals. By 0645, approximately twenty-five members of the rifle platoons had joined Runyon and Baker as they reached the south side of a draw approximately 250 yards from the castle. There they paused to catch their breath. With the objective in sight, Runyon ordered Baker to set up his machine-gun section to cover the approach of the riflemen for the final assault.

Baker again takes up the story:

> Upon moving forward to reconnoiter for a position, I observed two cylindrical objects pointing from a slit in a mount at the very edge of a hill overlooking the flat land. At first I took these objects to be machine-gun barrels, so crawling up under the opening, I stuck my M-1 into the slit and emptied the clip into the opening. Receiving no return fire, I looked into the aperture and discovered a BC-Scope—which I had mistaken for a machine-gun—and two men, one of who was slumped in a chair and the other, wounded, trying to crawl into a corner where some "potato-masher" grenades were piled. Seeing this, I moved to the rear of the OP and, pulling the pin from a hand grenade, tossed it into the rear entrance of the same. After the explosion of the grenade, I went into the position and discovered a powerful telescope, which was used to look down onto the flatland.

Baker cut the telephone lines, placed a hand grenade in the cradle of the periscope and pulled the pin, and moved away from the observation post.

Moving to another position in the same vicinity, he stumbled upon a well-camouflaged machine-gun position; its two-man crew was away from the gun eating breakfast. Baker shot and killed both men and ordered his machine gunner to set up his gun at the same position. Up to this point of the attack, Baker remembered, "we had killed an estimated number of twelve Germans, including one enemy officer, destroyed two machine-gun nests and an OP—without suffering any casualties." After Captain Runyon joined the group, a German soldier appeared from the draw and hurled a grenade. Baker was not sure what happened next, but the evidence indicates that three things occurred simultaneously: the grenade landed five feet from him, bounced, but did not explode; Baker squeezed off two shots, slamming the German in the back; and Runyon disappeared. Borrowing a Thompson submachine gun from one of his squad leaders, Baker then went down into the draw alone. There he blasted open the concealed entrance of second dugout with a hand grenade, shot one German soldier who emerged after the explosion, tossed another grenade into the dugout, and entered, firing his submachine gun and killing two more Germans.

Leaving the dugout, he returned to the summit of the hill, where he found Runyon. As the company commander was describing the hand grenade battle in which the other men had engaged in Baker's absence, the enemy zeroed in on the American position with heavy mortars, inflicting heavy casualties among the group of twenty-five soldiers around the two officers. The mortar's position was not obvious at the beginning of the barrage, but as the firing continued, one soldier, glancing up into the air, saw what he thought at first was a flock of birds. He soon discovered that the flock of birds was actually a barrage of mortar shells that had just been fired from a position behind a demolished house on the adjacent hill. Explosions followed in rapid succession, killing three of Baker's men and wounding three others. When he directed his forward observer to call for artillery support, Baker learned that regiment refused to fire because they could not believe that the men were so close to the castle. After much haggling, regiment finally fired the support and temporarily quieted the German mortars. By then, Baker's platoon had suffered an inordinate number of casualties. Nor did the Americans' respite last. The Germans launched another counterattack at 1430.

As Baker directed the defense, he searched in vain for his company commander. One of his men told him that Runyon was in a little stone house in an olive grove at the edge of the battlefield. Using the scant brush for concealment, Baker sprinted for the squat building and found Runyon sitting on the dirt floor, knees pulled up to his chest and arms wrapped around his legs. Runyon's face was "translucent," Baker later recalled, "the color of bleached parchment." Just then another barrage descended and completely unnerved Runyon. Fighting to control his shaking voice, Runyon ordered Baker to cover his withdrawal: "Look, Baker, I'm going for reinforcements." Baker replied, "All right, Captain. We'll be here when you get back," knowing he would never see any reinforcements and not sure why his company commander was deserting his men to do a job that any NCO could do. The next time Baker saw Runyon was days after the battle was over. Only then did he discover that his company commander had reported to battalion headquarters that Baker's platoon was "wiped out."

Baker's account of a panic-stricken white captain abandoning him on a fire-swept hill should not be considered race-specific. All armies of all wars have similar incidents as men break under the pressure of combat. What happened next marked Baker as an extraordinary combat soldier. With Runyon gone, he quickly collected the dog tags from his fallen soldiers and prepared for the inevitable German counterattack. An hour and a half after the initial request for reinforcements, another mortar barrage fell in the area; it preceded an attack by approximately a platoon of enemy soldiers disguised as medics and litter-bearers. After approaching to within fifty yards of Baker's command post under the protection of a Red Cross flag, the enemy dropped their disguise, took a machine gun from the litter, and prepared to assault the remnants of the beleaguered American platoon. Baker's men immediately returned fire, routing the attacking force.

By this time Baker had but eight men, in addition to the forward observer, remaining from the original detachment that had accompanied him up the hill. Down to a few clips per man and with no hope of reinforcements, Baker reluctantly ordered a withdrawal. It was a tough decision. "My men wanted to stay," he recalled, "but I wanted to ensure some of them stayed alive." "Let's get the hell out of here," he directed. Baker covered their withdrawal himself, killing one of four enemy soldiers who ventured out to get a clearer picture of the front. The remainder fled to the opposite side of the hill. After waiting a few minutes to see if any more Germans appeared, Baker moved out and joined his men.

Nearing a demolished house, Baker's survivors were spotted by an enemy mortar crew and immediately brought under indirect mortar fire. Another of his men was wounded, bringing the number in his platoon to seven. After another three hundred yards, a sniper shot and killed the only medic with the platoon, decreasing their number to six. Private James Thomas located the sniper and killed him with his BAR. Reaching the crest of Hill X, Baker discovered two additional machine-gun nests that the Americans had bypassed on their ascent to the castle. Directing Thomas to cover him, Baker crawled to the positions and destroyed them with white phosphorus grenades, thus clearing the way for the group to evacuate their casualties to the battalion aid station. Totally exhausted from the day's ordeal, Baker lowered himself to the side of the road, hung his head between his knees, and vomited. He had been in intense combat for twelve consecutive hours. In all, Lieutenant Vernon Baker had personally accounted for nine dead enemy soldiers and eliminated three machine-gun positions, an observation post, and a dugout.

Once he regained his composure, the embattled platoon leader reported to battalion headquarters, where Lieutenant Colonel Murphy, his commanding officer for the past six months, greeted him warmly. "Sit down, Bake; forget the formalities," his CO ordered. Murphy was the only white officer who had taken the time to learn Baker's nickname, and Baker was grateful. "Hear you had a pretty rough day up there," he motioned in the general direction of Castle Aghinolfi. "Rough. Yes sir, but we did it. We got within a few hundred yards of the castle. With more men we'd have taken it." Baker then recounted the basics and gave Murphy the pertinent information concerning enemy troop strength and dispositions. As Baker prepared to exit the command post, Murphy added, "Damn fine work today with those machine-gun nests and the bunkers. And snagging those telephone wires was smart soldiering. Tell your boys I appreciate it."[20] It was a refreshing change to hear praise for what his men had accomplished. A month later, Murphy would personally present Baker the silver bars that accompanied his battlefield promotion to first lieutenant.

Unfortunately, Baker's tumultuous day was far from over. Standard operating procedures dictated that Baker turn in the dog tags from his fallen comrades. Exhaustion again crept in and Baker fell asleep en route to regimental headquarters; only his driver's whispered announcement that they had arrived awakened him. Ordinarily, a commander would give the tags to the intelligence officer, but instead Baker encountered Colonel Raymond G. Sherman, the regiment commander. Unlike Murphy, Sherman had not earned the respect of the black officers and men in the 370th Infantry. He would later characterize the black troops as unreliable and prone to cowardice under fire. What followed would have been demeaning to any officer, black or white.

"You just out of the field?"

"Yes sir, with stops at the Command Post and Battalion HQ," Baker responded.

"Where's your helmet, Lieutenant?"

"At my quarters, sir."

Sherman looked Baker over and launched into one of the better "ass-chewings" the platoon leader had received in the army. Overall, Baker recalled, Sherman said he was a "disgrace to the universe, God, country, all for not wearing a helmet into battle." Baker's stupidity as well as his irreverence for authority was an abomination beyond words, Sherman continued. "Worse, lieutenant, you have a reputation . . . a reputation for never wearing a helmet. What kind of goddamn example do you think you are to your men? How about that, lieutenant, how about if none of your men wore their helmets into battle? 'I don't have to if Lieutenant Baker doesn't?' Huh? What about that? This will not stand, Baker, this will not stand. You hear me?"

"Yes sir."

Directing the intelligence officer to give Baker a helmet, Sherman continued, "Now that you're in uniform, lieutenant, I've got other news for you. The 473rd's taking over the advance to the castle tomorrow. They need somebody who knows the terrain. You're volunteering to lead them."

"Yes sir."

"Report to their regimental commander at 0430 hours tomorrow. Now get the hell out of here and wear your god-damned helmet tomorrow or I'll bust you to buck private. Dismissed."

"And damn glad to be," Baker added silently.[21]

Early the following morning Baker met a company commander from the 473rd Infantry Regiment, one of the all-white units assigned to the Buffalo Division in the recent reorganization. As he briefed the commander, Baker retraced his steps along the path he had taken the previous day. Dead soldiers, Americans and Germans, littered the field. Baker relived the thumping of mortar shells, the *rat-a-tat-tat* of machine-gun fire, and the dying cries of his men. Not a single round was fired in anger as the Americans reached the deserted castle. Only the remnants of a heroic struggle remained.

And what of Captain John Runyon, who deserted Baker on the hill? To his credit, Runyon recommended Baker for the Distinguished Service Cross. But he also wrote a scathing report on the day's actions in which he praised the platoon's marksmanship but then callously added, "The ideal situation with colored troops would be to have noncommissioned and commissioned officers who would never become casualties. . . . In my opinion the average colored soldier loses all control of his mind when subjected to overhead mortars and artillery fire. . . . I also learned that the colored soldier is for some reason or other terrified to fight at night. His imagination and fear overcome his sense of judgment. The colored soldier wants to be led in battle, but usually it's a foolish officer who leads colored soldiers because invariably he loses one half of his men. For when frightened and unless a very careful check is made, there will always be a few men who will take off and disappear. Any excuse is good enough, and they will manufacture excuses."[22] This from a company commander who advised his immediate superior that nothing could be done to save Baker's platoon.

Vernon Baker's shooting war ended the day his platoon fought the Germans to a standstill outside Castle Aghinolfi. And he was glad. Too many lives had been lost; he had seen too much suffering, too much death. His platoon and his company slowly regrouped after the battle and joined the remainder of the Fifth Army in early April as they advanced methodically through the Gothic Line into the Po River valley of northern Italy. When the Germans surrendered on May 2, Baker could finally relax. Like most soldiers who have experienced the intensity of combat, he was haunted by the memories of the fight at Aghinolfi. Then, to his surprise, he received a summons to report to

General Almond at division headquarters outside Genoa. This time Baker brought his helmet.

Baker had no idea why he had been directed to report to division headquarters. He had heard rumors that he was to receive the Distinguished Service Cross, but he had dismissed them out of hand as it was not the army's practice to award such a high decoration to a black lieutenant. It was thus with a degree of trepidation that Baker entered Almond's spacious office. He reported smartly and remained at attention. Almond offered no congratulatory remarks, no "well done," no praise at all. "I want you to write me a report about what happened up on that hill. I want it day after tomorrow. Any questions?"

"No sir."

"Dismissed."

Baker stewed as he left the general's villa. Obviously the rumors about the DSC were wrong. As directed, he hastily completed his report, delivered it to headquarters, and returned to his platoon the next day. Nothing more was said, but three weeks later the rumors about Baker's DSC became truth. Division held the ceremony on the Fourth of July in Viareggio. It was to be Baker's last encounter with both Runyon and Almond in Italy. General Truscott presided. To Baker's chagrin, Runyon joined him on the reviewing stand when Baker received the Distinguished Service Cross and became the most highly decorated black soldier in the Mediterranean Theater. Both Almond and Runyon received awards of their own; Almond, oak leaf clusters on his Silver Star; Runyon, the Silver Star. True to form, Almond and Runyon assumed the positions of honor to the right of Baker even though protocol dictated that the soldier receiving the highest award stand at the right of the line. Baker fumed at the lack of recognition for the black soldiers who had fought so gallantly.

Vernon Baker remained in Italy on occupation duty until February 1947. He took six months' leave, then reverted to his former enlisted status as master sergeant when his commission expired and the army demobilized its wartime force. The next day he appeared at the recruiting station and embarked on a new career as an army photographer. Assigned to Fort Bragg with the 82nd Airborne Division, Baker volunteered for combat duty with the 11th Airborne Division in order to regain his commission. He made his last jump at age forty-eight but never returned to combat. He tried to go to Korea, but the army refused to send—and risk losing—a DSC recipient. Baker soldiered on, rising to command an all-white company.

After the Korean War, Baker returned to the Signal Corps and photography. Lacking a college degree, he also relinquished his commission and reverted to NCO status. Baker served an additional thirteen years at Fort Ord, California, and was first sergeant of a training company. Transferred to Germany, Baker again encountered racism as the army coped with the socio-economic problems of the Vietnam era. Rampant drug use compounded the disciplinary problems. For Baker it was enough. On August 31, 1968, Vernon Baker retired from the army after nearly three decades of distinguished service.

Race ahead nearly three additional decades. Vernon Baker, the warrior, had at last found peace in the Idaho wilderness, where he enjoyed his favorite pursuits—hunting and living the life of a loner. Then Baker received a telephone call that "unraveled his peace." The voice belonged to Daniel Gibran, a professor from Shaw University who was the chief researcher on a study commissioned by the secretary of the army to determine why no black World War II veteran received the Medal of Honor. The cases of all black DSC recipients were being reviewed, and Baker's name had surfaced. Astonishment, Baker's initial reaction, was followed by anger because "it was something that should have been done a long time ago." Yet here was an opportunity to recognize the black soldiers who had performed valiantly during the war. As a tribute to his fallen comrades, Baker reluctantly agreed to meet Gibran and a Pentagon officer named Colonel John Cash. Baker characterized the two days of interviews with them as the toughest two days in his life outside combat as they forced him to relive memories he preferred to forget. To this day, the faces of the nineteen soldiers who died in the attack of Castle Aghinolfi haunt Baker.

As a result of the Shaw study, the records of ten black Americans were reconsidered for the award of the Medal of Honor. All ten were reconfirmed as worthy of the DSC; seven were nominated for the Medal of Honor. All but Baker were deceased. In January 1997 Vernon Baker finally received the recognition for heroism that he truly deserved. In the name of Congress, the president of the United States presented the nation's highest military award for valor to Baker for his actions a half-century earlier. Lieutenant Baker's "fighting spirit," noted the president, "and daring leadership were an inspiration to his men and exemplify the highest traditions of the military service." Former chairman of the Joint Chiefs of Staff Colin L. Powell also acknowledged Baker's achievement, telling the audience that he had risen on the shoulders of men like Baker, men who continue to be national treasures. For Baker, the chairman's presence was a singular honor. When asked why he repeatedly put his life on the line in Italy, Baker replied, "This was the only country I had. I knew things would get better. I just felt it in my heart. We've come a long way. We've got a little ways to go, but we're going to get there. I mean, look at Colin Powell."

Like most Americans, I first heard the name Vernon Baker on the occasion of his receipt of the Medal of Honor. Official army magazines were quick to pick up the story and express their outrage that recognition of some of this nation's most heroic servicemen had been so long in coming. I wasn't satisfied. Determined to find out more about Baker, I followed a circuitous route to acquire his phone number and address. He was a hard man to get hold of, but finally I reached him. I asked, "May I fly to Idaho and spend a day?" This was early October 1998. "Sure," he answered, "but you better make it fast as snow will be here in a few weeks." That was enough for me. We agreed to meet for dinner at one of Baker's favorite restaurants in Saint Maries. I was early, but he and his wife, Heidy, arrived right on time. The next day I drove to his cabin in the middle of the Idaho wilderness. Twice I was nearly run off the road by ponderous logging trucks that paid my rental car no respect. Finally I stopped one driver and asked the whereabouts of Baker's cabin. "Not sure," the trucker replied, "but if you go up to a dirt road about a mile ahead, take a right and then a left, I think you'll find it." Within ten minutes I was standing at Baker's front door.

For the next two hours Vernon Baker painfully recalled his combat experience and the loss of his men. On two occasions he had to stop as memories of his fallen comrades brought tears to his eyes. We talked about the current U.S. Army and its readiness. We both chuckled about how so many things about the army remain the same: troops complaining about chow, the importance of delivering mail to the front, after-duty activities in local towns, and so on. Then, over a bowl of elk stew, we tied up the afternoon. Before leaving, I asked for a photograph of the two of us, two old soldiers with nearly sixty years' service between them. Heidy took the first picture, then Vernon said, "Let me wear the medal for the next one." To my astonishment, he had to retrieve the nation's highest award for valor from a briefcase hidden in a corner among his private papers and newspapers. That seemingly insignificant incident told me a lot about Vernon Baker the man. Baker had accepted the award not for himself, but for his fellow Buffalo Soldiers. Here was a genuine American hero.

Did he have a message for the young men and women about to assume positions of leadership in today's army, I inquired? "Yes," he replied. "Conduct your life and your career in such a manner so that you don't have to say, 'If only I had done . . .' Second, be honest with yourself and be honest with everyone else." When I asked him how he would like to be remembered, he answered simply, "That is a hard question. I think I would like to be remembered as a 'regular fellow.'"

To this day Vernon Baker wears his hero's mantle uncomfortably, but his deeds at Castle Aghinolfi, coupled with later decades of selfless service, serve as quiet inspiration to future generations and as stark testimony that heroism outlasts prejudice.

Colonel Paul Tibbets, who piloted the Enola Gay on the Hiroshima mission, August 6, 1945. This copy of the author's original photo was presented to the author by Tibbets. *Paul Tibbets private collection*

Captain Joe Dawson receiving the Distinguished Service Cross from General Eisenhower for his actions at Omaha Beach, July 2, 1944. *U.S. Army Signal Corps photograph*

Captain Dick Winters outside battalion headquarters in Holland, October 1944. On D-Day, Winters assumed command of Easy Company, 506th PIR, 101st Airborne Division, and led it in the destruction of a German artillery battery overlooking Utah Beach. *U.S. Army Signal Corps photograph*

Lieutenant Len Lomell, 2nd Ranger Battalion, who destroyed the German battery at Pointe du Hoc and led the assault on Hill 400 in the Huertgen Forest. *Leonard Lomell private collection*

Right: Sergeant Lyle J. Bouck Jr. in 1941. On December 16, 1944, First Lieutenant Bouck commanded the Intelligence and Reconnaissance Platoon of the 394th Infantry Regiment, 99th Infantry Division, and bore the brunt of the initial German attack at Lanzerath. *Lyle J. Bouck Jr. private collection*

Below: Major Charity (Adams) Earley and Lieutenant General John C. H. Lee review the 6888th Postal Battalion in Birmingham, England, February 15, 1945. Sport and General Press Agency, Ltd., London. *Photo in the Women's Memorial collection and in Charity Earley's personal collection*

First Lieutenant Vernon Baker, 11th Airborne Division, 1951. First Lieutenant Baker earned the Medal of Honor for conspicuous gallantry in action at Castle Aghinolfi, Italy, in April 1945. V*ernon Baker private collection*

CHAPTER 12

HOLD AT ALL COSTS: LYLE J. BOUCK AND THE BATTLE OF THE BULGE

We were scared GIs trying to do what we were trained to do and maybe live through it.

—*First Lieutenant Lyle J. Bouck Jr.*

SOMETIMES THE OUTCOME OF A BATTLE turns on the actions of a single soldier. Such was the case with a twenty-year-old lieutenant who found himself in the path of Obersturmbannführer Jochen Peiper's 1st SS Panzer Regiment on the first day of the Battle of the Bulge. First Lieutenant Lyle J. Bouck Jr. was the unlikeliest of heroes, but on that immortal day his Intelligence and Reconnaissance Platoon single-handedly impeded the German advance for a precious eighteen hours, long enough to disrupt the enemy timetable and allow Lieutenant General Courtney Hodges's First Army to scramble to meet Hitler's last gamble in the West.

Born in St. Louis, Missouri, on December 17, 1923, Bouck was the second child of middle-class parents. Life was tough during the Great Depression, and Bouck enlisted in the Missouri National Guard at the tender age of fourteen to get the one dollar per drill each week and to attend summer camp with its three square meals a day. As he later testified before Congress, Bouck realized that he was underage, of course, but "they never asked me. I was able to drill at the armory in St. Louis and get a drill night on Thursdays, and in 1938, that was a big deal." Within two years he was the unit supply sergeant, earning considerably more than his civilian buddies. Though he had arranged Lyle's initial enlistment, Bouck's father, himself a veteran of the National Guard, was not exactly pleased that his son had not yet finished high school. He secured a promise that Lyle would complete his secondary education at the completion of his enlistment, but fate intervened. The 35th Infantry Division, comprising Missouri, Kansas, and Nebraska National Guardsmen, was mobilized at Camp Joseph T. Robinson, north of Little Rock, Arkansas, and ordered to one year of federal duty on December 23, 1940. Just prior to the termination of that service, the Japanese attacked Pearl Harbor; the 35th Division remained on active duty for the duration of the war.

In the interim Bouck made a name for himself as a good soldier. Along with most of the army, he participated in the Texas-Louisiana maneuvers in the late summer of 1941. Still junior in rank, he took over the duties of transportation sergeant for the regimental Headquarters Company and performed extremely well. He was attending the transportation course at Fort Benning, Georgia, when he received the news about Pearl Harbor. Three days later he was pulled from class and directed to return to the 138th Infantry Regiment and prepare for overseas deployment. The regiment deployed first to California to repel a possible enemy attack on the American mainland, then to Fort Lewis, Washington, to defend the Pacific Northwest and to prepare to ship out to the Aleutian Islands. Bouck deployed as part of the advance party, but the Arctic climate hardly suited him. Now eighteen years old and eligible for Officer Candidate School (OCS), he volunteered to join the newly organized Parachute School, the Army Air Corps, or the Infantry OCS in an effort to secure a better future and leave the frigid temperatures behind.[1]

The OCS Board results arrived first, and Bouck returned to Fort Benning in May to begin an intensive four-month training program. In his first day at the "Home of the Infantry," Bouck was ordered by the company tactical officer to drill the platoon. Falling back on his National Guard experience, Bouck performed reasonably well, attracting the attention of his classmates and the chain of command. The assessment of the men in his platoon was that several other soldiers were sharper than he, particularly the former first sergeants, but Bouck certainly knew basic soldier skills. Bouck absorbed the curriculum easily and graduated fourth in his OCS class of fifty-seven on August 26, 1942. As it was the policy at Fort Benning to keep the top ten graduates at the post to instruct future classes, Second Lieutenant Bouck soon found himself assigned to the Tactics Department, where his primary responsibility was to instruct OCS classes in small-unit defensive tactics. For the next year he served as a tactical officer before attending the Infantry Officer Advance Course from

December 1943 to February 1944. Most of the class consisted of field-grade officers, but there were a few general officers as well.

With his tour at Benning at an end, Bouck was sent to Fort Hood, Texas, where he helped organize a Basic Infantry Replacement Training Center. The commanding officer of the center, a brigadier general "bucking for his second star," created such a harsh command climate—twenty-hour days and outrageous orders—that Bouck and three other lieutenants volunteered to transfer to a unit preparing for combat. The next day, the four lieutenants departed for the 99th Division at Camp Maxey near Paris, Texas. Bouck joined the 394th Infantry Regiment, first as a rifle platoon leader and then as a weapons platoon leader, before becoming a company executive officer. In a subsequent corps-level operation, the regiment's Intelligence and Reconnaissance (I&R) Platoon performed so unsatisfactorily that the regimental commander was relieved. The new commanding officer brought along Captain Robert L. Kriz, a wounded veteran who had been awarded a Silver Star for his deeds with the 9th Infantry Division in North Africa, to reorganize the I&R Platoon.

One of Kriz's first acts was to select Bouck, "an extremely aggressive and intelligent young man," he thought, and "very clean cut," to command the platoon. Kriz was impressed to learn that the young officer had received more army education than many other lieutenants. Bouck also possessed the mental and physical capabilities to command this group of extremely intelligent, healthy, athletic individuals. The fortuitous coupling of Kriz and Bouck proved to be a match made in heaven. Kriz and Bouck together examined the records of the men in the regiment in order to select soldiers with extremely high IQ scores, athletic backgrounds, and expert rifleman skills; they also looked for ethnic diversity and for individuals with "outdoors experience." They initially selected about 135 soldiers and interviewed them. Only 32 men, including 2 from the original I&R Platoon, made the cut.

Kriz outlined a condensed training schedule and turned Bouck and his platoon sergeant, Technical Sergeant William Slape, loose. Slape was a product of the "old army," a rough-talking, stern disciplinarian who commanded respect from seniors and subordinates alike. Kriz checked on Bouck daily and critiqued him constantly. Within weeks Bouck had molded his men into a cohesive team that exceeded his initial expectations. Kriz agreed, stating that Bouck's training program had produced one of the sharpest platoons he had ever had the privilege of knowing.

By mid-September 1944 the platoon was ready for combat. Departing Camp Maxey, the regiment moved to Camp Miles Standish in Boston and boarded the USS *Excelsior* for the transatlantic crossing. Sixteen days aboard the craft were enough to convince Bouck and his platoon that life in the infantry was infinitely superior to maritime service. Boarding LSTs at Southhampton in late October, the 394th Regiment crossed the English Channel and arrived at Le Havre in early November. Mid-month found the men in the Ardennes, where the 394th received orders to relieve the 60th Regiment, 9th Infantry Division—Kriz's old unit from North Africa. For the next several weeks the I&R Platoon was used for the type of missions for which it was specifically trained: reconnaissance, establishing and maintaining regimental observation and listening posts, and gathering information. Kriz did not use the platoon for combat raids because the men had not been trained for missions that involved direct combat. As platoon leader, Bouck led numerous patrols, earning the coveted Combat Infantry Badge in the process.

On December 10 Bouck received a new mission when Kriz ordered him to move the platoon to the edge of a forest. The new site was on a hill overlooking a pasture about 150 yards northwest of Lanzerath, a small village about 300 yards south of a vital road junction. The left fork of the road ran westward to Buchholz Station, the right fork to Losheimergraben. Running northwest from Losheimergraben was the principal road in the area—and the best route between Sepp Dietrich's 6th Panzer Army and the Belgian town of Liège.[2] Lanzerath itself consisted of some eleven small wooden houses that were useless as protection against weapons fire of any sort.[3] Kriz's orders to Bouck were clear: "Occupy this prepared foxhole position—improve the position—you are to be the eyes and ears on this boundary of the regiment, division and the corps. Maintain contact with Task Force 'X' located in the little village down this hill to our right front."[4]

Bouck brought forward twenty men and immediately began improving the platoon's defensive position. The chosen site was on the German-Belgian border opposite the Siegfried Line in the Ardennes Forest. The men's first task was to construct a ten-foot-by-ten-foot hut, complete with overhead cover, to serve as a refuge from the freezing temperatures, an area to dry wet clothing, and a spot to get some sleep on a rotating basis. It snowed heavily on the thirteenth, and on the next day Bouck's platoon endured the heaviest snow to date. Improving the fighting positions was difficult, but here the months of intense training and the platoon leader's own experience from Fort Benning paid huge dividends. To augment the firepower of the platoon, Bouck obtained four additional carbines, one Browning automatic rifle, one light machine gun, and one .50-caliber machine gun mounted on a jeep, which he placed in defilade with the primary mission to fire on the road entering Lanzerath from the south.

The reinforced platoon now occupied what Bouck termed an ideal "Fort Benning school solution" position: perfect observation, flanks protected by dense underbrush and a deep ravine, clear fields of fire for the crew and automatic weapons, and an obstacle to the front. That obstacle was a farm fence that bisected the pasture to the platoon's immediate front. Two platoon members improvised a claymore mine by attaching hand grenades that could be detonated by wires running back to the defensive position. Thus was the stage set for Bouck's rendezvous with destiny. With one soldier confined to the hospital and two working at regiment with Kriz, Bouck had only seventeen men under his direct command on the hill overlooking Lanzerath when the Germans struck in force on the morning of December 16.

Sometime before dawn, German artillery flashes lit up the eastern sky. Bouck and his men were uneasy with the intensity of the bombardment. As the rolling barrage passed over the I&R Platoon's foxholes, the men noticed the swift withdrawal of the tank destroyers of the 14th Cavalry Group that had previously occupied their front. William James Tsakanikas (Sak), the most aggressive soldier in the platoon and the only soldier younger than Bouck, muttered, "If they can't sign off on the phone, they might at least wave goodbye as they leave." Bouck was a bit more sympathetic. "If we didn't have any more cover than those guys down in Lanzerath, we'd be pulling out too." Next Bouck did what he had been instructed to do. He immediately reported the action and requested instructions. Kriz's voice was on the other end of the line, and he directed Bouck to send a patrol to Lanzerath and report any additional enemy activity.

Bouck selected Private First Class John Creger, Slape, and Tsakanikas to accompany him, and the men scampered down the slope and entered Lanzerath. They quickly identified the building that offered the best observation point to view the surrounding countryside. Scrambling up the stairs to the second floor, they encountered a large man in civilian clothes sitting next to an open window and talking on a telephone. Sak readied his weapon, but Bouck screamed, "Let him go. This isn't how we do things. Besides we don't have room for prisoners. He can't cause any more trouble now." Bouck then moved to the window and reconnoitered the area around the town. The sight he saw would have unnerved many officers with more combat experience than Bouck. A long column of German troops was emerging from Losheim and moving in the direction of Lanzerath. Bouck had seen enough. Taking Sak with him, Bouck instructed

Slape and Creger to stay put until they were certain of the enemy's direction of march. As soon as he returned to his entrenched position he called headquarters to report the large number of Germans to his front. The voice at the end of the line was incredulous. Bouck blew up. "Don't tell me what I don't see! I have twenty-twenty vision. Bring down some artillery, all the artillery you can, on the road south of Lanzerath. There's a Kraut column coming up from that direction."[5] To the platoon leader's chagrin, no artillery followed.

Just then Bouck received an urgent call from Slape and Creger: "The Krauts are already downstairs. What shall we do?" Bouck immediately prepared a rescue mission, sending McGehee, Silvola, and Robinson to find Slape and Creger. No sooner had they departed than Slape and Creger appeared over the ridge. The three soldiers Bouck had dispatched to rescue them were soon pinned down by enemy fire. The trio escaped from Lanzerath once the firefight started, but all were subsequently captured as they attempted to reach the 1st Battalion at Losheimergraben.

The fate of the three rescuers was the last thing on Bouck's mind just then. Realizing the enemy would attack immediately once they ascertained the platoon's precise location, Bouck ordered the platoon to hold their fire until he gave the signal. Bouck later remembered his own heart pounding and sweat dripping from his forehead, even though it was the middle of December. He knew his men had itchy trigger fingers, but Bouck somehow convinced them to let the initial element pass by and wait for the main body. Soon the main column appeared, and three officers halted immediately to the front of the American position. As the GIs were about to commence fire, a young blond girl approached the German officers, pointed in a direction of the road junction, and then scurried inside the adjacent building. With the opportunity for ambush gone, Bouck's men opened fire at his command, pinning down the lead enemy battalion, which proved to be from the 3rd Fallschirmjaeger Division's 9th Fallschirmjaeger Regiment.

The intense fire continued for several hours, but the American line held. With no indirect fire support and snow so deep that they could hardly move, wave after wave of the Germans were cut to pieces. Private First Class Risto Milosevich fired his .30-caliber machine gun until the barrel was bright red. He later compared the platoon's defense to shooting clay ducks at the amusement park. It was unadulterated slaughter as the entrenched GIs mowed down the assaulting force. Historian Stephen Rusiecki likens the scene to a medieval battlefield littered by scores of bodies after a tremendous battle between phalanx formations.[6]

Again Bouck requested instructions from regiment. The reply was clear: Hold at all costs. Confident that he could maintain his position against the enemy's unimaginative attacks, Bouck made the critical decision that only a commander can make on a battlefield. He would stay. As the day wore on, however, he grew increasingly doubtful that his men would survive the next assault. In his own words, "An aura of modified shock surrounded me; the training gears meshed and instinct guided reaction." Rather than concentrate on what the future might bring, Bouck supervised the redistribution of ammunition and assessed the morning's events. No doubt about it; the platoon's situation was grim, and no reinforcements were forthcoming. Regiment merely acknowledged his transmissions and urged him to "hang on."

Around noon, a white flag appeared as the German commander requested a short truce to withdraw his wounded. Bouck complied, and the evacuation of the wounded lasted more than an hour. In the meantime, Bouck readied his men for another assault. It wasn't long in coming. At approximately 1400 the Germans attacked up the snow-covered hill, and this time they made it as far as the fence before they were mercilessly cut down by the I&R Platoon. With so many German soldiers bunched in front of them, it was virtually impossible for the men to miss. Private First Class Louis Kalil, who had been knocked unconscious earlier in the day by shell fragments from a rifle grenade and had sustained a fractured jaw, fired his M-1 until his ammunition was all but expended. The field to the platoon's front was now strewn with enemy bodies twisting in agony on the blood-covered snow.

As the battle continued unabated, Milosevich, now teamed with platoon sergeant Slape, delivered his own brand of destruction on the enemy. As German mortars forced most of the I&R men back into their foxholes, Milosevich noticed what he thought was a German medic administering aid to a fallen comrade. The man appeared to be speaking to the wounded man, but he looked up at the American position in short quick glances. Just then a barrage of mortar rounds descended on the American defenses.

"Sarge, get my rifle, behind you," screamed Milosevich.

"What for?" inquired Slape.

"I'm going to get that Kraut out there about 30 yards away on the left."

"Forget him!" said Slape. "There are too many coming up the front."

"He's the one calling in the mortars," said Milosevich. "He's got a radio and he's pretending to be a medic."

"Why, that son of a bitch," hollered Slape.

Grabbing Milosevich's M-1, Slape took careful aim and pulled the trigger. The German lurched backward, arms flailing, falling face up in the snow.

"That's that," exclaimed Slape.[7]

Tsakanikas, who was positioned next to the platoon leader, was amazed at the Germans' lack of ingenuity. "Whoever's ordering that attack must be frantic," he said to Bouck. "Nobody in his right mind would send troops into something like this without more fire support." He kept firing his M-1, then dashed behind the jeep, where Slape was firing the .50-caliber. As the Germans got closer, Sak continued to cut them down with his M-1. Later he would discover that the enemy battalion was a reconstituted force consisting of rear-echelon troops, and would express grief and anger at having to shoot and kill so many enemy soldiers, most of whom were teenage boys. "I had to do it. It was either them or us."

Aware that ammunition was running low, Bouck again requested permission to withdraw, but the answer from the regiment remained the same. Just then a direct hit from an automatic weapon destroyed the radio transmitter in his left hand while he was talking to First Lieutenant Ed Buenger, the assistant S-2 at regimental headquarters, and communication with the rear ceased. Realizing that the end was near, Bouck turned to Tsakanikas and said, "I want you to take the men who want to go and get out."

"Are you coming?"

"No," Bouck responded. "I have orders to hold at all costs. I'm staying."

"Like hell! You're coming with us or we'll all stay."

By now it was late afternoon and the I&R Platoon had repelled three attacks, inflicting tremendous casualties on the enemy. Darkness obscured the next and final German assault, this time by small teams advancing on Bouck's flanks. Soon the enemy was among the platoon's foxholes. Looking behind his own position, Bouck fired his final magazine at the two closest Germans, killing them both. He and Tsakanikas had expended their last rounds and were now totally defenseless. Just then an enemy soldier put his burp gun in Bouck and Sak's foxhole and yelled, "How many you? How many you?" Bouck didn't speak much German, but he responded, "Zwei, zwei." With that the enemy fired a burst and shouted, "How many you now?" Bouck pushed Tsakanikas aside as the German fired, but too late. The entire right side of Sak's face exploded; his right eyeball hung limply in the cavern where his cheek had been. As the two

Americans were pulled from the foxhole, one German soldier caught a glimpse of Tsakanikas. "Mein Gott! Mein Gott!" he exclaimed.

A German noncommissioned officer demanded to know who the American commandant was. Bouck identified himself, and the man asked his prisoner why his men were still firing. Bouck answered that his own men were out of ammunition and any firing had to be German in origin. Just then Bouck suffered his first wound of the day when a bullet pierced his leg. Before long almost the entire I&R Platoon had become casualties. One man had been killed and all the others except four were wounded. There was no surrender; the men were simply overpowered.

As the Germans mopped up the remainder of the platoon, Bouck was overwhelmed by guilt; his highly trained and capable unit had been destroyed. Depressed and angry that he had not withdrawn his men while there was still a chance to escape, Bouck considered himself a failure. Only later did he learn the magnitude of what they and he had accomplished. In assessing the impact of Bouck's I&R Platoon, historian John Eisenhower notes, "The action of the I&R Platoon, 394th Infantry was remarkable for the contribution that a handful of men was able to make on December 16." With less than twenty men Bouck had inflicted perhaps four hundred to five hundred casualties and had held up the German advance for nearly eighteen hours.[8] Other units in the 99th Division performed equally heroically, but elsewhere across the broad Allied front the Germans achieved spectacular success.

Bouck attributed the platoon's success to the quality of his men, all of whom were expert marksmen. The excellent defensive terrain and the supplemental weapons his platoon had acquired also contributed to the massive casualties the platoon inflicted on the enemy. The tremendous firepower sounded like a "battalion in the attack demonstration at Fort Benning," Bouck later recalled. Coupled with superior camouflage that created extremely effective deception, the intense fire from the platoon's position produced an extraordinarily high number of casualties. Nor, as Sak had noted, were the enemy tactics at all imaginative. Throughout the Battle of the Bulge, the Germans frequently attacked in waves. Their inferior training at this stage in the European war made more sophisticated tactics impossible. It was sheer madness to attack a fortified position across an open field with little indirect fire support, and the Germans paid a high price for their folly.

There was an additional factor that the platoon leader downplayed when the platoon's accomplishments were discussed, and that was his personal role. Units in combat reflect their commanding officers, and the I&R Platoon had one of the best in Lyle Bouck. Given the almost cavalier attitude that characterized the Allied forces as they settled in on a seemingly quiet part of the line, Bouck could have easily manned a simple outpost line. No one had forecast a major offensive. Rather than lowering his personal standards, however, Bouck demanded that the platoon construct a prepared defensive position with interlocking fire. He was relentless in preparing for the worst that might befall his platoon. It is an officer's responsibility to maintain the highest possible standard of preparation for combat, and Bouck did just that. It was this preparation that permitted the platoon to survive against an enemy attacking in overwhelming numbers.

By late afternoon an eerie calm blanketed the battlefield above Lanzerath. Under escort Bouck helped the injured Tsakanikas down the hill to the Café Scholzen, where the American wounded were being consolidated. En route an enemy soldier screamed in his ear, "Saint-Lô? Saint-Lô?" wanting to know if Bouck had been at the battle where the 3rd Fallschirmjaeger Division had suffered horrendous casualties the preceding July.

"Nein, nein!" Bouck replied, but the soldier put his rifle in Bouck's back and pulled the trigger anyway. To this day Bouck is unsure whether the gun was empty or misfired. What he does remember is walking over "lots of dead figures" in the snow. As for the badly wounded Tsakanikas, he leaned on Bouck's shoulder and whispered, "Let's take them." Discretion being the better part of valor, Bouck declined.

The saga of Lyle Bouck does not end with his capture on the ridge outside Lanzerath. As Bouck and Tsakanikas lay on the floor inside the Café Scholzen, the remainder of the platoon streamed in. German doctors did the best they could to treat the wounded, but many of the men were in very bad shape. Other officers attempted to interrogate the prisoners, but no information was forthcoming. Then one enemy officer whispered in Sak's ear, "*Ami*, you and your comrades are brave men." It was small comfort to Tsakanikas but a fitting tribute to the fallen heroes of the 394th Regiment's I&R Platoon.

Over the course of the evening Bouck took stock of what was occurring around him. German officers repeatedly interrogated him, and one took his OCS ring. Outside he could hear the rumbling of numerous tank formations passing through Lanzerath. One of the interrogators informed him that the tanks were going all the way to Paris and Antwerp, but told him not to worry because the Germans "intended to be good to the American people" as soon as the war was over. As the sound of battle echoed outside the café, all he could think about was his failure. If he had withdrawn when he had the opportunity, his men would have reached American lines with minimal casualties. His refusal to do so haunts him still. Yet, he did what he had been trained to do, and he accepted the consequences.

As he reflected on the day's carnage, Bouck sighted a cuckoo clock on the café wall. His mind conjured up images from his youth in St. Louis. When he was only thirteen years old, his Aunt Mildred, a gentle woman who studied horoscopes, visited the family and examined his palm. She told her nephew that if he reached twenty-one, he would have a very productive life. At midnight the clock struck twelve, marking that momentous milestone. With a sudden rush of adrenaline, Bouck reasoned that there wasn't a damn thing the Germans could do to him now that he had reached his twenty-first birthday. "What a hell of a way to become a man," he mumbled under his breath.

Late that evening several senior German officers entered the café, which was now being used as a command post. One hot-tempered commander, whom Bouck later identified as Peiper, demanded to know the enemy strength in the area. Peiper himself described the scene in a postwar interview:

> There [Lanzerath] I had a conference with the commanding officer of the parachute regiment. I asked him for all the information that he had on the enemy situation. His answer was that the woods were heavily fortified, and that scattered fire from prepared pill-boxes, plus mines in the road, were holding up his advance. He told me that it was impossible to attack under these circumstances. I asked him if he had personally reconnoitered the American positions in the woods, and he replied that he had averred the information from one of his battalion commanders. I asked the battalion commander, and he said that he had got the information from a Hauptman [captain] in his battalion. I called the Hauptman, and he averred that he had not personally seen the American advances, but it had been "reported to him."[9]

Holding up a lantern, Peiper examined a map pinned to the wall by several bayonets. Another officer informed Peiper that the enemy strength consisted of at least a regiment, an obvious overstatement, but testimony to Bouck's superb defense. Growing increasingly irritated that no one had a grasp of the tactical situation, Peiper demanded a battalion of troops that he personally intended to lead in the attack. Quickly organizing another assault, Peiper ordered his troops to deploy and attacked at 0400 the following morning. Meeting no opposition, the German column advanced on the 394th Regiment's rest area at Honsfeld and captured a large American contingent.

Bouck lay wounded on the café floor while Peiper prepared his attack. The next morning, December 17, the captors assembled their prisoners and prepared to send them to POW camps throughout Germany. Bouck was allowed to talk to Sak and his other wounded men before leaving. He told Tsakanikas that the Germans were evacuating him to a field hospital. "I told Sak that if he was alive, squeeze my hand." Tsakanikas couldn't speak, Bouck recalled, but "I felt his hand clench my fingers. I then told him when the war is over, we will get together again. I informed him that I was putting his Bible and the picture of his sweetheart, Chloe, which he always carried, into his pocket." Then I said, "I'll say a prayer for you. I have to go now."

The journey to the various camps was long and tortuous. At first the seventy-two American prisoners were crammed into a single railroad car and given no food or water for days on end. On December 23 they endured bombing by the Royal Air Force and the American 8th Air Force at Limburg, Germany. Seven in Bouck's car had died by Christmas; the remainder were so mentally and physically exhausted that they were merely going through the motions of survival. Finally, in late January while the prisoners were in Nürnburg, the Germans segregated them and loaded them into new cars, this time only thirty to a car. Bouck's ultimate destination was Hammelburg, an old training base for infantry officers. There the men were assigned to a flat-roofed stucco structure next to a riding stable, fifty men to a room. Upon entry to the compound each man received a burlap sack, a blanket, a bowl, a cup, and a spoon. Built for three hundred captives, the Hammelburg camp, designated Stalag XIII D, soon housed fifteen hundred officers.

Bouck remained at Hammelburg until March 27, when an expedition from the 4th Armored Division, commanded by Captain Abe Baum, was dispatched to liberate the prisoners. Baum was surprised at the number of captives and informed the men that he could take only a small number on his tanks. At dusk on the twenty-seventh Baum signaled his unit to advance, but the column immediately encountered German infantry. The Hammelburg raid proved a disaster. Baum and his entire command were captured and along with the former captives were returned to the compound. Attempting to escape on foot, Bouck and a fellow lieutenant from Providence, Rhode Island, by the name of Matthew Reid were soon recaptured, with Bouck sustaining another wound in the left knee. They were once again returned to Hammelburg, then taken to Nürnburg, and finally to Moosburg, a town about twenty miles east of Munich. There they remained until April 29, when elements from the 14th Armored Division liberated them. Bouck had weighed 185 pounds when he was captured, but his flesh now hung loosely on a 114-pound frame.

Grateful to see his liberators, Bouck noticed that one of the men wore the patch of the 99th Division, his old unit. He quickly scratched a short message and a map on the back of a dirt-covered K-ration box and asked the soldier to give it to Major Kriz if he was still with the 394th headquarters. The missive simply read: "Kriz 394 Bouck"; the map marked the POW compound's location with an X. On the evening of the twenty-ninth, Bouck was informed that someone was calling for him. Sure enough, it was Bob Kriz with a jeep towing a trailer. Kriz, now a lieutenant colonel and a battalion commander in the 394th Regiment, was shocked by Bouck's appearance. The lieutenant was "a skeleton of his former self," Kriz remembered years later. Taking Bouck to his command post, Kriz offered him chicken soup, but the lieutenant vomited uncontrollably. Major Gillespie, the regimental surgeon, was soon on the scene and immediately diagnosed a severe case of hepatitis.

Evacuated to a field hospital, Bouck found himself at Reims, where he remained until the war ended the next week. Next transferred to a hospital in Paris, Bouck began the slow road to recovery. In a ward with other hepatitis patients, he was nursed on a fat-free diet and given new uniforms. For the first time since his release, he felt that it would all be OK. In mid-June he was driven by ambulance to Orly Airport, where he boarded a DC-8 for the return to the United States. Eventually he reached O'Reilly General Hospital in Springfield, Missouri, where his recuperation continued. The war was finally over for Lyle J. Bouck, but the saga of the I&R Platoon would be replayed decades later.

Still in the army, Lyle returned to St. Louis for recruiting duty, and after "staying free almost a year" married his sweetheart, Lucy. In subsequent years he and Lucy raised a fine family of three sons and two daughters. Bouck had decided to apply for a regular army commission and was contemplating applying to West Point when an incident soured him on the postwar army. At that time one could accrue up to 120 days of leave. A new army regulation changed this policy, allowing only 60 days, but a soldier could apply for back pay for any days over 60 up to 120. Since Bouck had in excess of 120 days of accrued leave, he applied for 60 days' pay. When the payment arrived from Fifth Army Headquarters in Chicago, it was for $120—an enlisted man's pay and far less than he had expected. Angered that the pay was not based on his rank at the time he accrued the leave, Bouck called the finance officer at Fifth Army Headquarters. Obtaining no satisfaction, he cashed the check and tore up his application for a regular commission.[10]

Bouck soon put the war behind him and decided on another career. After obtaining a high school equivalency diploma, he entered Missouri Chiropractor College on the GI Bill in January 1947 and graduated two years later. He remained in private practice until 1997 and became an active participant in community affairs. As his community expanded, he helped start a Lion's Club and served as a charter member and president. He also played an advisory role with the Veterans Administration and initiated a lengthy correspondence with Congressman Richard A. Gephardt on a variety of issues involving St. Louis. Civic awards followed, including the DAR Medal of Honor from the Webster Groves Chapter of the Daughters of the American Revolution in spring 2002. The selection committee was searching for someone who epitomized the qualities of "Leadership, Trustworthiness, Patriotism, and Service." Bouck fit the bill and then some.

By the mid-1960s, now an established member of his community, Bouck thought that his platoon's exploits on that mid-December day in 1944 were long forgotten. The official history of the Battle of the Bulge published by the U.S. Army in 1965 seemed to confirm that; there was only a single mention of the Intelligence and Reconnaissance Platoon of the 394th Infantry Regiment, 99th Division. The incomplete and inaccurate account prompted a letter from William Tsakanikas, now William James, urging Bouck to contact members of the U.S. Senate to secure proper recognition for the platoon. James wrote:

> Bouck—We were responsible for blunting the main spearhead of the whole German offensive for that whole first 24-hour period. However, you would never know it without having been there and then reading the account from the American position and the German position.
>
> Listen Bouck, I would like to see our unit cited, but more importantly, I want the world to know, but for your calm determination, it could have been another story. Remember when you used to say, "F—— the torpedoes, straight ahead." What are your orders this time?[11]

Somewhat hesitant to reopen old wounds, Bouck balked, rationalizing that the men of his platoon hadn't done anything special. They were simply a bunch of scared young GIs trying to do what they were trained to do and maybe live through it. Thousands of other GIs had done much the same thing;

why talk about it, why even tell anyone at this late date? The opportunity to survive, come home, and marry and raise a family was reward enough for Bouck. James, however, wasn't buying it. The platoon deserved recognition for what they had accomplished on December 16. Ironically, in June 1966 a Silver Star—completely unsolicited—arrived in Bouck's mailbox. To his knowledge, no other soldier in his unit had received an award for the action on December 16. Angered by that injustice, Bouck finally took up the cause for his platoon.

At about the same time he received James's letter Bouck was contacted by John S. D. Eisenhower, son of the former supreme commander and president of the United States, who was researching the battle for his history of the Ardennes campaign. When Eisenhower published *The Bitter Woods* in 1969, the exploits of the platoon and the names of its members finally came into the public eye. Eisenhower, now U.S. ambassador to Belgium, hosted Bouck and several members of the platoon on a return visit to Lanzerath in December 1969. Also present were several of their former adversaries. The event was festive in the true spirit of national reconciliation. As the party returned to Bastogne in the twilight, a man named Vince Kuhlbach put his arm on Lyle's shoulder and the two shared a poignant moment. "Just as it was getting dark," Kuhlbach said, "our troops were helping the wounded. Do you remember someone asking you, 'Who is the commandant?' That was me." Twenty-five years after the battle, Bouck and Kuhlbach shook hands, not as adversaries but as friends.

The belated recognition brought a degree of relief to William James, who lived a prosperous life until he died from complications following his thirty-seventh operation on June 27, 1977. Unfortunately, he did not live to witness the final tribute to his former comrades. Following an unsuccessful campaign by columnist Jack Anderson to authorize the president to award the Medal of Honor posthumously to William James Tsakanikas for bravery above and beyond the call of duty on December 16, 1944, the Department of the Army belatedly hosted a World War II Valor Awards Ceremony at Fort Myer, Virginia, on October 26, 1981, to honor the men of the I&R Platoon.[12] Secretary of the Army John O. Marsh Jr. served as the ceremony's host. Fourteen members of the original platoon, including Lyle Bouck, were present. On a clear autumn afternoon thirty-seven years after they repelled three separate enemy assaults, the Intelligence and Reconnaissance Platoon, 394th Infantry Regiment, 99th Division became the most decorated platoon for a single day's action in the army's history. Four members—Bouck, platoon sergeant Slape, Milosevich, and Tsakanikas—received the Distinguished Service Cross, the nation's second highest award for valor. Corporals Aubrey P. McGehee Jr. and John B. Creger and Privates First Class James R. Silvola, Louis J. Kalil, and Jordan H. Robinson received the Silver Star; nine others were awarded the Bronze Star with Valor Device. All received the Presidential Unit Citation, which read:

> The Intelligence and Reconnaissance Platoon, 394th Infantry Regiment, 99th Infantry Division, distinguished itself by extraordinary heroism in action against enemy forces on 16 December 1944 near Lanzerath, Belgium. The German Ardennes Offensive that began the Battle of the Bulge was directed initially against a small sector defended by the Intelligence and Reconnaissance Platoon. Following a two-hour artillery barrage, enemy forces of at least battalion strength launched three separate frontal attacks against the small Intelligence and Reconnaissance Platoon of 18 men. Each attack was successfully repelled by the platoon. The platoon position was becoming untenable as casualties mounted and ammunition was nearly exhausted. Plans were made to break contact with the enemy and withdraw under cover of darkness. Before this could be accomplished, a fourth enemy attack finally overran the position and the platoon was captured at bayonet point. Although greatly outnumbered, through numerous feats of valor and an aggressive and deceptive defense of their position, the platoon inflicted heavy casualties on the enemy forces and successfully delayed for nearly 24 hours a major spearhead of the attacking German forces. Their valorous actions provided crucial time for other American forces to prepare to defend against the massive German offensive. The extraordinary gallantry, determination and esprit de corps of the Intelligence and Reconnaissance Platoon in close combat against a numerically superior enemy force are in keeping with the highest traditions of the United States Army and reflect great credit upon the Unit and the Armed Forces of the United States.

On November 23, 1981, Congressman Gephardt addressed the Speaker of the U.S. House of Representatives and respectfully requested that the heartfelt gratitude of Congress be added to that of the president and the American people for Bouck's heroic men.[13] Bouck used the occasion to write a short note to William James's son, telling him, "I am sure that the experience that happened to your father and me during these dark days and moments have caused us to be better citizens. . . . Always look up to your father with complete respect . . . and add the advantage of his experience to the things you learn from others."

I first met Lyle Bouck in New Orleans at a conference commemorating the fiftieth anniversary of D-Day in 1995, held by Stephen E. Ambrose and the Eisenhower Center. I was struck by Bouck's refusal to accept any credit for his platoon's success and his acknowledgment that any tribute to the I&R Platoon rightfully belonged to the soldiers, not to him. Bouck cited the unflinching courage, discipline, and devotion to duty displayed by his platoon in the face of overwhelming odds as representative of the highest traditions of the military service. Many leaders from World War II have said the same thing, but Bouck's comments seemed more genuine than most.

During a break between sessions I introduced myself and inquired if he would consider visiting the Military Academy to address the Corps of Cadets. He graciously consented and over the course of the next four years made annual pilgrimages to West Point to share his combat experiences with the cadets. His message was always the same: take care of your men and train them in the fundamental soldier skills necessary to survive in the crucible of war. He emphasized the unglamorous yet extremely critical aspects of basic training such as the care and cleaning of equipment. He spoke of courage under fire, citing Lou Kalil and Bill Tsakanikas. Never once did he mention his personal courage and heroism under fire or his own contribution to the platoon's success.

When one cadet asked if it had all been worthwhile, Bouck spoke of a visit he and several members of the I&R Platoon had made to Lanzerath in 1991. Bouck had examined the crumbling ruins of his foxhole. Closing his eyes, he had relived December 16 in its entirety for the first time. As goosebumps appeared on his arms, he knew that part of him would always remain in that hole. After dedicating a monument to the 99th Infantry Division, the old soldiers witnessed expressions of gratitude from the proud people of Belgium. Yes. It had been worthwhile.

In 1998 I paid Bouck a final visit at his home in St. Louis. He and Lucy met me at the airport and we spent an enjoyable two days together. On entering his home, I was shown to my room. Above the door was a sign that read: "VIP Quarters for COL Kingseed." He enjoyed a good laugh at my reaction. Then we got down to serious business, discussing combat leadership, his time in the POW camp, and the challenge of leading soldiers facing insurmountable odds. After fifty-plus years he could vividly recall the name of every soldier in his platoon, their individual strengths and weaknesses, and what each soldier did in civilian life after the war. Here was an officer in every sense of the word, one who knew his men inside and out.

I asked if he had any regrets, and he responded that he wished he had withdrawn his men when it became evident that the I&R Platoon would not be reinforced and that they could no longer hold their position. His orders were to hold, though, and hold he did. He realized that he and his men faced death, but he also knew that if they could impede the enemy advance for a few hours, headquarters might be able to organize a counterattack. Fate dictated otherwise, but in no way did the subsequent American withdrawal detract from the courage and determination of Bouck's platoon. Other questions followed and Bouck patiently answered each of my inquiries.

To my final question, "How would you like to be remembered?" he responded: "As a fair guy!" That simple expression says more about Lyle J. Bouck the man and the courage of America's citizen-soldiers than all the volumes written on the U.S. Army's greatest battle in World War II.

CHAPTER 13

BAND OF BROTHERS: DICK WINTERS AND THE MEN OF EASY COMPANY

I have found out just what is essential and what isn't in life. . . .
That I was alive each night was the big thing, the only thing.
And the only thing you ask for the future is that you'll be alive
tomorrow morning and be able to live through the next day. . . .
You can't be bothered or burdened with inessentials,
not when battle is the payoff.

—Captain Dick Winters

DICK WINTERS'S PATH TOWARD WAR mirrored that of millions of other American citizen-soldiers who fought World War II. Born in Lancaster, Pennsylvania, on January 21, 1918, Winters spent his formative years in eastern Pennsylvania. His early heroes were Babe Ruth and Milton S. Hershey, the founder of a school for boys in the town that now bears his name. After graduating as a business major from Franklin and Marshall College in June 1941, Winters worked for Edison Electric, digging holes for telephone poles, before volunteering for military service to escape the draft. His intent was to spend the mandatory one year in the army and then return to civilian life and pursue a private career. Following his induction in August, he spent his basic combat training at Camp Croft, South Carolina. He was still stationed there on December 7, 1941. Realizing that he would be in the army for a good deal longer than his one-year enlistment, Winters applied for Officer Candidate School (OCS). Rejecting an offer to attend the Armor OCS at Fort Knox, he selected the Infantry School because he already had seven months of training in that branch.

April 1942 found Winters at Fort Benning, Georgia, where he rapidly adapted to life as an officer candidate. Within a week he discovered an interest in airborne training. Of all the troops he had seen since his enlistment, the airborne troopers were the best-looking bunch. They were "hard, lean, bronzed, and tough," he later recalled, and "when they walked down the street, they were a proud and cocky bunch."[1] The airborne training appeared to be "interesting work," and the physical training was not at all intimidating to Winters, who stood six feet tall and weighed 177 pounds. Moreover, he was accustomed to lots of running and outdoor activity. And with the additional jump pay he could help to pay off the mortgage on his family's house. Although his parents were very much against the idea of him joining such a dangerous unit, Winters relied on his own judgment and volunteered. No slots for officers were available at the time, so Winters returned to Camp Croft. In early summer, an opening finally appeared.

When the 506th Parachute Infantry Regiment was formed in August, Winters became one of the original members of Easy Company, which comprised 8 officers (a company commander, executive officer, 3 platoon leaders, and 3 assistant platoon leaders) and 140 enlisted men. As in other elite units, the volunteers' washout rate was extraordinary. Of the 500 officers who volunteered, 148 graduated from basic airborne training; likewise the 5,300 enlisted volunteers were winnowed down to 1,800 graduates. Commanding Easy Company was First Lieutenant Herbert Sobel, an officer who commanded by fear and demonstrated little compassion for his men. It was only natural that he and Winters would lock horns, for their leadership styles were vastly different. Sobel was a petty tyrant who alienated his fellow officers and his men. Winters, in contrast, led by example and was quick to establish excellent rapport with his men. On the eve of the Normandy invasion, Sobel's noncommissioned officers would mutiny rather than go into combat with a commander in whom they had no confidence. But that was far in the future. In the interim, Sobel was producing an excellent company, highly skilled and proficient in its specialized tasks. Unfortunately, part of the glue that held the company together was the contempt the men shared for their commanding officer.

Airborne training at Camp Toccoa, Georgia, at the foothills of the Blue Mountains was rugged, but Winters relished the camaraderie and the challenges. The paratroopers' battle cry was "Currahee," after the twelve-hundred-foot mountain that overlooked the training camp. In the tongue of the region's original inhabitants *currahee* means "stands alone." The cry became a motto in which Winters and his fellow paratroopers took particular satisfaction. Officers and men trained sixteen hours a day. Physical training included a daily six-mile run to the top of Currahee and back to camp, an ordeal that later prompted Winters to remark that when the army gave out campaign ribbons for the war, they should have given one for the training at Toccoa. Winters's personal best time was forty-four minutes, just two minutes off the record. Assigned command of Easy's 2nd Platoon, Winters placed first in the regimental competition to determine who should serve as jumpmaster when the officers made their initial jumps. At Toccoa, he and Easy's other platoon leaders endured Sobel's ravings and coalesced into an effective team motivated not only by pride, but by their hatred for their commander as well. As their training ended, Winters completed his five qualifying jumps and received his airborne wings.

From the summer of 1942 through mid-1943 the 506th was not assigned to any division, but Winters was certain that the regiment, now commanded by Colonel Robert Sink, a 1927 West Point graduate, would soon join either the 82nd Airborne Division or the newly designated 101st Airborne Division. In mid-April 1943 he had assumed the duties of company executive officer, a position that brought new challenges. Promoted to first lieutenant, Winters remained with Easy Company when the regiment joined the 101st Airborne Division in June 1943. Three months later, the 506th PIR deployed to England to prepare for the invasion of Europe. The division encamped at Aldbourne, England, roughly eighty miles west of London.

In the year prior to the invasion of Europe, Winters quietly emerged as Easy Company's most dynamic and charismatic junior officer. He later attributed his success to his training and to the relationship he had developed with the enlisted men.[2] A teetotaler, Winters preferred quiet reflection and organized athletics to the rowdy social life of the other officers, although he understood that his refusal to join in might hold back his advancement. Although he was the only officer left who had started with Easy Company, he was still a first lieutenant on the eve of the invasion. He described himself as a "half-breed," an officer with the responsibility to train the men, but an enlisted man at heart. Nowhere was this bond more evident than in his description of a chance encounter with an enlisted man. The story is best told in Winters's own words.

> If you want to see a beautiful, pathetic, and touching picture, follow me. There you see a private, by his machinegun along an English roadside

> on a cold morning. He's been on the march and fighting for just about 24 hours without stopping. He's tired, dead tired, so tired his mind is almost a blank. He's wet, hungry, miserable. As his buddies sleep, he keeps watch, a hard job when you're so tired and know that when the sun's up in another half hour, you'll be on the move. What does he do? Pulls out a picture of his girl, who's over 3,000 miles away and then studies the picture. In a state of tranquility, he dreams of days when he can enjoy the kind of life she stands for. Down the road comes an officer—it's me, nobody else would think of being up at a pre-dawn hour. "How's it going, Shep? What are you doing?" Then together we study and discuss his girl's good features and virtues.[3]

And always weighing on his mind was the tremendous responsibility of preparing his men for combat. In a letter home he commented on his personal crusade to improve himself as an officer and to improve Easy Company as fighters and as men. The net result of months of intense training was a highly motivated company that was poised to inflict maximum punishment on the enemy when the "big day" (D-Day) arrived. Winters noted that he had "aged a great deal" in the process of training his men, not chronologically but in maturity; he had aged to the extent that he could keep going after his men fell over and slept from exhaustion, and to the point that if a decision or advice was needed, his was taken as if the wisdom behind it was infallible. "Yes," he stated, "old and tired from training these men to the point where they were efficient fighters who would return to their loved ones back home."[4]

With the invasion just a few days away, Easy prepared for the ultimate test—the crucible of combat. On June 5 Winters led his platoon to the airfield and aboard a C-47 Dakota. By 2300 they were airborne. Easy Company's mission was the same as that of other units within the 101st Airborne Division: to seize the causeways behind Utah Beach to facilitate the expansion of the beachhead. En route to Normandy, Winters prayed to live through the day and prayed that he would measure up in his first combat. "Every man, I think, had in his mind, 'How will I react under fire?'" As platoon leader, Winters stood in the open door. As soon as the red light flashed, he hollered, "Stand up and hook up." When the pilot turned on the green light, Winters was first to leave his plane. Describing the jump days later, he reflected: "We're doing 150 MPH. O.K., let's go. G-D, there goes my leg pack and every bit of equipment I have. Watch it, boy! Watch it! Jesus Christ, they're trying to pick me up with those machine-guns. Slip, slip, try and keep close to that leg pack. There it lands beside that hedge. G-D that machine-gun. There's a road, trees—hope I don't hit them. Thump, well that wasn't too bad, now let's get out of this chute."[5]

The men jumped from airplanes traveling 150 miles per hour at 500 feet, and the division's drop was scattered across the Cotentin Peninsula. Winters came down near the town of Sainte-Mere-Eglise, several kilometers from the intended drop zone. Rallying a couple of troopers, he set off for Sainte-Marie-du-Mont, the division's designated headquarters. En route they stumbled across the battalion staff and forty men of D Company. By 0700, E Company consisted of two light machine guns, one bazooka, one 60-mm mortar, nine riflemen, and two officers. No one knew the whereabouts of the company commander, First Lieutenant Thomas Meehan, so Winters took command. Winters later learned that Meehan, who had succeeded Sobel in the wake of the NCOs' mutiny, had been killed along with his entire stick of paratroopers when their plane crashed.

About a mile and a half from Sainte-Marie-du-Mont the column encountered sustained enemy fire, and Winters was summoned to the front. The battalion commander informed Winters that there was a four-gun battery of German 105-mm cannon two hundred yards to their front across an open field adjacent to a French farmhouse called Brecourt Manor. The battery was set up in a hedgerow and defended by a fifty-man German platoon. The guns were firing directly down a causeway leading to Utah Beach. The commander directed Winters to take the battery.

Assembling his company, Winters made a careful reconnaissance and then issued orders for an assault. The attack would consist of a flanking action led by Winters, with covering fire from several directions to pin down the Germans. Winters selected three soldiers for the assault: Second Lieutenant Lynn "Buck" Compton, "Popeye" Wynn, and Don Malarkey. Asked later why he selected those three, Winters recalled, "In combat you look for killers. Many thought they were killers and wanted to prove it. They are, however, few and far between." Winters assessed the impending attack as a "high risk opportunity." The key was "initiative, an immediate appraisal of situation, the use of terrain to get into the connecting trench, and taking one gun at a time." Crawling on their bellies, Winters and his men got close enough and knocked out the first gun. After mowing down the retreating Germans, Winters placed a machine gun to fire down the trench. He had also noticed that as soon as he got close enough to assault the first gun, the Germans in an adjacent hedgerow temporarily lifted their fire to avoid inflicting casualties on their own men. Winters realized that respite could be used to his advantage.

With the first gun out of action, Winters grabbed two other soldiers and charged the second. Throwing hand grenades and firing their rifles, they took the second howitzer and, of at least equal importance, a case containing a map that showed the locations of all the German artillery in the Cotentin Peninsula. Winters sent the map back to battalion headquarters and then directed another assault that rapidly captured the third gun. Reinforcements led by an officer from D Company soon arrived. Winters briefly outlined the situation and then watched D Company capture the last gun. With the mission complete, Winters ordered a withdrawal. It was 1130, roughly three hours since Winters had received the order to take the battery. In summarizing Easy's action, historian Stephen Ambrose notes that with twelve men, what amounted to a squad, later reinforced by elements of D Company, Winters had destroyed a German battery, killed fifteen Germans, wounded many more, and taken twelve prisoners. It would be a gross exaggeration to say that Easy Company saved the day at Utah Beach, but it certainly made an important contribution to the success of the invasion.

Winters's action at Brecourt Manor was a textbook infantry assault that is frequently studied at the U.S. Military Academy today. Ever the self-effacing leader, Winters described the action to S. L. A. Marshall, Eisenhower's chief historian, simply as laying down a base of fire to cover the assault. Left unsaid was his leadership by example. At every turn he made the correct decision, from selecting the right men for each task to making an accurate reconnaissance of the enemy position to leading the maneuver element in person. In his own analysis, Winters rated the destruction of the German battery as his "apogee" in command. When the day was finally over, he wrote in his diary that if he survived the war, he would find an isolated farm and spend the rest of his life in peace.

Colonel Robert Sink, the 506th PIR's commander, recommended Winters for the Medal of Honor for his leadership under fire at Brecourt Manor, but only one man in the 101st Airborne Division was to be given that medal in Normandy. Instead, Winters was awarded the Distinguished Service Cross, with Silver and Bronze stars awarded to the men of Easy Company who participated in the assault. Winters also formally received command of Easy when it was determined that the company commander had been killed in the airborne assault. Promotion to captain followed on July 2, but not before Winters led the company in the attack to capture Carentan, a small town at the base of the peninsula. Easy Company's spirited defense on June 13 prevented a vicious German counterattack from recapturing the town. Again Colonel Sink lauded Winters, stating that his personal leadership at a critical stage of the battle had been the crucial difference in Easy's success. Finally, on June 29, the 101st was relieved by elements of the 83rd Infantry Division.

In mid-July the 101st returned to England to prepare for contingency operations. By the time Easy Company was pulled from the line, it had suffered sixty-five casualties, including eighteen dead. Overall casualties for the 506th Parachute Infantry Regiment bordered on 50 percent. Though the campaign had proved costly, Easy had met its first test in combat, accomplishing every mission.

Normandy had been the proving ground both for Easy Company and for Captain Winters. He had earned his combat spurs and provided critical leadership when it was needed most. As he matured in company command, he developed a certain detachment from the men he had once befriended. "Now I am a captain and I find that the buddy stuff is out," he wrote in his journal. "I am all in favor of knowing each and every man, getting in bull sessions with them, knowing their background, likes, dislikes, capabilities, and weak points. I want to be their friend and the guy they go to when they want a favor or they're in trouble. But I am not their buddy, I am their captain, and when I say something, that's it, you jump. . . . I've been around three years in the army, but I can see that the old army is the right army, and the longer I am around, and the more I see of it. . . . I am convinced that you can't make a decision as quickly and thoroughly if your buddies are concerned in a life and death situation." Too close an affiliation with the men led to a breakdown in military discipline, anathema to Winters. To be alive to fight another day became an obsession, anything else was extra, unessential, and burdensome. A commander could not afford to let his guard down, not when "battle is the payoff."

For the next two months, Easy Company refitted and prepared to return to the Continent. A number of missions were scratched, including one in late August that prompted Winters to reflect on his three years in the army. As he looked back, it "seemed a lifetime in some respects, and as if I have aged three times three . . . there are not many in this outfit that have done as much in the same period of time." In fact, he knew of no one. "What I really want is to get this war over," he continued, "and the sooner they put me back in the fight the better I'll like it, for it's no good letting the other guy do it for you. Just doesn't seem right." Winters got his wish when Eisenhower directed the airborne divisions to mount Operation Market-Garden in mid-September. The

Allied plan called for the newly configured XVIII Airborne Corps—under the nominal command of Major General Matthew Ridgway, but with the 82nd and 101st airborne divisions initially assigned to the British 1st Airborne Corps for the operation—to seize a narrow road over which a British armor column would advance and capture the crossings over the Lower Rhine. In overall command of the Allied airborne divisions constituting the 1st Allied Airborne Army was Lieutenant General Lewis H. Brereton, a man who had never before commanded paratroops. British Lieutenant General Frederick "Boy" Browning, Brereton's deputy, was assigned actual command of the operation; like Brereton he had no prior experience with operational control of an airborne force. The mission of the 101st Division—the Screaming Eagles—was to seize the bridge over the Wilhelmina Canal at Son and then to liberate Eindhoven, a city of roughly one hundred thousand inhabitants.

Now a battle-tested company commander, Winters led Easy when it jumped into Holland on September 17. Unlike Normandy, the airborne drop was in broad daylight, so there was little of the confusion that permeated the ranks on D-Day. As the American column approached the Son bridge, the Germans blew it up and withdrew. The next day the Americans occupied Eindhoven, and Winters moved Easy Company east first to Nuenen, then toward Helmond, where he ran into determined opposition from the Germans. Forced to retreat, Easy congregated at Tongelre, several miles in the rear. Winters later confessed to his battalion commander that he had suffered 15 casualties and had taken a hell of a licking. Two days later, Winters personally led a counterattack at Uden that stalled an enemy attack to sever the road, which had become known as Hell's Highway. But Easy's fight did not end there. From September 17 through the 26th, Easy took an incredible pounding. They were often surrounded but never gave an inch. They paid a cost for their success; in ten days the company had lost 22 men. Overall Allied casualties for Market-Garden numbered in excess of 17,000, exceeding the total for D-Day. The British 1st Airborne Division, assigned to seize the bridge at Arnhem, nearly ceased to exist. American casualties reached nearly 4,000, with the 101st Airborne Division alone losing 2,118.[6] Market-Garden was destined from the beginning to fail, both because the Germans were in Holland in far greater strength than Eisenhower's headquarters surmised, and because the campaign called for an attack on far too narrow a front, which was extremely vulnerable to counterattack.

The service in Holland began a period of continuous combat for the 101st Airborne Division that lasted until November 25. The American airborne troops were trained for light infantry assault, not for sustained infantry combat. Excessive casualties within the Allied Expeditionary Force in Normandy and in subsequent operations, however, dictated that combat-hardened divisions, including the 82nd and 101st airborne divisions, remain in combat. For Winters and Easy Company, that meant defending a two-mile-wide "island" that lay between the Lower Rhine on the north and the Waal River on the south. At the time, Easy Company consisted of 130 men assigned to cover a little more than a mile along the front. "Our strength was low," Winters remembered, "and our front big." It was in defense of the island that Winters and Easy wrote another shining page in the history of the 506th PIR.

Arriving on the island on October 2, Winters deployed his men with two platoons forward and one in reserve along the south side of a dike that ran roughly parallel to the river. Keeping his first platoon in reserve, he placed combat outposts along the most likely avenues of enemy approach. He also sent reconnaissance patrols forward to keep an eye on enemy movements to Easy's front. At 0330 on October 5, one of the patrols encountered a full German company from the 363rd Volksgrenadier Division that had been given the mission of clearing the island. As soon as Winters received word that the Germans had penetrated his defenses, he gathered half his reserve platoon, roughly fifteen men, and immediately moved forward. Repeatedly halting the patrol to make personal reconnaissance, Winters brought his men up to a small ditch behind an enemy machine-gun nest. Under his personal supervision the paratroopers "beat the devil out of the machine-gun crew" and wiped out the enemy position.

Winters then called up the remainder of the platoon and carefully orchestrated another assault. Studying the landscape, he directed his men to attack toward the road, knowing only that beyond it an unknown number of enemy soldiers were huddling. With two squads providing covering fire, Winters ordered the remaining squad to fix bayonets and follow him across 175 yards of open ground. Running at full speed, Winters reached the road first, jumped over, and saw one hundred or so Germans preparing for an assault against Easy Company. Without hesitation he emptied two M-1 clips into their midst. As more Americans arrived, the Germans turned toward the river and fled. By now Winters had taken cover behind the ditch, but he rose to pour a withering fire on the retreating enemy. Other members of Winters's 1st Platoon did the same. Just then a second company of Germans arrived, but Easy's fire was too intense and they also took flight. For Easy Company it was a "duck shoot," with each man firing the equivalent of fifty-seven clips of M-1 ammunition into the enemy.

As he had done outside Brecourt on D-Day, Winters had executed a surprise attack with precision. He reacted quickly to the enemy penetration. Rushing to the front, he personally placed his men in a position from which they could inflict maximum punishment on the Germans. Calling for additional support, he carefully briefed his squad leaders, then personally led the charge. When confronted with the enemy in unexpected numbers, he reacted instinctively and then destroyed the cohesion of the enemy force. Calling for indirect fire support, he routed not only the company that confronted him but the second enemy company that appeared on the battlefield as well. Coming under artillery fire himself, Winters withdrew his platoon behind a dike to avoid unnecessary casualties. All in all, he demonstrated once again why Easy Company repeatedly found comfort under his charge.

Following the battle, Colonel Sink issued a general order citing the 1st Platoon's "daring attack and skillful maneuver." Four days later, he promoted Winters to executive officer of the 2nd Battalion. The promotion was bittersweet, for it meant that Winters had to relinquish command of the company in which he had served since Toccoa. His days in command of Easy had ended, but it had been a glorious close. With only thirty-five men he had routed two German companies of three hundred men, killing fifty, wounding approximately one hundred, and capturing eleven—all at a cost of one dead and twenty-two wounded, though his own casualties struck Winters to his core. Winters later said this attack was "the highlight of all E Company actions for the entire war, even better than D-Day, because it demonstrated Easy's overall superiority in every phase of infantry tactics: patrol, defense, attack under a base of fire, withdrawal, and, above all, superior marksmanship with rifles, machine gun, and mortar fire." October 5 was also the last day that Dick Winters fired his weapon in anger.

The war continued, but Winters was now an administrator. He found his staff duties boring, a far cry from the camaraderie of company command. Reflecting after the war, he noted that being "X.O. was a tremendous let down. The most fun I had in the army, the most satisfying thing I did was company commander. Being a junior officer was a tough job, taking it from both sides, from the men and from Captain Sobel. But as company commander, I was running my own little show. I was out front, making a lot of personal decisions on the spot that were important to the welfare of my company, getting a job done."[7] As battalion executive officer, Winters merely made recommendations to the commanding officer. He yearned for the front and sought every opportunity to maintain contact with Easy and the other forward companies. On one occasion he accompanied Easy's new commander on a patrol to inspect the forward outposts. As they returned to friendly lines, a tense American soldier fired at the two officers, seriously wounding his own commander. Miraculously, Winters emerged unscratched, but he had used another of his nine lives. For the most part, however, staff duties remained mundane. The only saving grace in his new job was his daily contact with Captain Lewis Nixon, a close friend, who served as the battalion operations officer.

The soldiers of the 2nd Battalion spent their days patrolling, improving their defensive positions, and training the replacements who began arriving in Holland. In late November the battalion was replaced on the line and moved to Mourmelon-le-Grand, some eighteen miles from the cathedral town of Reims. By then, many of the Toccoa men were gone; sixty-five had been casualties in Normandy, and another fifty-six fell in Holland. The constant strain of combat was beginning to tell. During the period of rest and relaxation, discipline broke down as the men tried to adjust to life away from the front lines. Too much drinking, too much fighting, and too much time on their hands led to frequent squabbles with sister units and resulted in non-battle casualties that Easy could not afford. The three-week stay at Mourmelon-le-Grand proved to be a short respite. Easy's most difficult fight still lay ahead.

When Hitler launched the Ardennes offensive on December 16, only Winters and Nixon were at battalion headquarters; the remaining officers were in Paris on passes. Leaves were immediately canceled and the 2nd Battalion was trucked to Bastogne, where the acting 101st Airborne Division commander, Brigadier General Anthony C. McAuliffe, improvised a hasty defense to defend the vital crossroads town. Many paratroopers arrived in Bastogne cold and wet from the ride in open cattle trucks from their camp at Mourmelon. Most lacked proper cold-weather gear and ammunition, and some even lacked helmets. The next several days were pure hell as the Germans repeatedly attempted to crack the American defenses. Winters and the 2nd Battalion held the line north of the town, but just barely.

Bastogne proved to be the battalion's toughest fight, "one of the most confused fights" Winters had seen since Normandy. With the battalion commander back in regimental headquarters rather than directing the unit's defense, Winters was the de facto commander of 2nd Battalion. When Patton's Third Army finally relieved the Bastogne garrison, the 101st Airborne Division had written the brightest page in its heralded history. But it had come at a terrific cost. The siege of Bastogne cost the 101st Airborne Division 1,641 casualties, and the end of the siege was not the end of the fighting.[8] Constant mortar and artillery fire, unspeakably frigid weather, and combat fatigue affected the entire command. Trench foot caused fully one-third of the American casualties. Lack of sleep, lack of rest, and too little food contributed to the decreasing effectiveness of units that spent too much time on the front lines.

Asked why he didn't break under the pressure, Winters replied, "I'm Pennsylvania Dutch. I won't quit. I made a commitment. Courage is willpower and determination. When I was assigned to battalion, that gave me a brief respite because I was now a little farther from the front. In combat fifty to seventy-five yards can be a tremendous difference in pressure. My responsibility increased, but the tension of direct fire decreased."[9] To keep his soldiers' heads in the game, as he termed it, Winters kept talking to them. If one was on the edge, he brought him back to the command post for a couple of days to rest from the tension of the front line. Most of the time, the GI was able to rejoin his comrades within a few days. As for officers, they needed to be the first ones up, even under artillery fire, to talk to the men in order to break the paralyzing fear that gripped those who encountered direct fire.

Officer replacements in Belgium posed another serious problem. Winters was far more understanding of weak soldiers than he was of weak officers. Leaders had to harden mentally in order to be emotionally ready to face stress. Officers needed to think during times of crisis. Far too many replacement officers wanted to get into combat before they were ready for it emotionally or physically. Too many were more concerned with promotions and medals than with the welfare of their men. In January, Winters observed an attack by Easy Company, now commanded by First Lieutenant Norman S. Dike Jr. In the middle of the attack, Dike froze, incapable of further action. As enemy fire began decimating the company, Winters relieved Dike on the spot and turned command of the company over to First Lieutenant Ronald C. Speirs, a veteran of Normandy and a man Winters once described as a "natural killer, but a man who could get the job done."[10] Speirs carried the day and remained Easy's commanding officer until the end of the war. But it was Winters, acting calmly under fire, who had recognized an officer paralyzed by fear and had taken the necessary step to remedy the problem.

Decades after the war, Winters spoke of the combat fatigue he witnessed at Bastogne. His battalion had already spent an inordinate amount of time at the front. The men were physically exhausted, and this in turn led to mental exhaustion and loss of discipline. Self-discipline keeps a soldier doing his job. Without it, the GI loses his pride and his sense of self-respect in the eyes of his fellow troops. Pride—in the company and in themselves—was the glue that held Easy Company together. Pride also drove Winters. "When you see a man break," Winters said, "he usually slams his helmet down and messes up his hair. You cannot talk to him then. That is precisely what happened to Dike. This breakdown occurs instantaneously. No one plans to become a combat fatigue casualty."[11]

No sooner had the Allies flattened the Bulge than the 101st was trucked to Alsace, some 160 miles south of Bastogne, where another German offensive threatened the Allied line. Initially in regimental reserve, the 506th PIR moved into the line in the city of Hagenau on February 5. Occupying a salient into the German lines, the 2nd Battalion was in daily contact with the enemy forces. Movement during the day was virtually impossible, so Winters dispatched nightly patrols to maintain contact and to man listening posts. After one successful raid that captured some prisoners, the regimental commander visited Winters's headquarters and directed him to send out another patrol to capture more. On this occasion, however, Colonel Sink had been drinking and the order didn't make tactical sense. Moreover, the temperatures were dropping, and the snow of the previous night had turned to ice, so the Germans would hear the patrol coming. What did Winters do? He said, "Yes sir," and then ignored the unwise order. With no time for preparation and a wide-open field to his front, he could do nothing else. He would have lost too many men for no purpose had he obeyed. He later wondered what he would have done had he been a career officer concerned about his own future and his promotion. The entire episode was "an ethical dilemma of the first magnitude," but Winters refused to compromise his beliefs and to this day has no regrets.

In the days following the aborted patrol, Captain Winters took time to gather his thoughts and reflect on events since the onset of Market-Garden. Between September 17, 1944, and January 22, 1945, he had jumped into Holland with the British 2nd Army and remained there for seventy-three days; had been surrounded at Bastogne for thirty days; and had been trucked to Alsace-Lorraine to plug a gap caused by the last major German offensive of the war on January 1 (Nordwind). When he slept, he dreamed of "fights, fighting Jerries, outmaneuvering, out-thinking, out-shooting, and out-fighting them. But they're tense, cruel hard, and bitter." The dreams were a part of his preparation. "When you dream over and over a problem," he wrote in a letter home, "you get the solution and crazy as it may seem in the cold morning light, it usually works." In the same letter he discounted the perception that he and all soldiers constantly raised all kinds of hell when they were on pass. Winters read his Bible for relaxation and remained all business, ever cognizant of his command responsibilities. "I've got my own conscience to answer to," he explained. "Next, my parents, and then I am an officer in the U.S. Army. I am damn proud of it and with the rank and position I hold, I wouldn't think of doing anything to bring discredit to my outfit, my paratroopers, boots, wings, patch or the army."[12]

After nine months of nearly continuous combat, Winters received a long-deserved promotion to major on March 8, 1945. Two weeks later, Sink elevated him to command of the 2nd Battalion, which he led with characteristic distinction until VE Day. Battalion command was the ultimate compliment: Winters had risen from junior second lieutenant to commanding officer in the same battalion in a period of two and a half years. Along with the promotion came a temporary lull in the fighting. As the Allied armies steamrolled into Germany, the 101st Airborne Division was reassigned to the U.S. Seventh Army under Alexander Patch for the duration of the war. The men enjoyed a brief break from the battlefield before they boarded trucks and moved to seal off the Ruhr pocket.

When the German resistance finally collapsed on April 18, the division once again boarded trucks and moved to Munich to prepare for a final assault on Hitler's Alpine redoubt. En route Winters encountered a German concentration camp near Landsberg. Even the battle-hardened veterans of Easy Company were shocked at the wretched condition of the prisoners. "The memory of starved, dazed men who dropped their eyes and heads when we looked at them . . . in the same manner that a beaten, mistreated dog would cringe, leaves feelings that cannot be described and will never be forgotten," Winters later recalled.[13] The sight convinced Winters of the need to end the war as expeditiously as possible. In the war's final week, General Maxwell Taylor released the 506th PIR for its final mission of the war, the assault on Berchtesgaden, Hitler's mountain retreat outside Salzburg. Winters's 2nd Battalion was first to enter the town and first to occupy Hitler's private residence.

The war ended for Winters at Berchtesgaden with the 2nd Battalion, but in all the years afterward his heart remained with the men of Easy Company. What made Easy so special to Winters? After all, he had been Easy's commander for only four short months. The answer was simple. "In combat," he stated, "your reward for a good job done is that you get the next tough mission. E Company kept right on getting the job done through Normandy, Holland, Bastogne, and Germany. The result of sharing all that stress throughout training and combat has created a bond between the men of E Company that will last forever." Their training in Georgia initially produced the bond among the "Toccoa men"; the stress of combat cemented the tie as the unit stuck together and fought together to survive. That bond among Easy's survivors still exists. The original members of Easy Company sit together at reunions because they formed the core of the company. The later replacements still hold the veterans of Normandy in awe. But everyone agrees on one point: To a man the survivors acknowledge that Captain Dick Winters was the best combat commander they had during the entire war. Winters shuns such acclaim, noting that "hardship and death bring a family together. Officers aren't family; the family belongs to the men. The officers are merely caretakers."[14]

The war changed Winters as war changes all men. His personal letters changed dramatically after he assumed command on D-Day. Prior to the invasion, he wrote of the carefree life in England and of the amenities of life in the United States that he hoped to share when the war was over. Afterward there was little time for tender thoughts. Those he "took off and left behind in the marshalling area prior to starting this war. There's no room for them. There's little thought about death, so how can one waste thoughts that are simply tender. Death? Yes, I think earnestly about the dead, but there is no time to mourn for them." Battle had made him "combat wise and in a position to do some good to help a lot of the men." He knew his job better than most and could not sit back and see less competent commanders take men out and get them killed. Maybe he would get hurt or killed for his trouble, he wrote, "but so what if I can make it possible for many others to go home. Their mothers want them too, the same as me. So what else can I do and still hold my own self respect as an officer and a man." He briefly contemplated volunteering for service in the China-Burma-India Theater or the Southwest Pacific Theater, but then reconsidered.

As they waited for their turn to ship back to the States, the men of Winters's battalion busied themselves with occupation duty. For veterans with so much time on their hands, it proved a frustrating experience. Drinking, looting, and reckless driving produced too many casualties among paratroopers who had miraculously survived the war. The transportation of prisoners of war and displaced persons was hardly exciting duty. "It's so quiet," Winters wrote. "And despite the fact that I have 25,000 Krauts under my charge, there seems like nothing to do, no reason to work." The men chafed at the wait, increasingly dissatisfied by the point system that determined priorities for returning home. Winters made his last jump on September 20, and on November 30, 1945, the 101st Airborne Division was deactivated and Easy Company ceased to exist.

In his analysis of Easy Company's service during World War II, Stephen Ambrose attempts to place Dick Winters's role in Easy in the proper perspective.[15] The company had three remarkable commanders: Herbert Sobel, Richard Winters, and Ronald Speirs. Of these, only Winters had been with the company from day 1 to day 1,095. Though each of the commanders had an impact, in the view of those who served in Easy, it was Dick Winters's company. The noncommissioned officers who formed the nucleus of the command certainly felt that way. One of those noncoms was Sergeant Floyd Talbert, who expressed his gratitude in a letter dated September 30, 1945. "The first thing I will try to explain," he wrote, "is . . . Dick, you are loved and will never be forgotten by any soldier that ever served under you or I should say with you because that is the way you led. You are to me the greatest soldier I could ever hope to meet. . . . You were my ideal, and motor in combat. . . . Well you know now why I would follow you into hell. When I was with you, I knew everything was absolutely under control." Another Easy Company noncom wrote Winters: "You were blessed with the utter respect and admiration of 120 soldiers, essentially civilians in uniform, who would have followed you to certain death. . . . I know as much about 'Grace Under Pressure' as most men, and a lot more about it than some. You had it."[16] No words were more sincerely spoken or more warmly received.

True to his word, when the war was over, Winters left the army and found solace far away from the battlefield. Though Colonel Sink attempted to keep his veterans in the regiment, Winters declined a regular army commission. The postwar army had simply changed too much. "In the paratroops, the money looked good. That's the end of it though, for it was a big party after that with a man growing lazy, both mentally and physically and going to hell fast." They could have it all; Winters would "dig ditches first." He was home by late November and placed on terminal leave.

After his separation from the service in January 1946, he joined his friend Lewis Nixon and went to work for Nixon's father in the Nixon Nitration Works in Nixon, New Jersey, and was promoted to personnel manager. He enrolled in Rutgers University and married his wife, Ethel, in 1948. The army recalled Winters to active duty during the Korean War, but training raw recruits at Fort Dix, New Jersey, was hardly his cup of tea. In his mind, the soldiers of 1950 were not the same caliber as the citizen-soldiers of World War II. When the opportunity arose for him to return to civilian life, he took it. A year later he purchased a farm outside Indiantown Gap, Pennsylvania, thus fulfilling the promise he made to himself on D-Day. Amid his neighbors in Bethel Township Winters found the calm for which he was searching. In the autographed copy of *Band of Brothers* that he donated to the local library, he urged his community to "enjoy each day the beauty, peace, tranquility of our fields and mountains. Take one day at a time and hang tough."

A highly successful businessman in civilian life, Winters marketed nutritional products to feed mills and became quite prosperous as a corporate manager and grain broker. He is now retired, but he remains active in promoting educational reform and serving as a consultant on a number of projects associated with his wartime service. He was a driving force in Time-Warner's "School Program" to educate children in a classroom environment. HBO's miniseries based on Ambrose's *Band of Brothers* brought Winters some undesired fame, but he is always quick to point out that the real heroes of Easy Company are those in the American cemeteries scattered across western Europe. He now spends his days in quiet contemplation, taking time to answer the many letters that arrive daily from people who saw the HBO series and want to thank Winters for his heroism and service to the nation. Some of the envelopes are addressed merely to Winters at "a farm somewhere outside Hershey, Pennsylvania." One came addressed to Winters in care of "the Mayor of the city of Hershey." Hershey does not have a mayor, but the letter ended up in Winters's hands nevertheless. To his credit, the former commander responds to each letter with a personalized message in his own hand. Of these letters Winters merely says, "They're very touching. I can only read so many, then I have to stop. It's very emotional."

A grateful nation has not yet forgotten Dick Winters. When the Franklin and Eleanor Roosevelt Institute awarded the veterans of World War II its prestigious Four Freedoms/Freedom from Fear award on May 4, 2001, representing the U.S. Army was Dick Winters, former company commander of Easy Company, 506th Parachute Infantry Regiment.

I first met Dick Winters when he traveled to the U.S. Military Academy to address the Corps of Cadets on the topic of combat leadership. I seldom "pulled rank" on my subordinates, but on this occasion I informed the officer who had invited Winters that I would host Winters for a quiet dinner at the Hotel Thayer on the grounds of West Point. I was immediately impressed by the quiet gentleman who introduced himself simply as Dick Winters. Over dinner we discussed an array of topics associated with his wartime experience and his thoughts on command in war. Why were some commanders more effective than others in inspiring their men? How did he identify the best soldiers in his company? Had he relieved any commander in combat? To what did he attribute his success in Easy Company? Minutes became hours as we discussed leadership under fire. By the time the evening was over I had received a primer on leadership unequaled in my twenty-five years of commissioned service.

Over the span of the next four years Winters made several more visits to West Point. His message to the cadets is always the same: Hang tough and take care of your soldiers. He admonished the cadets who said that they wished to become "killers" on the battlefield. "West Point needs to produce leaders," he responded, "not a bunch of 'Rambos' or killers." Asked by one cadet what his toughest challenge as a commander was, Winters instantly replied, "To be able to think under fire. In peace the toughest challenge is to be fair." As to what aspect of his military service provided him the greatest satisfaction, he answered without hesitation, "Knowing I got the job done; knowing that I kept the respect of my men. The greatest reward you can have as a leader is the 'look of respect.' The key to a successful combat leader is to earn respect, not because of rank, but because you are a man." The emphasis on building leaders of character is typical of Dick Winters.

Today, Dick Winters remains the gentlest of men. Ambrose recounts a visit to Winters's farm outside Hershey, Pennsylvania.[17] After Winters had finished telling him about practically wiping out an entire German rifle company on the dike in Holland on October 5, 1944, he and Ambrose walked down to one of the ponds near the cabin. A flock of perhaps thirty Canadian geese took flight, and one goose stayed behind, honking plaintively at the remainder. Ambrose had no idea that the goose had a broken wing and that Winters had been caring for it for several weeks. When Ambrose suggested they fetch a rifle and shoot the goose and freeze her for Thanksgiving dinner, Winters was horrified. "I couldn't do that!" With the war far behind him, Winters now seemed incapable of violent action.

I share a similar story that illustrates Ambrose's observation. When I visited Dick and Ethel Winters in 1999, they asked me if I would like to see the farm. It was a great honor to receive such an invitation. I knew the farm was Dick's personal refuge, and I suspected that its location was a secret shared with only a privileged few. We spent an enjoyable afternoon walking the farm, feeding the fish, and sharing childhood memories. Later in the afternoon, we drove to Hershey and Dick showed me his office and mementos from his service with the Screaming Eagles. Surrounded by company guidons, war trophies, and wall plaques depicting the various units in which he served, I asked the former commander to point out his most prized possession. I expected it to be the E Company guidon or perhaps a captured weapon. I couldn't have been more wrong. Surveying the walls of his office, he fixed on a glass frame that held a pressed edelweiss, a flower found only in the higher altitudes of the Austrian and Swiss Alps. "I picked this when I set up battalion headquarters in the Alpine village of Kaprun, just outside Zell am See, Austria," he said. It was just when his 2nd Battalion began their occupation duty following VE Day.

"Why edelweiss?" I inquired.

"Because the edelweiss is an expression of beauty and life," he answered. "After all the horrors of war I had observed, this flower symbolized a new birth of freedom for my world."

I would be remiss if I did not add a final postscript to the story of Dick Winters. When I retired from active duty following a thirty-year career, I tried to decide whom I most wanted to officiate at my retirement ceremony. From the back of my mind I recalled a newsletter from Easy Company's Sergeant Myron "Mike" Ranney that Ambrose selected to close *Band of Brothers*. "In thinking back on the days of Easy Company," Ranney recalled, "I'm treasuring my remark to a grandson who asked, 'Grandpa, were you a hero in the war?' 'No,' I answered, 'but I served in a company of heroes.'"[18] That sold it for me. I wanted the commander of Easy Company to preside over my ceremony. When I called Winters, he graciously consented to attend. As usual, he made me feel that I was doing him an honor when the reverse was true. His attendance at the retirement added a special luster to the ceremony. That evening we reminisced once again about our careers, and I asked him how he wished to be remembered. I was hardly surprised when he responded, "As company commander of Easy Company."

CHAPTER 14

SHATTERING STEREOTYPES: CHARITY ADAMS EARLEY AND THE WOMEN'S ARMY CORPS

In truth, I have accomplished much since my military service. I have opened a few doors, broken a few barriers, and, I hope, smoothed the way to some degree for the next generation.

—Lieutenant Colonel Charity Adams Earley

ASIDE FROM THE TRAILER ON CNN and the obituary in the January 22, 2002, edition of the *New York Times*, no national fanfare marked the passing of Charity Adams Earley at her home in Dayton, Ohio. Her own community remembered her more as an educator than for her wartime service. In fact, Earley was a pioneer in every sense of the word. One of only a few women to hold the wartime rank of major in the Women's Army Corps (WAC), Charity Adams Earley commanded the only all-black WAC unit to serve overseas during World War II. Her wartime memoir, *One Woman's Army,* introduced an entire generation of Americans to the contributions of the American women who served their country in uniform. Her death marked the closing of an important, albeit largely unknown, chapter in American history.

In the completely integrated armed forces of the twenty-first century, few Americans take the time to remember the men and women who broke down the barriers of gender and racism that once segregated the military forces of the United States. Prior to World War II, women had met with only limited success in their efforts to serve their country in the armed forces in wartime. Major General Jeanne M. Holm, USAF (Ret.), has noted that the scope and complexity of the war dictated the active recruitment of large numbers of women to fill not only "essential nursing positions, but to meet military requirements across a vast array of officer and enlisted skills." Before the war was over, some four hundred thousand American women joined the ranks of American warriors in an effort to contribute to the national defense. Major Beatrice Hood Stroup, who joined the Women's Army Corps, spoke for thousands of women when she said: "It wasn't just my brother's country, or my husband's country, it was my country as well. And so this war wasn't just their war, it was my war, and I needed to serve in it."[1]

The honor of becoming the first black commissioned officer in the Women's Army Auxiliary Corps (WAAC) fell to Charity Adams.[2] She was born in 1918, the oldest of four children of a minister and a teacher. Well acquainted with the racial bigotry that characterized Columbia, South Carolina, at that time, Adams studied hard and graduated valedictorian in her high school class at Booker T. Washington High School. Selecting Wilberforce University, one of the outstanding traditionally black colleges in the country, Adams graduated with a degree in mathematics and physics and returned to Columbia to teach in the same segregated school system where she had been a student. In the ensuing summers she attended The Ohio State University in Columbus, Ohio, expecting to pursue a graduate degree in vocational psychology.

Four years later, Adams received an unexpected invitation from the dean of women at Wilberforce University to apply for a position in a new organization called the Women's Auxiliary Army Corps. Such an organization promised new leadership opportunities, so Adams submitted her application and then went about her business. When three weeks passed without a response, she considered the matter closed and boarded a train to Columbus to complete her graduate education. En route her life took a dramatic turn.

When the train pulled into Knoxville, Tennessee, Adams was greeted by her aunt, who informed her that the army had finally responded to her application. Adams was to report to Atlanta immediately, a feat she later described as "a physical, if not financial impossibility."[3] Continuing on to Columbus instead, Adams reported to Fort Hayes, headquarters of the Fifth Service Command, and asked to have her records transferred from Atlanta. She took her physical that same day, and three days later passed an interview in which she told her inquisitors that if anyone could deploy ten thousand women overseas, she could. Surprised at her own brashness, Adams left the interview feeling somewhat ashamed at her cockiness. She needn't have worried. Within weeks her candidacy was approved, and on July 13, 1942, Charity Adams reported to Fort Hayes and was inducted into the WAAC. Although she was the only black in the group, the alphabetical spelling of her last name gave Adams the first number in the Fifth Service Command—A500001. Within a week she was en route to Fort Des Moines, Iowa, one of five WAAC training centers and Adams's home for the next two and a half years.[4]

As members of the first officer candidate class, the women found themselves objects of scrutiny by the press, who photographed and interviewed as many as possible as they arrived in camp. Reporters even followed the candidates into the mess hall. Immediately after the meal, the reality of the Jim Crow army of 1942 hit hard. By law the WAAC was limited to 10 percent black members, and barracks were assigned by race. That first officer candidate class comprised four hundred women, and a young second lieutenant ordered "all the colored girls to move over on this side." Adams joined thirty-eight other black officer candidates and moved to Quarters 54, a segregated barracks where they stayed for the duration of their training.[5]

Adams was assigned to the 1st Company, 1st Training Regiment, and as expected, the black women formed the third of the company's three platoons. Although they came from different socioeconomic backgrounds, the members of the 3rd Platoon made no distinctions among themselves. Adams later described the platoon as "thirty-nine personalities, from different family backgrounds and different vocational experiences. If our platoon had been referred to as thirty-nine 'characters,' it was meant to be complimentary." That aside, the term "third platoon" evolved into an enduring badge of honor for its members.

Within days the new members of the WAAC began their basic training. Commanding Company 1, 1st Training Regiment, was Captain Frank E. Stillman Jr. Training consisted of myriad classes ranging from close-order drill to map reading, property accountability, and physical training. Adams particularly relished drill, and after a few embarrassing moments when she gave some rather unorthodox commands to march her unit across the parade field became quite proficient at it. Unlike their male counterparts, the WAACs received no instruction in tactics. Every Saturday morning there were inspections followed by company parades.

Earley recalled her first two months at Des Moines as "most interesting. Remember, we were charting unexplored territory. The classes were pretty rigorous though we did not work with firearms. We had gym, lots of classes. There was no attrition rate. We knew we were going to take the place of men to free them up for the battlefield. We figured that we would find a way. It was a very close-knit class."[6] All in all, basic training proved to be a harrowing experience, with "as many unpleasant moments and disillusioning experiences, as there were pleasant and hopeful ones." This first officer candidate class was "the guinea pig for the WAAC," and its members encountered an unusually high number of changes in the rules and policies governing their training.

By late August, however, the initial officer candidate class of the WAAC had weathered the storm and was set to graduate. Charity Adams had the distinction of serving as acting company commander for the dress rehearsal. The next day, August 29, 1942, she and 438 members of her class were commissioned third lieutenants in the Women's Auxiliary Army Corps (equivalent to second lieutenant in the U.S. Army). On the reviewing stand stood Colonel Oveta Culp Hobby, director of the WAAC, and Representative Edith Nourse Rogers, sponsor of the bill that had created the WAAC. It was a proud moment for all. Adams, again by virtue of her last name, became the first black female to be commissioned an officer in the WAAC. Under ordinary conditions she would have been the first woman of either race to be sworn, but for this graduation the army broke with tradition and graduated the class by platoons. Still, it was a proud moment, one that Adams remembered as much because she was the first black woman to receive a commission as for the fact that she and her colleagues had "arrived." Black or white, all wore the gold bars of a third lieutenant.[7]

Adams next went before a classification board to determine her exact duty posting. To her delight she was assigned to 3rd Company, 3rd Training Regiment and stationed at Fort Des Moines. Her duties encompassed training newly arrived black auxiliaries assigned to the training command. Three weeks later, Adams was assigned as company commander of Basic Training Company 12, 3rd Regiment. Company 12 was the first all-black company in the WAAC, and Adams was its first commander.

To ensure proper supervision, the army assigned a male tactical officer to each WAAC company; he was a regular army officer who was familiar with company administration. Male commanders also served at every echelon above company level. Adams's regimental commander, Major Joseph Fowler, was another perfect role model for a young officer to emulate. Adams attributed most of her success as a commander to the things she learned from observing other commanders, and Fowler and Captain Frank Stillman, her OCS company commander, were particularly influential. Throughout her life she remembered both men with great admiration and affection. Initially, the army also assigned a small cadre of male officers to each of the training companies, but over the course of the next six months these officers were reassigned to more pressing duties. By the time the first black auxiliaries arrived in Company 12, Adams was on her own.[8] Since training schedules were developed at regimental headquarters, Adams's primary responsibility centered on seeing to the women's welfare and making sure they were at the right place at the right time. Because black recruits were so few, commissioned officers served in a variety of capacities ranging from squad leaders to platoon leaders, from supply officers to administrative officers. In the early days of the WAAC, black officers actually outnumbered enlisted personnel.

Lieutenant Adams and the graduates of the first WAAC officer candidate class continued leading the way for women in the U.S. armed forces. In late 1942 the army had not adequately considered the ramifications of the great influx of female personnel into the ranks. Questions concerning proper uniforms, the proper way to address WAAC officers, the lack of black recruiters, and the absence of black noncommissioned officers all remained unanswered. Not until December 1942 was the first group of WAACs assigned to various army posts across the United States. Because Adams's company was the only black company in the regiment, she personally endeavored to ensure that each soldier was trained in a variety of jobs, and this later facilitated their assignments in the field army. Given more flexibility than her white counterparts, Adams commanded a unit that actually served as a receiving company, a training company, and a staging company.

With new responsibilities came new opportunities for promotion. In the expanding WAAC force, all graduates of the initial Officer Candidate School class received promotions on December 23; Adams and twenty-three others were promoted to first officer (the equivalent of captain in the regular army), and the remainder of the class received promotion to second officer. Adams was one of four black women to be promoted to first officer. The promotion was so unexpected that Adams had to send someone into Des Moines to obtain the silver bars of a captain because the local post exchange had exhausted its supply.

At about this time Adams took her first leave to return home to South Carolina. Though the leave was pleasant in that she was "fêted as a hometown girl who made good," the ever present racial tension of the period surfaced repeatedly. Denied entry into the dining car of the Southern Railway system until a white officer demanded that she be allowed to dine, Adams quietly took the abuse with which she was familiar by virtue of growing up in the racist South. In Columbia, she attended a meeting of the NAACP; her father was president of the local chapter. Returning home, Adams and her family had to endure the jeers of Ku Klux Klan members who picketed her house. They were gone the next morning, but they were painful reminders that racism and prejudice were still defining elements of a country that prided itself on battling the forces of international racism and totalitarianism.

For the next two years Adams served as company commander and as one of the most visible examples of the advances black women had made in the military. She frequently visited other army posts, and she commanded vehicle convoys across the United States. Repeated inspection tours as an official representative of the WAAC also occupied her schedule. Company 8 became the showcase of the first WAAC training center, an honor that Adams attributed in large part to the retention of key personnel throughout her command tour. The downside, of course, was that the company was forced to maintain the incredibly high standards that Adams had demanded. Left unsaid in her wartime memoirs is the specific contribution that Adams made to ensure her unit's reputation. An old army adage is that any unit is only as good as its leaders, and Company 8 was no an exception. Adams instilled discipline, directly administered company punishment, personally supervised all training, and motivated her soldiers to be the best soldiers at the training center. She experienced failures, of course, but Company 8 established and maintained the standards for the remainder of the post. Following six months of highly successful command, Adams relinquished the company to First Lieutenant Alma Berry and reported for duty as the training supervisor in the Plans and Training Office of the WAAC training center.

As training supervisor Adams oversaw the training of the auxiliaries, participated in organizing new phases of training, and obtained necessary equipment for classroom instruction. Far more to her liking was an assignment to report to Washington and help convince congressional leaders to increase the quota of black women for motor transport training. Inspection tours of the various WAAC training centers followed, and by May 1943 Adams was once again at Fort Des Moines when news arrived that the WAAC was scheduled to receive official status within the army.

By summer 1943 the ranks of the WAAC had swelled to 60,000 women, and Congress passed a bill granting army women full military status. President Roosevelt signed the bill into law on July 1, and the Women's Army Corps (WAC) was born. Three months later, the WAAC ceased to exist. Its members were given the option of returning to civilian life or joining the WAC. More than 41,177 enlisted women joined the WAC, and some 4,600 WAAC officers accepted commissions in the WAC, among them Charity

Adams.[9] In the interim Adams received a well-deserved promotion to major on September 20; she was only the second black woman to be promoted to field-grade rank.[10]

Because she was one of only two WAC field-grade officers at Fort Des Moines, Adams naturally assumed increased responsibilities. As training center control officer, a position she likened to a civilian efficiency expert, she looked for innovative ways to enhance unit training. Adams campaigned hard against the formation of a separate black training center, which would further isolate the black women joining the U.S. Army. On the surface, this plan, endorsed by the president's black adviser, seemed promising and offered accelerated opportunities for promotion, but Adams doubted its efficacy. Having grown up in South Carolina, Adams was quite familiar with *Plessy* v. *Ferguson*, the 1896 U.S. Supreme Court decision that dictated "separate but equal" treatment of black Americans. It had legalized discrimination throughout the South, and Adams wanted no part of it in the WAC. Stating that she wanted promotion as a WAC officer, not a Negro officer, she refused to command any such training organization. In denouncing a plan that had presidential endorsement, Adams clearly put her career on the line. As she left the meeting she was ignored by her colleagues; it taught her a hard lesson: do not depend on the support of others for causes.[11] In the end, plans for a separate training regiment were drafted but never implemented.

Nineteen forty-four brought Adams new opportunities to develop her professional skills. As the only black officer at the training center headquarters, Adams pulled her fair share of additional duties, ranging from special courts-martial officer to Officer Candidate Selection Board member. Conducting routine investigations, writing routine reports and special reports when required, and lecturing at traditionally black universities broadly expanded her leadership skills. Concurrently she encountered her fair share of prejudice from white officers unaccustomed to seeing a black woman wearing the oak leaves of a U.S. Army major. On one occasion Adams was kept standing at attention for forty-five minutes while a senior officer berated her for attending a social function at the officers' club. Another time she was questioned by members of the military police who had received a complaint from white soldiers about the presence of a "Negro woman." In the latter case, Adams demanded to see the identification and papers of the MPs, who subsequently reported themselves for their unwarranted questioning of a military officer. All things considered, Adams recalled her tour at Des Moines with great satisfaction, preferring to remember the good times and not the bad.

By the fall of 1944, Adams was so firmly settled at the training center that she felt she had become a sort of "mother figure." In fact, there were few opportunities for a WAC major to serve elsewhere, save at WAC Headquarters in the Pentagon. Frequent temporary duty assignments in and out of Washington gave Adams a broader perspective of the army than she would have gained had she been assigned to any other unit. Colonel Frank W. McCoskrie had repeatedly refused to release her permanently from the training center because he saw no advantage in it for Adams unless she had the opportunity for promotion.

Two events soon changed McCoskrie's mind. In November an opportunity arose for a small contingent of WACs to attend the Army Command and General Staff School at Fort Leavenworth, Kansas. The Leavenworth school system was near the pinnacle of the army educational system during the war, and its graduates were earmarked for positions of increased responsibility and authority. Ever the pioneer, Adams was among the first group of WAC officers scheduled to attend the prestigious military school. Class was scheduled to start in early 1945, but in the interim another opportunity presented itself.

As had happened throughout her career, the army had other plans for Charity Adams. In December, Adams was summoned to the base commander's office and asked point-blank if she was interested in going overseas. Assuming the question was rhetorical, Adams said she would go if she were ordered to deploy but that she was quite comfortable with her current assignment. Although white WAACs had deployed overseas, no black members had done so. The first WAAC unit to serve overseas was the 149th WAAC Post Headquarters Company, which reported for duty at Eisenhower's Mediterranean headquarters in January 1943.[12] The 1st WAAC Separate Battalion arrived in England in July 1943 and was assigned for duty with the 8th and 9th air forces. Army policy at the time was that theater commanders had to request WAC units by race for duty at a specific military post. More than five thousand WACs served in the Southwest Pacific Area and in the China-Burma-India Theater, with large contingents serving in MacArthur's headquarters and in army-level commands.[13] With the pressing need to release male soldiers to the front to offset casualties inflicted in the Battle of the Bulge and related battles in late 1944, Eisenhower's headquarters petitioned Marshall to deploy eight hundred black women to Europe for a central postal directory unit. It was this request that generated McCoskrie's summons. In the ensuing days, additional requests for overseas duty flooded the training center, and by the first of the year Adams and hundreds of other women were en route to Fort Oglethorpe, Georgia, the overseas training center. At the time the precise organization to which the black WACs were going to be assigned had yet to be determined.

Training at Fort Oglethorpe resembled nothing that Adams had experienced at Des Moines. Instruction focused on gas mask drills, obstacle course drills, marching, physical examinations, and numerous tactical classes. Because of her rank, Adams frequently commanded the four companies during drill and ceremonies and for battalion parades. Adams also assumed the unpleasant task of addressing each company about the "stigmas some sectors of the public had attached to the WACs as a whole." The press had published unsubstantiated stories about high numbers of pregnancies, low morals, and poor discipline that had a debilitating effect on WAC recruitment. Investigations proved all the allegations groundless, but the episode left WAC commanders extremely sensitive about the corps's public image. Her elevated rank also dictated that Adams would hold an important position once the women deployed to England.

Within a few weeks, she and Captain Abbie Noel Campbell were summoned to Washington and instructed to report to the Munitions Building. From there Adams and Campbell were rushed through a series of briefings and meetings. The two officers were given sealed orders and then told to report to the ATC Terminal, where they boarded a flight, destination unknown. Three and a half hours later, their C-54 cargo plane touched down in Bermuda. Opening their orders, Adams and Campbell discovered that London was their destination. Following repeated delays caused by mechanical malfunctions and inclement weather, Adams and Campbell arrived in London on January 28, 1945.

Still unsure what their precise duties were to be, Adams and her colleague reported to Major Margaret L. Philpot, the WAC staff director in charge of all WACs in the United Kingdom. There Adams discovered that she had been assigned as the commanding officer of a battalion attached to the Postal Directory Service for the ETO. The organization was part of the adjutant general's service. Captain Campbell was assigned as the battalion's executive officer. The next day Adams and Campbell traveled to Birmingham and visited the King Edward School, where they were to be stationed. Four days later Adams and her exec flew to Paris to report to the WAC director for Eisenhower's headquarters. In Paris she met Brigadier General Benjamin O. Davis of the Headquarters Staff, Communications Zone, the only black general officer in the U.S. Army.

On February 3, Adams and Campbell accepted a dinner invitation from Lieutenant General John C. H. Lee, commanding general, Communications

Zone, ETO, and commander, Services of Supply (SOS). Lee, known as "Jesus Christ Himself" (a play on his initials), had commandeered a luxury suite at the Hotel George V in downtown Paris for his headquarters. The general was a strong proponent of the integration of frontline units, once even stating, "I believe it is right that colored and white soldiers should be mixed in the same company."[14] Adams, who had heard of Lee's rougher side, found him a delightful dinner companion. Over the course of the dinner Lee asked Adams if her troops could march. Without hesitation, Adams replied that her WACs were the best marching soldiers Lee would ever see. Demonstrating once again that there is never an innocent remark to a general officer, Adams had to make good on her boast. Lee inquired when the battalion would arrive in quarters and said he would be in Birmingham the following day to review the troops.

On February 12, the lead elements of Adams's battalion arrived in Scotland aboard the *Île de France*. General Davis joined Adams and Campbell when the WACs walked off the ship. Within an hour, the entire contingent was en route to Birmingham. True to his word, Lee arrived on the fifteenth to review the soon-to-be-designated 6888th Central Postal Directory. The parade was a tremendous success, and Lee complimented Adams for a sterling performance. On his return to Paris he wrote a letter to Adams's father to tell him what a wonderful unit his daughter commanded and "what a fine young woman" she was. Hundreds of Birmingham residents had also turned out for the parade, and they were equally impressed. The *Birmingham Sunday Mercury* reported that "these WACS are very different from the colored women portrayed on the films, where they are usually either domestics or the outspoken old-retainer type or sloe-eyed sirens given to gaudiness of costume and eccentricity in dress. The WACs have dignity and proper reserve."[15] The excellent impression they made on the local populace eased the unit's entry into Birmingham society. Adams later recalled that she was struck by the frequency which the local residents used the term "black." She had heard the term used as an adjective, but never as a racial designation. "Negro" was the accepted racial designation in World War II, although the term "colored" was also used. "Black" was considered derogatory and inflammatory.[16]

After the parade, the immediate task was to quarter the battalion. Adams spent most of the next few weeks finding housing for her WACs, planning their specific assignments, and putting them to work. Organizing the 6888th Central Postal Directory into five companies, Adams officially assumed command of the unit on March 2, 1945. Her assignment to command was a logical choice but not a foregone conclusion. True, Adams was the senior ranking officer with troop experience, and she had more troop time than any other black commander. Since Eisenhower had personally directed that no promotions in the WAC above the grade of captain could be made without his personal approval, Adams was and would remain one of the senior WAC officers in theater.[17] On the debit side, her entire career had been spent at a single post within the continental United States. There were other officers equally qualified to command the postal battalion, but in the end Adams's pluses far outweighed the minuses. To her relief Adams experienced no resentment from her colleagues with her elevation to command.

Adams's command consisted of approximately eight hundred officers and women. An estimated seven million American personnel were serving in the ETO at that time, and few of them stayed long in one place. It was the responsibility of the "Six Triple Eight" to redirect their mail. Redirecting the mail throughout the European Theater was a monumental task, but the 6888th adopted the motto No Mail, Low Morale and immediately moved to address the backlog. According to Adams, the system worked as follows. Every piece of mail was subjected to attempted delivery at the address listed on the envelope. If the mail could not be delivered at that address, it was sent on to the directory service, where one of Adams's soldiers would check an address card on file, readdress the envelope, and forward it to the new address. Every time a piece of mail was handled, the date and initials of the handler were noted on the face of the envelope. Each piece of mail was "worked" for thirty days; if it could not be delivered during that time, it was returned to the sender. Handling packages proved more difficult. Adams had to establish a "package restoration unit" because many packages from home were too poorly assembled to withstand transport. To accomplish their mission the 6888th worked three eight-hour shifts. Once they had established their standard operating procedures and reached peak efficiency, each shift handled in excess of sixty thousand letters a day, breaking all previous records within the ETO.

As commander of the largest American unit in the area Adams had numerous opportunities to visit surrounding communities as a representative of the U.S. Army. She accepted as many invitations as possible in order to maintain the good relations that the 6888th had established with the Birminghamites and to repudiate the slanderous stories that GIs and the press had told about the black WACs. Long accustomed to prejudice in the United States, Adams found acceptance in Birmingham society, which had become quite cosmopolitan over the course of the war. Her troops frequently attended local dances and were asked to visit local homes. When the Six Triple Eight's stay in Birmingham was extended, the interaction between the WACs and the local citizens increased significantly.

As is the case with all military commands, Adams encountered a few disciplinary problems. On one occasion she discovered that the unit's chaplain was encouraging her soldiers not to report for work and to see him in his office for counseling. Adams in turn counseled the chaplain about interfering with the unit's official duties. The next Sunday, the clergyman addressed the congregation, with Adams in attendance, and urged the women to pray for "their commanding officer because she needs it." Immediately after the service, Adams ordered the chaplain to her office and told him to pack his bags, because a driver would be parked in front of his quarters in one hour to take him to London to report to the chief of chaplains for another assignment. Though Adams confessed that she ran a "relaxed" unit and was often too lenient with her troops, she could be harsh when the situation dictated.

By far the most serious challenge to Adams in her capacity as battalion commander occurred on March 24, 1945, when a general officer in her chain of command paid a visit to the Six Triple Eight. Following an inspection of the postal directory, the officer directed Adams to line up the troops for an inspection. Adams understood his order to mean only off-duty personnel, because one shift was sleeping and another was at work. Rather than halt the mail directory, she fell out the remaining members of the command. Infuriated that the formation "didn't look like a battalion," the general demanded to know where the remainder of the troops were. Adams explained her understanding of the general's instructions, but her words fell on deaf ears. The general informed Adams that he intended to send "a white first lieutenant down to show you how to run this unit." Adams, who prided herself on her self-restraint, lost it on that occasion. "Over my dead body, Sir," she snapped back. The general dismissed her and departed in his limousine, but not before telling Adams that she would hear from him shortly.

Three days later, word reached the 6888th that senior headquarters was drawing up court-martial charges against Adams. With her career on the line, Adams prepared similar charges against the general for making "disparaging racial remarks" and thus violating instructions from SHAEF not to use offensive language that might be indicate racial disharmony within the American army. To make a long story short, the general dropped his charges because he "felt that it would take too much time to bring another WAC officer from the States to replace Adams." Adams, in turn, did not prefer her own charges and let the matter drop. The general was later relieved of duty but was assigned to Normandy at about the time that Adams and the 6888th deployed to the Continent at the end of the war. They would occasionally meet again, but their future encounters were quite pleasant.

As the only black female commander of a battalion-level unit, Adams experienced numerous challenges totally foreign to her white counterparts. She consistently resisted attempts to establish segregated facilities for her soldiers. When the Red Cross denied her soldiers entry into certain facilities and sent similar recreational equipment for Adams to establish a separate facility on her post, she directed that the equipment be immediately returned to the Red Cross. Later, the Red Cross coordinator in London asked Adams to come to the British capital and view a new hotel that was being "set aside for your colored girls." Adams inspected the hotel and then informed the coordinator that she was quite content with the current facilities that permitted integrated visits by all WAC personnel. When the director persisted and spent thousands of dollars to refurbish the hotel, Adams informed him that she was sorry he had gone to so much expense and trouble because the new hotel was not necessary. Adding emphasis to her displeasure, Adams continued, "I promise you that, as God is my witness, as long as I am commanding officer of the 6888th Central Postal Directory Battalion, not one member of that unit will ever spend one night here."[18] The next morning Adams assembled her entire command and gave them several options to govern their leaves and passes to London. None of the options included an overnight stay in the segregated hotel. As she later reflected on her command tour, her proudest moment as a commander occurred when every member of her command concurred with her decision to boycott the segregated hotel.

Adams continued to look after her soldiers with her characteristic vigor. In March 1945 she secured two Quonset huts for use as an NCO hut and an officers' lounge. She also established a beauty salon that proved critical in maintaining morale within her command. Once the word went out that the 6888th had a salon where women "could get their hair done just like in the United States," the postal directory was flooded with female visitors. To address the numerous telephone calls coming into the King Edward School, Adams next installed a telephone system with numerous in-house extensions and sufficient external lines for business and social use. Adams also made sure that her command was adequately fed, properly housed, and given ample time for leisure travel throughout England. For the most part she was uniquely successful in avoiding inconvenience to her troops and was able to maintain the trust and confidence of the WACs entrusted to her command.

On April 12, Adams received word from one of Birmingham's overseas operators that President Roosevelt had died unexpectedly in his Warm Springs, Georgia, home. As the senior U.S. officer in Birmingham, Adams officiated at numerous commemorative services. She personally attended five services, and her officers attended an additional twenty-five over the course of the next week.

The war went on, of course, despite Roosevelt's death, but it was beginning to wind down. When SHAEF decided to move the postal directory unit to the Continent to shorten the delivery distance, Adams prepared to move her command to Rouen. Adams and a small group of WACs arrived in mid-April to assess the directory unit's new site. Although her initial appraisal was not promising, the exigencies of war dictated that Adams would have to make the system work. Leaving a small group in Rouen to prepare for the arrival of the remainder of the 6888th, Adams returned to England to complete the deployment preparations.

VE Day found Adams in Paris. Having returned to the Continent to supervise the deployment of the 6888th to Rouen, Adams experienced firsthand the frenzied adulation of French citizens. Anyone wearing an American uniform was subject to the victory hysteria that gripped the City of Light, and Major Adams was no exception. The next day she was off to Rouen. Located seventy miles northwest of the French capital, Rouen proved to be an ideal location for the postal service. Three hundred POWs had been assigned to construct facilities and provide household maintenance. The presence of these workers, coupled with the rumors that a battalion of female soldiers had arrived in Rouen, generated an unusually high number of visitors to 6888th Headquarters and provided Adams with unusual leadership challenges. Adams recollected that the state of social euphoria lasted two weeks before she and her officers established new rules and regulations that governed the presence of visitors in the military compound.

Like the other commanders, Adams concentrated her efforts on maintaining morale within her own command now that the war was over. As the U.S. Army began its redeployment to the United States, the Six Triple Eight managed to escape most of the problems associated with troops with too much free time on their hands. Adams initiated a weekly "open door" policy during which soldiers of her battalion could address their personal concerns directly to the battalion commander without an appointment. Such policies have become routine at each level of the army's chain of command. Adams was not the first commander to recognize the importance of an open conduit between the troops and their officers, but she certainly used it to full advantage. She also initiated an expanded program of organized athletics to keep her soldiers fully engaged.

Personnel problems did occupy some of Adams's time. Members of the 6888th were frequently invited to visit other commands, and Adams found it necessary to regulate these visits so as not to interfere with the unit's duties. Not surprisingly, she encountered much resentment both inside and outside her command when she denied invitations. As far as prejudice and bigotry were concerned, Adams endured such attitudes with dignity and survived them "in a state of pleasant belligerency." Sadly, there was one real tragedy during the summer of 1945. Three of her soldiers on an authorized social visit to another unit were killed in a vehicle accident. When I spoke to her fifty years after the war, Adams could still identify the soldiers by name.

By late summer, the point system determining priorities for repatriation was taking its toll on the 6888th. The women who had joined the Women's Army Corp at its inception had accumulated sufficient points to begin returning home. Ever mindful of their contribution, and feeling a little nostalgic as her command diminished in numbers, Adams organized several parades in their honor.

In October the 6888th bid farewell to Rouen and moved to Paris. That provided its own set of challenges, but Paris was still the crown jewel of Europe, and the soldiers of the Postal Service Command enjoyed their time there. Officers' quarters for Adams's command were in the Hotel Etats-Unis, a far cry from the cramped quarters in Rouen. Routine disciplinary problems were easily handled, but it became increasingly apparent to Adams that with her command diminishing daily, her elevated rank precluded her retention in theater. When notified that her next assignment would be WAC Headquarters in the Pentagon, Charity Adams requested release from the European Theater and rotation home for release from active duty.

An event that occurred at the start of the homeward voyage reaffirmed Adams's caliber as a commander. Designated "group commander" of the troop transport ship by virtue of her rank, Adams discovered that several white nurses refused to sail home under command of a "colored" officer. Adams's solution was swift and effective—she informed the nurses that they were free to disembark and remain in England while the ship sailed home. She gave them twenty minutes to leave. The *George Washington* sailed on time, with all nurses aboard. For Charity Adams, the war was finally over.

The *George Washington* docked at New York Harbor twelve days later. After debriefing at Camp Shanks, the returning soldiers scattered to the four winds. Adams traveled to Fort Bragg, North Carolina, the army post designated as her separation center. With orders in hand relieving her of active duty effective March 26, 1946, Adams spent an enjoyable holiday season with her family in Columbia, South Carolina. In the interim she received her promotion to lieutenant colonel, effective the day after Christmas. By law she had reached the pinnacle of rank within the Women's Army Corps because full colonel rank was authorized only for the WAC director in Washington, D.C.

Adams had come full circle. Cognizant that she was a role model for young black women, Adams decided to return to Ohio State and complete her graduate degree. Taking a circuitous route to Columbus, she visited Washington, D.C., where noted educator Mary McLeod Bethune presented her with an award for distinguished service on behalf of the National Council of Negro Women. It was the first of numerous awards that Adams would receive in her lifetime. Following graduation from Ohio State, she accepted a job with the Veterans Administration as a claims officer in Cleveland. Adams found the position neither challenging nor satisfying. She remained in Cleveland, however, where she managed Miller Music Academy and became engaged to her future husband. Eventually she returned to the field of education and served as the dean of students at Tennessee A&I College; she later accepted a similar post at Georgia State College. Perhaps remembering her own freshman year, Adams concentrated her efforts on working with freshmen. After a year and a half at Georgia State College, she married Stanley A. Earley Jr., a medical student from the University of Zurich in Switzerland. Adams lived in Zurich until her husband completed his medical training, then returned to the United States and settled in Dayton, Ohio, where she raised her family.

Over the course of the next several decades Earley dedicated her life to community service and to being a spokeswoman for women's and civil rights. She gained both satisfaction from and recognition for her efforts: member of the Ohio Women's Hall of Fame, listing on the Smithsonian Institution's list of the 110 most important historical black women in 1982, Montgomery County (Ohio) Citizen of the Year in 1991, and member of the Ohio Veterans' Hall of Fame are among the awards she received.

In 1989 Earley penned *One Woman's Army: A Black Officer Remembers the WAC* to urge the nation to reflect and to remember the female veterans of World War II. Six years later Lieutenant Colonel Earley introduced President William Jefferson Clinton at a ceremony saluting African Americans in World War II. Afterward the *Washington Post* noted: "The commander-in-chief and the military brass were out in force last night, but it was one of the troops whom everyone saluted at a tribute to African American World War II veterans."[19] The veteran whom everyone saluted was none other than Charity Adams Earley, a true pioneer in every sense of the word. The following year the Smithsonian's National Postal Museum honored Earley for her wartime service. The ceremony proved a fitting climax to a stellar career of public service.

I had the distinct privilege of meeting Charity Adams Earley in the autumn of 1998. I first heard of her from the 1995 Department of Defense ceremony honoring black veterans of World War II and came across her name again a few years later during discussions for Women's History Month at the U.S. Military Academy. When I took leave and traversed the country interviewing the veterans whose stories fill these pages, I called on Lieutenant Colonel Earley. I discovered a congenial woman who was happy to have me stop by her home for a short visit. To my surprise, I found she lived only two blocks from my old college dormitory at the University of Dayton, Ohio. As she gave directions to her home, I told her to go no further as I was intimately familiar with her neighborhood. We soon found that we had another common bond; both of us attended graduate school at The Ohio State University in Columbus, one of the Midwest's premier academic institutions.

I arrived in Dayton in early afternoon on October 11, 1998, having recently visited Vernon Baker, another distinguished black officer from the war, in Saint Maries, Idaho. Charity Earley and her husband graciously greeted me at the door, and for the next two hours Earley patiently answered my many questions concerning her role and that of the Women's Army Corps. Why did she join? Did she realize that she was making history? "Not really," she replied. "You don't know you're making history when it's happening. I just wanted to do my job." She added that most of her soldiers prefer to remember the camaraderie that existed within the Six Triple Eight above all their other experiences. "You would be surprised how many women come up to me," she said, "and inform me that they served under my command. Now we all remember the 'memory part,' not the war part. During the first reunion in New York City, for example, so many came up to me and told stories from those early years." It was evident that she remained quite proud of her old command, which she described as a "terrific outfit." Personal achievement gave way to unit pride as Earley recalled that the women of the 6888th had ventured into a service area where they were not really wanted and had assumed jobs formerly held by men. In performing in a "valiant and praiseworthy manner, they had survived racial prejudice and discrimination with dignity. They were proud and had every right to be."

Other questions rapidly followed. What was her toughest leadership challenge? Did she have any regrets? As she patiently answered my inquiries, I was struck by her mental alertness and her keen memory. She vividly recalled names and places from a conflict fifty-plus years in the past. Never once did she attempt to steal the spotlight. The focus remained on her fellow soldiers and their contributions. Indeed, Adams dedicated her memoir to all the women who served the Allied cause during the war. Although the future of women in the modern military seems assured, she expressed personal joy that female warriors in the U.S. Army of the twenty-first century no longer endure the barriers of sex and race that subjected her contemporaries to ridicule and disrespect. If she had a single message for today's military leaders, she would urge them to "be true to yourselves and the troops under your command." She remembered the members of the Women's Army Auxiliary Corps and the Women's Army Corps by expressing her gratitude "for all the heartaches, hard work, and companionship" that they shared during the war.

As for herself, Charity Adams Earley took immense pride in being a "veteran of service to my country." And that is how she wished to be remembered, as a "caring leader who remained thoughtful of my troops. I want my troops to remember me as a person who never forgot any of them," she told me. "That is the reason I wrote my book, to inform the world about women in service, especially black women. Most of the general public do not understand and do not believe these women played such an important part in the war."[20] Such unselfish patriotism has earned Charity Adams Earley a rightful place alongside her male counterparts in America's pantheon of military heroes.

CHAPTER 15

TO HELL AND BACK: THE SAGA OF AUDIE MURPHY

When I was a child, I was told that men were branded by war. Has the brand been put on me? Have the years of blood and ruin stripped me of all decency? We have been so intent on death that we have forgotten life. I may be branded by war, but I will not be defeated by it.

—*First Lieutenant Audie L. Murphy*

AUDIE LEON MURPHY EMERGED FROM WORLD WAR II as the U.S. Army's most decorated soldier. In nearly three years of combat, Murphy cut a bloody swath across the enemy's ranks like no other soldier who served in the European Theater of Operations. Over the course of the war he personally killed 240 enemy soldiers in combat in Sicily, Italy, and France, and the toll would undoubtedly have been higher had not the army removed him from combat in the spring of 1945 while his nomination for the Medal of Honor was being processed. Sixty years after the war, his combat exploits still defy description. A battlefield genius, Murphy was the recipient of every major award for valor that his grateful nation could bestow. The official tabulation of his decorations compiled by the Department of Defense lists twenty-four medals, including the Medal of Honor, the Distinguished Service Cross, two Silver Stars, the Bronze Star with "V," and the Purple Heart with two clusters.[1] When he finally discarded the uniform, he was still too young to vote. Only his untimely death in an airplane crash in 1971 prevented Murphy from receiving the adulation afforded to America's combat veterans on the fiftieth anniversary of the conflict.

Audie Murphy was born in Hunt County, Texas, on June 20, 1924, the third son of an impoverished sharecropper family. Murphy was one of twelve children born to Emmett and Josie Bell Murphy. By the time he was seventeen, his father had deserted the family and his mother was dead. Life in Hunt County, notes Murphy biographer Don Graham, was always lived in the shadow of the American dream. Murphy himself described his youth as devoid of the normal amenities associated with growing up in America. He had to fight for survival long before he joined the army. "Poverty dogged my every step," he later wrote. "It was a full-time job just existing."[2]

Hunting was one of few sure ways to put food on the table, and Murphy was a crack shot. He seldom missed his target, and his fame spread throughout the neighboring counties. One friend recalled that Audie "had the eyes of a hawk" and could smell and hear his prey long before he could see it. Another said that he could hit darting rabbits from a moving car. Long after the war, Murphy remembered that he was happiest when he was alone and hunting. "In solitude, my dreams made sense; nobody was there to dispute or destroy them."

In the rough-and-tumble world of midland Texas, Murphy matured into a scrawny but tough-minded teenager unafraid of anything or anybody. By the time his mother died in 1941, Audie was seventeen and drifting. With only a fifth-grade education, his prospects were bleak. He worked menial jobs just to scrape out a living and support his brothers and sisters. The limited horizons that circumscribed Murphy's life expanded dramatically with the Japanese attack on Pearl Harbor. "Half-wild with frustration," Murphy attempted to enlist right away, but he was only seventeen years old and too small. Standing five feet five and a half inches tall and weighing a meager 112 pounds, Murphy was turned down by the Marine Corps and then the paratroopers. The local army recruiter told him to come back when he had put on some weight. On June 20, now legally old enough to enlist and slightly heavier, Murphy returned and signed up for the infantry. Ten days later he was off to Camp Wolters, Texas, the same camp to which Vernon Baker had reported for basic training.

At Wolters, the pint-sized recruit encountered real army training. He passed out from the heat during his first session of close-order drill. Nicknamed "Baby" for his youthful appearance, Murphy fought hard to keep his combat classification when his commanding officer tried to have him reclassified as a cook. As a field soldier he was average, earning his highest scores in bayonet training. As a marksman he was mediocre at best, never earning expert status despite his background in rural Texas. At Camp Meade, Maryland, where his unit underwent the final stages of predeployment training, Murphy warded off attempts to have him assigned to the local post exchange. To his immense relief, he was soon en route to North Africa aboard a troop transport.

Murphy and his friends landed at Casablanca as infantry replacements in February 1943. The invasion of Africa was in full swing by then, with the Americans suffering a severe reversal at Kasserine Pass in mid-February. Murphy was assigned to Company B, 1st Battalion, 15th Infantry Regiment, 3rd Infantry Division, a unit that would serve as his home for the remainder of the war.[3] He was hoping to see action right away, but the war in Morocco was nearly over. The next several months were just another "long, monotonous period of training." In late spring, just before the fighting ended in North Africa, Murphy received his first promotion, to private first class. Disappointed at being denied the chance to fight Germans, Murphy prepared for the upcoming invasion of Sicily. Operation Husky was scheduled for the second week in July, and the 3rd Infantry Division was destined to play a key role. To prepare the division for the impending assault on a hostile shore, the commanding general, Lucian K. Truscott Jr., told his men: "You are going to meet the Boche! Carve your name in his face!"[4]

Murphy waded ashore with Company B just east of Licata in the early hours of July 10. Shortly thereafter Baker Company suffered its first casualties during an artillery exchange. His first sight of dead American soldiers killed any compassion Murphy might have felt prior to his initial encounter with the enemy. His commander still thought he was too small for combat, but Murphy repeatedly volunteered for frontline patrols. In front of his company with a group of scouts just a few days after the invasion, Murphy and his patrol saw two Italian officers attempting to escape on a couple of magnificent white horses. Reacting instinctively, Murphy dropped to one knee, fired twice, and killed both officers. He had shed his first blood, killed his first enemy soldiers. Surprisingly, he felt "no qualms; no pride; no remorse." All empathy for the enemy had vanished when his platoon lost those first men. "I saw a couple of guys I knew get blown up. I was very serious after that. Very serious. I wanted to take what toll on the enemy I could," he later recalled.[5] From that point on, he was saddled with "a weary indifference" that would follow him throughout the war. Murphy's commander cautioned him to be careful but also promoted him to corporal and continued to send him back to the front lines, instructing his new squad leader to "get up there and give 'em hell." Murphy always went, but he got so sick of action that he would vomit.

Audie Murphy's first experience in killing followed years of honing his skills as a hunter. His friend David McClure later recalled that he had never seen a man with faster reflexes. With Murphy, to think was to act. "If he thinks too much," McClure continued, "he loses the advantage of reflex. . . . If Audie fires on instinct, he is deadly accurate, but if he starts tracking the bird with his gun, he is apt to miss. . . . His vision is fabulous and his sense of smell is very acute. During the war, he was sent out to capture prisoners for intelligence on night patrols, and was able to locate the Germans by the smell of the tobacco they smoked and thus gain the advantage by surprise."[6] Although Murphy's marksmanship skills became legendary during combat, during basic training he had received the lowest possible classification. The reason is no mystery. All GIs fired from a static position during training, but combat placed a higher premium on instinct and fire and movement, and in this style of fighting Murphy excelled.

Instinct was hardly the sole reason for Murphy's success. Combat experience also proved an able teacher. In the weeks that followed the amphibious assault, Murphy continually honed his skills as a soldier. With the Italians and Germans in retreat, Baker Company and the 3rd Division pushed on to Palermo and then east toward Messina. Using the "Truscott trot," marching at a rate of five miles per hour over rugged terrain, the division kept steady pressure on the retreating enemy. Along the way, malaria did what no enemy could do—it put Murphy on the sideline. He was back in action within days, however, this time facing the best German troops on the island. The division's progress was slow and painful. From his position on a ridge overlooking a fire-swept valley, Murphy watched his company commander die outside Mount Fratello. In *To Hell and Back* he admitted that he contributed little to this particular battle but gained much experience. He came to understand that his adversaries were seasoned fighters who never gave an inch and were particularly proficient in directing indirect fire and covering the approaches to their defensive positions with interlocking direct fire. Murphy realized that to succeed, he had to be able to outthink and outfight his enemy. Reflecting on his battlefield experience, Murphy remembered that Sicily took "the vinegar out of my spirit. I have seen war as it actually is and I don't like it." There was no denying that war had seasoned him—making him battle-wise and intensely practical. Combat against the Germans had also hardened him into a veteran who clearly understood that survival required killing the enemy before they killed him.

In mid-September the 3rd Division participated in Operation Avalanche, the invasion of the Italian mainland. For the next two months Murphy remained in almost continuous combat. The men of the 15th Regiment crossed the Volturno River in October and plodded north until they reached the outskirts of Monte Cassino a month later. Murphy directed his squad in daily combat, usually against isolated German machine-gun emplacements. Trapped for three days in a cave with his men, Murphy watched helplessly when one of them lost his composure, exposed himself to enemy fire, and was cut down by a German sniper on the opposite side of the river.

Outside Mignano, astride Highway 6, Murphy and his squad encountered a German combat patrol "intent to kill without an instant's hesitation or an atom of mercy." Murphy's squad ambushed them, killing them all with a machine-gun burst followed by systematic fire from their individual weapons. After two months in the line, they were finally pulled off and given a short respite. In the interim Murphy and his squad had become proficient in the business of killing. Taking numerous casualties themselves, they accepted that "the only safe Germans are dead ones." More battles, more dead. The strains of daily combat dulled Murphy's senses. "My eyeballs burn; my bones ache; and my muscles twitch, from exhaustion. Oh, to sleep and never awaken. The war is without beginning, without end. It goes on forever." His words were to prove prophetic, for memories of the war would haunt the young Texan for the remainder of his life.

Malaria and influenza again felled Murphy on the eve of the amphibious attack at Anzio. A week later he was back, ignoring orders to remain in the rear to perform mundane duties. He preferred to be with his comrades in Baker Company, which had now been reduced to thirty-four men. Murphy's platoon had been especially hard hit, and he was anxious to rejoin them. The company clerk informed Murphy that he had received a battlefield promotion to staff sergeant and directed him to report to the company commander. Murphy's first assignment was to take out a reconnaissance patrol to decipher the enemy's intentions. The patrol determined that the enemy was preparing defensive positions in anticipation of an Allied offensive. The next day, acting platoon sergeant Murphy led the remnants of the 3rd Platoon into the first battle for Cisterna, a small village several miles inland. The battle raged for several days, with the Germans conducting "fanatical and desperate" resistance before they were finally driven from their entrenchments. Baker Company incurred tremendous casualties before the battle evolved into a stalemate.

For the next two months, the front lines remained essentially where they were; constant artillery barrages and periodic patrolling were the only actions on both sides. On March 2, Murphy earned his first award for valor—a Bronze Star with "V" device—when he led a patrol that knocked out an enemy tank, an incident that is vividly portrayed in the cinematic version of *To Hell and Back.* In the process he attracted the attention of his new battalion commander, who labeled Murphy "a soldier, a born leader, potentially a fine officer."[7] In May, Murphy received the Combat Infantryman Badge and an oak leaf cluster to his Bronze Star. At the end of the month, the 3rd Division finally broke out of the Anzio beachhead and joined the advancing Fifth U.S. Army in its final push toward Rome, a city that Murphy called "but another objective on an endless road called war." Rome fell the first week in June, and for Murphy and Baker Company the Italian campaign was over. The absence of combat provided little respite for Murphy, who prowled Rome "like a ghost, finding no satisfaction in anything" he saw or did. He was relieved to have a "brief reprieve from death," but his thoughts remained with the men on the fighting fronts.

For the 3rd Division, the lull in the battle was temporary. In mid-August the 15th Regiment deployed in the first assault wave that waded through the swirling waters onto the beaches of the French Riviera in what Murphy described as "a near-perfect landing." Code-named Anvil, the invasion was designed to soften up the German defenses and take the pressure off the Allied forces engaged in Normandy. The ensuing combat was the beginning of an incredible six-month period in which the Murphy legend was born. For his deeds during that period, when he was virtually in daily contact with the enemy, Audie Murphy was awarded the three highest awards for valor that his country offered. Receiving either the Medal of Honor, the Distinguished Service Cross, or the Silver Star is remarkable; to receive all three is beyond belief. Yet that is exactly what Murphy did, beginning on the first day he and his comrades waded ashore.

A mile inland from the beach, Murphy and his platoon encountered a German pillbox whose fire raked the valley below and killed two of Murphy's men. Leaving his men in a covered position, Murphy dashed forty yards through withering fire to a draw. Two Germans exposed themselves, and Murphy killed them both with his carbine. Just then Murphy was joined by his best friend, Brandon, a man Murphy had once described as closer to him than a brother. Refusing to allow his friend to make the assault on his own, Brandon had left the concealed position in which Murphy had ordered him to remain. As Murphy and Brandon continued up the hill, they came under intense machine-gun fire. They fired back, silencing some of the enemy guns. Brandon saw the remaining Germans hold up a white flag and rose to accept their surrender. It was a trick. When Brandon stood up, a machine gun sliced him in two. Now alone, Murphy instinctively spun about to find the machine gun a few yards to his right. He hurled a grenade and killed the two German defenders. Finding the machine gun in good working order, he cradled it like a BAR and started up the hill, firing from the hip. What happened next is best told in his own words: "I remember the experience as I do a nightmare. A demon seems to have entered my body. My brain is coldly alert and logical. I do not think of the danger to myself. My whole being is concentrated on killing. Later the men pinned down in the vineyard tell me that I shout pleas and curses at them, because they do not come up and join me. . . . I find the gun crew that betrayed Brandon . . . and have time to take careful aim before pulling the trigger. As the lacerated bodies flop and squirm, I rake them again; and I do not stop while there is a quiver left in them." Private First Class Norman Hollen, one of Murphy's men, confirmed Murphy's account, stating that "Staff Sergeant Murphy killed 8, wounded 3, and captured 11 of the enemy in approximately an hour, single-handedly cleaning out the entire enemy position."[8]

Only after he had wiped out all resistance did Murphy return to Brandon and collapse from sheer mental and physical exhaustion. Then he sat by his buddy's side and cried like a baby. After a little while he got up, wiped the tears from his eyes, and walked over the hill to rejoin his company. For his extraordinary heroism resulting in the capture of a fiercely contested enemy-held hill and the annihilation and capture of the entire enemy garrison, Murphy received the Distinguished Service Cross.[9]

German resistance in southern France rapidly collapsed, and by mid-September Murphy's unit had joined elements of Patton's Third Army in its sweep across northern France. Murphy received his first wound near Genevreuville, France, when an exploding mortar shell knocked him unconscious. The five soldiers surrounding Murphy were all killed or wounded. Miraculously, Murphy's luck held, and after a few days in the field hospital he returned to the front lines. With Brandon's death Murphy's war became more personal. He repeatedly volunteered for dangerous missions, many of which he conducted himself.[10]

German resistance intensified as September merged into October. As the enemy began fortifying the heavily wooded approaches to the Vosges Mountains, Murphy lost yet another close comrade and swore he would never get close to any man again. Murphy continued his private war during the first week of October, and for his exploits within a three-day period was awarded two Silver Stars. In the first instance, he "inched his way over rugged, uneven terrain, toward an enemy machine gun which had surprised a group of officers on reconnaissance. Advancing to within fifteen yards of the German gun, Murphy stood up and disregarding a burst of enemy fire delivered at close range and which miraculously missed him, he flung two hand grenades into the machine-gun position, killing four Germans, wounding three more and destroying the position."[11] Murphy remembered that the eighth German, "a fat, squat man," tried to escape, running down the hill "like a duck being chased by an ax-man." Murphy fixed his sights on the man's helmet and then hesitated; killing him would be like "killing a clown." But in this instance the clown had a gun. Murphy slowly squeezed the trigger, and the enemy fell "as if struck in the head with a club."

The next day he took it upon himself to eliminate a German sniper simply because "he needed a release from taut nerves." Offended that his company commander ordered him to take two men to provide covering fire, Murphy reluctantly agreed. Once they were in position, he deposited them behind a boulder and went after the sniper himself. Murphy crawled forward on his belly and then leaned against a rock for support as he waited for some sound or movement to give away the sniper's position. As he later told the story, he heard a rustle and his eyes snapped forward. Noticing that the branches of a neighboring bush moved ever so slightly, Murphy dropped to one knee and fired twice at a "face as black as a rotting corpse; his cold eyes filled with evil." Throwing two grenades to take care of any companions the man might have had in the area, Murphy advanced and saw the devastation he had wrought. The sniper had two bullet holes in the center of his forehead, and the grenades had torn off his arm. Murphy vomited at the sight—as he did again when he came across two more German dead from the previous day's action, "soggy corpses [that] had taken on a wooden appearance." Returning to headquarters, he made his report and then casually took his carbine apart and started cleaning it. Another mission completed.

Years later Murphy told a friend: "I took my time on that one. That sniper sonofabitch was lethal." In 1955 Murphy recalled his duel with the sniper in different terms. According to this version, "They say I killed 241 men in

World War II. I only really remember one. He was a sniper in Germany. He had accounted for a couple of my buddies and I didn't feel anything as I squeezed the trigger. When the bullet hit him, I saw the expression on his face in the rifle sights . . . then he collapsed like a rag doll and fell to the ground."[12] By now Murphy was the most famous soldier in the Marne Division. After being featured in *Stars and Stripes*, he was recognized wherever he went.

The second Silver Star was awarded for an action on October 5. Company B ran into a heavily defended position astride a dry stream bed at the base of a slope. Murphy's platoon walked into a perfectly executed ambush and was cut to pieces. Under intense machine-gun and rifle fire, Murphy moved down the slope "like a lizard," crawling fifty yards to a point two hundred yards from a strongly entrenched enemy who prevented further advance. From that site Murphy directed artillery fire on enemy positions for an hour, killing fifteen Germans and inflicting approximately thirty-five additional casualties.[13] The artillery did the trick. After rousting the enemy from their positions, Murphy and his remaining men "bore into them" with their rifles, shooting down the fleeing enemy as if in a turkey shoot. As the remainder of Baker Company came up, he and his platoon slung their weapons and continued their advance to the slope beyond. For his courage and audacity, which enabled his company to advance and attain its objective, Murphy was again cited for gallantry in action and awarded the Silver Star.

One week later, Murphy and two other noncommissioned officers received battlefield promotions to second lieutenant. This time his commander forced him to accept the promotion, which he had previously declined in order to remain with his platoon. There was no refusing this time, as platoon leaders were in increasingly short supply. As the battalion commander pinned the bars of an officer on Murphy's shoulders, he stated, "You are now gentlemen by act of Congress. Shave, take a bath, and get the hell back into the lines." Two weeks later, near Les Rouges Eaux, France, Murphy suffered his second wound, this time taking a sniper's bullet in the hip. Typically, Murphy drilled the sniper between the eyes at thirty-five yards' distance before being evacuated to the rear. That night Murphy's entire platoon was nearly wiped out.

Gangrene and infection delayed his convalescence, and it was January 1945 before Lieutenant Murphy returned to action. By that time the 3rd Division had pushed through the Vosges, cracked the enemy's "winter line," and reached the Rhine River at Strasbourg. Assigned to clean up the Colmar pocket, the Marne men now embarked on yet another dangerous campaign. Murphy's regiment joined the attack in mid-January and immediately encountered stiff resistance. After suffering numerous casualties, Murphy's platoon dug in near the Riedwihr Woods outside Holtzwihr, France. As he slept that night his hair literally froze to the ground. Awakened by a gunshot, he raised his head and left "patches of his hair in the ice." As they were lining up for another attack the next morning, the Americans were struck by a heavy mortar barrage. The two officers who had been commissioned along with Murphy were killed instantly, but again Murphy escaped, this time with a superficial wound in the leg.

The next day, January 26, Company B commenced another attack. Of the seven officers who had initiated the advance two days earlier, only Murphy remained. Headquarters ordered him to take command of Company B, drive to the edge of the woods facing Holtzwihr, dig in, and hold at all costs. Another company would pass through Murphy's lines and continue the attack. By dawn, no company had appeared and Company B, now reduced to eighteen effectives, prepared to meet the full onslaught of a German attack. Fortunately, two tank destroyers reinforced the company during the evening, but still no infantry arrived to fill Murphy's depleted ranks.

At 1400 Murphy noticed the Germans deploying for an attack. Six tanks and two companies totaling 250 infantry started across the field toward Murphy's front. The two tank destroyers were immediately hit and put out of action. At that moment, Murphy "knew we were lost." Calling for immediate artillery, Murphy ordered the remainder of the company to pull back. Characteristically, he remained at the edge of the woods to adjust the counter-barrage fire against the oncoming infantry, now within two hundred yards of his position. He emptied his carbine and had begun to pull back when he noticed that the machine gun on the damaged tank destroyer on his flank was still intact. Murphy rushed to the turret and emptied a full belt of ammunition into the advancing enemy, all the while adjusting the artillery fire by radio. The tank destroyer was repeatedly struck by direct enemy fire, but Murphy remained where he was, "conscious only that the smoke and the turret afford a good screen, and that, for the first time in three days, my feet are warm."

The German attack intensified and still Murphy held his position. Noticing twelve Germans just ten yards from the side of the tank destroyer, Murphy fired and killed them all just as the blast from a German 88-mm gun knocked him off the turret. His right leg now throbbing with pain, Murphy slid off the tank destroyer just minutes before the vehicle exploded, and then hobbled down the road through the forest to rejoin Baker Company. The entire experience left him with "no sense of triumph, no exhilaration at being alive. . . . Existence had taken on the quality of a dream in which I was detached from all that was present. I could hear the shells bursting among the trees, see the dead scattered on the ground; but did not connect them with anything that particularly concerned me." Once back with his command, he refused medical attention and organized the company in a counterattack that forced the Germans to withdraw. The next day the remnants of Baker Company were replaced on the front line.

For heroism above and beyond the call of duty, Murphy was nominated for the Medal of Honor. The award citation notes that Murphy, alone and atop a burning tank destroyer, "killed dozens of Germans and caused their infantry attack to waver. The enemy tanks, losing infantry support, began to fall back." For an hour the Germans tried every available weapon to eliminate him, but he continued to hold his position, all the time "directing artillery fire. . . . Murphy wiped out many of the enemy and killed or wounded about 50. Lieutenant Murphy's indomitable courage and his refusal to give an inch of ground saved his company from possible encirclement and destruction, and enabled it to hold the woods which had been the enemy's objective."[14]

Murphy's heroism was subsequently confirmed by Lieutenant Walter Weispfenning, Sergeant Elmer C. Brawley, and Private First Class Anthony Abramski. Weispfenning, an American artillery officer who observed the action, stated that Murphy "was clearly exposed [to the enemy], making a silhouette against the snow and leafless trees." It was, he said, "the bravest thing I ever saw a man do in combat."[15] Brawley added his own description of events: "[Enemy] tanks added their murderous fire to that of the kraut artillery and small-arms fire that showered the Lieutenant's position without stopping. The German infantrymen got within ten yards of the Lieutenant, who killed them in the draws, in the meadows, in the woods—wherever he saw them. Though wounded and covered with soot and dirt which must have obscured his vision at times, he held the enemy at bay, killing and wounding at least 35 during the next hour."[16] Abramski called Murphy's one-man battle "the greatest display of guts and courage I have ever seen. There is only one in a million who would be willing to stand up on a burning vehicle, loaded up with explosives, and hold off around 250 raging Krauts for an hour and do all that when he was wounded."[17]

Murphy's company returned to the line after the action at Holtzwihr. As acting company commander, Murphy told the replacements that B Company specialized in killing. Lacking time for a pep talk, he merely instructed them to follow the example of the veterans and said that as far as he was concerned they were able men until they proved otherwise. Then he led them forward to the front line to tempt fate. Murphy described the unit's move as "a phantom body of troops doing a forced march through hell." More battles, more casualties. Eventually the Colmar pocket was cleared, but over the course of seven weeks the division had suffered forty-five hundred casualties. At long last Murphy's unit was pulled from the line and sent to a rest camp to recuperate before the next mission. On February 16, Murphy received a battlefield promotion to first lieutenant.

With the end of the war finally in sight, Baker Company's training concentrated on house-to-house fighting, an indication to Murphy that the unit was preparing to march into Germany itself as soon as the weather improved. The lull in the fighting caused the GIs, Murphy included, to reflect on the end of the war and their personal survival. Murphy refused to be optimistic, noting that "the road across Germany is a long one; and each mile of it must be bought with somebody's blood. Why not mine? My luck has been extraordinary, but there is an end even to the extraordinary. So until the last shot is fired, I will go on living from day to day, making no postwar plans."[18] For Murphy, however, the fighting *was* nearly over. His former company commander returned, and Murphy was transferred to liaison duty away from the front lines. Receiving the "gift of life without inward emotion because" he was "so much a part of the war that it does not matter," Murphy refused to hope that his new duties would save him, fearing that when he returned to the front, as inevitably he would, "somewhere, sometime, the bullet bearing my name will find me." To improve his chances of survival, he added a few rifles, two German machine guns, and a case of grenades to his jeep's basic armament.

Not content to remain in the rear after he heard that B Company's commander had been killed, Murphy returned to the men with whom he had fought since North Africa. "Oh, hell," he once told a nurse who was dressing his wounds, "as long as there's a man in the lines, maybe I feel that my place is up there beside him." Officially he returned only to check a telephone line, but once he was forward Murphy abandoned his jeep and moved ahead armed with his familiar carbine. On reaching the company, even Murphy was surprised at the men's condition. They looked as if they had experienced a "thorough psychological beating . . . a mass collapse of nerves." He immediately rallied the noncommissioned officers and ordered an advance. B Company penetrated the Siegfried Line against little opposition. The Marne Division crossed the Rhine River on March 26–27 in the vicinity of Worms and Mannheim. Now in Germany, they liberated Nürnburg and drove toward Munich in the war's final weeks. The Germans were finished, exhausted by six years of war. Near Salzburg, Austria, Murphy had his last contact with the enemy when he accepted the surrender of a German officer. For all intents and purposes, the war in Europe was over.

VE Day officially marked the end of Murphy's fighting war, but the conflict never really ended for him; it had indelibly altered his psyche. He heard the official news of the German surrender while he was en route to the French Riviera for a well-deserved leave. While the other GIs were wildly celebrating and chasing women, Murphy lay in a bathtub reflecting on the first moments of peace since the end of the war, and then took a nap. "I didn't know a body could get so tired," he later said. When he awoke in mid-afternoon, the town was relatively quiet and Murphy decided to walk the streets. Searching for his necktie, he spied his service revolver and automatically picked it up, "removed the clip, and checked the mechanism. . . . I weigh[ed] the weapon in my hand and admired the cold, blue glint of its steel. It is more beautiful than a flower; more faithful than most friends." Murphy put the pistol aside and strolled the crowded streets, but his mind was elsewhere. "There is VE-Day without, but no peace within," he reflected in his memoirs.[19] First Lieutenant Audie Murphy, the hero of the 3rd Infantry Division, was a troubled man haunted by the carnage of war.

Back from leave, Murphy assumed command of Company B, 15th Infantry Regiment, on May 20, 1945. Four days later, word arrived that he was to be awarded the Medal of Honor. By any standard Murphy's achievements had been remarkable. A veteran of nine campaigns, he had risen from buck private to company commander. All in all it had been a brilliant performance by a lone GI from midland Texas. On June 1 the Texas House of Representatives passed a resolution honoring him for his many valorous deeds during the war. The next day Lieutenant General Alexander Patch, Seventh Army commander, presented the Medal of Honor to Murphy at an airfield near Werfen, Austria. Murphy was three weeks shy of his twenty-first birthday. With the Legion of Merit—awarded to every member of the armed services who had distinguished themselves by conspicuous service—added to his total, Murphy edged ahead of legendary soldier Maurice Britt, a fellow "Marne" man, and became the most decorated soldier of the war. His final medal tally, including foreign decorations, totaled thirty-seven, of which eleven were for valor.[20]

The medals themselves meant little to Murphy. In his view, the real heroes remained behind, buried under wooden crosses. The true recipients were the soldiers as a unit, not individuals. Murphy viewed himself merely as the unit's caretaker. The ghosts of the men who had been killed or wounded haunted him. Of the original 235-man roster of Company B who had deployed to the Mediterranean, only 2 remained—Murphy and a supply sergeant. Small wonder that he described his combat experiences as a "horror film run backwards, images of the war flickering through my brain." Always present were the men who had stood shoulder to shoulder with him at Anzio, on the beach near Ramatuelle, France, and near Holtzwihr—men "who went and would go again to hell and back to preserve what our country thinks right and decent."

In his brilliant analysis of America's combat experience in World War II, Gerald F. Linderman identifies the evolution of comradeship as personified by Murphy's combat career. So fully did Murphy believe that "comradeship was war's sole redemptive element and thus that war's only positive function was as the vehicle of comradeship, that World War II became for Murphy, in effect, a comrade" in itself. In Italy, Murphy held the dead Brandon and could not accept the fact that his friend was dead, because if Brandon "was dead, the war was all wrong and Brandon had died in vain." Soldiers like Murphy went to extraordinary lengths to help their comrades survive to fight another day. In the Riedwihr Woods near Holtzwihr, for example, Murphy sent his men to the rear and then fought a one-man battle against the advancing Germans. Calling friendly artillery down on his own position, Murphy fought on because "I don't give a damn. . . . If the Germans want to shoot me, let them. I am too weak from fear and exhaustion to care." Without comradeship, notes Linderman, there is nothing.[21]

In the conclusion of his wartime memoir, Murphy expresses his sincere hope that he has not been so intent on death that he has forgotten life. He longed to learn to work in peacetime, to "experience life through uncynical eyes." On June 13, Texas's favorite son returned to the United States, landing at San Antonio after more than two years overseas. But there was little rest for Murphy amid the tumultuous homecomings and plethora of "Audie Murphy Days" in Hunt County and the surrounding communities. In Farmersville, Texas, the entire town stood in ninety-eight-degree heat to cheer while he made a brief, bashful speech. Then it was off to get his hair cut in the Greer Barbershop, where Mrs. J. C. Greer remembered how she had frequently cut his hair before Murphy's enlistment. He also visited Miss Hattie Neathery, for whom he had once delivered newspapers. In Farmersville, Murphy celebrated his twenty-first birthday with his sister and her husband before driving to Dallas for another appearance.

By the time his face graced the cover of *Life* magazine on July 16, 1945, Audie Murphy was already famous as America's most decorated soldier of the war. *Life*'s photographic essay glamorized the boyish soldier fresh from the battlefields of Europe and made Murphy a national hero. Murphy spent the summer of 1945 being entertained by an adoring public, the recipient of numerous civic honors and accolades. Unknown to all but his closest associates were the restless nights disturbed by recurring dreams of combat. Once he told his sister Corinne, "I didn't sleep a minute last night. I fought the damned war all night long." Another time Corinne awoke and found all the lights in the house on. Murphy had turned them on to keep from falling asleep and having those bad dreams.[22] Away from the daily stress of combat that had accompanied him for two years, but released without any psychological debriefing, Murphy was suffering from chronic war weariness. Like hundreds of thousands of other GIs, he was totally unprepared to return to civilian life.

His life changed dramatically when actor Jimmy Cagney wired him and invited him to come to Hollywood in late summer 1945. Always looking for new talent, Cagney recognized the potential bonanza of signing Murphy to a long-term contract. After his discharge from the army on September 21, Murphy boarded a plane and flew west to embark on what proved to be a twenty-year career in feature films. In all, he appeared in forty-four films, starring in all but three of them. His most memorable performance was in *The Red Badge of Courage*, Stephen Crane's Civil War classic, in which he portrayed troubled Henry Fleming. Typecast as a good-guy gunslinger in numerous B-movie westerns, Murphy reached his apogee in the western genre with *Destry,* which began shooting in mid-1954. The next year brought the release of *To Hell and Back*, an autobiographical portrayal based on his wartime memoir of the same name. If *Life* had made Murphy a household name in 1945, *To Hell and Back* achieved the same results a decade later. Then, unfortunately, the good scripts dried up and Murphy's cinematic career faded rapidly.

During the last two decades of his life, Murphy attempted to stay active in civic affairs. He received numerous awards during this period. He returned to France in 1948 to be decorated with the insignia of the 159th Alpine Infantry Regiment at a luncheon hosted by the mayor of Ramatuelle. The following week he received the National Order of the Legion of Honor, grade Chevalier, from a grateful France, along with the French Croix de Guerre with Palm from General de Lattre de Tassigny. Belgium would award Murphy its Croix de Guerre with Palm for combat in 1955. In 1949 the governor of Texas presented Murphy with an honorary commission in the Texas Rangers, and the following year Audie Murphy was sworn in as a member of the Texas National

Guard's 36th Infantry Division. He remained active in the reserve components through 1957, retiring with the rank of major in 1969.

All the awards and citations could not conceal that fact that the life of America's greatest war hero was out of control. By the mid-1960s Murphy's personal life paralleled the demise of his movie fortunes. One failed marriage, a troubled second union, and a penchant for gambling and chasing women led Murphy into a downward spiral from which he never fully recovered. With his movie career behind him, he found pleasure in writing lyrics for country and western songs, achieving limited success. He also wrote poetry as an outlet for his energy. Always present was his need to stay active. "That's what two years of combat did to me," he later exclaimed. Through it all, the big money always eluded him. After several failed business ventures he was bankrupt by 1968. It was during an attempt to reach financial solvency by resurrecting his acting career that Murphy boarded a two-engine Aero-Commander for a short commute from Atlanta to Martinsburg, Virginia, in May 1971. His plane never arrived. It crashed into a mountain outside Roanoke on Memorial Day weekend.

Audie Murphy died as he had lived, a restless spirit wound tight as a coiled spring. He lived life at an accelerated pace, with his war memories giving constant chase. Unable to adjust to a tranquil lifestyle following three years of living on battle's edge, he could never be still. By the age of fifty, no longer a Hollywood commodity, Murphy had become an old man. His friend Casey Tibbs summed up the final decade of Murphy's life thus: "Audie was one of my best friends and I really loved the guy, and he was a great guy, but I think he was the closest man to self-destruction I ever knew in my life."[23] Another observer noted that the "tension between man and image had become a permanent fact of Murphy's life. It was as though he had never lived except as our war hero."[24]

How ironic that Murphy, who had escaped death a hundred times in war, surrendered his life on the holiday when Americans traditionally honor their war veterans. The news of Audie Murphy's demise brought numerous tributes. Keith L. Ware, who once served as Murphy's battalion commander and who himself received the Medal of Honor, remembered Murphy as "the finest soldier" he had ever seen. The wartime commanding general of the 3rd Infantry Division, John W. "Iron Mike" O'Daniel, stated emphatically that Audie Murphy was "the greatest combat soldier I have ever known. He even outshone the host of Medal of Honor heroes produced by the immortal 3rd Infantry Division in World War II. . . . [Murphy] led that breed of gallant men who gave the Marne Division its spirit, heart and success . . . from Casablanca to Berchtesgaden." Army Chief of Staff William C. Westmoreland praised Murphy, noting that his "example to fellow Americans served as an inspiration to all persons during World War II."

In 1996, twenty-five years after Murphy's death, the Honorable Ralph M. Hall of the U.S. House of Representatives paid a lasting tribute to one of his district's native sons by entering a tribute to Murphy in the *Congressional Record*.[25] In closing, Hall cited two odes that Murphy himself had composed to express his feelings for his fallen comrades. They reveal the truest measure of a genuine American hero.

"Alone and Far Removed"

Alone and far removed from earthly care
The noble ruins of men lie buried here.
You were strong men, good men
Endowed with youth and much the will to live.
I hear no protest from the mute lips of the dead.
They rest; there is no more to give.

"Freedom Flies in Your Heart Like an Eagle"

Dusty old helmet, rusty old gun,
They sit in the corner and wait—
Two souvenirs of the Second World War
That have withstood the time, and the hate.

Mute witness to a time of much trouble.
Where kill or be killed was the law—
Were these implements used with high honor?
What was the glory they saw?

Many times I've wanted to ask them—
And now that we're here all alone,
Relics all three of a long ago war—
Where has freedom gone?

Freedom flies in your heart like an eagle.
Let it soar with the winds high above

Among the spirits of soldiers now sleeping,
Guard it with care and with love.

I salute my old friends in the corner,
I agree with all they have said—
And if the moment of truth comes tomorrow,
I'll be free, or By God, I'll be dead!

In death Audie Murphy finally achieved the peace that had eluded him throughout his life. He was laid to rest with full military honors in Arlington National Cemetery on June 7, 1971. Hundreds of mourners were present, among them future president George Bush and forty members of Murphy's old 3rd Infantry Division. In his will Murphy stipulated that he wished to be buried in a simple soldier's metal casket with no outer casing. Years later, when the federal government replaced the headstones of all Medal of Honor recipients with the standard gold leaf inlaid lettering, Murphy's family requested that his be kept inconspicuous. That's the way Murphy would have wanted it—plain and simple.

Today few monuments to America's most decorated war hero remain. The Audie L. Murphy Memorial Veterans Hospital stands in San Antonio, Texas, and in the year 2000 the U.S. Postal Service honored Murphy with a postage stamp. Other than that, he has nearly faded from memory. To that extent, Audie Murphy was himself a casualty of the war, twenty-six years removed from the day the guns fell silent in central Europe. At Arlington he remains today "among the soldiers now sleeping," finally at ease among the other veterans who have paid the last full measure of their devotion.

EPILOGUE

WITH THE RETURN OF PEACE, the American military machine that had successfully waged war across the globe began the process of demobilization. Major combat operations terminated in Europe with the unconditional surrender of Germany to General Eisenhower on May 7, and in the Pacific with the Japanese delegation signing the articles of capitulation on the deck of the USS *Missouri* on September 2, 1945. At the war's end roughly 8,267,958 officers and enlisted men and women were actively serving in the U.S. Army and Army Air Forces. Army and air force casualties from 1941 to 1945 totaled 234,874 killed directly from hostile action and 565,861 wounded. Of the 16 million Americans who served in World War II, 405,399 persons died during their service.[1]

How to summarize the U.S. Army's contributions to Allied victory? Writing on the eve of World War II, Dwight D. Eisenhower warned that Hitler should be wary of the "fury of an aroused democracy." He was correct. The future supreme commander of the Allied Expeditionary Force was stationed in Manila when Hitler invaded Poland. He hastily penned an entry into his diary when he heard the news: "This crisis has made me more than ever anxious to get home. I want to be back with my own army to watch and be a part of our own development and preparations . . . to keep in closer touch with the daily record of the war as it is made."[2] That expression of the American spirit found an outlet in the U.S. Army.

The American army that fought World War II reflected both the strengths and the weaknesses of a democracy at war. In the two decades between the wars, senior military planners had laid the foundation for a mass citizen army without the benefit of conscription. Budgetary constraints hindered the modernization and mechanization of the armed forces, causing undue hardships on a succession of army chiefs of staff, from John J. Pershing to George C. Marshall. Hitler's attack against Poland on September 1, 1939, finally gave impetus to a series of Selective Service acts that reintroduced the draft, but the expanding army was ill trained when America joined the Allied cause in 1941. As chief of staff, Marshall moved quickly to prepare for global warfare, but the U.S. Army entered the war with an imbalance between air and ground forces, a shortage of armored and mechanized forces, and an individual replacement system that proved inadequate once casualties decimated the ranks of the frontline units. Prewar training also failed to meet the needs of modern combat; Kasserine Pass and Buna demonstrated the army's inadequacies with respect to logistics, battlefield tactics, and combined arms warfare. Battlefield leaders, including Bob Eichelberger, George S. Patton, and Omar Bradley, carefully analyzed the results of battles and conducted after-action reviews that corrected many of the deficiencies. By the end of the Sicilian and New Guinea campaigns, the army had made marked improvements in virtually every aspect of combat and combat service support. Additional combat eventually transformed the American army into an institution that was arguably the finest national army on Earth.

The U.S. Army also reflected the multiple strengths of American democracy. Although lacking the professionalism that marked the Wehrmacht in 1939, the individual GI proved a quick learner. The enlisted ranks constituted one of the best-educated armies of the world; nearly 50 percent were high school graduates, and one in ten had attended a college or university. All division- and higher-level commanders were products of the army's emphasis on institutionalized professional education. Moreover, the GIs were more independent minded and more accustomed to taking initiative than their German and Japanese adversaries. The average American soldier was twenty-six years old, five feet eight inches tall, and weighed 144 pounds.[3] The vast majority of American draftees and volunteers had been born in the decade between America's entry into World War I and the mid-1920s. All were products of the Great Depression, and few were optimistic about future opportunities. But as soon as Japan attacked Pearl Harbor, they were ready to fight. On Monday, December 8, the floodgates opened and the army recorded more enlistments than on any other day in American history.

No assessment of the American army in World War II would be complete without a word concerning the contributions of Army Chief of Staff George C.

Marshall. Although he was not a commander in the strictest sense, no officer had a more profound impact on the performance of the U.S. Army as a whole. It was Marshall who supervised the expansion of the army from 174,000 to 8.25 million between 1939 and 1945. To achieve this miraculous growth Marshall employed four principal means: (1) establishing control over the promotion and retirement of regular army officers; (2) generating manpower in quantity by initiating and continuing the draft; (3) teaching new recruits in large numbers through the service schools, cadre systems, and large-scale military exercises; and (4) fighting for increased budgetary allocations from the president and Congress.[4] The "Victory Program" that Marshall and his aides coauthored with Chief of Naval Operations Harold R. Stark provided the blueprint for the size of the armed forces and the industrial mobilization required to defeat Germany and Japan. But it was in the selection of the army's leaders that Marshall made his most direct contribution to the U.S. Army's success.

While serving as a personal aide to General John J. Pershing in 1920, then-Major Marshall outlined the qualities he would like to see in a young officer going to war. They encompassed tactical and technical proficiency, a cheerful and optimistic disposition, the ability to put aside any thought of personal fatigue and to display marked energy in looking after the comfort of one's organization, and extreme loyalty in thought and deed. "The less you approve" of your senior's decisions, Marshall wrote, "the more energy you must direct to their accomplishment." The final point Marshall emphasized emerged as the hallmark of his selection of the senior leaders of the American army two decades later: "The more alarming and disquieting the reports received or the conditions viewed in battle, the more determined must be your attitude."[5]

What Marshall wanted most were commanders who kept cool under fire and then made rapid yet thorough analyses of tactical situations, men who then demonstrated the initiative to bring problems to successful solutions. He also wanted "team players" who sacrificed personal ambitions for the betterment of the army as a whole. Where did he find such officers? Many historians credit Marshall with keeping a "black book" on promising and enterprising officers, although no actual book has ever surfaced. Still, there seems little doubt that Marshall at the very least kept a "mental book" in which he recorded the names of officers destined for senior command.

With the exception of Douglas MacArthur, who had established a superlative war record in World War I in his own right and remained outside the Pershing circle, the vast majority of the army- and corps-level commanders who served during World War II owed their rise to prominence to the patronage of George C. Marshall. Vinegar Joe Stilwell and Matthew Ridgway were old China hands with Marshall in the 15th Infantry Regiment in Tientsin. While serving as assistant commandant of the Infantry School at Fort Benning, Georgia, Marshall encountered "the most brilliant, interesting, and thoroughly competent collection of men" he had ever been associated with. Joseph Stilwell headed the Tactical Section; Omar Bradley the Weapons Section; and "Pinky" Bull, destined to become Ike's operations officer in Europe, served in Marshall's Second Section, responsible for logistics, supply, training, and signal communications. Joe Collins, the future VII Corps commander in Europe, was one of Stilwell's instructors. During the five years that Marshall served at Benning, the staff and graduates of the Infantry School included Matthew Ridgway, James Van Fleet, Clarence Heubner, Walter Bedell Smith, Terry Allen, Leven Allen, Norman Cota, and scores of other officers who would eventually rise to command the army's corps and divisions in World War II. Bradley, Ridgway, and Smith would later serve on Marshall's staff in the War Department. Another prominent officer, Courtney Hodges, sat with Marshall on the Infantry Board. Combine these future commanders with George S. Patton, whom Marshall knew intimately from the Great War; Dwight D. Eisenhower, brought to his attention by Major General Fox Conner, Marshall's boss in World War I; and Mark Clark, who had previously impressed Marshall with his training techniques and supervision of a series of war games, and you have a virtual roll call of the army's senior leadership. In each instance Marshall identified a promising officer, promoted him, assigned additional responsibility and offered him the opportunity to display his initiative and judgment, then reevaluated him for positions of increasing importance.

To command the army's smaller units Marshall established a series of officer training programs, most notably the Officer Candidate Schools located at the largest training centers. Graduates of these institutions demonstrated the same characteristics Marshall demanded of his senior commanders: initiative, physical and mental toughness, and the ability to think clearly under the rigors of combat. While West Point may have produced the majority of corps- and army-level commanders in World War II, the various officer training and air cadet programs produced junior officers the likes of Charity Adams, Vernon Baker, Lyle J. Bouck, Joe Dawson, Paul Tibbets, and Dick Winters. Battlefield promotions from the enlisted ranks added Len Lomell, Audie Murphy, and scores of battle-tested commanders who commanded the platoons, companies, and battalions. Battlefield attrition removed a high percentage of these junior commanders from combat, and the officer replacement system failed to deliver highly trained personnel in a timely manner. Too often replacements learned their trade on the job. If they survived, they were promoted. Far too many did not live through their initial experience in combat.

Naturally it took time for these leaders to emerge, and in the early campaigns the U.S. Army paid an exceedingly high cost in men and matériel. To Dwight Eisenhower, the solution was simple. In selecting senior commanders, Ike advised his future Fifteenth Army commander, Gee Gerow, "Officers who fail must be ruthlessly weeded out. Considerations of friendship, family, kindliness and nice personality have nothing whatsoever to do with the problem. . . . Get rid of the lazy, the slothful, the indifferent or the complacent [or] you will have to spend the rest of your life writing letters explaining your actions."[6]

Contrary to the conventional interpretation that the United States prevailed in World War II simply because it outproduced and overwhelmed its adversaries, there seems little doubt that American combat effectiveness increased over the course of the war while that of the Axis powers decreased. It was the leadership of the American army, coupled with the industrial mobilization of the American economy, that turned the tide from defeat to victory.[7]

Ike, who commanded in excess of four million Allied soldiers—including three million Americans—at the end of the European war, gets the final word. Speaking on behalf of those who fought for the Allies, the supreme commander honored all the soldiers of democracy:

> The route you have traveled through hundreds of miles is marked by the graves of former comrades. Each of the fallen died as a member of the team to which you belong, bound together by a common love of liberty and a refusal to submit to enslavement. . . . Let us have no part in the profitless quarrels in which other men will inevitably engage as to what country, what service, won the . . . war. Every man, every woman, of every nation here represented has served according to his or her ability, and the efforts of each have contributed to the outcome. This we shall remember—and in doing so we shall be revering each honored grave, and be sending comfort to the loved ones of comrades who could not live to see this day.[8]

NOTES

Chapter 1. The Theater Commanders: MacArthur, Eisenhower, and Stilwell

1. Quoted in William Manchester, *American Caesar: Douglas MacArthur 1880–1964* (Boston: Little, Brown, 1978), 5.
2. Dwight D. Eisenhower, *At Ease* (New York: Doubleday, 1967), 212.
3. Douglas MacArthur, *Reminiscences* (New York: McGraw-Hill, 1964), 109.
4. D. Clayton James, *The Years of MacArthur*, 3 vols. (Boston: Houghton Mifflin, 1975), 2:13.
5. For two versions of MacArthur's arrival in Australia, see ibid., 108–09; and MacArthur, *Reminiscences*, 142–45.
6. See James, *The Years of MacArthur*, 2:119–21, for the specific wording of MacArthur's charter.
7. For the best analysis of the New Guinea campaign, see Stephen R. Taaffe, *MacArthur's Jungle War* (Lawrence: University Press of Kansas, 1998).
8. Eric Larrabee, *Commander in Chief: Franklin Delano Roosevelt, His Lieutenants and Their War* (New York: Harper and Row, 1987), 348.
9. Ibid.
10. MacArthur, *Reminiscences*, 275.
11. Larrabee, *Commander in Chief*, 350–51.
12. As quoted in Dwight D. Eisenhower, *Crusade in Europe* (New York: Doubleday, 1948), 12.
13. See efficiency report dated June 16, 1926, in Dwight D. Eisenhower Personal Records, Series III, Efficiency Reports (1926–30), Records of the Office of the Adjutant General, RG 407.
14. See Cole C. Kingseed, "Eisenhower's Prewar Anonymity," in *Parameters* (Autumn 1991): 87–97, for an elaboration of the three watershed events in Eisenhower's career.

15. Endorsement by Major George Moseley as quoted in ibid., 94.
16. Letter from Marshall to the students in Miss Craig's Class, dated March 15, 1944, as quoted in Larry I. Bland and Sharon Ritenour Stevens, eds., *The Papers of George Catlett Marshall* (Baltimore: Johns Hopkins University Press, 1996), 4:345. Hereafter cited as *Papers of GCM.*
17. Alfred D. Chandler Jr. et al., eds., *The Papers of Dwight D. Eisenhower: The War Years* (Baltimore: Johns Hopkins University Press, 1970), 1:5–6. Hereafter cited as *Papers of DDE.*
18. Eisenhower, *At Ease*, 249.
19. Chandler et al., *Papers of DDE*, 1:205–08. See also Cole C. Kingseed, "Ike Takes Charge," *Military Review* 72 (June 1992): 75.
20. E. K. G. Sixsmith elaborates on this theme in his analysis of Eisenhower in *Eisenhower as Military Commander* (New York: Da Capo Press, 1972), 1.
21. Bernard Law Montgomery, *The Memoirs of Field-Marshal Montgomery* (New York: World Publishing Company, 1958), 484.
22. Brooke's assessment is found in his diary dated January 20, 1943, as quoted in Arthur Bryant, *The Turn of the Tide 1939–1943* (New York: Doubleday, 1957), 454–55.
23. Clay Blair and Omar Bradley, *A General's Life* (New York: Simon and Schuster, 1983), 130.
24. Martin Blumenson, ed., *The Patton Papers, 1940–1945* (Boston: Houghton Mifflin, 1974), 202.
25. For the best summary of the evolution of Eisenhower as a combat commander, see Joseph Hobbs, *Dear General: Eisenhower's Wartime Letters to Marshall* (Baltimore: Johns Hopkins University Press, 1971).
26. Chandler et al., *Papers of DDE*, 4:2696.
27. For full text of the Eisenhower-Marshall exchange, see ibid., 6:14–15.
28. Quoted in Winston Churchill, *The Second World War: Triumph and Tragedy* (Boston: Houghton Mifflin, 1953), 547.
29. Montgomery, *Memoirs of Field-Marshal Montgomery*, 315.
30. As quoted in Larrabee, *Commander in Chief*, 513.
31. As quoted in Barbara Tuchman, *Stilwell and the American Experience in China 1911–45* (New York: Macmillan, 1970), 303. Subsequent quote by Stilwell on the end of the Pacific war is on 521.

Chapter 2. Army Group Commanders in Europe and the Mediterranean: Travails and Triumphs

1. Bradley and Blair, *A General's Life*, 283.
2. See Martin Blumenson, *The Battle of the Generals* (New York: William Morrow, 1993), 272–73; and Carlo D'Este, *Patton: A Genius for War* (New York: HarperCollins, 1995), 643.

3. Forrest Pogue, *George C. Marshall: Education of a General, 1880–1939* (New York: Viking Press, 1963), 258.
4. Ed Cray, *General of the Army: George C. Marshall, Soldier and Statesman* (New York: Cooper Square Press, 2000), 106.
5. For Bradley's reaction to the change of assignments, see Bradley and Blair, *A General's Life*, 113.
6. See Eisenhower's assessment of Bradley in *Crusade in Europe*, 214–15.
7. Eisenhower to Marshall, March 3, 1943 as quoted in Hobbs, *Dear General*, 106.
8. Ernie Pyle, *Brave Men* (New York: Henry Holt, 1944), 312.
9. Eisenhower to Marshall, September 6, 1943, quoted in Chandler et al., *Papers of DDE*, 3:1388.
10. Ibid., 2:1357.
11. Williamson Murray and Allan R. Millett, *A War to Be Won: Fighting the Second World War* (Cambridge: Belknap Press of Harvard University Press, 2000), 418.
12. Bradley and Blair, *A General's Life*, 298–99.
13. Ibid., 363–64.
14. Chandler et al., *Papers of DDE*, 4:2368.
15. Ibid., 4:2426.
16. All numbers of German prisoners are extracted from Bradley's operational records. This particular report is from Headquarters, Twelfth Army Group, ACoS, G-2, "Destruction of the German Armies in Western Europe," 27, on file in the Department of History, U.S. Military Academy, West Point, New York.
17. Chandler et al., *Papers of DDE*, 6:207.
18. Martin Blumenson, *Mark Clark* (New York: Congdon and Weed, 1984), 42.
19. Blumenson, *Patton Papers*, 2:83.
20. Chandler et al., *Papers of DDE*, 2:800.
21. Quoted in Blumenson, *Mark Clark*, 112.
22. Ibid., 114.
23. Ibid., 216.
24. Ibid., 235.
25. Murray and Millett, *A War to Be Won*, 378.
26. Truscott's assessment is found in his wartime memoir, *Command Missions* (New York: E. P. Dutton, 1948), 547.
27. As quoted in Bland and Stevens, *Papers of GCM*, 4:596–97.
28. Winston Churchill, *The Second World War: Triumph and Tragedy* (Boston: Houghton Mifflin, 1953), 529–30.
29. Marshall to Devers, personal and confidential, June 13, 1942, as cited in Bland and Stevens, *Papers of GCM*, 3:237.
30. Devers replied that he found Eisenhower's report "disturbing," particularly in light of his own inspection two months earlier, in which he found some "over-

confidence and signs of lack of thorough training among the units at the front," but "found no softness nor complacency." Ibid., 564–65.

31. Bradley and Blair, *A General's Life*, 210; Blumenson, *Patton Papers*, 2:414.
32. Eisenhower to Marshall, dated December 25, 1943, OPD Exec. 17.
33. Eisenhower, *Crusade in Europe*, 216.
34. Chandler et al., *Papers of DDE*, 3:2000.
35. David Eisenhower, *Eisenhower at War, 1943–1945* (New York: Random House, 1986), 524.
36. Russell Weigley, *Eisenhower's Lieutenants: The Campaign of France and Germany, 1944–1945* (Bloomington: Indiana University Press, 1981), 554.
37. D. K. R. Crosswell, *The Chief of Staff: The Military Career of General Walter Bedell Smith* (Westport, Conn.: Greenwood Press, 1991), 306.
38. Chandler et al., *Papers of DDE*, 3:2009–10.
39. Ibid., 4:2426, 2468–69.
40. Larry I. Bland et al., *George C. Marshall: Interviews and Reminiscences for Forrest C. Pogue* (Lexington, Va.: George C. Marshall Research Foundation, 1991), 627.

Chapter 3. Army Commanders in the Pacific: Forgotten Warriors

1. Duane Schultz, *Hero of Bataan* (New York: Saint Martin's Press, 1981), 3
2. See *Howitzer*, West Point Class of 1906, 67.
3. As quoted in Schultz, *Hero of Bataan*, 10.
4. See Table 1: Strength of Philippine Division, July 31, 1941, as quoted in Louis Morton, *The Fall of the Philippines* (Washington, D.C.: Government Printing Office, 1985), 22.
5. Schultz, *Hero of Bataan*, 59–60.
6. Ltr Order, CG USAFFE to CG North Luzon Force, December 3, 1941, subject: Defense of Phil, AG 381 Phil Rcds, as quoted in Morton, *The Fall of the Philippines*, 69.
7. James, *The Years of MacArthur*, 2:25.
8. See Memorandum for the President, March 19, 1942, as quoted in Bland and Stevens, *Papers of GCM*, 3:139.
9. Morton, *The Fall of the Philippines*, 463.
10. Jonathan Wainwright, *General Wainwright's Story: The Account of Four Years of Humiliating Defeat, Surrender, and Captivity* (New York: Doubleday, 1946), 122–23.
11. See James, *The Years of MacArthur*, 2:150–51. See also Forrest Pogue, *George C. Marshall: Ordeal and Hope, 1939–1942* (New York: Viking Press, 1966), 258.
12. MacArthur, *Reminiscences*, 272.

13. As quoted in Schultz, *Hero of Bataan*, 420.
14. See Carlo D'Este, *Eisenhower: A Soldier's Life* (New York: Henry Holt, 2002), 280–281.
15. Chandler et al., *Papers of DDE*, 2:921.
16. Christopher Gabel, *The U.S. Army GHQ Maneuvers of 1941* (Washington, D.C.: Center of Military History, 1991), 187.
17. As quoted in Walter Krueger, *From Down Under to Nippon* (Washington, D.C.: Combat Forces Press, 1953), 3.
18. Krueger, *From Down Under to Nippon*, 211.
19. Robert L. Eichelberger, *Dear Miss Em: General Eichelberger's War in the Pacific, 1942–1945,* ed. Jay Luvaas (Westport, Conn.: Greenwood Press, 1972), 214.
20. Robert Ross Smith, *Triumph in the Philippines* (Washington, D.C.: Government Printing Office, 1984), 212–13.
21. As quoted in Ronald Spector, *The American War with Japan* (New York: Free Press, 1985), 521. See also Manchester, *American Caesar*, 410.
22. James, *The Years of MacArthur,* 2:669.
23. Smith, *Triumph in the Philippines*, 652.
24. As listed in Krueger, *From Down Under to Nippon*, 318.
25. Eisenhower to Marshall, Cable S 74971/SG 962, dated January 14, 1945, in Chandler et al., *Papers of DDE*, 4:2426–27.
26. As quoted in Courtney Whitney, *MacArthur: His Rendezvous with History* (New York: Alfred A. Knopf, 1956), 187.
27. Brian Garfield, *The Thousand-Mile War* (New York: Bantam Books, 1969), 312.
28. Memorandum for War Plans Division, dated March 18, 1942, subject: Joint Army-Navy Plans for Alaska, as quoted in *Papers of GCM,* 3:134–35.
29. As quoted in Forrest Pogue, *George C. Marshall: Organizer of Victory, 1943–45* (New York: Viking Press, 1973), 152–54.
30. DeWitt was initially inclined to replace Buckner, but following lengthy meetings with both Buckner and Theobald he concluded that the two men had settled their differences amicably and neither ought to be relieved. Marshall and King temporarily accepted the recommendation but transferred both officers following the reconquest of the Aleutians. For texts of DeWitt's recommendations and Marshall's response, see Bland and Stevens, *Papers of GCM,* 3:379–81, 590–92.
31. Roy E. Appleman et al., *Okinawa: The Last Battle* (Washington, D.C.: Government Printing Office, 1984), 25–26.
32. David Nichols, ed., *Ernie's War* (New York: Random House, 1986), 404–05. Pyle was killed on April 18 as Buckner directed the capture of Ie Shima, a small island three and one-half miles off the western tip of Okinawa. He was temporarily buried in the 77th Division's cemetery on Ie Shima under a crude marker

that the division later replaced with a monument; the inscription reads: "At this spot the 77th Infantry Division lost a buddy, Ernie Pyle, 18 April 1945."

33. In January 1944, the western Allies conducted an amphibious assault at Anzio in order to break the stalemate in front of General Mark Clark's Fifth Army. Unfortunately, a less than zealous commander took too much time to consolidate the beachhead before attacking toward Italy's Alban Hills. When the Germans counterattacked in force, a five-month stalemate ensued.
34. See Allan R. Millett, *Semper Fidelis: The History of the United States Marine Corps* (New York: Macmillan, 1980), 435–36.
35. Appleman et al., *Okinawa: The Last Battle*, 473.
36. James, *The Years of MacArthur,* 732–33, 735. Eichelberger refers to the criticism by the navy in *Dear Miss Em*, 278.
37. Eichelberger, *Dear Miss Em*, 230.
38. As quoted in Spector, *The American War with Japan*, 539.
39. MacArthur, *Reminiscences*, 170.

Chapter 4. Army Commanders in Europe: A Formidable Array of Warriors

1. FM 100-15, *Field Service Regulations: Larger Units, 1942*, 51; War Department FM 101-10, *Staff Officers Field Manual: Organization, Technical and Logistical Data* (Washington, D.C.: War Department, 1943), 108, as quoted in David W. Hogan Jr., *A Command Post at War: First Army Headquarters in Europe, 1943–1945* (Washington, D.C.: Center of Military History, 2000), 285.
2. For Hodges's background and command style, see Hogan, *A Command Post at War*, 121–22.
3. Bradley and Blair, *A General's Life*, 95.
4. Ibid., 218.
5. Hogan, *A Command Post at War*, 121.
6. Chandler et al., *Papers of DDE*, 3:1669–70.
7. Ibid., 293.
8. Ibid., 212.
9. Quoted in Daniel Bolger, "Zero Defects: Command Climate in First US Army, 1944–1945," *Military Review* 71 (May 1991): 63–64.
10. Chandler et al., *Papers of DDE*, 4:2564, 2598.
11. Omar Bradley, *A Soldier's Story* (New York: Henry Holt, 1951), 226.
12. Chandler et al., *Papers of DDE*, 2:938–39.
13. As quoted in Blumenson, *Patton Papers*, 2:169.
14. Eisenhower to Marshall, August 24, 1943, as quoted in Hobbs, *Dear General*, 121.
15. As quoted in Blumenson, *Patton Papers*, 2:393.

16. As quoted in Pogue, *GCM: Organizer of Victory*, 372.
17. Eisenhower, *Crusade in Europe*, 225.
18. D'Este, *Patton: A Genius for War*, 596–97.
19. Patton Diary entry for January 18, 1944.
20. James M. Gavin, *On to Berlin* (New York: Viking Press, 1978), 43.
21. Max Hastings, *Overlord* (New York: Simon and Schuster, 1984), 247.
22. Chandler et al., *Papers of DDE*, 4:2466.
23. Blumenson, *The Battle of the Generals*, 34.
24. George Patton, *War as I Knew It* (New York: Houghton Mifflin, 1947), 331.
25. Bradley and Blair, *A General's Life*, 340.
26. Weigley, *Eisenhower's Lieutenants*, 431.
27. As quoted in J. D. Morelock, *Generals of the Ardennes: American Leadership in the Battle of the Bulge* (Washington, D.C.: National Defense University Press, 1994), 210.
28. Chandler et al., *Papers of DDE*, 4:2466–67; Eisenhower, *Crusade in Europe*, 376.
29. Bradley and Blair, *A General's Life*, 395.
30. Harry C. Butcher, *My Three Years with Eisenhower* (New York: Simon and Schuster, 1946), 247–48.
31. David Eisenhower, *Eisenhower at War*, 177. David Eisenhower claims that Gerow was one of the few general officers who "irrevocably" lost Marshall's favor.
32. When Marshall refused to transfer Truscott from the Mediterranean, command of the second assault corps fell to J. Lawton Collins.
33. David Eisenhower, *Eisenhower at War*, 223; Bradley, *A Soldier's Story*, 227, both quoted in Adrian R. Lewis, *Omaha Beach: A Flawed Victory* (Chapel Hill: University of North Carolina Press, 2001), 165.
34. Lewis, *Omaha Beach*, 168.
35. Chandler et al., *Papers of DDE*, 4:2466.
36. Blumenson, *Patton Papers*, 2:739.
37. Hobbs, *Dear General*, 223.

Chapter 5. America's Dual-Theater Commanders: Interlopers from the Pacific

1. For the best biography of Alexander Patch, see William K. Wyant, *Sandy Patch: A Biography of Lt. Gen. Alexander M. Patch* (New York: Praeger, 1991).
2. Bland and Stevens, eds., *Papers of GCM*, 3:191. See also Chandler et al., *Papers of DDE*, 1:287–89.
3. Responsibility for Guadalcanal resided with Admiral Chester Nimitz, CINCPAC, who was based at Pearl Harbor. Dissatisfied with the navy's support for Vandegrift's marines, Nimitz relieved Admiral Robert L. Ghormley and replaced him with Halsey on October 18. Wyant, *Sandy Patch*, 59.

4. As quoted in Wyant, *Sandy Patch*, 69.
5. Cable, Marshall to Patch, dated March 19, 1943, cited in Bland and Stevens, *Papers of GCM*, 3:596.
6. Ibid.
7. For the complete text of Marshall's cable and Patch's reply, see Bland and Stevens, *Papers of GCM*, 4:39–40.
8. Ibid., 4:556.
9. Ibid., Radio No. WAR-34206, Marshall to Eisenhower, dated September 21, 1944, 4:595–96.
10. Butcher, *My Three Years with Eisenhower*, 793.
11. Chandler et al., *Papers of DDE*, 4:2665.
12. As quoted in Wyant, *Sandy Patch*, 215.
13. Chandler et al., *Papers of DDE*, 4:2467.
14. As quoted in Wyant, *Sandy Patch*, 215.
15. Telephone conversation, Marshall to Emmons, dated December 16, 1941, as recorded in Bland and Stevens, *Papers of GCM*, 3:21–22.
16. For details of Collins's training program, see J. Lawton Collins, *Lightning Joe: An Autobiography* (Baton Rouge: Louisiana State University Press, 1974), 137–40. Nimitz's remarks are on p. 143.
17. Marshall, Memorandum for the President, February 11, 1943, as cited in Bland and Stevens, *Papers of GCM*, 3:541.
18. Chandler et al., *Papers of DDE*, 3:1715–16.
19. Martin Blumenson, "Ranks of the WWII Greats Grow Thinner: A Lament," *Army* 37 (November 1987): 18.
20. Collins, *Lightning Joe*, 279.
21. Ike's commendation is in a memo that appears in Butcher's diary, dated February 1, 1945, as quoted in Chandler et al., *Papers of DDE*, 4:2467. Bradley's assessment appears in Bradley, *A General's Life*, 400.
22. See Philip A. Crowl and Edmund G. Love, *Seizure of the Gilberts and Marshalls* (Washington, D.C.: Government Printing Office, 1955), 170–71, 289–90, for a detailed discussion of the operation.
23. Radio No. 124, Marshall to Eisenhower, dated February 17, 1944, as quoted in Bland and Stevens, *Papers of GCM*, 4:306.
24. See Cable W 11493, Eisenhower to Marshall, dated February 19, 1944, quoted in Chandler et al., *Papers of DDE*, 3:1736.
25. Diary entry of February 18, 1944, in Diary of George S. Patton Jr., Feb. 9, 1944–Aug. 1 1944, on file at the U.S. Military Academy. See also Blumenson, *Patton Papers*, 2:306-07. For Bradley's assessment, see Bradley and Blair, *A General's Life*, 224.
26. Murray and Millett, *A War to Be Won*, 419.

27. Charles H. Corlett, *Cowboy Pete: The Autobiography of Major General Charles H. Corlett* (Santa Fe, N.M.: Sleeping Fox Enterprises, 1974), 88.
28. For the circumstances surrounding Corlett's relief, see Weigley, *Eisenhower's Lieutenants,* 363; Corlett, *Cowboy Pete*, 103–05; Bradley, *A General's Life*, 337. Not surprisingly, Bradley's and Corlett's views of the relief are diametrically opposed.
29. Cable S 63258, Eisenhower to Marshall, dated October 20, 1944, in Chandler et al., *Papers of DDE*, 4:2233–34.

Chapter 6. Commanders in Desperate Situations: Restoring the Fighting Spirit

1. Matthew B. Ridgway, *The Korean War* (New York: Doubleday, 1967), 79.
2. Robert Eichelberger, *Our Jungle Road to Tokyo* (New York: Viking Press, 1950), xxiv; Pogue, *GCM: Ordeal and Hope,* 335.
3. James, *The Years of MacArthur*, 243.
4. Ibid., 243–44. Eichelberger relates his side of the meeting with MacArthur in *Our Jungle Road to Tokyo*, 23. See also James Shortal, *Forged by Fire: General Robert L. Eichelberger and the Pacific War* (Columbia: University of South Carolina Press, 1987), 47–48.
5. Eichelberger, *Our Jungle Road to Tokyo*, 22.
6. Relieving combat commanders is never an easy task. The postwar historian of the 32nd Division felt that Harding received a raw deal and that Eichelberger had been less than honest in dictating Harding's relief. In reality, MacArthur and Eichelberger had simply lost confidence in Harding's ability to get the job done. The War Department elevated Harding to command the Department of the Canal Zone and Antilles in May 1943. Eichelberger later expressed his feelings about the Harding affair: "I was very sorry the way that turned out but there was nothing else I could do." See James, *The Years of MacArthur*, 263.
7. For conditions at Buna, see Eichelberger, *Dear Miss Em,* 38–39.
8. See Samuel Milner, *Victory in Papua* (Washington, D.C.: Government Printing Office, 1985), 245.
9. Eichelberger, *Our Jungle Road to Tokyo*, 29.
10. As quoted in Milner, *Victory in Papua*, 323.
11. Eichelberger, *Our Jungle Road to Tokyo*, 48.
12. Shortal, *Forged by Fire*, 60–61.
13. See text of Eichelberger's DSC citation in MacArthur, *Reminiscences*, 165. MacArthur himself received his third Distinguished Service Medal for the Buna victory.
14. Eichelberger, *Dear Miss Em*, 65.
15. Ibid.
16. As quoted in Shortal, *Forged by Fire*, 126.

17. George F. Howe, *Northwest Africa: Seizing the Initiative in the West* (Washington, D.C.: Government Printing Office, 1985), 471.
18. E. N. Harmon, *Combat Commander* (Englewood Cliffs, N.J.: Prentice-Hall, 1970), 66. See also Donald Houston, *Hell on Wheels: The 2d Armored Division* (Novato, Calif.: Presidio Press, 1977), 112.
19. As summarized in Harmon, *Combat Commander*, 111–12.
20. Cable 1895, Eisenhower to Fredendall, February 20, 1943, in Chandler et al. *Papers of DDE*, 2:968.
21. See Harmon, *Combat Commander*, 114–15; and Martin Blumenson, *Kasserine Pass* (New York: Jove Books, 1983), 289.
22. For a complete account of Harmon's activities, see L. K. Truscott Jr., *Command Missions* (1954; reprint, Novato, Calif.: Presidio Press, 1990), 170–72.
23. As quoted in Howe, *Northwest Africa*, 474.
24. Patton's assignment as II Corps commander naturally meant that Fredendall was out of a job. Ike cabled Marshall on March 3, stating that Fredendall had failed to make the most of the tools at his disposal. This was Ike's way of saying that Fredendall had difficulty picking good men and, even worse, getting the best from his division commanders. In short, with II Corps about to become an independent organization away from British control, a more aggressive commander was needed. Fredendall returned to the United States to a hero's welcome, received a promotion, and trained armored troops as commanding general of the Second Army at Memphis for the remainder of the war. He was a good trainer; he simply could not handle the rigors of combat command. See Cable, Eisenhower to Marshall, dated March 3, 1943, in Chandler et al., *Papers of DDE*, 2:1006.
25. See E. N. Harmon, "Notes on Combat Experience during the Tunisian and African Campaigns," undated.
26. Cable, Eisenhower to Harmon, dated March 12, 1943, in Chandler et al., *Papers of DDE*, 2:1026.
27. Ward returned to the United States to take command of the Tank Destroyer Center. Eventually, he returned to Europe in command of the 20th Armored Division and compiled a distinguished record.
28. Truscott, *Command Missions*, 548.
29. Cable, Eisenhower to Marshall, dated August 24, 1944, in Chandler et al., *Papers of DDE*, 2:1354.
30. Harmon, *Combat Commander*, 15.
31. Martin Blumenson, "Anzio: Dilemma on the Beachhead," *Army* 33 (March 1983): 41.
32. Lucas returned to the United States to command a stateside corps and ultimately assumed command of the Fourth Army.
33. As quoted in Cable W11279, Eisenhower to Marshall, dated February 16, 1944, in Chandler et al., *Papers of DDE*, 3:1730.

34. For the best analysis of Truscott's philosophy of command, see his *Command Missions*, 540–42.
35. Ibid., 331.
36. Ibid., 179–80.
37. Ibid., 338.
38. Memo in Butcher diary, dated February 1, 1945, as recorded in Chandler et al., *Papers of DDE*, 4:2467.
39. Truscott, *Command Missions*, 546.
40. Quoted in Pogue, *GCM: Organizer of Victory*, 374.

Chapter 7. Airborne Commanders: The Stuff of Instant Legends

1. See Ridgway's dedication in *The Korean War*.
2. Bland and Stevens, *Papers of GCM*, 1:505. At the time, Ridgway was stationed in Chicago as assistant chief of staff, G-3, of the Second Army and VI Corps.
3. Matthew Ridgway, *Soldier: The Memoirs of Matthew B. Ridgway* (New York: Harper and Brothers, 1956), 58. Ridgway's early career and his recollections of his tour on the General Staff are outlined on pp. 47–50.
4. Training Memorandum Number 43, Allied Force Headquarters, Subject: Employment of Airborne Forces, dated August 2, 1943.
5. Ibid., 74.
6. Gavin, *On to Berlin*, 54.
7. See Report on Airborne Operations, "Husky," dated July 24, 1943, in Joseph M. Swing's Cullum File (CU 5350), in box marked Swing, Joseph M., U.S. Military Academy, West Point, New York.
8. Clay Blair, *Ridgway's Paratroopers* (New York: Dial Press, 1985), 348.
9. Marshall to Bradley, in Bland and Stevens, *Papers of GCM*, 4:517. Taylor was commanding general of the 101st Airborne Division.
10. As quoted in Chandler et al., *Papers of DDE*, 4:2427, 2467, 2616.
11. As quoted in Blair, *Ridgway's Paratroopers,* 60.
12. Ibid., 61.
13. Gavin's observations appear in his *Airborne Warfare* as quoted in Ridgway, *Soldier*, 70.
14. T. Michael Booth and Duncan Spencer, *Paratrooper: The Life of Gen. James M. Gavin* (New York: Simon and Schuster, 1994), 200.
15. Gavin's promotion became effective October 20, 1944. See Bland and Stevens, *Papers of GCM*, 4:633.
16. Booth and Spencer, *Paratrooper*, 251.
17. Taylor's companion was Colonel Gardner, U.S. Air Forces. See Eisenhower, *Crusade in Europe*, 183.
18. Maxwell D. Taylor, *Swords and Plowshares* (New York: W. W. Norton, 1972), 70.

19. Historian Clay Blair puts Taylor's casualties at 4,670 officers and men.
20. Blair, *Ridgway's Paratroopers*, 36.
21. Blumenson, *Patton Papers,* 2:615. Patton discusses relieving Miley on p. 627.
22. Blair, *Ridgway's Paratroopers*, 540.
23. Copies of the War Department order activating the Airborne Operations Board are in Swing's Cullum File 5350 in box Swing, Joseph M.
24. Letter, Swing to March, dated February 24, 1945, in folder: Letters to Peyton March, December 1944–September 1945, in box Swing Cullum File 5350.
25. For background on the 503rd PIR, see Blair, *Ridgway's Paratroopers*, 626.
26. The rift between Taylor and Gavin was widely known in army circles. Taylor died on April 19, 1987, and lies in Arlington National Cemetery among the nation's honored dead. Gavin died on February 23, 1990, a victim of Parkinson's disease. He is buried in the West Point Cemetery on the grounds of the U.S. Military Academy.
27. Butcher, *My Three Years with Eisenhower*, 767–68.

Chapter 8. Enola Gay: Paul Tibbets of the Army Air Forces

1. Interview with the author, May 4, 1998; transcript on file with the author.
2. Frank Armstrong was later featured in the novel *Twelve O'Clock High.* The fictional general in that story, Frank Savage, is based on Armstrong.
3. As quoted in the *Chicago Tribune*, March 10, 1968. The *Tribune* ran a series of articles on Tibbets's career in the March 10–22, 1968, issues.
4. Norstad would later rise to four-star rank and become supreme Allied commander, NATO.
5. For Tibbets's side of the story, see his *Return of the Enola Gay* (Columbus, Ohio: A Paul Tibbets Book, 1998), 127–36.
6. Ibid., 159–64.
7. For Sweeney's version of this meeting, see Charles W. Sweeney, *War's End* (New York: Avon Books, 1997), 40–44.
8. Interview with the author. Tibbets claimed he also used "silverplate" to procure washing machines for his command. He was not reluctant to use his broad authority to do anything to improve the morale of men isolated from the outside world and cloaked in secrecy.
9. Tibbets, *Return of the Enola Gay*, 188.
10. As quoted in "Atomic Bomb Crews Practice Lone Plane Strikes," *Chicago Tribune*, March 18, 1968.
11. Several versions of this exchange appear in various accounts of the atomic mission. See Tibbets, *Return of the Enola Gay*, 189, for Tibbets's own story.
12. Four days after departing Tinian for the Philippines, the *Indianapolis* was torpedoed by a Japanese submarine, resulting in the loss of nearly nine hundred sailors.

13. Interview with the author.
14. Tibbets's exact words were recorded by Bill Laurence, a *New York Times* science writer who was in attendance.
15. Tibbets's flight announcements and Lewis's log entries are recorded in Tibbets, *Return of the Enola Gay*.
16. Not surprisingly, Tibbets's and Sweeney's versions of the success of the second atomic mission are diametrically opposed. Tibbets faults Sweeney for not taking decisive action and for losing valuable time at takeoff and over Iwo Jima (*Return of the Enola Gay*, 245–51). Sweeney relates his first meeting with Tibbets in *War's End*, 230.
17. Tibbets expresses similar views in Bob Greene, *Duty* (New York: William Morrow, 2000), 89.
18. Oral interview with the author; and Tibbets, *Return of the Enola Gay*, 330.

Chapter 9. Measuring Up: The Epic Tale of Joe Dawson

1. Joseph T. Dawson, World War II Letters, copyright 1990, Joseph T. Dawson, published with permission of the Joseph T. Dawson Estate. Hereafter cited as Dawson Letters. Over the course of the war Dawson wrote in excess of one hundred letters to his family, in which he described virtually every aspect of military life. Copies of the letters are on file at the First Infantry Division Museum at Wheaton, Illinois.
2. Texas A&M at College Station remains one of the premier ROTC colleges in the United States. Dawson was merely reflecting on the merits of receiving a commission through university studies versus OCS.
3. Dawson assumed command from Captain Edward F. Wozenski, one of the standout combat officers in the regiment. By the end of the war Wozenski commanded the 3rd Battalion. His awards included the DSC with cluster and the Silver Star with cluster.
4. As quoted in the eulogy for Dawson given by Major General Albert H. Smith Jr. on December 12, 1998.
5. For the best account of Dawson on D-Day, see Stephen Ambrose, *D-Day, June 6, 1944: The Climactic Battle of World War II* (New York: Simon and Schuster, 1994), 355–57.
6. Monthly strength figures for Company G are on file in Historical Records of the 1st Infantry Division and Its Organic Elements, WWII, 1940–1945, NA, RG 319, box 147, reel 3.24, 301-INF (16)-1.6. Microfilm on file at the McCormick Research Center, First Infantry Division Museum, Wheaton, Illinois.
7. In addition to Dawson, the awardees included Brigadier General Willard Wyman; Colonel George Taylor; Lieutenant Colonel Herbert Hicks; Major Charles Tetgmeyer; Captains Kimball Richmond, Thomas Marendino, and

Victor Briggs; Lieutenants Carl Giles and John Spaulding; First Sergeant Lawrence Fitzsimmons; Staff Sergeants Curtis Colwell, Philip Clark, David Radford, James Wells, and Kenneth Peterson; Tech/Sergeants Raymond Strojny and Philip Streczyk; Sergeants Richard Gallagher and John Griffin; T/4 Stanley Appleby; and Private First Class Peter Cavaliere. Colonel William Waters and Master Sergeant Chester Demich received the Legion of Merit. As cited in H. R. Knickerbocker et al., *Danger Forward* (Washington, D.C.: Society of the First Division, 1947), 217–19.

8. See Stanhope Brasfield Mason, "Reminiscences and Anecdotes of World War II," 228–29, on file at the McCormick Research Center.
9. Reporter W. C. Heinz of the *New York Sun* recorded the saga of Dawson's company in a series of stories for the *Fort Worth Star-Telegram*. Copies of the October 22, 23, and 31 reports are on file at the McCormick Research Center.
10. See also Stephen Ambrose, *Citizen Soldiers* (New York: Simon and Schuster, 1997), 117, 140, and 149–53, for an account of Dawson's defense.
11. Other companies, particularly I Company, contributed to the defense.
12. Ambrose, *Citizen Soldiers*, 149–53.
13. Interview with the author, June 4, 1998, copy on file at the McCormick Research Center.
14. An autographed copy of Dawson's remarks is on file at the McCormick Research Center.

Chapter 10. Rangers Lead the Way: Len Lomell and the 2nd Ranger Battalion

1. The U.S. Army Ranger School is located at Fort Benning, Georgia, the traditional home of the infantry.
2. See Tom Brokaw, *The Greatest Generation* (New York: Random House, 1998), 125–33, for a journalistic account of Lomell's life.
3. Bradley discusses Rudder's mission and their training techniques in *A Soldier's Story*, 269.
4. See Gordon Harrison, *Cross-Channel Attack* (Washington, D.C.: Government Printing Office, 1950), 196, for Allied plans for counterbattery fire against the German emplacement.
5. With a macabre sense of humor, rangers still kid the "swimmers," as they call the survivors of Slater's craft, for their inability to get ashore.
6. As quoted in Ambrose, *D-Day*, 406. Subsequent quotes concerning the fighting at Pointe du Hoc are from the same source or from Lomell's oral history on file at the Eisenhower Center at the University of New Orleans.
7. Interview with the author. See also Gerald Astor, *The Greatest War: Americans in Combat 1941–1945* (Novato, Calif.: Presidio Press, 1999), 505–6.

8. As authorized by Executive Order No. 9396 and General Orders, No. 34, Headquarters 1st Infantry Division, 11 July 1944, as approved by the Commanding General, First Army [Omar Bradley].
9. Cornelius Ryan, *The Longest Day* (New York: Simon and Schuster, 1959), 239.
10. As quoted in Ambrose, *D-Day*, 417.
11. As quoted in Ambrose, *Citizen Soldiers*, 173.
12. On the morning before the attack, Rudder received a promotion to command the 109th Infantry Regiment of the 28th Division. Command of the rangers fell to George Williams, his executive officer.
13. As quoted in Ambrose, *Citizen Soldiers*, 176.
14. Astor, *The Greatest War*, 705.
15. Sundby was awarded the Silver Star for his bravery.
16. As quoted in Ambrose, *Citizen Soldiers*, 176.
17. Interview with the author, August 18, 1999.
18. Ambrose, *Citizen Soldiers*, 177.
19. Thomas H. Taylor, *Rangers Lead the Way* (Paducah, Ky.: Turner Publishing Company, 1996), 66.
20. Interview with the author, August 18, 1998.
21. As quoted in Brokaw, *The Greatest Generation*, 130.

Chapter 11. Heroism Outlasts Prejudice: Vernon J. Baker and the Buffalo Soldiers

1. Recipients included Private George Watson, 29th Quartermaster Regiment; Sergeant Edward A. Carter Jr., 12th Armored Division; Private Willy F. James Jr., 104th Infantry Division; Sergeant Ruben Rivers, 761st Tank Battalion; First Lieutenant Charles L. Thomas, 103rd Infantry Division; and First Lieutenant John R. Fox, 92nd Infantry Division.
2. Interview conducted with Vernon Baker in his home in Saint Maries, Idaho, October 9, 1998. See also Vernon J. Baker with Ken Olsen, *Lasting Valor* (Columbus, Miss.: Genesis Press, 1997), 62.
3. Ibid., 85–87.
4. Ambrose, *Citizen Soldiers*, 345.
5. Ulysses Lee, *The Employment of Negro Troops* (Washington, D.C.: Government Printing Office, 1966), 536.
6. Interview with the author, October 9, 1998.
7. For Baker's assessment of the 92nd Division, see *Lasting Valor*, 72–75.
8. Pogue, *GCM: Organizer of Victory*, 538–39.
9. Blumenson, *Mark Clark*, 224, 237.
10. "Recollections and Reflections: Transcripts of the Debriefing of Gen. Edward M. Almond by Captain Thomas G. Fergusson," March 25, 1975, Edward

M. Almond Papers, Archives, U.S. Army Military History Institute, Carlisle Barracks, Pa. As quoted in Dale E. Wilson, "Recipe for Failure: MG Edward M. Almond and Preparation of the U.S. 92d Infantry Division for Combat in World War II," *Journal of Military History* 56 (July 1992): 474.

11. Ibid.
12. Lee, *The Employment of Negro Troops*, 543.
13. Truscott, *Command Missions*, 468–69, 473–74.
14. Memorandum, HQ 371st Infantry; Subject: Summation of Tactical Notes, dated June 21, 1945, s/James Notesteio, COL, 371st Infantry, Commanding, copy in Vernon J. Baker's private papers; hereafter cited as Baker Papers. Lest the reader think that Baker fabricated these reports, they are exact duplicates of official Fifth Army records presented by an army team that later interviewed Baker and recommended his consideration for the Medal of Honor.
15. William T. Bowers, William M. Hammond, and George L. MacGarrigle, *Black Soldier, White Army: The 24th Infantry Regiment in Korea* (Washington, D.C.: U.S. Army Center of Military History, 1996), 23.
16. Ernest Fisher Jr., *Cassino to the Alps* (Washington, D.C.: Government Printing Office, 1984) 407, 460–61.
17. As quoted in Wilson, "Recipe for Failure," 482.
18. See Hondon B. Hargrove, *Buffalo Soldiers in Italy* (Jefferson, N.C.: McFarland, 1985), 151, for an account of the effect of Truscott's actions on the morale of the 92nd Division.
19. On June 10, Baker was summoned to Almond's headquarters and ordered to write an account of the day's actions. See Memorandum, Headquarters, Company "C" 370th Infantry, Subject: Narrative of Action 5 April 1945, dated 12 June 1945, s/Vernon J. Baker, Baker Papers.
20. Baker's account is in *Lasting Valor*, 186–87.
21. Ibid., 188–90.
22. April 12, 1945, Report on the Combat Operation 5–6 April 1945 by Captain J. F. Runyon, commander, Company "C," 1st Battalion, 370th Infantry, copy in Baker Papers. See also Lee, *The Employment of Negro Troops*, 583. Copies of both Runyon's and Baker's reports are also in WDSSP RG 113 (MTO) (a II).

Chapter 12. Hold at All Costs: Lyle J. Bouck and the Battle of the Bulge

1. In an interview with the author on August 22, 1999, Bouck freely admitted that he volunteered for OCS to get out of the Aleutians. Because he had only two years of high school, he falsified his records to meet the eligibility requirements. See also Stephen M. Rusiecki, *The Key to the Bulge* (Westport, Conn.: Praeger, 1996), 84–85, for a description of Bouck's early life.
2. John S. D. Eisenhower, *The Bitter Woods* (New York: G. Putnam's Sons, 1969), 183.

3. Rusiecki, *The Key to the Bulge*, 86.
4. Interview with the author.
5. Ibid. See also John Eisenhower, *The Bitter Woods*, 186. For subsequent quotations, see ibid., 187–92; Astor, *The Greatest War*, 760–66; Charles MacDonald, *A Time for Trumpets* (New York: William Morrow, 1985), 177–79; and Rusiecki, *The Key to the Bulge*, 85–105. These sources carry vivid accounts of the I&R Platoon's battle.
6. Rusiecki, *The Key to the Bulge*, 99–100.
7. Ibid., 101.
8. This figure has appeared in various accounts of the battle. Bouck himself never reported any number, stating only, "I do not know and cannot even think of a number. I feel it is quite accurate to say what I have said at all times when the question has been presented: 'There were many.'"
9. Interview with Obst. Joachim Peiper by Major Kenneth W. Hechler on September 7, 1945, copy on file in Lyle J. Bouck's personal papers.
10. See Rusiecki, *The Key to the Bulge*, 153, for an analysis of Bouck's postwar career.
11. Ibid., 153–54.
12. For congressional testimony involving a bill authorizing the president to award the Medal of Honor to William James Tsakanikas, see Military Personnel Subcommittee Hearings on HR 3407, HASC No. 96-20, dated July 11, 1979.
13. See *Congressional Record*, Proceedings and Debates of the 97th Congress, 1st session, November 23, 1981.

Chapter 13. Band of Brothers: Dick Winters and the Men of Easy Company

1. Interview with the author, April 11, 2000.
2. Winters's observations on training are found in his personal papers and private correspondence, both in his possession.
3. Letter, Winters to De Etta Almon, May 6, 1944; Winters's private papers.
4. This and subsequent quotations from Winters are found in his private papers.
5. Excerpts from Winters's diary are quoted extensively in Stephen E. Ambrose, *Band of Brothers* (New York: Simon and Schuster, 1992). See p. 70 for Winters's account of his first combat jump.
6. Cornelius Ryan, *A Bridge Too Far* (New York: Simon and Schuster, 1974), 599.
7. As quoted in Ambrose, *Band of Brothers*, 163–64.
8. MacDonald, *A Time for Trumpets*, 532.
9. Interview with the author.
10. Ibid.
11. Ibid.
12. Letter, Winters to De Etta Almon, January 22, 1945, Winters's private papers.

13. Interview with the author.
14. Quoted in Ambrose, *Band of Brothers*, 270.
15. Ibid., 298–99.
16. See remarks of Sergeant Robert "Burr" Smith as quoted in Stephen Ambrose, *Comrades* (New York: Simon and Schuster, 1999), 115–16.
17. Ibid., 316.
18. Letter is in Winters's personal papers.

Chapter 14. Shattering Stereotypes: Charity Adams Earley and the Women's Army Corps

1. Both Holm's and Stroup's quotes are from Jeanne M. Holm, *In Defense of a Nation: Servicewomen in World War II* (Washington, D.C.: Military Women's Press, 1998), xiii, 1.
2. The Women's Army Auxiliary Corps was signed into law by President Roosevelt on May 15, 1942. A year later, Roosevelt signed an act that created the Women's Army Corps on July 1, 1943. With women fully integrated as a separate corps within the army, the need for the WAAC no longer existed. The WAAC officially went out of existence on September 30, 1943.
3. Direct quotations, unless otherwise noted, are extracted from Earley's memoir, *One Woman's Army: A Black Officer Remembers the WAC* (College Station: Texas A&M University Press, 1989).
4. The other camps were at Daytona Beach, Florida; Fort Oglethorpe, Georgia; Fort Devens, Massachusetts; and the combined Camps Polk and Ruston in Louisiana.
5. Earley lists the names of the thirty-nine women in the Third Platoon, First Company, First WAAC Training Center in *One Woman's Army*, 22–23.
6. Interview with the author, October 11, 1998.
7. When the WAAC was officially disbanded and the Women's Army Corps formed in 1943, the WAC assumed the regular army rank structure, and the rank of third lieutenant passed into history.
8. After several months, Company 12 was first redesignated Company 14 and subsequently Company 8.
9. Holm, *In Defense of a Nation*, 48–49.
10. The other was Major Harriet West.
11. See Earley, *One Woman's Army*, 100, for Adams's analysis of the plan to establish an all-black training regiment.
12. In a message to his chief of staff, Eisenhower referred to the assignment of the WAAC as a "God-send." Chandler et al., *Papers of DDE*, 2:694.
13. Figures extracted from Holm, *In Defense of a Nation*, 46–47.
14. Quoted in Ambrose, *Citizen Soldiers*, 348.

15. As quoted in the *New York Times* obituary, January 22, 2002.
16. Adams, *One Woman's Army*, ix.
17. Chandler et al., *Papers of DDE*, 4:2454. Eisenhower's directive did not indicate any reluctance on his part to make such promotions where clearly deserved; his purpose was to see that a proper balance was preserved among the several activities to which WACs were assigned.
18. Adams, *One Woman's Army*, 164.
19. *Washington Post*, February 18, 1995.
20. Interview with the author.

Chapter 15. To Hell and Back: The Saga of Audie Murphy

1. The most current biography of Audie Murphy is Don Graham's *No Name on the Bullet* (New York: Viking Press, 1989). Murphy's own account of the war can be found in his autobiography, *To Hell and Back*, originally published in 1949 by Henry Holt and Company. Unless otherwise noted, all direct quotations by Murphy are extracted from this source, which was republished by Tab Books in 1988. See also Thomas B. Morgan's "The War Hero," in *Esquire* (December 1983): 597–604, for a provocative portrayal of Murphy as America's most decorated soldier in war and one of its most troubled veterans in peace.
2. As quoted in Graham, *No Name on the Bullet*, 8.
3. The 3rd Infantry Division was commanded by Major General Lucian Truscott Jr., arguably the finest division commander in the European war. His tough, realistic training program produced one of the finest infantry divisions in World War II. Over the course of the conflict, soldiers from the Marne Division garnered thirty-nine Medals of Honor, roughly 11.6 percent of the total awarded during the war.
4. Truscott's personal account of the invasion of Sicily is found in his autobiography, *Command Missions*, 174–243.
5. As quoted in Morgan, "The War Hero," 602.
6. Letter, McClure to Colonel Red Reeder, dated March 27, 1964. Copy of letter is in folder Audie Murphy-Sgt Parillo Fan Club, Copied Articles (3), Audie Murphy Papers, U.S. Military Academy Library, West Point, New York.
7. As quoted in Graham, *No Name on the Bullet*, 53.
8. Hollen's description of Murphy's action was sworn and subscribed to First Lieutenant Abraham Weiner in December 1944 as part of the investigation to substantiate the award of the Distinguished Service Cross.
9. For the citation, see Headquarters Seventh Army, General Orders Number 21, dated January 28, 1945.
10. Graham discusses Murphy's private vendetta against the enemy in detail in *No Name on the Bullet*, 69–71.

11. Citation for Silver Star presented by Headquarters 3rd Infantry Division, General Orders Number 66, February 25, 1945.
12. Graham, *No Name on the Bullet*, 76.
13. See citation in Headquarters 3rd Infantry Division, General Orders Number 83, March 3, 1945.
14. Citation for the Medal of Honor is located in Audie Murphy Papers. Murphy's own account of the action is in *To Hell and Back*, 238–43.
15. Weispfenning's account is extracted from a letter from David McClure to Colonel Red Reeder, dated March 27, 1964, on file in the Audie Murphy Papers. See also Donald G. Taggart, ed., *History of the Third Infantry Division in World War II* (Washington, D.C.: Infantry Journal Press, 1947), 311.
16. Taggart, *History of the Third Infantry Division in World War II*, 311.
17. Abramski's statement was subscribed and sworn to First Lieutenant Charles Blossom on February 27, 1945, as part of the investigation into the circumstances surrounding Murphy's valor at Holtzwihr.
18. Murphy, *To Hell and Back*, 263.
19. Ibid., 272–73.
20. There remains some dispute concerning the number of medals Murphy accumulated over the course of the war, but no one disputes that he was the war's most decorated soldier. Figures cited in this paragraph come from Graham's *No Name on the Bullet*, 101.
21. As paraphrased in Gerald F. Linderman, *The War within War: America's Combat Experience in World War II* (New York: Free Press, 1997), 296–98.
22. Graham, *No Name on the Bullet*, 122–23.
23. Ibid., 335.
24. Morgan, "The War Hero," 598.
25. *Congressional Record*, Proceedings and Debates of the 104th Congress, 2nd session, May 30, 1996.

Epilogue

1. Casualties figures appear in Murray and Millett, *A War to Be Won*, 558; and the undated fact sheet entitled "World War II," compiled by the Department of Defense in support of the 50th Anniversary of World War II Commemoration Committee.
2. Daniel D. Holt and James W. Leyerzapf, eds., *Eisenhower: The Prewar Diaries and Selected Papers, 1905–1941* (Baltimore: Johns Hopkins University Press, 1998), 446–47.
3. Ambrose, *D-Day*, 48.
4. These categories are extracted from Larabee, *Commander in Chief*, 116.

5. As quoted on the dust jacket cover of George C. Marshall's *Memoirs of My Services in World War 1917–1918* (Boston: Houghton Mifflin, 1976). See also Bland and Stevens, *Papers of GCM*, 1:202–3.
6. Quoted in Stephen Ambrose, *The Wisdom of Dwight D. Eisenhower* (New Orleans: Eisenhower Center, 1990), 15.
7. See Peter Mansoor, *The GI Offensive in Europe* (Lawrence: University Press of Kansas, 1999), for an elaboration of this theme.
8. Eisenhower, *Crusade in Europe*, 428.

BIBLIOGRAPHY

Primary Sources

Collections in the U.S. Military Academy, West Point, New York

Bradley, Omar Nelson, USMA 1915, CU 5356, Papers
Krueger, Walter, Papers
Murphy, Audie, Papers
Patch, Alexander McCarrell Jr., USMA 1913, CU 5187, Papers
Patton, George Smith Jr., War Diary, 7 vols., August 5, 1942–March 23, 1945
Ridgway, Matthew Bunker, USMA April 1917, CU 5657, Papers
Swing, Joseph May, USMA 1915, CU 5350, Papers

Interviews in Collections

Bouck, Lyle J. Jr.
Dawson, Joseph T.
Howard, John
Lomell, Leonard G.
Von Luck, Hans
Winters, Richard D.

Interviews Conducted by the Author

Baker, Vernon, October 9, 1998
Bouck, Lyle J. Jr., August 22, 1999
Dawson, Joseph T., May 31–June 2, 1998
Earley, Charity Adams, October 11, 1998
Howard, John, August 1, 1997
Lomell, Leonard G., August 18, 1998

Tibbets, Paul, May 4, 1998
Winters, Richard D., September 22–23, 1999; January 18, 2001

Manuscripts

Eisenhower Center for American Studies, Metropolitan College, University of New Orleans, Oral Histories

Newspapers and Periodicals

Chicago Tribune, March 10–22, 1968
Life, July 16, 1945, 94–97
Stars and Stripes, 1942–45

Private Collections

Baker, Vernon, Private Papers
Dawson, Joseph T., World War II Letters
Lomell, Leonard G., Private Papers
Winters, Richard D., Private Papers

Published Sources

Arnold, H. H. *Global Mission*. New York: Harper and Brothers, 1949.

Baker, Vernon J., with Ken Olsen. *Lasting Valor*. Columbus, Mississippi: Genesis Press, 1997.

Bland, Larry I., and Sharon Ritenour Stevens, eds. *The Papers of George Catlett Marshall*. 4 vols. Baltimore: Johns Hopkins University Press, 1996.

Bradley, Omar N. *A Soldier's Story*. New York: Henry Holt, 1951.

Bradley, Omar N., and Clay Blair. *A General's Life: An Autobiography*. New York: Simon and Schuster, 1983.

Cawthon, Charles R. *Other Clay: A Remembrance of the World War II Infantry*. Niwot, Colorado: University Press of Colorado, 1990.

Chandler, Alfred D. Jr., et al., eds. *The Papers of Dwight D. Eisenhower: The War Years*. 5 vols. Baltimore: Johns Hopkins University Press, 1970.

Collins, J. Lawton. *Lightning Joe: An Autobiography*. Baton Rouge: Louisiana State University Press, 1979.

Corlett, Charles H. *Cowboy Pete: The Autobiography of Major General Charles H. Corlett*. Santa Fe, New Mexico: Sleeping Fox Enterprises, 1974.

Earley, Charity Adams. *One Woman's Army: A Black Officer Remembers the WAC*. College Station: Texas A&M Press, 1989.

Eichelberger, Robert. *Our Jungle Road to Tokyo*. New York: Viking Press, 1950.

Eisenhower, Dwight D. *At Ease: Stories I Tell My Friends*. New York: Doubleday, 1967.

———. *Crusade in Europe*. New York: Doubleday, 1948.

Harmon, E. N. *Combat Commander: Autobiography of a Soldier*. Englewood Cliffs, New Jersey: Prentice-Hall, 1970.

Hodenfield, G. K. "I Climbed the Cliffs with the Rangers." *Saturday Evening Post*, August 19, 1944, 18–19, 98.

Krueger, Walter. *From Down Under to Nippon: The Story of Sixth Army in World War II*. Washington, D.C.: Combat Forces Press, 1953.

Lang, Will. "Lucian King Truscott Jr." *Life*, August 2, 1944, 97–111.

MacArthur, Douglas A. *Reminiscences*. New York: McGraw-Hill, 1964.

Montgomery, Bernard Law. *The Memoirs of Field-Marshal Montgomery*. New York: World Publishing Company, 1958.

Morgan, Thomas B. "The War Hero." *Esquire* (December 1983): 597–604.

Murphy, Audie. *To Hell and Back*. 1949. Reprint. Blue Ridge Summit, Pennsylvania: Tab Books, 1988.

Patton, George S. Jr. *War as I Knew It*. Boston: Houghton Mifflin, 1947.

Ridgway, Matthew B. *Soldier: The Memoirs of Matthew B. Ridgway*. New York: Harper and Brothers, 1956.

Sledge, E. B. *With the Old Breed at Peleliu and Okinawa*. New York: Oxford University Press, 1981.

Standifer, Leon C. *Not in Vain: A Rifleman Remembers World War II*. Baton Rouge: Louisiana State University Press, 1992.

Sweeney, Charles. *War's End: An Eyewitness Account of America's Last Atomic Mission*. New York: Avon Books, 1997.

Taylor, Maxwell. *Swords and Plowshares*. New York: W. W. Norton, 1972.

Tibbets, Paul W. *Return of the Enola Gay*. Columbus, Ohio: A Paul Tibbets Book, 1998.

Truscott, L. K. Jr. *Command Missions*. 1954. Reprint. Novato, California: Presidio Press, 1990.

Wainwright, Jonathan M. *General Wainwright's Story: The Account of Four Years of Humiliating Defeat, Surrender, and Captivity*. New York: Doubleday, 1946.

Wilson, George. *If You Survive*. Canada: Ivy Books, 1987.

Unpublished Documents

Allen, Terry de la Mesa. "Combat Operations of the 1st Infantry Division during World War II." Undated. U.S. Army Military History Institute, Carlisle Barracks, Pennsylvania.

Harmon, E. N. "Notes on Combat Experience during the Tunisian and African Campaigns." Undated. U.S. Army Military History Institute, Carlisle Barracks, Pennsylvania.

Secondary Sources

Ambrose, Stephen E. *Band of Brothers: E Company, 506th Regiment, 101st Airborne from Normandy to Hitler's Eagle's Nest*. New York: Simon and Schuster, 1992.

———. *Citizen Soldiers: The U.S. Army from the Normandy Beaches to the Bulge to the Surrender of Germany June 7, 1944–May 7, 1945*. New York: Simon and Schuster, 1997.

———. *D-Day June 6, 1944: The Climactic Battle of World War II*. New York: Simon and Schuster, 1994.

———. "I Learn a Lot from the Veterans." *American Heritage* (November 1998): 64–73.

———. *Pegasus Bridge June 6, 1944*. New York: Simon and Schuster, 1985.

———. *The Victors: Eisenhower and His Boys: The Men of World War II*. New York: Simon and Schuster, 1998.

Astor, Gerald. *The Greatest War: Americans in Combat 1941–1945*. Novato, California: Presidio Press, 1999.

Blumenson, Martin. "Anzio: Dilemma on the Beachhead." *Army* 33 (March 1983): 38–48.

———. *The Battle of the Generals: The Untold Story of the Falaise Pocket—the Campaign That Should Have Won World War II*. New York: William Morrow, 1993.

———. *Heroes Never Die: Warriors and Warfare in World War II*. New York: Cooper Square Press, 2001.

———. *Mark Clark*. New York: William Morrow. 1984.

———. *Patton: The Man behind the Legend, 1885–1945*. New York: William Morrow, 1985.

———. *The Patton Papers, 1940–1945*. Boston: Houghton Mifflin, 1974.

Bolger, Daniel. "Zero Defects: Command Climate in First US Army, 1944–1945." *Military Review* 71 (May 1991): 61–73.

Bowers, William T., William M. Hammond, and George L. MacGarrigle. *Black Soldier, White Army: The 24th Infantry Regiment in Korea*. Washington, D.C.: Center of Military History, 1996.

Bryant, Arthur. *The Turn of the Tide 1939–1943*. New York: Doubleday, 1957.

Churchill, Winston. *The Second World War*. Chartwell Edition. Boston: Houghton Mifflin, 1953.

D'Este, Carlo. *Eisenhower: A Soldier's Life*. New York: Henry Holt, 2002.

———. *Patton: A Genius for War*. New York: HarperCollins, 1995.

Eichelberger, Robert L. *Dear Miss Em: General Eichelberger's War in the Pacific, 1942–1945*. Ed. Jay Luvaas. Westport, Connecticut: Greenwood Press, 1972.

Eisenhower, John S. D. *The Bitter Woods*. New York: G. P. Putnam's Sons, 1969.

Fisher, Robert F. Jr. *Cassino to the Alps*. Washington, D.C.: Government Printing Office, 1984.

Fuller, J. F. C. *Generalship: Its Diseases and Their Cure*. Harrisburg, Pennsylvania: Military Service Publishing, 1936.

Garfield, Brian. *The Thousand-Mile War: World War II in Alaska and the Aleutians.* New York: Bantam Books, 1969.

Graham, Don. *No Name on the Bullet: A Biography of Audie Murphy.* New York: Viking Press, 1989.

Greene, Bob. *Duty: A Father, His Son, and the Man Who Won the War.* New York: William Morrow, 2000.

Hargrove, Hondon B. *Buffalo Soldiers in Italy: Black Americans in World War II.* Jefferson, N.C.: McFarland, 1985.

Harrison, Gordon A. *Cross-Channel Attack.* Washington, D.C.: Government Printing Office, 1950.

Hobbs, Joseph P., ed. *Dear General: Eisenhower's Wartime Letters to Marshall.* Baltimore: Johns Hopkins University Press, 1971.

Hogan, David W. *A Command Post at War: First Army Headquarters in Europe, 1943–1945.* Washington, D.C.: Center of Military History, 2000.

Holland, Matthew. *Eisenhower between the Wars.* Westport, Connecticut: Praeger, 2001.

Holm, Jeanne M. *In Defense of a Nation: Service Women in World War II.* Washington, D.C.: Military Women's Press, 1998.

Houston, Donald E. *Hell on Wheels: The 2d Armored Division.* Novato, California: Presidio Press, 1977.

Howe, George F. *Northwest Africa: Seizing the Initiative in the West.* Washington, D.C.: Government Printing Office, 1985.

Kingseed, Cole. "Eisenhower's Prewar Anonymity: Myth or Reality?" *Parameters* (Autumn 1991): 87–98.

———. "Ike Takes Charge." *Military Review* 42 (June 1992): 73–76.

Larrabee, Eric. *Commander in Chief: Franklin Delano Roosevelt, His Lieutenants and Their War.* New York: Harper and Row, 1987.

Lee, Ulysses. *The Employment of Negro Troops.* Washington, D.C.: Government Printing Office, 1966.

Linderman, Gerald F. *The World within War: America's Combat Experience in World War II.* New York: Free Press, 1997.

MacDonald, Charles B. *A Time for Trumpets.* New York: William Morrow, 1984.

Manchester, William. *American Caesar: Douglas MacArthur 1880–1964.* Boston: Little, Brown, 1978.

McPherson, James M. *For Cause and Comrades: Why Men Fought in the Civil War.* New York: Oxford University Press, 1997.

Milner, Samuel. *Victory in Papua.* Washington, D.C.: Government Printing Office, 1985.

Morelock, J. D. *Generals of the Ardennes: American Leadership in the Battle of the Bulge.* Washington, D.C.: National Defense University Press, 1994.

Morton, Louis. *The Fall of the Philippines*. Washington, D.C.: Government Printing Office, 1985.

Murray, Williamson, and Allan R. Millett. *A War to Be Won: Fighting the Second World War*. Cambridge: Belknap Press of Harvard University Press, 2000.

Pogue, Forrest C. *George C. Marshall.* 3 vols. New York: Viking Press, 1973.

———. *The Supreme Command.* Washington, D.C.: Government Printing Office, 1954.

Ridgway, Matthew B. *The Korean War*. New York: Doubleday, 1967.

Rusiecki, Stephen M. *The Key to the Bulge: The Battle for Losheimergraben.* Westport, Conn.: Praeger, 1996.

Shortal, James. *Forged by Fire: General Robert L. Eichelberger and the Pacific War.* Columbia: University of South Carolina Press, 1987.

Taaffe, Stephen R. *MacArthur's Jungle War: The 1944 New Guinea Campaign.* Lawrence: University Press of Kansas, 1998.

Taggart, Donald G. ed. *History of the Third Infantry Division in World War II.* Washington, D.C.: Infantry Journal Press, 1947.

Tuchman, Barbara. *Stilwell and the American Experience in China 1911–45*. New York: Macmillan, 1970.

U.S. Army Center of Military History. *Generalship: Historical Perspectives.* Washington, D.C.: Government Printing Office, undated.

Weigley, Russell F. *Eisenhower's Lieutenants: The Campaigns of France and Germany.* Bloomington: Indiana University Press, 1981.

Wilson, Dale E. "Recipe for Failure: Major General Edward M. Almond and Preparation of the U.S. 92d Infantry Division for Combat in World War II." *Journal of Military History* 56 (July 1992): 473–88.

Wyant, William K. *Sandy Patch: A Biography of Lt. Gen. Alexander M. Patch*. New York: Praeger, 1991.

Symposia

Eisenhower Center. D-Day Remembered: 50 Years After. New Orleans, Louisiana, May 16–17, 1994.

Robert R. McCormick Tribune Foundation and the U.S. Naval Institute. End of World War II Seminar. Cantigny, Wheaton, Illinois, March 1–2, 1995.

Robert R. McCormick Tribune Foundation and the U.S. Naval Institute. Normandy Seminar. Cantigny, Wheaton, Illinois, March 2–3, 1994.

INDEX

Page numbers followed by the letter *n*, plus a number, refer to endnotes.

ABOUT THE AUTHOR

COLONEL COLE C. KINGSEED, U.S. Army (Ret.), is a thirty-year army veteran who commanded infantry units at the platoon, company, and battalion levels. His last military assignment was Chief of Military History at the U.S. Military Academy at West Point. A 1971 graduate of the University of Dayton, Ohio, Kingseed graduated from the U.S. Naval War College in 1992 and holds a Ph.D. in history from The Ohio State University. He is the author of *Eisenhower and the Suez Crisis of 1956* and *The American Civil War* and coauthor of the acclaimed *Beyond Band of Brothers: The War Memoirs of Major Dick Winters.* Kingseed is also an assistant editor of the five-volume *Encyclopedia of World War II.* Now retired from active military service, he is the founder and president of Brecourt Leadership Experience, Inc., a leadership consulting firm that conducts leadership seminars at Gettysburg and Normandy.